Ghosts of Old Companions

Lloyd George's Welsh Army, the Kaiser's Reichsheer and the Battle for Mametz Wood, 1914–1916

Lieutenant General Jonathon Riley CB DSO PhD MA FRHistS FRGS

There are no gaps in a battalion on the march, though many have fallen, but the closing-up that follows losses tells its own tale. The faces of many silent and hard-eyed men showed that they were but half-aware of their new neighbours, newcomers who jostled the ghosts of old companions, usurpers who were themselves struggling against the same griefs and longings, marching forward with minds that looked backwards into time and space…

Llewelyn Wyn Griffith
Up to Mametz

Helion & Company

For Clare
with love

Helion & Company Limited
Unit 8 Amherst Business Centre
Budbrooke Road
Warwick
CV34 5WE
England
Tel. 01926 499 619
Fax 0121 711 4075
Email: info@helion.co.uk
Website: www.helion.co.uk
Twitter: @helionbooks
Visit our blog http://blog.helion.co.uk/

Published by Helion & Company 2019
Designed and typeset by Mach 3 Solutions (www.mach3solutions.co.uk)
Cover designed by Paul Hewitt, Battlefield Design (www.battlefield-design.co.uk)
Printed by Gutenberg Limited, Tarxien, Malta

Text © Jonathon Riley 2019
All images open source unless individually credited.
Original maps drawn by Paul Hewitt, Battlefield Design (www.battlefield-design.co.uk) and © Helion
& Company 2019

ISBN 978-1-911628-86-6

British Library Cataloguing-in-Publication Data.
A catalogue record for this book is available from the British Library.

For details of other military history titles published by Helion & Company Limited contact the above
address or visit our website: http://www.helion.co.uk.

We always welcome receiving book proposals from prospective authors.

Contents

List of Illustrations   iv
List of Maps   ix
Introduction   x
Acknowledgements   xii
Note on Titles   xiii
A Note on the Archaeology of Mametz Wood Composed after a Reconnaissance of the
    Ground, June 2018   xiv
Glossary of Military Terms and Abbreviations   xviii

1   Lord Kitchener, the British Army and the Expeditionary Force 1904–1914   21
2   Lloyd George's Welsh Army, 1914–1915   32
3   'England's best sword knocked out of her hand': German Strategy
    and Operational Plans for 1916   61
4   'Ending the war by fighting': Allied Strategy and Operational Plans for 1916   90
5   Christmas in France: The 38th (Welsh) Division's Deployment and Early Days at
    the front, December 1915–January 1916   110
6   In the Line: The 38th (Welsh) Division from February to July 1916   129
7   'The place was a ruin before, now it is a dust-heap': The First Assault at Mametz:
    1–5 July 1916   144
8   'They want butchers, not brigadiers': Mametz Wood, 5–7 July 1916   169
9   'We are stuck in the wood': Mametz, 8–9 July 1916   209
10 'Another day of heavy fighting': Mametz Wood, The Attack of 10 July 1916   217
11 'Dead and mangled bodies were strewn everywhere': Final Acts, 11–12 July 1916   259
12 'A Dulac picture of some goblin forest': Subsequent Operations Around Mametz Wood   273
13 Aftermath: 'The price paid for Mametz Wood'   288

Annexes
A   Honours and Awards, December 1915–July 1916   304
B   Welsh Army Corps Outside 38th Welsh Division   310
C   Welsh Regular, Special Reserve and Territorial Force Units   318
D   British and Imperial Divisions World-Wide Deployment 1916   321
E   Mametz Wood Writers, Poets and Artists   324

Bibliography   330
Index   339

List of Illustrations

The famous recruiting poster featuring Lord Kitchener, urging voluntary enlistment.   27

A recruiting office overwhelmed with potential soldiers in 1914.   28

1 R.W. Fus near Mons in August 1914.   29

David Lloyd George in 1914.   32

David Jones. (RWF Mus)   35

15 R.W. Fus memorial in Gray's Inn. (Author's collection)   36

A Welsh enlistment poster: 'Freedom demands her best men'.   38

Brigadier General Owen Thomas, Commander 113 Infantry Brigade, and his sons: all three were commissioned into the R.W. Fus and all three were killed during the war. (RWF Mus)   38

Officers of 15 R.W. Fus, the 1st London Welsh. Noel Osbourne-Jones is first on the left in the back row, Goronwy Owen is fifth from the left in the back row; Harold Gladstone Lewis is second from left in the middle row. (RWF Mus)   41

CSM John Bradshaw. (Family of John Bradshaw)   41

Two jingoistic cartoons promoting enlistment into the 38th (Welsh) Division.   43

Llewelyn Wyn Griffith. (Wyn Griffith family)   44

Brigadier General H.J. Evans, Commander 115 Infantry Brigade. (RWF Mus)   47

The badge of the 38th (Welsh) Division.   50

Salisbury Plain, two line drawings by David Jones. (RWF Mus 2998b)   51

18 R.W. Fus at Kinmel Park camp. (Author's collection)   52

A group of 130th Field Ambulance with their vehicle, presented by the people of Abertillery. (www.130thstjohnambulance.co.uk)   53

Three contemporary diagrams showing the arrangement of rank badges, cap decoration and armbands for Regimental and staff officers during the Great War.   54

General Erich von Falkenhayn.   61

Two German photographs of civilians being evacuated from the frontline area on the Somme. (163 I.R. Regimental History)   71

A contemporary diagram of German trench systems on the Western Front.   72

British diagrams showing the layout of German defences.   73

An Allied air photograph of German trenches in early 1916.   74

A German trench in late 1915.   75

German artillery preparing to move up to the front. (James Payne collections)   75

A German Pfalz E-1 aircraft.   76

Crown Prince Rupprecht of Bavaria.   76

General Sir Henry Rawlinson.   93

(Edmonds, *Military Operations France and Belgium 1916*, Vol. I)   99

A German MG 08 team.   101

A British artillery barrage map illustrating the timed lines supporting an advance by infantry.   103

Haig and Joffre at Chantilly, 23 December 1915.   107

Brigadier General Llewellyn Price-Davies.   110

Ellis Evans, 'Hedd Wyn' who joined 15 R.W. Fus in 1917.   111

Llewelyn Wyn Griffith and his company in tents behind the line. (Family of John Bradshaw)   114

British trench layout in late 1915.   115

Using a trench periscope in the line, a drawing by David Jones. (RWF Mus 2998b)   116

British troops being fed hot rations in trenches. (IWM Q4843)   117

A cross-section of a British trench.   117

Laventie trenches Christmas 1915 where the second Christmas Truce occurred. (RWF Mus)   120

A field kitchen being enjoyed by British soldiers in a dugout. (IWM E1219)   121

The scene in a German dugout at Christmas 1915. (James Payne collections)   121

Robert Keating: Witness to the 1915 Christmas Truce. (RWF Mus)   123

A German officer in the sort of uniform described in the scene at Richebourg l'Avoué. (James Payne collections)   130

Four drawings by David Jones of front-line trench conditions in the early months of 1916. (RWF Mus 2998b)   133

Second Lieutenant Noel Osbourne-Jones, killed on the night of 7/8 May 1916.   137

The problem of rats was not confined to the British lines: a photograph of German soldiers dealing with the same problem.   140

A German sketch of the positions of the 16th Bavarian Infantry Regiment in the Second Line and its failed counter-attack on 1 July 1916. (16th Bavarian Regimental History)   147

Lieutenant Colonel (later Major General) John Minshull Ford. (NPG X154642)   149

A diagram showing the method of training and organising bombers for trench clearance.   150

Major General Herbert Watts, G.O.C. 7th Infantry Division, 1916.   150

Lieutenant Colonel Clifton Stockwell. (Major Miles Stockwell)   151

The ground in front of Mametz before the attack on 1 July 1916.   152

German prisoners from the 28th Reserve Infantry Division being escorted to the rear by British troops.   152

A British mine being blown before the assault on 1 July 1916.   152

British air photograph of the Quadrangle. (RWF Mus)   159

The Battalion Commanders of the 16th Bavarian Infantry Regiment who held the Second Line on 1 July 1916. (16th Bavarian Regimental History)   160

Mametz Village after the attack. (*Illustrated London News,* 22 July 1916)   162

Siegfried Sassoon with a group of bombers. (Burntwood family)   162

1 R.W. Fus in its bivouac field before operations on 3 and 4 July. (RWF Mus)   163

1 R.W. Fus' German opponents enjoying a similar rest behind the lines. (James Payne collections)   163

1st RWF on the Somme. (The *Illustrated London News*)   164

Royal Garrison Artillery gunners shifting ammunition, Somme 1916.   166

British air photograph of Mametz Wood. (RWF Mus)   172

An oblique British air photograph of Mametz Wood. (RWF Mus)   173

An oblique German air photograph of Mametz Wood and Bazentin Ridge. (16th Bavarian
    Regimental History)   173

The sketch map of Mametz Wood issued to all units as an Annex to the Divisional Operation
    Order. (T.N.A. WO 95//2539/4, 38th Division War Diary (G.S.)   174

British air photograph of Acid Drop Copse and Contalmaison. (RWF Mus)   175

A contemporary photograph of Mametz Wood from Marlborough Wood on 7 July 1916.
    (greatwarphotos.com)   176

British air photograph of Caterpillar Copse. (RWF Mus)   176

Modern photograph of the trench at the northern edge of Caterpillar Copse. (A.M. Goulden)   177

Modern photograph of a section of narrow-gauge railway track now doing duty as a fence-post
    outside Caterpillar Copse. (A.M. Goulden)   177

Modern photograph of the forming-up place on the northern side of Caterpillar Copse and the
    axis of advance on 7 July, from Marlborough Wood. (A.M. Goulden)   178

Modern photograph of Flatiron and Sabot Copses (to the right) and the southern edge of the
    Hammerhead, from Marlborough Wood. (A.M. Goulden)   178

Modern photograph of the defenders' view from the Hammerhead towards the direction of
    attack on 7 July. (A.M. Goulden)   179

Modern photograph of Queen's Nullah from the south, which can be made out by the line of
    bushes. (A.M. Goulden)   179

A German sketch of the positions held around Mametz Wood on 4/5 July, before the relief by
    the *Lehr* Regiment, showing the new entrenchments. (16th Bavarian Regimental History,
    p. 186)   180

Two photographs of the Regimental and 2nd Battalion headquarters staffs of the 163rd I.R. (163
    I.R. Regimental History)   181

A German sketch showing their entrenchments around the Mametz Wood area. (Lehr
    Regimental History)   182

The Regimental Colour of the *Lehr* Infantry Regiment. (Lehr Regimental History)   182

A German sketch showing the positions held on 7 July. (16th Bavarian Regimental History, p.
    187)   183

The Kaiser reviews the Guards Fusilier Regiment before the opening of the Somme battles.
    (Guard Fusiliers Regimental History)   184

Positions of the Guards Fusilier Regiment. (Guard Fusiliers Regimental History)   184

Pommiers Redoubt, the headquarters of 115 Infantry Brigade.   192

Modern photograph of the culminating point of the attack on 7 July. (A.M. Goulden)   196

Officers of 16 Welsh before the battle. (RWF Mus)   198

British 4.7-inch gun in action, June 1916.   205

Lieutenant Colonel Graham Gwyther   210

A postcard sent by *Feldwebel* Hoffmann of the 3rd Battalion, *Lehr* Regiment. (http://
    roadstothegreatwar-ww1.blogspot.co.uk/2013/07/the-german-experience-at-battle-of-
    somme.html)   215

A German photograph of the N.C.O.s of the *Lehr* Infantry Regiment who defended sections
    of Mametz Wood throughout the battle. (http://roadstothegreatwar-ww1.blogspot.
    co.uk/2013/07/the-german-experience-at-battle-of-somme.html)   215

Colonel Bonham-Carter, the GSO I of the 7th Division, who accompanied Major General
    Watts to the 38th Division. Seen here with his brother, Admiral Sir Stuart Bonham-Carter.   218

Modern photograph taken from the probable position of Cliff trench, the start line of the attack on 10 July, towards Mametz Wood. (A.M. Goulden) — 220

Modern photograph taken of the line of the cliff, on the abandoned railway line at its base. (A.M. Goulden) — 220

Modern photograph taken at the bottom of the cliff, looking upwards. (A.M. Goulden) — 221

Modern photograph of the remains of Strip trench, just inside the current western edge of Mametz Wood. (A.M. Goulden) — 222

Modern photograph of the defenders' view from the south-west corner of Mametz Wood. (A.M. Goulden) — 223

Modern photograph of the defenders' view from the Hammerhead, looking towards the Welsh Memorial and the direction of attack on 10 July. (A.M. Goulden) — 223

German troops detraining, as described in the British air reconnaissance report quoted. (James Payne collections) — 226

A sketch of the German entrenchment on the edge of Mametz Wood by W.R. Thomas. (RWF Mus) — 227

A German trench on the edge of a wood; the hasty defences constructed around Mametz Wood between 3 and 7 July 1916 would have looked like this. (James Payne collections) — 227

A smashed German artillery limber outside Mametz Wood as described in the sketch by W.R. Thomas, possibly where Robert Graves later picked up his carved chalk memento (see Chapter 12). — 228

Modern photograph of the trench line inside the southern edge of Mametz Wood, as shown in the sketch by W.R. Thomas. (A.M. Goulden) — 228

Modern photograph looking towards Mametz Wood, matching the view in the sketch by W.R. Thomas. (A.M. Goulden) — 228

A group of men of II./*Lehr-Infanterie-Regiment*. (http://roadstothegreatwar-ww1.blogspot.co.uk/2013/07/the-german-experience-at-battle-of-somme.html) — 229

Sketch of the German positions to the west of Mametz Wood on 10 July. (Regimental History, 122nd R.I.R.) — 230

Modern photograph taken at the bottom of the cliff, towards Mametz Wood. (A.M. Goulden) — 230

Christopher Williams's painting *The Welsh at Mametz*. (National Museum and Galleries Wales) — 235

A fanciful picture of the fighting in Mametz Wood; the Germans are wearing uniforms that are at least a year out of date. — 237

Captain Macdonald and RSM Jones, 15 R.W. Fus. (RWF Mus) — 237

Modern photograph of the attack on the Hammerhead. (A.M. Goulden) — 239

A German sketch of the British attack on 10 July and the German retirement. (16th Bavarian Regimental History, p. 189) — 239

The Assault on Mametz Wood, by David Jones. (RWF Mus 2998b) — 241

Brigadier General Thomas Marden. (R. Welsh Museum Brecon) — 243

10-18 Inside a German command post in Mametz Wood, similar to that of Major von Zeppelin, 122nd Reserve Infantry Regiment. (James Payne collections) — 245

A wrecked German bunker in Mametz Wood, possibly the command post of Major von Zeppelin. (James Payne collections) — 245

The Funeral of Major von Zeppelin at Bertincourt on 12 July. (122 I.R. Regimental History) — 246

Modern photograph of the remnants of Major von Zeppelin's H.Q. bunker; Professor David Austin (right) and Mr Nick Keyes (left). (A.M. Goulden) — 246

British patrol advancing into Mametz Wood. 248

A British reconnaissance aircraft prepares to take off. 253

Brigadier General Horatio Evans, Major Charles Veal and an unknown officer in Mametz Wood, 11 July 1916. (IWM Q868) 261

Modern photograph of the central ride in Mametz Wood, taken from the probable German line inside the northern edge of the Wood. (A.M. Goulden) 264

Modern photograph of the line of Middle Alley trench. (A.M. Goulden) 264

A German communication trench leading to a position in a wooded area, similar to Middle Alley trench from the II *Stellung* to the northern edge of Mametz Wood. (James Payne collections) 264

Modern photograph of the German Second Line, running this side of the wood, from the northern edge of Mametz Wood and looking up the disused railway line. (A.M. Goulden) 264

Mametz Wood, by Henry Handley-Read. (National Museums and Galleries Wales) 265

A German *Flammenwerfer* in action. (http://roadstothegreatwar-ww1.blogspot.co.uk/2013/07/the-german-experience-at-battle-of-somme.html) 266

German artillery concealed in a wood. (James Payne collections) 267

Trench digging. 269

The British and German positions prior to the assault on the Second Line. (Miles, *Military Operations France and Belgium 1916*, Vol. II) 274

A German panoramic sketch of the view along the Second Line from Longueval towards Bazentin le Grand. (16th Bavarian Regimental History) 275

A German sketch of the British attack on the Second Line. (16th Bavarian Regimental History) 277

A German air photograph centred on Bazentin le Grand. (16th Bavarian Regimental History) 278

Bazentin le Grand village, depicting location of the captured 16th Bavarians' Regimental Headquarters. (16th Bavarian Regimental History) 278

German dead interred in temporary burials. (James Payne collections) 283

2nd Lieutenant Glyn Roberts. (RWF Mus) 283

A contemporary view from Bazentin le Petit Wood looking north-east towards 1 R.W. Fus' position. 284

Modern photograph taken from the Windmill towards Bazentin le Petit Cemetery – the line held by 1 R.W. Fus. (A.M. Goulden) 284

Modern photograph taken from 1 R.W. Fus' position towards the direction of the attack by the Guards Fusiliers. (A.M. Goulden) 285

Modern photograph of Bazentin le Petit Cemetery. (A.M. Goulden) 285

Modern photograph showing the enduring effects of British artillery fire, shell-holes and unexploded ordnance inside Mametz Wood. (A.M. Goulden) 293

Fricourt German cemetery. (A.M. Goulden) 296

Mametz Wood Memorial in 1987. (*The Western Mail*) 297

Battle centenary, 7 July 2016. 297

List of Maps

1.i   The B.E.F. in relation to French, Belgian and German Armies in August 1914.   23
3.i   The German Plan for 1914 and French counter-moves.   62
3.ii   Verdun, February to June 1916.   68
3.iii   German and Allied Armies on the Western Front, 1916.   77
3.iv   The Layout of the German Second Army on the Somme, 1916.   79
4.i   The Somme Battlefield.   94
5.i   A contemporary sketch of the trenches around Laventie.   119
6.i   A contemporary trench of the Neuve Chapelle sector.   131
6.ii   A sketch showing the area around Richebourg l'Avouvé, described in the report above.   132
6.iii   A trench of the Givenchy area.   135
6.iv   A trench of the Moated Grange sector.   139
7.i   The area of assault between Mametz and Trônes Woods.   145
7.ii   The area south-west of Mametz Wood, 1–5 July 1916.   146
7.iii   A contemporary of the defences in the Mametz – Contalmaison area.
        (Source: *German Official History Somme-Nord*)   148
7.iv   The assault on 1 July, 1 R.W. Fus in the extreme south. (*Official History*)   154
7.v   The action at the Quadrangle.   157
8.i   Mametz Wood and environs.   170
8.ii   The German Dispositions in Mametz Wood, 5 July 1916. (Source: *German Official History Somme-Nord*)   171
8.iii   German dispositions in Mametz Wood, 7 July 1916. (Source: *German Official History Somme-Nord*)   186
8.iv   The assaults by 115 Infantry Brigade, 7 July 1916.   195
10.i   The German Dispositions in Mametz Wood, 10 July 1916. (Source: *German Official History Somme-Nord*)   225
12.i   The Assault on Bazentin Ridge.   276

Introduction

When I was asked to put together a full account of the service of the 38th (Welsh) Division from its formation to the end of the Battle for Mametz Wood, I was very conscious that, as far as the fighting in Mametz Wood was concerned, a great deal of work had already been published. I have included more observations on that work in the acknowledgements below. To that I have added a detailed survey of the war diaries and papers in the National Archives and elsewhere, along with personal accounts, to provide as detailed an account as possible of the bitter fighting in and around the Wood in July 1916. I have further supplemented this with a detailed study on the ground with a noted archaeologist. As a result, I believe that I have been able to add some new information, or details that have been forgotten since the battle, such as the extent to which the Germans had entrenched the edges of the Wood between 1 and 7 July and then connected these new entrenchments to their second line positions. I have also, I believe, explained the failure of the smoke screen on 7 July which led to so much loss of life during 115 Brigade's assault that day. In addition, I have carried out a full investigation of the casualties incurred by the 38th Division and recorded these by unit. Finally, I have carried out the first full detailed examination of the German casualties from an analysis of the Regimental Histories: the results are startling.

In the analytical sections of this book, I have also tried to bring the perspective of my own experience, that of a General Officer in command of troops from many nations on active service, to the way in which commanders and senior staff officers carried out their tasks during the Great War; in doing so I am not seeking to damage the reputations of any who cannot now answer back, nor to second-guess their decisions. What I am seeking to do, however, is point out where those responsibilities were and were not accepted and carried through and what, as a result, were the consequences. No-one who has held command in war on a post-modern battlefield can possibly compete or compare with the magnitude of the struggle in 1916; however, in principle, the exercise of command as a human activity, divorced from the advances of technology which allow the rapid passage of information and almost universal visibility over the battlefield, has not changed. For this reason, I have not been kind to either Lieutenant General Sir Henry Horne, or Major General Ivor Philipps; or at times General Sir William Rawlinson, Major General Herbert Watts, Brigadier General Llewellyn Price-Davies and Brigadier General Horatio Evans.

This book is not, however, just a survey of the Battle for Mametz Wood. It is a full account of the raising of what was intended to be the Welsh Army Corps and the early training and front-line service of the 38th (Welsh) Division. There is, of course, an official history of the Division published after the war and cited in the bibliography, but it is sketchy in the extreme on the first two years of the war, concentrating for the most part on 1917–18. This is, therefore, the first complete survey of the Welsh Division from its raising to the end of its part in the Battle of the Somme. Because there is a particularly Welsh angle to the narrative, I have also included brief summaries of the participation of Welsh battalions not in the 38th Division around Mametz in two chapters covering the period 1–5 July and 12–15 July; a summary of what happened to the remaining units raised in Wales for the Welsh Army Corps in one of the Annexes; and summaries of other relevant general and specific information as appendices to particular chapters, or stand-alone Annexes. I have also commented on some aspects of the politics and cultural *mores* of the day as they affected Wales and Welsh nationalism, since these were factors in the raising and the command of the Welsh Army Corps.

In any battle there are of course two sides. It would be very easy to concentrate exclusively on the Welsh experience in and around Mametz, for all the cultural and historical reasons outlined by Chris Williams and Colin Hughes. But as one wise old soldier once said to me, 'never forget that the enemy always has a vote'. Although German sources are fewer and many were destroyed during the Second World War, they are still there. With the help of researchers in the archives in Dresden, Munich, Stuttgart and Berlin, with the generous assistance of Jonathan Hicks, and drawing on the work of Jack Sheldon, I have done my best to represent the German side of the battle and to pay tribute to the soldierly qualities of the German Army in 1916. A German Army meant something very different to my father's and grandfathers' generations from what it means to us now: it should not be forgotten that the amateur soldiers of the 38th (Welsh) Division who were, as Shakespeare puts it, 'but warriors for the working day', faced some of the most professional units in what was the greatest and most consistently successful field army in Europe at the time – the Kaiser's *Reichsheer*.

Some readers may well take me to task for the preponderance of source material related to my old Regiment, The Royal Welch Fusiliers. I have tried wherever possible to cite the experience of veterans of the South Wales Borderers, the Welch Regiment and the combat support arms; however, it is an unavoidable fact that the records of The Royal Welch Fusiliers surpass all others in quality and quantity. This is true both of the formal archival material held in Wrexham, Aberystwyth and Kew, and of the personal accounts of the battle. As the Annex on writers and poets shows, the great majority of published accounts come from Fusiliers. At Mametz, these writings come from Robert Graves, Siegfried Sassoon, James Dunn, Frank Richards, Llewelyn Wyn Griffith, Emlyn Davies, Wynn Powell Wheldon, Bill Tucker and the poet, writer, calligrapher and artist David Jones. During the War, the Regiment's ranks also included other notable writers and artists of the period: the poet Vivian de Sola Pinto, the Welsh-speaking bard Ellis Humphrey Evans, or Hedd Wyn, Bernard Adams, Edward Vulliamy, J.N. More and the painter and illustrator Richard Lunt Roberts. It is almost easier to list the writers and artists of the War who did *not* serve in the Royal Welch Fusiliers, than those who did. This was not an isolated phenomenon but has been a feature of the Regiment since the 18th Century and one which continued through the Second World War and into modern times – but that is another story.

Lieutenant General Jonathon Riley, CB, DSO
February 2019

Acknowledgements

In putting together this account of the 38th (Welsh) Division I must first acknowledge my debt to the scholarship of Colin Hughes, Michael Renshaw, Chris Williams and Jonathan Hicks – and Colin Hughes in particular. Their accounts and analysis, their coverage of the experience of individuals, and their rebuttal of the criticisms made of the division's performance both at the time and later have provided the spine of this account. Jonathan Hicks also gave me a great deal of help with German sources for the fighting in Mametz Wood. I hope that I have fully and properly acknowledged their work throughout the text. Next, I acknowledge the huge work of Sir J.E. Edmonds in his official history, as well as C.H. Dudley Ward and Thomas Marden in their records of the service of The Royal Welch Fusiliers and the Welch Regiment. Marden's account is particularly important as he was a Commander 114 Infantry Brigade before, during and after the battle for Mametz Wood. Last but by no means least I would like to acknowledge my debt, and probably that of many others, to Jack Sheldon for his works on the German Army in the Great War, cited throughout the text. I am much indebted for photographs of the German experience of the war to James Payne and the on-line resource *Roads to the Great War*. They have provided images not previously seen and which bring the German perspective sharply into focus.

I would also like to acknowledge the easy partnership with Duncan Rogers and his team at Helion & Co, their excellent editing and production, and the production of the maps and research into the German original sources held in Berlin, Stuttgart, Munich and Dresden.

I would also like to thank a number of institutions and individuals for their invaluable assistance and their time, freely given. Mr Allan Poole and Ms Karen Murdoch in the R.W.F. Archives, who have spent many hours researching and copying documents and images; Mrs Anne Pedley, Secretary of the R.W.F. Trust for her help with the Stockwell papers; the Board of Trustees for permission to use material from the R.W.F. Regimental collections, especially the papers of Brigadier General Horatio Evans, David Jones, J.C. Dunn, Siegfried Sassoon and Robert Graves; the Stockwell family for permission to quote from the diary of C.I. Stockwell; Mr Richard Davies at the Brecon archives of the Welch Regiment, now the Royal Welsh; Mrs Jennifer Platt and Mr Tim Platt for permission to quote from the account of Captain C.J. Jones; the staff at the National Archives, Kew; the archivists at Churchill College, Cambridge; the staff at the National Library of Wales, Aberystwyth; Mr Alasdair Goulden and Mr Nick Keyes for proof-reading and suggesting amendments – especially Alasdair Goulden who has done this for me now on four occasions – and for helping me with research on the ground in France from 21–23 June 2018; Professor David Austin for his eye as an archaeologist on the battlefield of Mametz during the same period, and who has written the note on the archaeology of the battlefield. Finally, to my daughter Victoria for inspiring the cover and to my partner Clare for constant encouragement, help and support, for the benefit of her literary talents, and for suggesting the title of this book.

Note on Titles

According to the *Army List* at the time of the action of this book, the official spelling in the titles of The Royal Welch Fusiliers (23rd Foot) and the Welsh Regiment (41st/69th Foot) was 'Welsh', not Welch; this was not changed until 1920 (Army Order 56). The contemporary spelling has therefore been used throughout. Likewise, the abbreviated titles of all Regiments as listed at the time in *Field Service Regulations* have been used throughout this book and these are noted in the list of abbreviations below. For complete consistency with the practice of the time, private men in the R.W. Fus are given the rank of Private, not Fusilier, since this was the contemporary usage and again not changed until 1923 (AO 222).

A Note on the Archaeology of Mametz Wood
Composed after a Reconnaissance of the Ground, June 2018

Professor David Austin, Trinity St David's Lampeter

The landscapes of the area around Mametz Wood have not changed much in the course of the 100 years that separate us from the time before the battle in 1916. The battle itself was for a moment transformative as the accounts and images enshrined in records of all kinds tell us. No longer living, however, are those who can recall and recount what they saw and felt. So, what remains is no longer a truly memorial past; it is now, rather, a monumental one. That is, whatever we wish to learn must come from the abundant archives or from the ground itself. These are monuments not memories.

The momentary transformation was quickly past and human endeavour and the desire to win a living and forget the trauma was strong. Trenches in the open farmland were quickly back-filled burying a rich array of structures, artefacts and, sadly, human remains which, because they were sealed hermetically beneath millions of tons of alkali soils and rock, have a remarkable rate of survival.[1] Not only were the wartime trenches, block-houses and other military installations back-filled by farmers and the recovery teams despatched by the War Office, but also the rich grain fields were re-established and have been ploughed for nigh on a 100 years. So now, out in the fields, little is visible to the naked eye, except where modern tracks or roads may briefly follow a lost trench or light railway line. Modern archaeological techniques of geophysics or LiDAR can locate and delineate, but these are expensive and time-consuming. Sometimes after ploughing, when the crops are not yet growing in the Autumn, Winter or early Spring, differentiation of soil colour or very shallow linear depressions can be detected, but really only become trenches because we know from the records they are there. Elsewhere we, as professional field archaeologists, might pay them no heed at all. So ironically, we can today, standing among the growing wheat or rape, see little. But in reality, what is there is wonderfully preserved, as many archaeological projects in recent years have shown.[2] The Western Front as a landscape is thus a remarkable monument, one of the largest in the world, almost rivalling the Great Wall of China and thus, in its entirety, worthy of World Monument status.

Therefore, in the open fields of Mametz, where modern farming has even swept away many of the old hedgerows of the pre-war landscapes, I could stand with detailed maps of the trenches and still see nothing. In fact, as a medievalist, I could more easily reconstruct the great open field systems of the 14th century villages engraved into the land by hundreds or years of human labour, than I could catch a glimpse of the momentary horror of 1916 – however catastrophic was the intervention into the surface of the earth. Even this invisibility is an archaeological fact; a testament to the human spirit of survival and endeavour.

In Mametz Wood, however, it was entirely different. Robertshaw and Kenyon[3] have brilliantly described the survival of archaeological features in Thiepval Wood, another slaughter ground of the Somme campaign. There, as in Mametz Wood, archaeological features can be found everywhere. For a landscape archaeologist such as myself, the noticeable thing is how the woodland floor is covered in earthworks. These are mostly ill-shapen and eroded hollows which are most readily interpreted as shell holes, but only because of what we know took place there and nothing intrinsic. In the woodlands of the Weald these would be the pits and small quarries of the iron industry. They look the same. Even the command posts look like kilns and furnaces until you start to plan them and can see the structures they once were. These are very large earthworks and we can recover information about what they were and where they were. The hard truth, however, is that actually, we know all this and more from the records and photographs. This is true also of the more fugitive former trenches. Their remains are intermittent among the 100-year-old trees and undergrowth. Much has eroded and we can only see their lines in the landscape, for a moment so bold in 1916, and now gone, by joining together the fragments that represent each little stretch of earthwork. In the wood too and along the line of a new trench skirting it, this time for a gas pipeline, we could also find the artefacts of trench warfare.

There is however some certainty. In 2015, an archaeological team commissioned by Bearhug Television carried out excavation work in and around the Wood to investigate trench positions.[4] In addition to a LiDAR survey using hyper-spectral laser scanners and geophysical surveys, five excavation trenches were opened. The results identified vestiges of the trenches to the west of the Wood – such as Strip, Wood and Wood Support trenches; also, a series of features inside the Wood along the report lines of the 38th Division's assault. These excavations were dug entirely by hand. The excavations also confirmed the un-named German trench on the southern and south-eastern face of the Wood. As the report states:

> A visible earthwork was discerned a few metres inside the edge of the wood, it is in places up to 1m deep, measured from the top of the up-cast parapet to the top of the internal fill … The project felt that, as a German-built defence, this trench was likely to contain German artefacts and construction techniques, and so it proved. As an area not marked on trench maps, this location would certainly benefit from future topographic surveys to contribute to an overall study of the battle.

As a digging archaeologist, I found myself pondering my contribution to the already detailed and lengthy account of the Battle of Mametz Wood. This was unfamiliar territory in all sorts of ways. The archaeology, the material culture of war, is immensely rich. It is being dug up at precisely the moment when the Great War is passing from memory to monument. But why? This is the question elegantly addressed and answered by Robertshaw and Kenton. Their attempt to justify it as recovering details lost, and thus misremembered or forgotten in the fog of war, is only partly convincing. It is a very expensive way of recovering tiny details and even these can be contested, since they also depend on the process of interpretation. Their account of the excavations at Thiepval, however, gets closer to the truth. The very act of digging and exposing the past, of finding the human remains of those 'known only to God' is a performance of war, a shadow show of a trauma still not laid to rest in the national psyche. The proper burial of the dead in war cemeteries is an act of kindness amongst all this, but it is incidental.

As a landscape archaeologist I could certainly lend another pair of eyes to Jonathon Riley, and ones quite used to the task of reading traces and signs. We could follow the maps and confirm the position and nature of the things shown on them. It is also a mantra of the landscape archaeologist that we unravel the palimpsest of human action over long periods of time. We write narratives of place as they evolve and change. There is no sense of this in Conflict Archaeology as a sub-discipline. How did the acts of war fit into, adapt and change the world people lived in? The truth may be very little if at all. The acts of peace, sustained over much greater lengths of time than those of war, reinstated the status. Even Mametz Wood, which was blown to bits in July 1916, regenerated largely of its own accord – but also perhaps because the local people wanted it back in their world for complex economic and social reasons.

Finally, I asked myself how I would design an archaeological project of my kind at Mametz. I would first define the area as Jonathon has done in this book and as we did in the field: the land fought over from 6 to 11 July 1916. Then I would use maps and fieldwork to reconstruct the cultural terrain of the pre-war era as the base point and I would as a matter of course assess the historical evolution prior to that, largely from field morphology. Next, I would intensively survey with geophysics to find all the features which lie below ground. This would be an expensive business. This information can then be correlated with maps and documents to see where exactly everything was and, if there was anything, missing or misplaced in the accounts, it could be used to alter the narrative. In some cases, excavation might be needed to disentangle sequence such as what belonged to July 1916, and what to 1918 – or even to the Iron Age. This would define much more precisely the archaeological resource and give the data for a real landscape archaeology of the place and the event. But I would not dig to find remains unless it was to keep the memory alive.

When we had finished in the field and Jonathon went back to amend his account of the Battle of Mametz Wood, he wrote the following, which is what he got out of the presence of an occasionally bemused archaeologist:

> Changing land use patterns have had an effect on the surface of what was the battlefield. This is especially apparent outside the wooded areas. Here, a century of ploughing – and, since the 1960s, deep ploughing – has obliterated all signs of where the trench lines ran. These can be inferred only by comparing contemporary photographs and maps with the shape of the terrain, and also applying the principles of defence, inter-visibility and the ranges of weapons. Examples are the lines of Cliff, Quadrangle, Wood and Wood Support trenches. In one or two cases, such as Middle Alley, modern tracks follow the probably lines of the trenches where it seems possible that debris and rubble were used to form a hard road for wheeled agricultural vehicles.
>
> Another set of features that can be picked out from the lines of hard tracks is the network of light railway lines that ran around Mametz Wood, connecting the outlying agricultural areas with the station in Mametz village which was served by the main line from Peronne to Albert. Not all of these have survived, for example the siding or spur to the west of Mametz Wood, but most can still be followed. Indeed, in one place investigation revealed a section of rail doing duty as a fence post on the edge of Caterpillar Copse.
>
> Another feature that survives outside the wooded areas, in spite of ploughing, is the large amount of shrapnel from artillery fire, both British and German, which can be seen on the surface of the ground – a testament to the weight and intensity of the fire in July

1916. In some areas, most notably the south-west corner of Mametz Wood, a large quantity of horse-shoes, horse furniture and metal wagon parts were observed. The sketch in the text of this book by W.R. Thomas suggests that a horse-drawn German artillery battery was located in this area and from this, and the description by Robert Graves of wrecked artillery limbers, it seems possible that the battery's horses were killed by British counter-battery fire. Given that the Germans were having, as we know, great difficulty in supplying their troops, it seems possible that the dead horses were dismembered and used for food – the metal shoes are all that remains of them.

Inside the wooded areas the story is somewhat different. Many of these woods – and in particular Mametz Wood – were reduced to stumps during the heavy fighting; they have now fully regenerated and are in some cases being managed for both wood and for the preservation of game. Since no ploughing has taken place inside the woods, the trenches can be traced relatively easily by the lines of hollows and embankments, the parados being especially well preserved in many cases. Strip Trench, running down the western fringe of Mametz Wood, is readily identifiable. So too is the German trench running along the northern edge of Caterpillar Copse, a trench clearly sited to fire into the valley between the cliff and the Wood itself, using the protection of the cliff to hide from observed direct or indirect British fire, rather than being sited on the exposed southern crest line at the top of the Copse to fire forwards at the line of approach from the British line. Similarly, entrenchments inside Marlborough Wood are still clearly visible, especially at the north-western corner.

Of particular interest is the line of the un-named German trench running along the southern edge of Mametz Wood and the Hammerhead, as shown on the German maps and the sketch by W.R. Thomas as well as the various accounts cited in the narrative. This line can be readily identified along the whole of its length as far as its junction with the communication trench across to Flatiron Copse, where it disappears under the plough. Also of interest is the former regimental command post inside the southern edge of Mametz Wood, overlooking Wood and Wood Support trenches. This was, and is, a considerable earthwork with a network of trenches around it to provide local defence, and saps running forward to observation posts on the edge of the Wood. This is clearly marked on the German maps of the time and described in the account of *Leutnant* Köstlin; the remains are exactly where one would expect to find them from these descriptions.

Notes

1   Andrew Robertson and David Kenyon, *Digging the Trenches: the Archaeology of the Western Front* (London, 2007), p. 41 ff.

2   See, for example, Nicolas J. Saunders, *Killing Time: Archaeology and the First World War* (London, 2007).

3   Robertson and Kenyon.

4   Richard Osgood, *A Certain Cure for Lust of Blood: Archaeological Excavation Report, Mametz Wood, Somme* (Bearhug Television, 2005).

Glossary of Military Terms and Abbreviations

A.A. & Q.M.G.	Assistant Adjutant and Quartermaster General. The administrative department of a division, corps or army
A.D.C.	*Aide de Camp*, personal staff officer to a General.
A.M.	Albert Medal
A.N.Z.A.C.	Australia and New Zealand Army Corps
A.S.C.	Army Service Corps
B.E.F.	British Expeditionary Force
B.M.	Brigade Major, the senior General Staff Officer in a brigade headquarters
C.B.	Companion of the Most Honourable Order of the Bath
C.C.R.A.	Corps Commander Royal Artillery
C.H.	Companion of Honour
C.I.D.	Committee for Imperial Defence
C.I.G.S.	Chief of the Imperial General Staff
C.I.H.	Central India Horse
C.-in-C.	Commander in Chief
C.M.G.	Commander of the Order of St Michael and St George
C.R.A.	Commander Royal Artillery (at divisional level)
C.O.	Commanding Officer
D.C.M.	Distinguished Conduct Medal
D.G.	Dragoon Guards, heavy cavalry
D.L.	Deputy Lord Lieutenant (of a county)
Dorsets	The Dorsetshire Regiment
D.S.O.	Distinguished Service Order
E. Yorks	The East Yorkshire Regiment
Fd	Field
G.B.E.	Grand Commander of the Order of the British Empire
G.C.B.	Grand Commander of the Most Honourable Order of the Bath
G.C.M.G.	Grand Commander of the Order of St Michael and St George
G.H.Q.	General Headquarters, the command of the B.E.F. in France
G.C.V.O.	Grand Commander of the Royal Victorian Order
G.O.C.	General Officer Commanding

G.S.O. I	General Staff Officer Grade 1; the senior General Staff Officer in a divisional headquarters
I.R.	Infantry Regiment (German Army)
J.P.	Justice of the Peace, a magistrate
K.C.	King's Counsel
K.C.B.	Knight Commander of the Most Honourable Order of the Bath
K.C.I.E.	Knight Commander of the Indian Empire
K.G.	Knight of the Garter
K. St J.	Knight of the Order of St John of Jerusalem
K.T.	Knight of the Thistle
Leicesters	The Leicestershire Regiment
L.I.R.	*Lehr* Infantry Regiment
M.C.	Military Cross
M.G.	Machine Gun
M.i.D.	Mentioned in Despatches
M.M.	Military Medal
M.M.G.	Motorised Machine Gun
M.P.	Member of Parliament, Military Police
M.V.O.	Member of the Royal Victorian Order
N.C.O.	Non-Commissioned Officer
N.F.	Royal Northumberland Fusiliers
O.B.E.	Officer of the Order of the British Empire
O.M.	Order of Merit
P.C.	Privy Councillor
R.A.M.C.	Royal Army Medical Corps
R.A.P.	Regimental Aid Post
R.E.	Royal Engineers
R.F.A.	Royal Field Artillery
R.F.C.	Royal Flying Corps, the precursor, with the Royal Naval Air Service, of the Royal Air Force
R.F.L.	Restricted Fire Line. A line across which no unit or formation might fire without prior arrangement. Usually a boundary or forward control line
R.G.A.	Royal Garrison Artillery
R. Irish	The Royal Irish Regiment
R.I.R.	Reserve Infantry Regiment (German Army)
R.W. Fus	The Royal Welsh Fusiliers
Shrops L.I.	The King's Shropshire Light Infantry
S.R.	Special Reserve
S.W.B.	South Wales Borderers
T.D.	Territorial Force Decoration
T.F.	Territorial Force

T.M.	Trench Mortar
V.C.	Victoria Cross
Welsh	The Welsh Regiment
W.G.	Welsh Guards
Yorks	The Yorkshire Regiment, or the Green Howards
Z, Zero	The time at which an attack or major phase of operations began

Key to Military Symbols

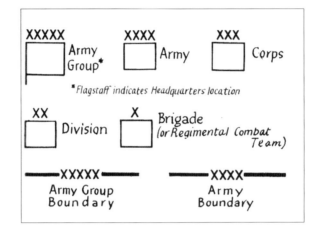

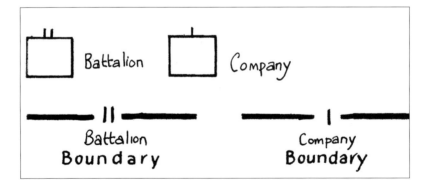

1

Lord Kitchener, the British Army and the Expeditionary Force 1904–1914

Like many young men of his age, 24-year-old Llewelyn Wyn Griffith was on holiday on 4 August 1914, enjoying the hot summer weather of that year. Again, like so many others, he returned home immediately to enlist when war with Germany was declared that day, lest he should miss the chance of action in what everyone – or nearly everyone – assumed would be a short war.[1] Wyn Griffith did not finish his service and return to his peace-time occupation as an inspector of taxes until 1919, by which time nearly 800,000 of his fellow citizens had been killed and four times as many injured, gassed shell-shocked or crippled by illness.

This short war was in the first instance fought by the British Expeditionary Force (B.E.F.), the original organisation of which had begun in 1906–1907, but it was at first, at least in the opinion of Parliament, the British public and the Committee for Imperial Defence (C.I.D.), destined for India. The work of the Extraordinary Committee under Lord Esher between November 1903 and February 1904,[2] and the Sub Committee of the C.I.D. under Lord Morley in 1907 had formalised the requirement for a military organisation at home capable of sending 100,000 men to India in the first year of a war.[*] These measures were aimed at a perceived continued threat to India from Russia rather than a major war with Germany on the continent of Europe. Esher himself wrote in 1905 that the Army:

> … is not to be organised for the defence of these shores, but is intended to take the field, at any threatened point where the interests of the Empire are imperilled, and especially on the North-West Frontier of India.[3]

The defence of Britain was to be in the hands of the Fleet, backed up by a Militia and Volunteer force should naval protection alone prove inadequate. A study by the C.I.D. in 1908 assessed that a home army should be 70,000 Volunteers and Militia backed by up to two divisions of regular troops,[4] a target never actually met. There was also, and remained, a body of opinion led by The National Service League which proposed conscription as the basis of a mass army to defend the country, but this never achieved official backing. Balfour's view was that Britain's continental neighbours had only one war to fear: a war on a large scale, with their own neighbours and so they needed large armies available to be called up in times of threat to the homeland. By

---

[*]   Ironically in 1914–1915, Indian troops were deployed to fight alongside the British Army in France and Flanders.

contrast in Britain: 'Our Army is wanted for purposes abroad … it is necessarily a professional army … because of the limited nature of its function – to strike at a distance – it ought to be of strictly limited dimensions.'[5]

However, as early as 1906, the embryonic British Imperial General Staff had urged the need to reconstitute Russia as a counterweight to Germany,[6] and had begun to espouse the idea of creating an effective expeditionary army of up to 200,000 men. This had its origins in a series of studies in the preceding year, 1905, which examined the feasibility of British military intervention on the Continent in the event of involvement in a Franco-German war. Study focused on what contribution a British army could make to redressing the military balance, and especially on the moral effect of British troops fighting alongside French, even though in comparatively small numbers. A war game was played based on the involvement of 473,000 German troops in an attack on France – but only four corps operating west of the Meuse,[7] a serious underestimation. However, this war game did much to lay the basis of British strategic thinking for the next nine years, for it deduced correctly that the main weight of a German attack on France would come through the Low Countries, and that if British help was to be effective it would have to be prompt. In September 1905, Balfour gave official authorisation to study the military implications of a violation of Belgian neutrality. The resulting memorandum stated:

> An efficient Army of 120,000 troops might just have the effect of preventing important German successes on the Franco-German frontier and of leading up to the situation that Germany, crushed at sea, also felt herself impotent on land … [8]

Subsequently, Balfour authorised contact for preliminary staff talks with the French which lasted from 15 December 1905 to 31 December 1906, in order to begin preliminary work on: '… arrangements for the mobilisation and transport to the northern French ports of [an expeditionary force] of 120,000 men.'[9] On 18 January 1906, Anglo-Belgian staff talks lasting three months began, for the Belgians, well-aware of the threat posed by Germany and of their guarantees under the Treaty of London (1831),[10] were anxious to see British troops in Belgium as soon as possible after landing in France.

Despite misgivings, these discussions were taken forward by the Liberal Government. Sir Edward Grey, the Liberal Foreign Secretary, fearing the growth of German power, resolved that Britain would not face Germany alone.[11] With the backing of Secretary for War Richard Haldane, Grey advised Prime Minister Campbell-Bannerman to continue the Anglo-French military co-operation; indeed the relationship with France grew so rapidly that: 'By 1907 the preservation of the *Entente Cordiale* had become the cardinal feature of Grey's diplomacy … '[12]

From 1909, both Army and Royal Naval plans were based on the assumption that a German attack on France or Belgium would be a *casus belli* for Britain, and that the B.E.F. would fall in on the French left flank. This planning derived directly from the political calculation that a German victory would upset the balance of power, and that the presence of a British force at the decisive point would be enough to tip the scales in favour of the French. The B.E.F. was not to be a masive Prussian-style force but a small, mobile and strategically decisive *balancing* force, ' … to make up for the inadequacy of the French Armies for their great task of defending the entire French frontier … '[13] This, however, was not revealed by Asquith or his government to Parliament or the public, and he was rescued from embarrassment only by the German violation of Belgian neutrality which Britain as a guarantor of the 1831 treaty could not ignore.

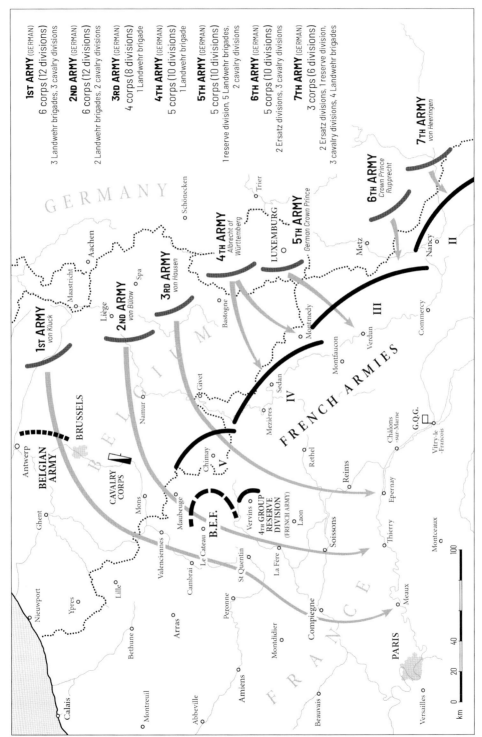

1ST ARMY (GERMAN)
6 corps (12 divisions)
3 Landwehr brigades, 3 cavalry divisions

2ND ARMY (GERMAN)
6 corps (12 divisions)
2 Landwehr brigades, 2 cavalry divisions

3RD ARMY (GERMAN)
4 corps (8 divisions)
1 Landwehr brigade

4TH ARMY (GERMAN)
5 corps (10 divisions)
1 Landwehr brigade

5TH ARMY (GERMAN)
5 corps (10 divisions)
1 reserve division, 5 Landwehr brigades,
2 cavalry divisions

6TH ARMY (GERMAN)
5 corps (10 divisions)
2 Ersatz divisions, 3 cavalry divisions

7TH ARMY (GERMAN)
3 corps (6 divisions)
2 Ersatz divisions, 1 reserve division,
3 cavalry divisions, 4 Landwehr brigades

Map 1.i The B.E.F. in relation to French, Belgian and German Armies in August 1914.

Initially, the conclusions of the Imperial General Staff specified a B.E.F. of four divisions (in two corps) and a cavalry division to reinforce the left flank of the French Army, landing in France and ready for action on the twentieth day after mobilisation. In 1911, however, the Wilson-Dubail memorandum specified 150,000 troops under French command in six divisions and one cavalry division, with two additional mounted brigades.[14] Thus the Force which was produced would, once the reforms of Lord Esher and of Haldane had done their work, and with the effort of the Imperial General Staff:

> Mobilise for service overseas a force consisting of four cavalry brigades and six divisions (each of three brigades) with the necessary troops for Lines of Communication, or roughly 150,000 officers and men. Of these about 50,000 would be regulars serving with the Colours, about 70,000 reservists, and about 30,000 men employed on a militia basis.[15]

The scale of war in 1914 was determined by the trained manpower available to the major protagonists: France 3.3 million, Germany 2.73 million, Russia 3.9 million, Austria-Hungary 2.3 million.[16] The six British divisions could be dwarfed by the French ability to mobilise 85 divisions, and Germany's (albeit to fight on two fronts) 110.[17] The B.E.F. therefore stood open to the charge that it was merely a political expedient bearing little correspondence to actual needs or obligations.[18] Nor was it sustainable in anything but a short war.

Sir William Nicholson, the Chief of the Imperial General Staff (C.I.G.S.) in 1906, put his finger on the nub of this issue when he said that: 'History teaches us that the crises of war on a large scale do not always – I might say do not generally – occur at the beginning of a campaign.'[19] In April of that year it was estimated that the B.E.F. would need up to 50,000 men in drafts trained and ready to replace the expected losses in a continental war. It was, however, abundantly clear that the existing structure of the Regular Reserves, Militia and Volunteers could not cope with this scale of reinforcement, dealing with which became one of the major achievements of the Haldane Reforms:

> If we engaged in a war of great severity and prolonged existence, what provision is made for further support and for expansion if necessary? The answer under the present circumstances is that provision is deficient … [20]

To remedy this situation, Haldane first re-formed the Militia into the Special Reserve, allocating 74 militia infantry battalions, one to every line regiment as its 3rd Battalion, as draft finders; an additional 24 formed militia infantry battalions to relieve Regular troops in garrison overseas; and a number of militia combat support and combat service support units.[21] This was an important step since the overseas garrisons contained the up-to-strength units of the army while those at home which were to form the Regular element of the B.E.F. were often under strength since their primary purpose was to supply drafts of trained men to those battalions overseas.

Associated with this was the structure of the Regular Reserve and the associated mobilisation procedures. By 1914, the standard Regular Army engagement was seven years with the Colours and five in the reserve,[22] which had produced an available manpower of 145,090.*

---

*   5,823 Class A men who had volunteered for recall in an emergency short of general war; 104,096 seven-year men; and 35,171 12-year men.

An efficient recall and mobilisation process existed, by which men knew to which unit they belonged, and this was backed up by a comprehensive movement plan and reception plan at regimental and corps depots. When put to the test in 1914, the system in general worked extremely smoothly.

Next, Haldane paved the way for *The Territorial and Reserve Forces Act* (1907). This re-formed the Volunteer forces of late Victorian Britain into the Territorial Force (T.F.), whose units were to be linked directly to, indeed part of the order of battle of, Regular Regiments and Corps. The T.F. would comprise 14 divisions and four Yeomanry brigades organised on the Regular Army model,[23] and offered the great advantage that it was organised on a war establishment basis and therefore more complete than Regular divisions in peacetime.[24] The T.F. would be mobilised in order to train for war and be ready after six months. It came into being on 1 April 1908 with an Establishment of 302,199. By 1 June it had reached 144,620; by 1 December 207,000; and by 25 February 1910, 276,618.[25]

By 1914 the B.E.F. was thus well organised for its limited task and backed by sufficient machinery of reserves and the T.F. to keep it in the field for a limited time. But when it *was* committed to war in 1914 it was not considered by many that its size would grow as it did during the course of the ensuing war. The instructions to Sir John French were quite clear in this respect:

> The numerical strength of the British Force and its contingent reinforcements is strictly limited, and with this consideration kept steadily in view it will be obvious that the greatest care must be exercised towards a minimum of loss and wastage … [26]

By December 1914, however, it was clear that the war was not going to be a short one and that all the assumptions which had led to the formation of the B.E.F. were invalid. If the war was to be prosecuted to a victorious ending, the British Army would have to be hugely expanded in size. Quality would be an issue, given the massive losses suffered by the Regular Army during the first five months of the war. A government report, published in 1922, summarised the losses of the B.E.F. in 1914:[27] out of a total of 165,000 officers and men employed in the B.E.F. and on the lines of communication, 3,627 officers and 84,275 other ranks had been killed, wounded, taken prisoner or gone missing – that is, half the total deployed. The effect on the Army was dramatic, for many professional officers and N.C.O.s were lost, with the consequent effect on the efficiency of the Army. Its entire peace-time strength in 1914 had been 223,000, with another 145,000 in the Regular Reserve and 64,000 in the Special Reserve. Close on a quarter of this total had therefore been killed, wounded or captured.

Many Regular units had to be rebuilt from scratch; the example of one Welsh Regular battalion tells the story. The 1st Battalion of The Royal Welsh Fusiliers (1 R.W. Fus) had shipped from Malta, landing on 7 October 1914 at Zeebrugge, at a strength of 1,150 men – of whom 342 were reservists – and joined the 7th Division.[28] During the First Battle of Ypres, 1 R.W. Fus had been ordered to advance eastwards from Ypres. By 20 October it was no more than 400 men strong and it was almost annihilated by a German attack to the west of Zandvoorde where it was reduced to only 90 all ranks. Its Commanding Officer, Lieutenant Colonel H.O.S. ('Hal') Cadogan, was among those killed. By 31 October only 30 men and a Quartermaster Sergeant were still alive and unwounded, and the battalion was temporarily amalgamated with 1 Queen's, which has sustained similar losses, until it could be rebuilt. A final action took place at Zillebeke on 7 November.[290] The battalion's losses at this point amounted to 37 officers and 1,024 men, of whom 22 officers and 796 men were either dead or had become prisoners of war.

To begin the task of expansion there was of course the Territorial Force, as already described; moreover, the Indian Army, with its 155,000 men in nine divisions,[30] of which two infantry divisions and a cavalry brigade were earmarked for service in the case of a European War. In the early days of the war, Indian Army units relieved British regular units in garrisons overseas, permitting the formation of two new regular divisions, the 7th and 8th, which were sent to France.

When added together, these resources were far short of what was needed to field an Army capable of taking on a long war with the Germans, even in alliance with the French. Among the first to realize this was the newly-appointed Secretary of State for War, Lord Kitchener. Kitchener was still a serving soldier, with enormous prestige in the country after his conquest of the Sudan and his victory in South Africa. He had also reformed the Indian Army and been Consul-General in Egypt – the effective ruler of that country under British domination. *The Times* had firmly endorsed him over the other contender, Lord Haldane, declaring that:

> It is necessary that the army should be in the firm hands of a man in whom the public have confidence; and we do not know where we can find any head for the War Office who would be more completely secure in this confidence than Lord Kitchener … a capable adminis-trator, and a first-rate organiser.[31]

This was more than a little unfair to Lord Haldane, the man who had reorganised the Army reserves and put them on a footing for modern war, but Haldane was an admirer of Germany and so disqualified in the eyes of most people. Kitchener therefore took office 'without in any way identifying himself with any set of political opinions.'[32]

As early as 1911 Kitchener had estimated that a Great War would last at least three years, and in this he differed markedly from his new Cabinet colleagues and the assumptions outlined above. He also believed that British military strength could not be fully deployed until 1917.[33] On appointment, Kitchener immediately re-stated his view that the war would last for years and that the Regular Army was wholly inadequate for the task. The Territorial Force he regarded as partly trained and poorly equipped, and not fully under War Office Control, for it was answerable to the County Associations in the areas in which it was recruited, even though Haldane had seen it as the basis for augmenting an expeditionary force. Its members were, moreover, not liable for service overseas unless they volunteered. One of his first acts was to demand that the County Associations reorganise the Territorials into Home Service units and foreign service units, so that those who were willing and able to go overseas could do so.[34] This permitted the immediate movement of three Territorial divisions to the Mediterranean, relieving regular troops in garrisons there, and permitting the formation of three new regular divisions – the 27th, 28th and 29th. The formation of second and third line Territorial units followed, with battalions, brigades and then divisions moving to France. By the end of the war the Territorial Force had expanded to 28 divisions, of which 22 served overseas.[35]

Kitchener's model for expansion was not, however, the T.F., but the Regular Army, for which General Mobilisation had been declared on 4 August.[36] On the evening of 6 August 1914, as Kitchener arrived to take office, Prime Minister Herbert Asquith asked Parliament to increase the size of the Army by half a million, by which Kitchener aimed to create:

... such a force as would enable us continuously to reinforce our troops in the field by fresh divisions ... so that at the conclusive period of the war we should have the maximum trained fighting army this country could produce.[37]

Kitchener would no doubt have welcomed conscription to raise this number of men, but there was a view that compulsory military service would not be tolerated by the British people. This is an odd view when one considers that for most of British history, military service *was* compulsory. From Anglo-Saxon times to the middle of the 19th century, service in the Militia had been a requirement. The Militia indeed had been for centuries the biggest part of the British military establishment; its control had been a root cause of the civil wars of the 17th century. Most people alive in 1914 would have known that.

The famous recruiting poster featuring Lord Kitchener, urging voluntary enlistment.

Instead of compulsion, therefore, Kitchener called for volunteers, asking on 7 August for 100,000 men to join the regular Army for either three years, or the duration of the war, whichever was longer.[38] 30,000 men applied in the first week, as many as the recruiting organisation dealt with in a normal year. additional recruiting offices had to be opened to deal with the numbers: the target of 100,000 was reached by late August and by September, the rate of enlistment had gone from 30,000 a week, to 30,000 a day. Asquith had to return to Parliament and ask sanction for a further half a million. It was with Kitchener therefore that total commitment to a continental war began.[39]

Whilst the B.E.F. fought for its life in France and Belgium during late 1914, Kitchener's New Army began to take shape. Army Orders in August and September laid down the formation of six new infantry divisions, consisting of 80 battalions, and army troops units, for the First Army (K1).[40] It was soon followed by a Second Army (K2),[41] and then a Third. The order for the last of these, for example, specified the regulations:

2. These Divisions will be numbered from 21 to 26.

3. The new battalions will be raised as additional battalions of the regiments of Infantry of the Line and will be given numbers following consecutively on the existing battalions of those regiments. They will be further distinguished by the word "Service" after numbers.[42]

There were in the end five 'Armies', listed in the Appendix to this chapter, but they never took the field as such. The divisions were sent abroad to various theatres as they became available, joining field formations in various theatres. The divisions were numbered in sequence following on from the eight regular divisions and taking precedence over the Territorial Force formations, with a break for the three regular divisions formed in the Middle East; they were initially named after the regional Army Commands from which they were drawn.

Of course, this method was not efficient in terms of the allocation of manpower between formations and theatres, not to mention the needs of the Royal Navy, the Royal Flying Corps,

A recruiting office overwhelmed with potential soldiers in 1914.

the technical arms and services, the Territorial Force, the Special Reserve as the supplying agency for the regular Army – and of course the needs of the merchant marine and war industries such as munitions, steelworks, shipbuilding and the mines. In due course this had to be addressed, as the competition for manpower was fierce.

By June 1915, with stalemate on Western Front, a real choice had to be made between total commitment in the west or retaining some freedom of action: there were still significant forces in the Mediterranean and Middle East and although these might have knocked out Germany's ally Turkey, they could also, by weakening the Western Front, have lost Britain's major ally, France. Although Churchill won the argument in the short term, and the Dardanelles campaign was duly launched, Kitchener was in no doubt as to the only possible course of action: that Britain should: ' … act with all our energy and do our utmost to help the French.'[43] This commitment to the Anglo-French alliance lay at the very heart of Kitchener's policy and is something for which he received little acclaim until recent times, due mainly to his support for what were to be abortive and costly offensive operations in France in 1915, in spite of the failure of the Gallipoli operation.[44] It was Kitchener, therefore, who laid the basis for the expansion of the British Army as a force on the world stage.

1 R.W. Fus near Mons in
August 1914.

Appendix

Kitchener Armies in Order of Formation

Kitchener Army	Date of Formation	Divisions	Sent To
K1	7 August 1914	9th (Scottish)	France/Flanders
		10th (Irish)	Egypt/Gallipoli
		11th (Northern)	Egypt/Gallipoli
		12th (Eastern)	France/Flanders
		13th (Western)	Mediterranean
		14th (Light)*	France/Flanders
K2	11 September 1914	15th (Scottish)	France/Flanders
		16th (Irish)	France/Flanders
		17th (Northern)	France/Flanders
		18th (Eastern)	France/Flanders
		19th (Western)	France/Flanders
		20th (Light)	France/Flanders
K3	13 September 1914	21st	France/Flanders
		22nd	France/Flanders
		23rd	France/Flanders
		24th	France/Flanders
		25th	France/Flanders
		26th	France/Flanders
K4†	October 1914‡	30th	France/Flanders
		31st	France/Flanders
		32nd	France/Flanders
		33rd	France/Flanders
		34th	France/Flanders
		35th	France/Flanders

Kitchener Army	Date of Formation	Divisions	Sent To
K5	10 October 1914	36th (Ulster)	France/Flanders
		37th	France/Flanders
		38th (Welsh)	France/Flanders
		39th	France/Flanders
		40th	France/Flanders
		41st	France/Flanders
K6	10 October 1914	42nd (Ulster)§	All renumbered in April
		43rd (Welsh)	1915 as K5
		44th	
		45th	
		46th	
		47th	

*   Originally the 8th Division but renumbered when the regular Army raised the 8th Infantry Division.
†   In April 1915 the divisions of the original fourth Kitchener Army were broken up to provide reinforcements. The Fifth Army was re-designated as the Fourth and a new Fifth was raised with the same numbers. Thus the 38th (Welsh) Division was originally 43rd Division.
‡   There are no Army Orders directing the formation of K4, K5 and K6 in the contemporary HMSO printed calendar.
§   Raised as the Ulster Division and renumbered on 28 August 1914.

Notes

1   Llewelyn Wyn Griffith (ed. and annotated by Jonathon Riley), *Up to Mametz ... And Beyond* (Barnsley, 2010), pp. xiii-xiv.
2   Report of the War Office (Reconstitution) Committee, 1904 (Esher Report) (Parliament Command Paper 1932).
3   M.V. Brett (ed), *Journals and Letters of Reginald Viscount Esher Vol. II* (London, 1934) p. 75.
4   Michael Howard, *The Continental Commitment: The dilemma of British defence policy in the era of the two world wars* (London, 1989), p. 40.
5   Colonel John R. Dunlop, *The Development of the British Army 1899–1914* (London, 1938), p. 250. A characteristic of military thinking during the 18th and 19th Centuries had been that forward operations on the continent by a field army might at times be required to supplement the defence of Britain itself by the fleet.
6   Howard, p. 34.
7   S.R. Williamson, *The Politics of Grand Strategy. British and French Preparations for War, 1904–1914* (OUP, 1969), pp. 46–47.
8   T.N.A. WO 106/46/E2.10 Memo by Colonel Callwell dated 3 October 1905.
9   T.N.A. CAB /18/24 dated 19th December 1905. See also Williamson, p. 61.
10   Report of the Mowatt Commission (HMSO, 1904), p. 74.
11   Williamson, p. 6.
12   Williamson, p. 96.
13   Dunlop, p. 243.
14   Howard, p. 60. The Royal Navy had aided this commitment by refusing to guarantee disembarkation ports above the line Dover-Calais.
15   Memorandum by the Secretary of State for War on Army Reorganisations, 30 July 1906 (Haldane Report) (Parliament Command Paper 2993), p. 2; Major General W.H. Anderson CB, *An Outline of the Development of the British Army up to the Commencement of the Great War 1914. Notes on four lectures delivered at the Staff College, Camberley* (London, 1920) p. 49. See also Peter Simkins, *Kitchener's Armies: The Raising of the New Armies, 1914–16* (Manchester, 1988), pp. 6–8.
16   Martin Van Creveld, *Command in War* (Cambridge, Massachusetts,1985), p. 149.
17   Winston Churchill, *The World Crisis 1911–1918* (London, 1931), p. 53.

18 Williamson, p. 99.
19 E.M. Spiers, cited in Beckett and Gooch, p. 75.
20 Memorandum by the Secretary of State for War on Army Reorganisations, 30 July 1906 (Haldane Report) (Parliament Command Paper 2993). See also E.M. Spiers, *Haldane: An Army Reformed* (Edinburgh, 1980).
21 Haldane Report, p. 8.
22 *The Times History of the War* (Published Weekly, 1914–1919), Vol. I, p. 130.
23 Anderson, p. 48.
24 Haldane Report, p. 8.
25 Williamson, p. 279.
26 Sir J.E. Edmonds, *History of the Great War based on Official Documents by direction of the Historical Section of the Committee of Imperial Defence. Military Operations France and Belgium, 1916* (London, 1932), p. 499.
27 *Statistics of the Military Effort of the British Empire during the Great War 1914–1920* (War Office, March 1922).
28 C.H. Dudley Ward, *Regimental Records of the Royal Welch Fusiliers, Vol. III, 1914–1918* (London, 1928).
29 See the account in Henry Cadogan, *The Road to Armageddon* (Wrexham, 2009).
30 Graham Watson, *1914 Indian Army Order of Battle* <http://www.orbat.info> (Accessed 29 August 2017).
31 *The Times,* 4 August 1914.
32 Hansard's *Parliamentary Debates,* House of Commons Official Report, dated 6 August 1914, column 2082.
33 Ian Beckett and John Gooch (ed), *Politicians and Defence: Studies in the Formulation of British Defence Policy* (Manchester, 1981), p. 97.
34 Formalised in A.O. 399 of 1914 dated 21 September 1914, in *Army Orders* (London, 1915).
35 Colin Hughes, *Mametz. Lloyd George's 'Welsh Army' at the Battle of the Somme* (London, 1982), p. 20.
36 A.O. 281 of 1914 dated 4 August 1914.
37 Beckett and Gooch, p. 97; for a full explanation of the process see Peter Simkins *Kitchener's Armies: The Raising of the New Armies, 1914–16* (Manchester, 1988).
38 *The Times,* 7 August 1914.
39 Rhodri Williams, 'Lord Kitchener and the Battle of Loos' in *War, Strategy and International Politics*, ed Freedman *et al,* (Oxford, 1992), p. 123; Esher's Journal, 24 December 1914.
40 A.O. 324 of 1914 dated 21 August 1914.
41 A.O. 382 of 1914 dated 9 September 1914.
42 A.O. 388 of 1914 dated 11 September 1914.
43 Kitchener to Haig, in Robert Blake (ed), *The Private Papers of Douglas Haig 1914–1919* (London, 1952) p. 102. See also David French, p. 21 and Kennedy, pp. 458–460.
44 Rhodri Williams, pp. 118–119.

2

Lloyd George's Welsh Army, 1914–1915

David Lloyd George, the most eminent, prominent and recognisable Welshman of his day, was 41 years old in 1914 and had been Chancellor of the Exchequer in Asquith's government for six years.* He had opposed the Anglo-Boer War and had been originally against war with Germany. However, as a member of a small nation, he was roused by the spectacle of another small nation, Belgium, resisting the demands of a much larger nation, Germany, for passage across its sovereign territory. It was in this spirit

David Lloyd George in 1914.

that he made his famous intervention into the raising of Kitchener's New Armies and Wales's part in this great endeavour. In his speech on 19 September at Queen's Hall in London he set out his vision:

> I should like to see a Welsh Army in the Field. I should like to see the race that faced the Norman for hundreds of years in a struggle for freedom, the race that helped to win Crecy, the race that fought for a generation under Glendower against the greatest Captain in Europe – I should like to see that race give a god taste of its quality in this struggle in Europe; and they are going to do it.[1]

Two days later, on 21 September, a conference of prominent Welshmen was convened at 10 Downing Street; among those present, in addition to Lloyd George, were the Rt Hon Reginald

---

*   David Lloyd George, 1st Earl Lloyd-George of Dwyfor OM PC (1863–1945). He became Prime Minister of the Wartime Coalition Government from 1916 in succession to Asquith and remained in post until 1922. He was a major contributor to the Paris Peace Conference of 1919 that reordered Europe, the Ottoman Empire and the Middle East, and the former German Imperial territories. His two sons both served in The Royal Welsh Fusiliers during the war.

McKenna M.P.,[*] the Earl of Plymouth,[†] Lord Mostyn,[‡] Lord Kenyon,[§] Sir David Brynmor Jones K.C.,[¶] Lord Treowen,[**] Mr William Brace M.P.;[††] Mr R.T. Jones; and Mr O.W. Owen acting as secretary. The conference was in no doubt that public feeling in Wales was very much in favour of the war, but those present saw a pressing need to improve the recruiting organisation; and to group those joining the Army in Wales as well as many London Welshmen, into a Welsh Army Corps. As the minutes record: 'It is well within the recollection of all how the military pride of Wales was gratified when the Welsh units of the Territorial Force were formed into a Welsh Division under a Welsh Officer – General Sir Francis Lloyd.'

Wales already provided six infantry battalions of the Regular Army – the 1st and 2nd Battalions of The Royal Welsh Fusiliers (R.W. Fus), the Welsh Regiment (Welsh) and the South Wales Borderers (S.W.B.) – the last only partly Welsh as the Regiment recruited in Monmouthshire, which was an English county in 1914 although closely associated with Wales. Each of these Regiments had a training depot – at Wrexham, Cardiff and Brecon respectively – and a Special Reserve battalion tasked with providing drafts in wartime to keep the regular battalions in the field up to strength as described in Chapter 1. Wales also found two Regular Cavalry Regiments, the 3rd (Prince of Wales's) Dragoon Guards and the 12th (Prince of Wales's) Royal Lancers. In February 1915, a single battalion of the Welsh Guards was formed by Major General Sir Francis Lloyd,[‡‡] General Officer Commanding London District, as part of the effort to raise enough battalions for the Guards Division.[2] Lloyd was a Welshman and a Grenadier; the Grenadier Guards at that time recruited in Cardiff and it was from the Grenadiers that the cadre of this new Regiment was formed.

In the Territorial Army, Wales found the 53rd (Welsh) Division, headquartered at Shrewsbury, with its three brigades (158, 159 and 160) and divisional troops in North Wales, South Wales and the Welsh and English counties of the Marches. In January 1915 the 2nd Welsh Division was formed as a second-line T.F. division, a duplicate of the 53rd. It also included units from Cheshire and Herefordshire. In August 1915 it was numbered as the 68th (2nd Welsh) Division. It served on home defence duties throughout the war, while also recruiting, training and supplying drafts to overseas units. It was stationed for most of the war in East Anglia. Also within the Territorial Force was the Monmouthshire Regiment, one of five infantry Regiments

---

[*]   Reginald McKenna (1863–1943) was a banker and Liberal politician who served under Henry Campbell-Bannerman as President of the Board of Education, and then First Lord of the Admiralty. He was Home Secretary and Chancellor of the Exchequer under Asquith.

[†]   Robert George Windsor-Clive, 1st Earl of Plymouth GBE CB PC (1857–1923).

[‡]   Llewelyn Neville Vaughan Lloyd-Mostyn, 3rd Baron Mostyn (1856–1929).

[§]   Lloyd Tyrell-Kenyon, 4th Baron Kenyon (1864–1927).

[¶]   David Brynmor Jones (1851–1921), barrister, historian and Liberal Member of Parliament for Swansea.

[**] Major General Ivor John Caradoc Herbert, 1st Baron Treowen CB CMG KStJ (1851–1933), a Liberal politician and officer in the Grenadier Guards. He was General Officer Commanding the Militia of Canada from 1890 to 1895.

[††] William Brace (1865–1947) was a trade unionist, Liberal and later Labour politician.

[‡‡] Later Lieutenant General Sir Francis Lloyd GCVO KCB DSO (1853–1926) was Major General Commanding the Brigade of Guards and General Officer Commanding London District from 1913 to 1918. He was also Colonel of The Royal Welsh Fusiliers.

in the Army which existed only in the T.F.[*] This Regiment, which formed 10 battalions during the course of the war, was permitted to contribute only three battalions (2/1, 2/2 and 2/3) to one of the Welsh Divisions, the 68th; the remainder served in other Regular and T.F. divisions in the Middle East and on the Western Front.[3] Finally there were two Yeomanry cavalry brigades: the South Wales Mounted Brigade, formed from the Yeomanry regiments of Glamorgan, Montgomeryshire and Pembrokeshire; and the Welsh Border Mounted Brigade, formed from those of Denbighshire, Cheshire and Shropshire. The Welsh Horse was formed subsequently.

The manpower bill for these units and formations came to more than 27,000 men, without counting the turnover from casualties. The proposal for the Welsh Army Corps required that over and above these existing commitments, Wales would raise an additional formation of two divisions and corps troops, around 40,000 men. As the report on the project put it: '… it is only when taken as an addition to, and not part of, the national requirements that the task… will be appreciated in its proper perspective.'[4] One must therefore pause and consider whether this was at all feasible. The male population of Wales and Monmouthshire between the ages of 20 and 40 was just over 400,000 in 1914, and half of these were in Glamorgan. One man in 10 would be needed for the initial formation of the corps, without considering the turnover required by casualties and discharges for other reasons. When the existing commitment was added, this rose to 67,000 men plus turnover, or almost one in six. Given also the competing requirements of the Royal Navy and merchant marine; and the requirements of war industry in Wales – especially the coal mines, docks and steel works – this figure appears challenging.

Nevertheless, a conference was convened at Park Hall, Cardiff on 29 September; the meeting was called on 25 September, a Friday, only five days ahead of the actual date. Present at this conference were all the Welsh Anglican bishops, most of the peers, and the military, political and commercial leaders of Wales. The Conference adopted a resolution to raise enough men, some 40,000, to form the Corps with the endorsement of Lord Kitchener and appointed a National Executive Committee of 27 members under chairmanship of the Earl of Plymouth.[5]

The Committee met for first time on 2 October. Unsurprisingly, the first problem to be addressed was the relationship of the Welsh Army Corps with the Regular Army, Special Reserve and T.F. The Committee had no control over the machinery of recruiting, which was geared to maintaining the existing Regular divisions via the Special Reserve and the T.F.; recruiting offices were therefore allocating all recruits to the Special Reserve battalions of the Regular regiments and to the T.F. as required. A firm measure of control was therefore needed and the Committee asked for the authority the General Officer Commanding–in–Chief (G.O.C.-in-C.), Western Command, Lieutenant General Sir Henry Mackinnon,[†] for a Superintendant of Recruiting. The Committee recommended Major General Lord Treowen for this role, which was, however, not sanctioned, although in 1916 Lord Derby's Scheme adopted a similar model.

The pool of available manpower was already shrinking. By 30 September 1914, 50,000 Welsh men had joined the Royal Navy, the Regular Army and the T.F. Another complicating factor was that many men in South Wales were not Welsh but were Irish or West Country men who

---

[*]   The other four were the Cambridgeshire Regiment, the Herefordshire Regiment, the Hallamshire Regiment and the London Regiment. The last was not really a regiment, but an umbrella for 26 battalions formed locally in Greater London, some but not all of which were affiliated to Line Regiments.

[†]   General Sir William Henry Mackinnon GCB KCVO (1852–1929).

had arrived to work in the steel works, pits and dockyards. To kick things off, therefore, the Committee asked that three battalions from Swansea, North Wales and the Rhondda,* which were about to be allocated by the Special Reserve to K4 divisions, should be allocated to the Welsh Army Corps. Permission was also sought to raise Welsh battalions in London, Liverpool and Manchester from among expatriate Welshmen there.[6] Nothing came of this scheme in Manchester and Liverpool, although many Welshmen from those cities enlisted as individuals; but in London the 15th (1st London Welsh) Battalion of The Royal Welsh Fusiliers was quickly formed. 15 R.W. Fus. was inaugurated at a meeting of London Welshmen on 16 September 1914, presided over by Sir Vincent Evans.† It was officially recognised on 29 October and for its first few months, drilled in the garden and square of Gray's Inn under the command of Lieutenant Colonel I. Bowen, and soon after, a Regular officer, Lieutenant Colonel William Fox-Pitt of the Grenadier Guards: it was here, after the war, that its memorial was placed and here it still remains. W.A. (Bill, or sometimes Tommy) Tucker‡ recalled that:

> The growing unit assembled every day in the grounds of Gray's Inn, London, and we all returned to our homes every night. To recompense for this burden on our private finances our pay was (temporarily) raised to three shillings (15p) a day. The basic pay was one shillng (5p).[7]

David Jones, the artist and writer, who was then 19 years old, joined the battalion after his father had written personally to Lloyd George, and he had heard Lloyd George's speech on 19 September.[8] Initially, he was de-barred from enlistment by a weak chest but was accepted, like many others, when the requirements were relaxed in January 1915. The Committee further decided that in order to be manageable, recruiting had to be carried out on a county basis. Wales was to be divided into 13 county recruiting districts, with each Lord Lieutenant in charge of a county committee which would include employers and working people, and which would operate through the county council. Service units would be created by and in each county, with all expenses met by the National Executive Committee.

The Committee would also see to the clothing, housing and feeding of recruits until the War office

David Jones. (RWF Mus)

---

*   13th (1st North Wales) R.W.F., a 'Pals' battalion raised in Rhyl on 3 September; 10th Welsh, formed in the Rhondda on 1 October; 14th Welsh was raised in Swansea from the local football and cricket clubs during September.

†   Sir (Evan) Vincent Evans CH (1851–1934) was a journalist and promoter of the Welsh national revival.

‡   W.A. Tucker (1897–1987) later worked for *The Times* as head of special publications and helped to launch *The Times Atlas of the World*. His autobiography, *The Lousier War*, is a fascinating memoir of life as a prisoner of war in German hands.

took over the new units, providing arms and all military equipment. This scheme was, however, only taken up in Caernarvonshire and Carmarthenshire. Finally in the initial period, the Committee asked the War Office to reduce the minimum height restriction for enlistment to 5 feet 3 inches (160 cm); in addition, 'Bantam' battalions were to be created from men between 5 feet (150 cm) and 5 feet 3 inches tall.[9]

15 R.W. Fus memorial in Gray's Inn. (Author's collection)

Official sanction for the Corps was not easily obtained, in spite of the enthusiasm of the Committee.[10] Kitchener went so far as to question the reliability of Welsh units and objected strongly to an all-Welsh formation of corps size. There were further clashes in Cabinet between Lloyd George and Kitchener; these were at least partially resolved on 10 October, when Kitchener gave tacit approval for the scheme. Authority to form the Welsh Army Corps of two divisions was then given by the War Office in a letter to the G.O.C.-in-C Western Command:

> I am commanded by the Army Council to inform you that sanction is given to raise the necessary troops in Wales and Monmouthshire and from Welshmen resident in London, Liverpool and Manchester to form a Welsh Army Corps consisting of two divisions… The infantry battalions will be service battalions of the Royal Welsh Fusiliers, South Wales Borderers, and Welsh Regiment.[11]

The association of new battalions with old Regiments was important, for it was in its Regiments that the traditions, the strength and the morale of the British infantry rested. E.S. Turner wrote of this that:

> No subaltern on the Western Front had read, or heard of, Wolseley's Pocket Book, but all grew to recognise the truth which Wolseley set out; "The soldier is a peculiar being that can alone be brought to the highest efficiency by inducing him to believe that he belongs to a regiment that is infinitely superior to the others round him." That was the Old Army's source of strength; and that faith in the regiment could be agreed through 20 battalions with very little dilution.[12]

Robert Graves, who was commissioned into the Special Reserve of the Royal Welsh Fusiliers, discoursed on the same subject:

> I used to congratulate myself on having chosen, quite blindly, this of all regiments. "Good God!" I used to think, "Suppose that when war broke out I had been living in Cheshire and had applied for a commission in the Cheshire Regiment …"

The regimental spirit persistently survived all catastrophes. Our First Battalion, for instance, was annihilated within two months of joining the British Expeditionary Force… In the course of the war at least 15 to 20,000 men must have passed through each of the two line battalions[*27]… the ranks were filled up with new drafts from home, with lightly wounded from the previous disaster returning after three or four months' absence, and with the more seriously wounded returning after nine months or a year.[13]

This did not stop the Regular and Special Reserve officers (and men) looking down on the 'temporary gentlemen' of the New Armies, however. Pre-war Regular and Militia (later S.R.) officers were generally drawn from the families of gentlemen, and often followed several generations of forebears in the same Regiment. They were educated at Public Schools and in the case of Regulars, went through Sandhurst as Gentleman Cadets. The Territorial Force officers were for the most part drawn from the local landed gentry. By contrast the New Armies took their officers from wherever they could find them, selection being based on patronage or educational achievement. Many New Army officers were therefore middle-class: the sons of tradesmen or school teachers and as such, not quite the thing as far as the pre-war standards of the Regiments saw it. Their commissions were therefore strictly limited to the duration of the war.

Official sanction for the Welsh Army Corps, moreover, included several conditions: first, that all recruiting was done through the Regular offices, which would keep existing units filled up before allocating men to new ones; secondly, that all recruiting until further notice would be for the infantry and so for the time being, the Corps would have no artillery, engineer, medical or service units; and last that the T.F. was *not* to be made available as part of the Corps. These constraints were severe. The existing priorities for recruits remained as before; there were no divisional or corps troops units and no combat support or service support units for the infantry; and the 53rd Division, the two Yeomanry brigades and the Monmouthshire Regiment were to remain outside the construct of the Welsh Army Corps. The participation of the Welsh Regular Army infantry battalions and cavalry Regiments was not even considered. It must be concluded therefore that Kitchener and the War Office were at best lukewarm about the idea of a Welsh Army Corps; at worst, it might be thought that the whole idea was being quietly sabotaged.

There were further reports of anti-Welsh bias in official circles which caused great anger. Welsh recruits were forbidden to speak Welsh on duty or even in billets, presaging another row in Cabinet.[14] In North Wales in particular, this had to be overcome by promising that recruits, especially Welsh-speaking recruits, would be given training under Welsh officers.

Even so, following the grant of official sanction, hundreds of meetings were held around the country and much effort devoted to advertising. Fortunately, the stipulation on raising only infantry battalions was lifted almost at once. Some particularly energetic individuals made significant contributions to the effort. In South Wales, Lieutenant Colonel Frank Gaskell of Llantwit Major raised the Cardiff City Battalion, the 13th, of the Welsh Regiment almost single-handedly. He commanded the battalion until his death in 1916. The battalion formed

*   The best available research, by Mr Richard Ward, gives a maximum figure of 70,019 men who served in the R.W. Fus during the war years; of these, research by John Krijnen records that 10,967, or 15.5 percent, were killed, or died of wounds, sickness and other causes while serving. This broad figure masks huge variations in the casualty levels in different battalions, depending on where they served.

at Sophia Gardens in Cardiff 23 October and soon raised 500 men. 14 Welsh originated with the Swansea Cricket and Football Club, which formed a Club Training Corps on 13 August 1914 and turned part of its ground into a rifle range. This battalion was subsequently adopted by the City and £7,000 was raised by subscription for its maintenance. By September, 200 men had been enlisted and by December it had joined the Welsh Army Corps.[15]

Once the restriction on raising non-infantry units was relaxed, Lieutenant Colonel C.A. Pearson of the Royal Engineers set about forming the four field companies needed to support the division and its brigades. However, perhaps the greatest individual contribution was made by Colonel, later Brigadier General Sir, Owen Thomas. Owen Thomas began his military career in 1886 in the newly-formed 3rd (Militia) Battalion of the Manchester Regiment. Soon afterwards, he was ordered to raise a company of volunteers; this he did, successfully, from 1887 onwards by raising a company of the 2nd Volunteer Battalion of The Royal Welch Fusiliers in Anglesey. During the South African War of 1899–1902, Thomas was attached to the 1st Battalion the Essex Regiment. He later joined the 2nd Brabant's Horse, a light cavalry unit whose task was to out-Boer the Boers, as it were. Thomas remained with them until the end of November 1900 when he was invited by Lord Kitchener to raise a regiment of Welsh light horse in Cape Town and at home – the Prince of Wales's Light Horse. Within a few months, the new regiment was 500 strong, of whom half had come from Wales. It eventually enlisted 1,350 men – a feat of recruiting and training that was described as 'superhuman'. Thomas was twice mentioned in despatches, received the King's and Queen's campaign medals with six clasps and was made an honorary lieutenant clonel.

Thomas had now shown on two occasions that he had a talent for raising and training troops. When war was declared in 1914, Thomas was

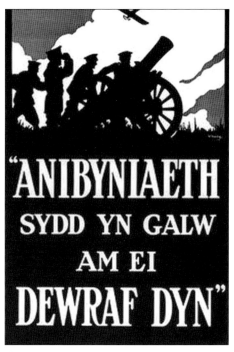

A Welsh enlistment poster: 'Freedom demands her best men'.

Brigadier General Owen Thomas, Commander 113 Infantry Brigade, and his sons: all three were commissioned into the R.W. Fus and all three were killed during the war. (RWF Mus)

among the first to answer the call to arms. In late August 1914 he joined the newly-formed recruiting committee in Anglesey, rousing the young men of the island to join up in a series of public meetings along with other prominent men of the island, such as the M.P. Ellis Griffith, Lord Boston, Dr Thomas Jones and several prominent non-conformist ministers.

In spite of the efforts of Thomas and others, however, early recruiting was poor all across North Wales. Anglesey produced only 36 recruits by September, Caernarvonshire only 60. Merioneth was the worst county in Wales and even Denbighshire gave a poor showing.[16] Why was this? Probably it was the product of a long tradition of volunteer soldiering, along with the pacifist tradition in North Wales evident in religious non-conformity. There was, too, a general disapproval of soldiers and their lax way of life, especially their drinking, which did not fit with the cultural mores of the time and place. Finally, there had been the use of troops in industrial disputes, which had led to much bad feeling on the part of trade unionists.

Even so, Lloyd George recognised in Owen Thomas the man to change local opinion in North Wales: an experienced soldier, a would-be Liberal politician, a local man and a Christian father-figure. Thomas threw himself into the task throughout Wales, as well as in the Welsh *diaspora* of London, Birmingham, Liverpool and Manchester. On 30 October, he accompanied Lloyd George to the War Office. Frances Stevenson was Lloyd George's secretary and mistress and left a memoir of her time with him in which she recorded the meeting between Lloyd George and Lord Kitchener that day, at which doubts were expressed about who should command the new North Wales Brigade:

> Kitchener agreed and asked C. [the Chancellor, Lloyd George] if he had anyone in mind. C. suggested Colonel O.T. [Owen Thomas] and K. rather fell in with the idea. He asked where the colonel was, and when he heard he was in the building, sent for him and appointed him brigadier general on the spot. C. said it was a most dramatic touch, and very magnanimous on K.'s part as he must have known it was the colonel who had been supplying C. with complaints about the War Office and the Welsh army corps. C. was very pleased with the appointment. The new brigadier seemed dazed at the sudden elevation.'[17]

How Thomas went about the task of forming his brigade, and the dramatic turn-around he achieved in recruiting, is well described in his biography;[18] the *Welsh Outlook* went so far as to say that no man had done more than Thomas to create the new Welsh Army.[19] His personal sacrifice as well as his commitment was immense, as all three of his sons were commissioned into the R.W. Fus and all three were killed during the war.

In North Wales, once Thomas had mobilised the support of trade union leaders and Nonconformist clergy, the 13th (1st North Wales Pals), 16th, 17th (2nd North Wales), were rapidly raised in Rhyl, Llandudno and Blaenau Ffestiniog. 15 R.W. Fus. was forming in London. In South Wales the picture was much better: 22,500 men had enlisted in Glamorgan by the end of September, and recruiting was brisk even in a hotbed of Socialist fervour like Tonypandy.[20] The 10th, 11th and 13th Welsh were raised in the Rhondda and Cardiff by the end of October and that date, the nucleus of the Corps was about 3,000 men. All that existed of the structure of an army corps was, however, a collection of infantry battalions composed of untrained men with no equipment and few leaders or experienced instructors. An infantry battalion at this date consisted just over 1,100 officers and men, organised into a Headquarters Company with the command elements of the battalion, the heavy weapons sections, administrative personnel and attachments; and four infantry companies each with four platoons. The chart below shows how each unit was organised as follows:

Headquarters	Rifle Company (x4)
Lieutenant Colonel Commanding	*Headquarters*
Major, Second-in-Command	Major or Captain Commanding
Captain & Adjutant	Captain or Lieutenant Second-in-Command
Regimental Sergeant Major	Company Sergeant Major
Signal Section	Company Quartermaster Sergeant
Orderlies/batmen	Orderlies/batmen
Horse Transport drivers and grooms	Horse transport drivers and grooms
Captain R.A.M.C. and stretcher bearers	Storemen and cooks
Quartermaster, Regimental Quartermaster Sergeant and staff	*Sub Total 2 officers and 47 men*
Paymaster, Pay Sergeant and staff	**Rifle Platoon (x4 per company)**
Orderly Room Sergeant and clerks	Lieutenant or Second Lieutenant
Sergeant Drummer and drummers	Sergeant
Cook Sergeant and Cooks	Orderly/runner
Pioneer Sergeant and pioneers	Lewis Gun section, 2 men
	4 sections each 1 corporal, 1 lance-corporal and 8 men
Machine Gun Section	*Sub Total 4 officers and 172 men per company*
Lieutenant, 5 sergeants and 28 men	*Total 6 officers and 219 men per company, 24 officers and 876 men per battalion*
Total 7 officers and 258 men including attached personnel	
Grand Total	*31 officers and 1,134 N.C.O.s and men*

The rapid pace of recruiting highlighted a series of major problems: the lack of leadership, experience, professional competence and even basic military knowledge. To command the new battalions, many Indian Army officers were brought in as instructors or to command battalions. Other British Army officers were kept back from the front. K1 units received about six Regular Army officers per battalion, but later tranches, including the Welsh, were lucky to have one. This meant that retired officers had to be recalled along with militia or S.R. officers.

With exclusion of the Regular Army and the T.F. from the Welsh Army Corps, the officers were largely selected not on any basis of military efficiency but on the basis of patronage – usually in the gift of the Lords Lieutenant of the counties who had been given the authority to appoint officers on 2 November 1914 – and even in the gift of Lloyd George himself. The 38th Division had a number of Liberal M.P.s among its officers, in addition to Philipps: Hamar Greenwood, later the Conservative Peer Lord Greenwood, in command of 10 S.W.B.; David Davies, later Lord Davies of Llandinam, in command of 14 R.W. Fus.[21] Cronyism was rife: Major V. Paget, late of the Royal Horse Artillery, was recommended as Commander Royal Artillery in the 38th Division, a Brigadier General's appointment: he was the brother-in-law of Lord Plymouth, Chairman of the Committee. He was not in the end appointed. In 15 R.W. Fus, Noel Evans came from a noted Merionethshire family. He was later Deputy Director of Public Prosecutions, a J.P., High Sheriff and Deputy Lord Lieutenant of the County; Goronwy Owen was related to Lloyd George by marriage: he had a very good war, ending as a Lieutenant

Officers of 15 R.W. Fus, the 1st London Welsh. Noel Osbourne-Jones is first on the left in the back row, Goronwy Owen is fifth from the left in the back row; Harold Gladstone Lewis is second from left in the middle row. (RWF Mus)

Colonel with a DSO and was later Liberal M.P. for Caernarvonshire and President of British Controlled Oilfields. Llewelyn Wyn Griffith had the backing of the Liberal M.P. for Anglesey, Ellis Griffith. The most obvious example was Lloyd George's two sons, Richard and Gwilym. Both were commissioned into the Royal Welsh Fusiliers and began their service with the 15th Battalion. Richard, aged 25 in 1914, later transferred to the Royal Engineers; Gwilym joined 15 R.W. Fus for a short while before becoming Aide de Camp (A.D.C.) to the General Officer Commanding the 38th (Welsh) Division. He transferred to the Royal Garrison Artillery in 1916. Neither had any previous military experience.

Few of the junior officers had any experience, although many would have spent time in the junior or senior divisions of the Officers Training Corps, formed under the Haldane reforms, at public schools and universities respectively. As far as possible, the N.C.O.s were drawn from Regular Reservists and re-enlisted men, who provided a measure of experience missing among the commissioned officers. Sergeant John Bradshaw, who

CSM John Bradshaw.
(Family of John Bradshaw)

became a Company Sergeant Major, was a good example. Bradshaw had been a regular soldier in the King's Royal Rifle Corps during the South African War and enlisted into the Royal Welch Fusiliers in London in January 1915.[22]

Initially, most men continued to wear plain clothes until khaki could be issued, although the 'Pals' battalions – those recruited on a very close local basis from local urban or rural districts, wore the distinctive serge 'Kitchener blues'. In late November 1914 the Committee conceived the idea of clothing the Corps in a distinctive shade of uniform, *brethyn llwyd,* literally 'grey cloth'. His was homespun of greyish-pink hue which was manufactured in the thousands of small cloth mills that sprang up across Wales, powered by streams, taking advantage of the need for cloth by the Army. The clothing and equipment sub-committee of the Corps discussed contracts in November at Carlton House.[23] The uniforms made in this shade were worn by some units while in Britain but were discarded in favour of the regulation khaki before going overseas. Despite the large amount of cloth produced, almost none has survived to the present and supply never kept up with demand.[24]

On 11 November 1914, the Committee invited St John's Ambulance to form one of the three field ambulances – a medical unit which was the first level of care where surgery could be performed, and commanded by a lieutenant colonel – for the first division of the Corps. This was 130 (St John's) Field Ambulance R.A.M.C., under the command of Lieutenant Colonel J.E. Davies.

It was also decided to make Llandudno the training centre for R.W. Fus battalions, Colwyn Bay for the S.W.B., and Rhyl for the Welsh.[25] The officers of 15 R.W. Fus were given a farewell banquet in London on 1 December 1914 before their departure for Llandudno, which Lloyd George found time to attend in the midst of government business. Proposing the Loyal Toast, he said that he was: 'Proud to be the President of the battalion, and still more proud to find among the list of officers a young officer called Captain Richard Lloyd George.' Gwilym joined his brother a few weeks later, before moving to the G.O.C.'s staff.[26]

On 31 December the people of Cardiff turned out in their thousands to cheer the Cardiff City battalion on its way to Colwyn Bay. On arrival, the battalion, along with 10 S.W.B., was met at the station by the Mayor, Aldermen and Councillors, and by the local clergy, and given a warm welcome in the pouring rain.[27] It was in Rhyl that 15 Welsh was formed, originally with a draft of Lancashire men, but later supplemented by drafts from Porthcawl and then a large number of men from Carmarthenshire.[28] Emlyn Davies recalled that the Lancashire men were 'grand lads', who had joined up in the expectation of a few months training by the sea, in their favourite holiday destinations.[29]

In these seaside towns, recruits were billeted in boarding houses and local hotels: more comfortable than where many farm labourers, miners or steel-workers had come from, with regular meals and proper medical attention for perhaps the first time in their lives. Most men put on height and weight during their service. Civilians on whom troops were billeted bene-fitted from an allowance of 3/4½d (£14.71 at today's prices)[30] per man per day, later reduced to 2/6d (£11.01), which brought more than £400,000 (£35 million) into the town of Llandudno alone.[31] One soldier remarked, 'we are in clover, and cannot wish for greater comfort.'[32] Bill Tucker recalled that: 'The troops were received almost as holiday visitors. They occupied ordinary bedrooms and were catered for by the hotel waitresses and general staff.'[33]

Recruits had to be in their billets by 21.00 hrs and all public houses were closed at this time. Attendance at Chapel was strongly encouraged by Owen Thomas and others. Schoolrooms and

If der Royal Welsh Fusiliers haf gone by, den I kan kom out.

THE ROYAL WELSH FUSILIERS
"THE NANNY-GOATS"

Two jingoistic cartoons promoting enlistment into the 38th (Welsh) Division.

public libraries were made available for reading and writing; soccer and rugby matches, sports days, target shooting, concerts and *eisteddfodau* were all held to enhance the Welsh character of the units.[34] David Jones remembered the quality of Welsh singing as opposed to that of the cockneys in his own battalion; like others, he also noted the amount of Welsh spoken in the rest of his brigade, by: 'That kind of Welshman little known to the English – silent and without any of the exterior enthusiasm of the supposed "Celt", large of body, kindly, but a terrible disciplinarian.'[35]

The question of the Welshness of Lloyd George's Army merits some discussion. As has already been mentioned, units raised in South Wales and Monmouthshire contained many men who were not Welsh, or if they were, did not speak the Welsh language. Although the ability to speak Welsh and the idea of *being* Welsh were not the same, the two concepts were and are closely allied and need to be considered together. Research into this subject within the Royal Welsh Fusiliers indicates that it is not possible to determine the nationality of all those who served in Regiment during the Great War, because of the destruction by German bombing during the Second World War of the personal files of many (not all) of those who had served. However, most entries in the records *Officers Died in the Great War*, and *Soldiers Died in the Great War*, give the place of birth. From this, it is possible to obtain a good indication of the Welshness of that Regiment. During the War, the Regiment raised 40 battalions (not counting the Volunteer Force), of which 22 served abroad. Of these, 15 sustained over 200 casualties. In these 15 battalions, an average of 47 percent gave Wales or Monmouthshire as their place of birth. The figure was highest in the Territorial battalions at around 60 percent, and generally lowest in the regular battalions which had, in peacetime, recruited strongly in London and Birmingham. The service battalions in 38th (Welsh) Division averaged just over 40 percent: in the 15th (1st London Welsh), this figure is a mere 27 percent. Further research by Dr Chris Williams[36] has provided figures in the mid-60 percent range for the Service battalions of the Welsh Regiment, except for 15 Welsh which was 51.5 percent; and figures in the mid-40 percent range for the two battalions of the South Wales Borderers.

There was therefore a very significant Welsh national character to most of the battalions but the idea that any unit in the 38th Division *spoke* only Welsh during the war is not sound, and in danger of creating yet another myth of the Great War: care is needed here. In North and Mid Wales, more Welsh *was* undoubtedly spoken and there was a good deal of Welsh used by men from these areas in the trenches. Llewelyn Wyn Griffith speaks of it frequently in *Up to Mametz* and in *Beyond Mametz*, as does Wynn Wheldon in his article on 14 R.W. Fus in the Ypres Salient in *The Welsh Outlook*. The bonding value of this shared culture during danger and hardship must have been immense; although in the case of Welsh speakers in, for example, 15 R.W. Fus, it could also be exclusive. Nor does any notion that *only* Welsh was spoken do service to the many patriotic men who gave their lives, and who spoke no Welsh, but considered themselves no less Welsh for it.[37]

Llewelyn Wyn Griffith.
(Wyn Griffith family)

Training in North Wales was limited by the lack of instructors and the want of equipment – broomsticks did duty as rifles and handcarts as machine-guns. The training regime concentrated on three aspects: training the body physically through P.T., sports, and – most importantly – close order drill; secondly, developing a soldierly spirit, ethos and bearing through Regimental history, traditions, and ceremonies; and thirdly the technical aspects of training in the use of the rifle, bayonet, grenade and entrenching tool. Drill, as the means of teaching instant obedience, discipline, the sense of togetherness and the bearing of a soldier, was of paramount importance. According to *Infantry Training 1914,* 'The first and quickest method of teaching discipline is close order drill… close order drill compels the habit of obedience, and stimulates, by combined and orderly movements, the man's pride in himself and in his unit.'[38] Robert Graves remarked on the significance of drill in *Goodbye to All That*:

> … in every division of the four in which I served there were three different kinds of troops. Those that had guts but were no good at drill; those that were good at drill but had no guts; and those that had guts and were good at drill. These last fellows were, for some reason or other, much the best men in a show.[39]

Some courses were also begun for specialists such as signallers, medical orderlies, drivers, clerks and cooks. Emlyn Davies, who joined 17 R.W. Fus with Watcyn Wyn Griffith, younger brother of Llewelyn, recorded that:

> First parade was at 7 a.m. One hour of physical jerks à l'armée. Arms and legs and feet and back reacted too unkindly at first… Followed, after breakfast at 9 a.m., by two or three hours daily of square bashing and rifle drill… Other forms of training included rifle drill and bayonet fighting. Of all experiences the latter was most exhausting. Straw-filled sacks were suspended from a cross-bar fixed to two upright poles about six feet high. Instructions were that from a distance of about 30 yards the assailants rushed at the double with rifle and bayonet firmly grasped at the ready…[40]

Some platoon and company training was possible; so too were mock battles in company or battalion strength, such as that carried out on 15 December on the Great Orme near Llandudno by 15 R.W. Fus., after which the Commanding Officer, William Fox-Pitt, 'was loud in his praise of the way the men had carried out these operations, especially in the way they took cover.'[41] The atmosphere was, however, one of amateurish games.

On 18 November, three brigades formed: the 1st Brigade, initially numbered 128, was to be formed from R.W. Fus battalions, since this regiment was the oldest and most senior Regiment of Wales and was to be commanded by Owen Thomas. The 2nd Brigade, 129, was to be formed at Rhyl from Welsh Regiment battalions, under the command of Colonel R.H.W. Dunn, a former T.F. officer who had already commanded a brigade but had retired in 1911.[42] The 3rd Brigade, 130, composed of R.W. Fus, S.W.B and Welsh Regiment battalions, was formed at Colwyn Bay under the command of Colonel Ivor Philipps.[*] Like Owen Thomas, Philipps had experience of field command in war: he had been commissioned in the Indian Army in 1883 and promoted to Major in 1901. He served in the Anglo-Burmese War from 1885 to 1889, in the Miranzai Expedition in 1891, the Isazai Expedition in 1892, with the Tirah Field Force from 1897 to 1898. He then served in China from 1900 to 1901 during the Boxer Rebellion as Quartermaster-General. He retired from the Regular Army in 1903, and joined the Pembrokeshire Yeomanry as Second-in-Command, becoming its Commanding Officer from 1908 to 1912. He was also, perhaps most importantly given the politics of the time, the Liberal Member of Parliament for Southampton.[43]

The brigade was the smallest military grouping that could be considered as a 'formation' and because it consisted of units of several arms and services; its commander was normally a Brigadier General. Each of the three Welsh brigades consisted of a small headquarters that commanded the formation; and four – or sometimes five – infantry battalions. In early 1915, a machine-gun company equipped with the .303-inch Vickers water-cooled medium machine gun was added to each brigade;[44] and in early 1916 a light trench mortar battery followed, equipped with the Stokes mortar. Each brigade could also expect to have units attached to it from the divisional troops: a field ambulance from the Royal Army Medical Corps, a field company Royal Engineers, and the observation parties of a field artillery brigade which would routinely

---

[*]   Later Major General Sir Ivor Philipps KCB DSO (1861–1940). He later commanded the 38th (Welsh) Division and held a seat in the House of Commons as a Liberal M.P. from 1906 to 1922.

fire in support of the brigade: the artillery was *controlled* at battalion level, but *commanded* at divisional level and thus the fire of the guns could be shifted to support the point of most need, or greatest danger.

To assist him to command the brigade, the Brigadier General had a very small staff: a Brigade Major, who would usually have been a professional officer, trained at the Army Staff College. The three B.M.s appointed to the Welsh brigades were Major O.S. Flower, R.W. Fus; Major P. Umpfreville of the Royal West Kents; and Captain Charles Veal of the Welch Regiment.[45] In addition, each would have a staff captain and it was not uncommon for at least one junior officer to be attached as a 'staff learner'. Moreover, there would be a small number of batmen, drivers and signallers. This headquarters would maintain contact with the next highest level of command, the division, to receive orders from the Commanding General and in return keep him abreast of the situation facing the brigade. It would maintain contact with the subordinate units of the brigade, and with flanking formations. It would frame and transmit the brigade commander's orders to his subordinates and keep him informed of the situation in order that he could make timely decisions. Finally, it would provide the administrative support needed by the commander both in and out of the line. *Field Service Regulations* defined the brigade major's task as follows:

i.   To assist [his] commander in the execution of his functions of command.
ii.   To assist the fighting troops and services in the execution of their tasks.[46]

This rather general guidance was supplemented by specific responsibilities laid on the G, or General Staff, branch, to which the Brigade Major's post was assigned. These were laid down in the slightly later, but still relevant, *Field Service Pocket Book* as:

i.   To obtain and communicate information about our own troops, the enemy, and the theatre of war.
ii.   To prepare plans and issue orders for operations.
iii. To arrange for communication, cipher, censorship. The provision and distribution of maps, secret service, guides, interpreters and propaganda.
iv.   The organisation, training and efficiency of troops.
v.   To draft despatches.[47]

That November, the Committee agreed to the incorporation of four additional infantry battalions into the Corps: 14 (Caernarvon and Anglesey) R.W. Fus; 10 (1st Gwent) S.W.B., raised from the Monmouthshire collieries; 15 (Carmarthenshire) Welsh; and 16 (Cardiff City) Welsh; and also 129 Field Ambulance R.A.M.C. under Lieutenant Colonel R.J. Simons. This period also saw the formation, importantly, of the cadres of the Royal Field Artillery (R.F.A.) and Army Service Corps (A.S.C.) units. At the 9 December meeting, the Committee further sanctioned the formation of another infantry battalion, 11 S.W.B., in Gwent. The final meeting of 1914 took place just before Christmas at Shrewsbury and approved the raising of 17 Welsh, 123 and 124 Field Companies R.E., and a signal company R.E. for the first divisional headquarters.

The two field companies R.E. were formed from 13 Welsh, which had within it a great many skilled tradesmen; 300 of these were transferred to form the two companies and once at Abergavenny, they also formed 151 Field Company from surplus manpower. In April 1915, they contributed men to the formation of the divisional pioneer battalion, 19 Welsh.[48] The field companies would provide mobility and counter-mobility support to the brigades, constructing field fortifications and wire entanglements, providing drainage and duckboards in trenches, helping to breach enemy obstacles, and issuing defensive stores such as pickets, wire, sandbags and revetting material to the infantry while the pioneers would mostly dig trenches although they were also trained as infantry soldiers.

The formation of field artillery batteries and brigades was placed on hold, pending the appointment of a Commander, Royal Artillery (a Brigadier General) in the first divisional headquarters; a cavalry squadron or regiment at divisional level was also on hold (the Wiltshire Yeomanry subsequently fulfilled this role). By 31 December, following a series of recruiting marches and events all around Wales, the strength of the Corps was reported as around 10,000 officers and men.[49]

An important step was taken on 19 January 1915: the formation of the first divisional headquarters of the Corps and the assignment of brigades and divisional troops to the new formation. This was initially numbered 43rd (Welsh) Division. The division was, at this period, the *highest* level of command that was fixed in terms of organisation and assigned units. At corps and army level, subordinate formations moved repeatedly. The division was the *lowest* level that could simultaneously plan and conduct operations; and which controlled both the contact

battle with the enemy as well as the security of the rear area, the administration and the supply of the formation. A divisional commander at this date, however, had no means of observing the enemy's depth and had no weapons capable of firing into the enemy rear in order to disrupt his supply, administration and command. The order of battle of the division is in the Appendix to this chapter.

Command of the division was given to Ivor Philipps, who was promoted to Major General and his place as Commander 115 Brigade taken by Brigadier General Horatio Evans, late of the King's (Liverpool) Regiment,* who was then in command of the 4th District of Western Command. At 55, Evans was at the top end of the age bracket for field command, but he was an experienced soldier, having served in the Second Afghan and South African Wars – and experience was sorely needed. Llewelyn Wyn Griffith, who later served on his staff, described him as 'physically strong, with a hard and clear face, and the bearing of a man who has lived wisely.'[50] Although there is no direct evidence to suggest that Lloyd George had a hand in getting Ivor Philipps a Brigadier General's cap, his influence in Philipps's promotion to Major General is not open to doubt as he

Brigadier General H.J. Evans, Commander 115 Infantry Brigade. (RWF Mus)

---

*   Brigadier General Horatio James Evans CMG DL JP (1859–1932).

wrote in a letter to his wife that: 'I have seen Ivor Philipps and confirmed Gwilym's appointment with him [as his aide de camp, or A.D.C.] if P. gets the generalship of the division. Have seen K. about that now and think all will be all right.'[51] Philipps' appointment was felt to be unsound by many, however, and neither Lieutenant General Sir Richard Haking, commanding XI Corps, nor Lieutenant General Henry Horne of XV Corps, later demonstrated confidence in him.[52]

Major Geoffrey Drake-Brockman, a Regular officer later attached to the divisional headquarters, and one who will be cited later in this book, commented on the political influences in the 38th Division, saying that Lloyd George's pulling of strings on behalf of certain individuals was:

> … almost a record instance for political interference and dishonesty with the fighting portion of the army in France. Particularly is it an illustration of the disadvantages under which the 38th Division functioned, which in no small measure accounts for the very poor performance put up by it during the period under review.[53]

The appointment of Lloyd George's son to a relatively safe position out of the line was probably not, however, the deciding factor in his decision to recommend Philipps for the command; however Frances Stevenson provides a possible motive when she recorded on 25 January 1915 that Lloyd George had mentioned to her that years before, Philipps's older brother, Lord St David's, had offered a loan of £500 (£50,000 at today's rate) at a time that Lloyd George was in political and financial trouble:[54] 'C. was mightily touched, for he said the man had nothing to gain from his generous offer then, nor could he know that C. would ever be in a position to repay him. But although C. did not accept the offer, yet he has never forgotten St. Davids's generosity and St.D. will never ask him for anything in vain.'[55]

Divisional headquarters was larger than that of brigade and demanded a good many more trained and qualified officers to run it. In 1914, there were 15 officers and 67 N.C.O.s and men in the headquarters, which was organised into three principal branches: G, or General Staff; A, or Administration; and Q, or Quartermaster. G was the primary branch and was commanded by a Staff Officer Grade I, a Lieutenant Colonel. G dealt with intelligence, operations, plans, deployments, organisation and training. Another Lieutenant Colonel headed up the A and Q branches as Assistant Adjutant & Quartermaster General (A.A. & Q.M.G.). A dealt with personnel and discipline; and Q with supply, transport, housing, equipment and ammunition. In addition, there were the staffs supporting the commanders of the divisional artillery, engineer and medical units; plus the signal company, drivers, cooks, batmen and clerks.

In late January 1915 the Committee sanctioned the formation of the second London Welsh battalion, 18 R.W. Fus, and the transfer of 17 Welsh to a new fourth brigade which would be composed of bantam battalions: 19 R.W. Fus, 12 S.W.B., and 17 and 18 Welsh. At the same time, it was also decided to raise an additional company in each infantry battalion, bringing the established strength to 1,325 officers and men. To support the divisional level of command, the first R.F.A. brigade and 151 Field Company R.E. were also sanctioned. At the end of January, the strength of the Corps had reached 16,300; a month later this figure had risen to 20,000, or half the target, which had been achieved in five months.[56]

On St David's Day, at Owen Thomas's suggestion, Lloyd George visited Llandudno for a review of 128 (North Wales) Infantry Brigade, which could now boast a strength of 5,500 men who marched along the promenade, all wearing a leek in their caps or on their epaulette, past a dais where the salute was taken by Lloyd George along with General Mackinnon, Major General Philipps and the Earl of Plymouth.[57] Thousands of spectators turned out in spite of very cold weather. Lady Boston presented Owen Thomas with a ceremonial sword in honour of his achievements, the gift of the women of Anglesey. Thomas afterwards posed for a famous photograph with his three sons. The local press reported that:

> Llandudno has today entertained the largest crowd of excursionists that has ever honoured the town with a visit in the winter season. They came, thousands upon thousands of them… from all parts of North Wales… to take part in the first inspection of the First Brigade of the Welsh army corps, to lionise the Chancellor of the Exchequer, and to celebrate St David's Day in an entirely new fashion.
>
> … The four battalions comprising Brigadier General Owen Thomas's command were drawn up on the wind-swept promenade, the whole length and width of which appeared carpeted with blue and khaki – the blue uniforms of the 'Pals' and the khaki of the three other battalions including the stalwart London Welsh… The march past, first in column and afterwards in platoon formation, was splendidly done. The men were, of course, delighted to be on the move, and were aglow with the exercise, marching with a rhythmic swing and sure tread to their own excellent bands…'[58]

Lloyd George appeared most impressed; General Mackinnon was more cautious even though he congratulated the Commanding Officers:

> There was doubt in the minds of many whether a Welsh corps could be raised at all, and whether if raised it could be efficient.' The reason for the initial doubt was the comparatively late date in starting the project and therefore finding it difficult to get experienced instructors and staff. He felt that further training was essential before the troops could take their place in the field army.[59]

David Jones recollected listening to Lloyd George's address and feeling inspired; although when he read the printed account a few days later he was dismayed to find it 'appalling bloody tripe.'[60]

During March 1915 it became clear that the formation of technical units for the first division of the Corps and the formation of the second division were urgent, but that a second division could not be formed without a revision of the current recruiting methods. A meeting of the Committee on St David's Day at Llandudno had reiterated that it would be necessary for all recruiting, whether Regular, T.F. or New Army, to come under the authority of 'the Welsh contingent of His Majesty's Army', with an Inspector-General of Recruiting in charge. A memorandum to this effect was sent on 3 March to the G.O.C.-in-C, Western Command. General Mackinnon, however, did not support this concept and left matters very much as they were, except for some adjustment in the stationing of the Special Reserve battlions.

The argument rumbled on through April, during which time the first division was renumbered as the 38th (Welsh).* The three brigades were also renumbered as 113 (Royal Welsh), 114

---

*   See Chapter 1, Appendix.

and 115. Meanwhile, the brigading of the artillery batteries was completed: the original four batteries each split into two; and the eight thus formed were also later divided to create the 16 batteries, in four brigades, that made up the divisional artillery.[61] Horses began to arrive in small numbers in April; all the greys were allocated to 121 Brigade where they were a feature until just before the Somme battle when they were exchanged for browns.

The A.S.C. organization was also rounded out. In the Engineer group, 215 Fortress Company R.E. was formed. A cyclist company was raised at Conwy on 22 April:[62] these men were trained in reconnaissance and

The badge of the 38th (Welsh) Division.

message carrying; they were armed as infantry and could act as a mobile reserve if required. Bill Tucker, who joined the company at its formation, remembered that:

> … a battalion notice appeared inviting volunteers to form a Divisional Cyclist Company. Preference would be given to those knowing something about maps and one or more foreign languages. As I had a rudimentary knowledge of German and an acquaintance with maps (I had been the touring secretary of a cycling club) I was accepted …
>
> The bicycles, when they eventually did arrive, were incredibly heavy. They were made to fold with the idea of being portable. But the genius responsible for their construction must have imagined he was working for a tribe of Herculean cyclists because it was only by help from at least two other people that the folded machine could be hoisted and strapped to one's back….in due course these crazy machines were replaced by cycles of a standard design…'[63]

By late May, Corps strength stood at 29,660 and after great efforts in North and Mid Wales, all units were reported to be at full strength. The division was, however, well dispersed: the A.S.C. companies were in Pwllheli and Portmadoc; R.A.M.C. units at Prestatyn; and the Engineer companies were far off, near Abergavenny.[64] Properly co-ordinated unit and formation training was not possible under these circumstances. The three brigades managed only one day's training together, in May 1915.[65]

Once camps and training areas in the south of England were vacated by the K1 and K2 formations, however, the remaining divisions could concentrate there. On 14 June, the 38th Division began to move to hutments at Winchester, close to Salisbury Plain, where further training was to be carried out: this included shooting, longer route marches, field manoeuvres, training in trench warfare and live drills for the engineers, artillery and machine-gunners.[66] Some troops were under canvas at first: 'Allotted 24 to a bell tent did not leave much room for manoeuvre,' as Emlyn Davies remarked. When the hutted camp at Hazeley Down was occupied it was 'only half completed. One mettled [sic] road only ran through the camp. Consequently there was considerable overcrowding and the parade ground was covered with a sea of oozing mud half way to the knees.'[67] Equipment was still woefully short: the artillery practiced limbering up with pairs of old bus wheels with long poles attached to simulate guns.[68] It was only in the weeks that immediately preceded embarkation for France that every man was put through the

Salisbury Plain, two line drawings by David Jones. (RWF Mus 2998b)

shortened war course in musketry, a poor substitute for the ability to fire 30 aimed shots a minute demanded by the pre-war Regular Army. The artillery, however, had to delay departure for several weeks in order to complete firing practices with live ammunition.[69]

The infantry battalions left 25 percent of their strength behind in North Wales and these men were formed into reserve battalions, whose task was to supply reinforcements to the first-line units to replace casualties. These battalions, which were formed into 14 (Reserve) Infantry Brigade, were 20 R.W. Fus with five companies; 17 S.W.B. with three companies; and 21 Welsh with six companies.[70] The brigade moved to Kinmel Park Camp, near Rhyl: a vast, purpose-built infantry training camp of corrugated iron huts constructed by McAlpine's. The camp also boasted a rifle range, hospital and a huge reconstructed trench system in the grounds of nearby Bodelwyddan Castle which gave recruits the best possible preparation for war on the continent.

On 14 July, a meeting was held to conclude how the formation of the second division of the Corps would be formed, now that the 38th Division was on the order of battle. General Mackinnon, however, continued to insist, in keeping with direction from the War Office, that providing drafts for Regular and T.F. units at the front and reserve companies for the New Army formations was more important than forming anther division, even though the available manpower had now reached the target of 40,000. No progress was therefore made on the

18 R.W. Fus at Kinmel Park camp. (Author's collection)

subject. Three days later, on 17 July, the four Bantam battalions became 119 Infantry Brigade, which was detached to the 40th Division at Aldershot, joining 120 and 121 Brigades.

The final meeting of the Committee was held on 27 October 1915, with Lord Derby present. Derby told the Committee firmly and finally that the War Office did not require any more formations, but given the casualties being suffered in France and Flanders, as well as in Mesopotamia and Gallipoli, the creation of reserves was crucial. The Committee had no option therefore but to agree that the recruitment and formation of a second division should be brought to a close. Further reserve units were therefore formed and passed to War Office control at Kinmel Park – these were 18 (2nd London Welsh), 21 and 22 R.W. Fus; 13 S.W.B.; and 20, 21 and 22 Welsh.[71]

It was ironic that by this time, 50,000 recruits had been raised for the Welsh Army Corps over and above existing needs. It is also clear that had the 53rd (Welsh) Division and at least one of the two Welsh Yeomanry brigades been assigned to the Corps, and had the Welsh battalions of the Regular Army been permitted to provide at least some stiffening in terms of officers and N.C.Os, then the Corps could well have been brought into existence *and sustained throughout the war.* One must conclude that the War Office had no intention of allowing this to happen, despite Kitchener's endorsement. Even allowing for the very correct insistence on providing the existing field formations with proper sustainment, there had to be another reason. Although it is nowhere stated, it is entirely possible this reason was tied up with political nationalism. The great issue of the day immediately before the outbreak of war had been, after all, Irish Home Rule, which had been shelved for the duration of the war.

Why was this an issue? Certainly, there was not the same urgency for independence in Wales as in Ireland. During the latter part of the 19th century and early part of the 20th century the notion of a distinctive Welsh political identity had gained some traction. In 1881 the Welsh Sunday Closing Act was passed, the first legislation exclusively concerned with Wales. The Central Welsh Board was established in 1896 to inspect the grammar schools set up under the Welsh Intermediate Education Act of 1889, and a separate Welsh Department of the Board of Education was formed

A group of 130th Field Ambulance with their vehicle, presented by the people of Abertillery.
(www.130thstjohnambulance.co.uk)

in 1907. The Agricultural Council for Wales was set up in 1912. In parallel, institutions like the National *Eisteddfod*, established in 1861; the University of Wales, set up in 1893; and the National Library of Wales, established in Aberystwyth in 1911, reinforced the sense of nationhood. The campaign for disestablishment of the Anglican Church in Wales, achieved by the passage of the Welsh Church Act in 1914 (although like Irish Home Rule shelved for the duration of the Great War), was also significant in the development of Welsh national consciousness.[72]

Around the time of the Great War, Welsh voters were overwhelmingly Liberal and the Welsh Liberal M.P.s were deeply tied into the Liberal Party machine at Westminster. Here, they were far more concerned with the issues and reforms outlined above, than with Welsh Home Rule. Outside the Liberal Party, however, as early as 1894, *Cymru Fydd* ('Young Wales') was formed and initially, Lloyd George used this body as a vehicle to call for Welsh Home Rule. However, a series of hostile mass meetings in South Wales made it clear that many influential Liberals and indeed ordinary working people were deeply opposed to the idea.[73] After one such meeting in Newport, Monmouthshire, in January 1896, where he was shouted down, Lloyd George turned away from Home Rule altogether.

Welsh Home Rule was not, therefore, in itself issue. Nevertheless, the formation of a distinctively Welsh national Army Corps might well have been a powerful engine in developing national consciousness: it certainly proved to be so in Canada and Australia during the Great War. An Army is, after all, one of the hallmarks of a nation and no proper state can do without one, for it defines relations with other states and strongly influences how any country is viewed by its friends and foes alike. If Wales had been allowed to go down this path then inevitably there would have been calls for the formation of similar bodies for Scotland and Ireland, thus re-igniting the issue of Irish nationalism that no-one in the Westminster political establishment wished to encourage. The Welsh Army Corps was therefore a dead duck, and Wales was represented in the *British* Army by its Regular Regiments, its three divisions – the 38th, 53rd and 68th – and its Yeomanry brigades.

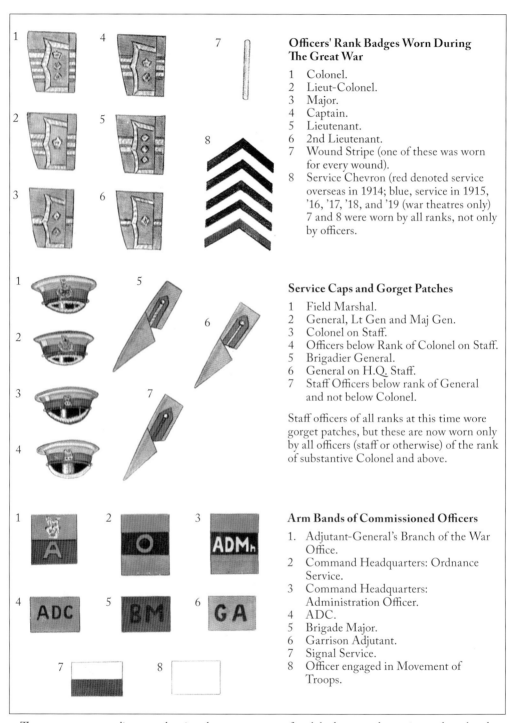

Officers' Rank Badges Worn During The Great War

1   Colonel.
2   Lieut-Colonel.
3   Major.
4   Captain.
5   Lieutenant.
6   2nd Lieutenant.
7   Wound Stripe (one of these was worn for every wound).
8   Service Chevron (red denoted service overseas in 1914; blue, service in 1915, '16, '17, '18, and '19 (war theatres only)
7 and 8 were worn by all ranks, not only by officers.

Service Caps and Gorget Patches

1   Field Marshal.
2   General, Lt Gen and Maj Gen.
3   Colonel on Staff.
4   Officers below Rank of Colonel on Staff.
5   Brigadier General.
6   General on H.Q. Staff.
7   Staff Officers below rank of General and not below Colonel.

Staff officers of all ranks at this time wore gorget patches, but these are now worn only by all officers (staff or otherwise) of the rank of substantive Colonel and above.

Arm Bands of Commissioned Officers

1.   Adjutant-General's Branch of the War Office.
2   Command Headquarters: Ordnance Service.
3   Command Headquarters: Administration Officer.
4   ADC.
5   Brigade Major.
6   Garrison Adjutant.
7   Signal Service.
8   Officer engaged in Movement of Troops.

Three contemporary diagrams showing the arrangement of rank badges, cap decoration and armbands for Regimental and staff officers during the Great War.

Appendix

38th (Welsh) Division Order of Battle, 1914–1916
Changes to the order of battle are shown in italics

Divisional Headquarters

Appointment	Name	Date
G.O.C.	Major General Sir Ivor Philipps KCB DSO	9 January 1915
	Major General Herbert Watts (Acting) CB CMG	10 July 1916
	Major General C.G. Blackader CB DSO ADC	15 July 1916
G.S.O.I	Lieutenant Colonel H.E. ap Rhys Pryce CMG DSO	June 1915
A.A. & Q.M.G.	Lieutenant Colonel H.E. ap Rhys Pryce CMG DSO*	April 1915
	Lieutenant Colonel C.E. Willes	September 1915
	Lieutenant Colonel H.M. Pryce-Jones DSO MVO MC	September 1915
C.R.A.	Brigadier General W.A.M. Thompson CB CMG	July 1915
C.R.E.	Lieutenant Colonel C.A. Pearson	November 1914
	Lieutenant Colonel E.H. de Vere Atkinson CB CMG CIE	August 1915
A.D.M.S	Colonel F.J. Morgan CMG	January 1915

Divisional Troops Units

Unit	Commander	Date
Wiltshire Yeomanry (Divisional Cavalry) (H.Q., D Squadron and M.G. Section)	Lieutenant Colonel U.O. Thynne DSO	January 1915
38th Divisional Signal Company	Captain S. Bowyer	May 1915
	Captain H.P. Jesson	June 1916
38th Cyclist Company	Lieutenant R.E. Burrell	April 1915
		Disbanded June 1916
115th (Glamorgan Pioneer) Battalion, the Welsh Regiment	Major J. Owen James	March 1915
	Lieutenant Colonel S.J. Wilkinson	October 1915
	Lieutenant Colonel D. Grant-Dalton CMG DSO	April 1916
Artillery		
119 Brigade R.F.A.	Lieutenant Colonel P.J. Paterson DSO	November 1915
120 Brigade R.F.A.	Lieutenant Colonel C.O. Head	May 1915
121 Brigade R.F.A.	Lieutenant Colonel F.A. Tighe	July 1915
	Lieutenant Colonel W.C.E. Rudkin CMG DSO	November 1915
122 Brigade R.F.A.	Lieutenant Colonel J. Gardner	July 1915
	Lieutenant Colonel H.G. Pringle DSO	November 1915
38th Heavy Battery R.G.A.	Major O.W. Owen	*Withdrawn November 1914*
38 X Heavy Trench Mortar Battery	Lieutenant W.J. Peters	*Added June 1916*
38 Y Heavy Trench Mortar Battery	Lieutenant L.W. Fox	*Added June 1916*
38 Z Heavy Trench Mortar Battery	Captain F.R. Watson MC	*Added June 1916*
No 5 Medium Machine Gun Company	Major P. Hammond DSO	*Added June 1916*
38th Divisional Ammunition Column	Lieutenant Colonel G.W. Hayward DSO	July 1915
119 Brigade Ammunition Column	Lieutenant S.H. Hildyard	
	Captain H. Lewis	
120 Brigade Ammunition Column	Captain J.H. Palmer	January 1916
121 Brigade Ammunition Column	Captain J.P. Plummer	January 1916
	Lieutenant J.S. Arnold	June 1916

Unit	Commander	Date
122 (Howitzer) Brigade Ammunition Column	Major B.F. Burroughs	January 1916
	Captain F. Pavey	July 1916
B Echelon Ammunition Column	Lieutenant T. Hayes-Sheen	*Formed in July 1916*
Engineers		
123 Field Company R.E.	Major I.W. Lamonby	May 1915
124 Field Company R.E.	Major J.R.N. Kirkwood	May 1915
151 Field Company R.E.	Captain F.H. Cory	May 1915
	Captain C.G.V. Fenton	January 1916
215 Fortress Company R.E.	Capt A.S.W. Best	January 1915
	Captain W.F. Newton	May 1916
		Transferred to Fifth Army troops, May 1916.
Army Service Corps		
38th Divisional Supply Train	Lieutenant Colonel H.E. Sykes	February 1915
	Lieutenant Colonel H.F.T. Fisher	June 1915
	Lieutenant Colonel T.E. Bennett DSO OBE	March 1916
H.Q. Company	Major R.S. Smallwood	December 1915
330 Company A.S.C.	Lieutenant J.E. Affleck	June 1916
331 Company A.S.C.	Captain T.N. Cross	December 1915
332 Company A.S.C.	Captain M. Williams	June 1916
333 (Divisional Troops) Company A.S.C.	Captain H.F. Lambert	December 1915
38th Division Mechanical Transport Company	Major R.S. Smallwood	*Incorporated into H.Q. Company, Divisional Train, December 1915*
Medical Services		
129 Field Ambulance R.A.M.C.	Lieutenant Colonel R.J. Simons	March 1915
	Lieutenant Colonel W.G. Edwards	August 1915
130 (St John's) Field Ambulance R.A.M.C.	Lieutenant Colonel J.E.H. Davies DSO	March 1915
131 Field Ambulance R.A.M.C.	Lieutenant Colonel W.P. Gwynne	March 1915
	Lieutenant Colonel R.H. Mills-Roberts CMG	April 1915
77 Sanitary Section	Captain D. Llewelyn Williams	November 1914
No 5 Mobile Bacteriological Section	Captain E. Emrys Roberts	*Withdrawn December 1915*
49th Mobile Veterinary Section	Lieutenant W. Tully Christie	
38th Divisional Field Ambulance Workshop	Lieutenant S.H. Lambert *A.S.C.*	December 1915

Unit Headquarters	Name	Date
113 (Royal Welch) Infantry Brigade		
Commander	Brigadier General Owen Thomas MP	October 1914
	Brigadier General Ll. A.E. Price-Davies VC DSO CMG	November 1915
Brigade Major	Major O.S. Flower	September 1914
	Captain H.R. Bently *Cheshire*	October 1915
Staff Captain	Captain H. Campbell	
13 R.W. Fus (1st North Wales Pals)	Lieutenant Colonel R.H.W. Dunn	October 1914

Unit Headquarters	Name	Date
	Lieutenant Colonel C.E. Willes	December 1914
	Lieutenant Colonel O.S. Flower	October 1915[b]
	Captain H.W. Hardwick (acting)	July 1916
14 R.W. Fus	Lieutenant Colonel D. Davies MP	November 1914
	Major G.H. Gwyther	June 1916[c]
	Captain J. Glynn Jones (acting)	July 1916
15 R.W. Fus (1st London Welsh)	Lieutenant Colonel I. Bowen	September 1914
	Lieutenant Colonel W.A.L. Fox-Pitt *Gren Gds*	November 1915[d]
	Lieutenant Colonel R.C. Bell DSO *C.I.H.*	July 1916
	Major J.E. Edwards (acting)	
16 R.W. Fus	Lieutenant Colonel T.A. Wynne-Edwards	December 1914
	Lieutenant Colonel R.J. Carden *17L*	November 1915[e]
113 M.G. Company	Captain B.H. Badham	February 1916
	Captain W.S. Roberts	April 1916
113 Light Trench Mortar Battery	Lieutenant A. Ferrier Kerr	May 1915
	2nd Lieutenant R.C. P. Shopland	April 1916[f]
Bombing Officer	Lieutenant J.R. Humphries *R.W. Fus*	December 1915
	Lieutenant H.J. Cundall	June 1916
Signal Section	Lieutenant R. Shearburn *R.E.*	November 1915
114 Infantry Brigade		
Commander	Brigadier General R.H.W. Dunn	October 1914
	Brigadier General T.O. Marden CB CMG DSO[g]	December 1915
Brigade Major	Major P. Umpfreville *R.W.K.*	March 1915
	Captain C.H.R. Crawshay *R.W. Fus*	December 1915[h]
	Major A.P. Bowen MC *Shrops L.I.*	June 1916
Staff Captain	Captain A.P. Bowen MC *Shrops L.I.*	December 1915
	Captain A.E. Redfern	June 1916
10 Welsh (1st Rhondda)	Lieutenant Colonel E.L. Holloway	October 1914
	Lieutenant Colonel P.E. Ricketts MVO	December 1915[i]
13 Welsh (2nd Rhondda)	Colonel Sir W. Watts KCB	November 1914
	Lieutenant Colonel W. Gifford	June 1915
	Lieutenant Colonel F.E. Packe	March 1916
	Major C. Bond	July 1916[j]
	Major D.A. Edwards (acting)	July 1916
14 (Swansea) Welsh	Lieutenant Colonel H.W. Benson DSO	September 1914
	Lieutenant Colonel L.R. King	December 1915
	Lieutenant Colonel J.H. Hayes DSO	April 1916
	Major G. d'A. Edwards (acting)	July 1916[k]
	Captain – Johnson (acting)	July 1916
15 (Carmarthenshire) Welsh	Lieutenant Colonel M.J.G. Scobie CB	October 1914
	Lieutenant Colonel T.W. Parkinson DSO	November 1915[l]
	Major C.G. Phillips *King's Own*	July 1916
	Major P. Anthony	July 1916
114 M.G. Company	Captain P. Evans[m]	November 1915
	Captain C. Guy	December 1915

Unit Headquarters	Name	Date
114 Light Trench Mortar Battery	Lieutenant G.L. Ross	May 1915
115 Infantry Brigade		
Commander	Brigadier General Ivor Philipps DSO MP	October 1914
	Brigadier General H.J. Evans CMG	January 1915
Brigade Major	Captain C.L. Veal *Welsh*	December 1915[n]
	Captain Ll. Wyn Griffith *R.W. Fus* (acting)	July 1916
Staff Captain	Captain H.V. Hinton *Welsh*	December 1915[o]
17 R.W. Fus	Lieutenant Colonel H.R.H. Lloyd Mostyn	March 1915
	Lieutenant Colonel J.A. Ballard	December 1915[p]
	Major J.B. Cockburn (acting)	July 1916
10 S.W.B. (1st Gwent)	Lieutenant Colonel Sir Hamar Greenwood Bt MP	November 1914
	Lieutenant Colonel J.N.R. Harvey	June 1916
11 S.W.B. (2nd Gwent)	Lieutenant Colonel H.E. Porter	December 1914
	Lieutenant Colonel R. Gaussen	December 1915
16 Welsh (Cardiff City)	Lieutenant Colonel F. Gaskell	December 1914[q]
	Lieutenant Colonel F.W. Smith	May 1916
115 M.G. Company	Captain T.M. Jenkins	April 1915
	Captain E.D. Job	April 1916[r]
	2nd Lieutenant F.W. Evans *R.W. Fus*	July 1916
115 Light Trench Mortar Battery	Lieutenant K.E. Noel	May 1915
Signal Section	Lieutenant A.J. Taylor *R.E.*	November 1915

Notes to Appendix

a   Later General Sir Henry ap Rhys Pryce KCB CMG DSO (1874–1950), mentioned in despatches seven times during the Great War, he was later Quarter-Master General of India.

b   Died of wounds 11 July 1916.

c   Wounded at Mametz, 10 July 1916.

d   Wounded at Mametz 10 July 1916.

e   Killed at Mametz Wood 10 July 1916.

f   Wounded at Mametz 11 July 1916.

g   Later Major General Sir Thomas Owen Marden KBE CB CMG (1866–1951) later commanded 6th Division. Following the war, he commanded the British occupation force in Turkey during the Chanak Crisis in 1921–1922.

h   To command 2 R.W. Fus.

i   Wounded 10 July 1916.

j   Killed at Mametz, 10 July 1916.

k   Killed at Mametz, 10 July 1916

l   Wounded at Mametz 10 July 1916.

m   Died of wounds 23 December 1915.

n   Wounded in Mametz Wood 11 July 1916.

o   Wounded in Mametz Wood 11 July 1916.

p   Wounded 10 July 1916.

q   Killed May 1916.

r   Killed July 1916.

Notes

1　Cited in N.L.W. MS 3556E, Welsh Army Corps Draft Report, prepared for The Executive Committee.

2　A.O. 124 of 1915, Royal Warrant dated 26 February 1915.

3　*The Monmouthshire Regiment TF World War I. Fact Sheet: 7-B07-11.* Regimental Museum of the Royal Welsh (Brecon).

4　N.L.W. MS 3556E, Welsh Army Corps Draft Report.

5　N.L.W. MS 3556E, Welsh Army Corps Draft Report.

6　N.L.W. MS 3556E, Welsh Army Corps Draft Report.

7　W.A. Tucker, *The Lousier War* (London, 1974), p. 13,

8　Thomas Dilworth, *David Jones in the Great War* (London, 2012), p. 35.

9　Sidney Allinson, *The Bantams: The Untold Story of World War One* (Barnsley, 2009). N.L.W. MS 3556E, Welsh Army Corps Draft Report.

10　See, for example, Peter Simkins, *Kitchener's Army: The Raising of the New Armies 1914–1916* (M.U.P., 1988), pp. 96–99.

11　T.N.A. WO 20/Gen. No. 3449 (A.G.1) dated 10 October 1914.

12　E.S. Turner, *Gallant Gentlemen. A History of the British Officer, 1600–1956* (London, 1956), p. 6.

13　Robert Graves, *Goodbye to all That* (London, 1929) pp.106, 115.

14　Peter Rowland, *Lloyd George* (London, 1975), pp. 289–290.

15　Lieutenant Colonel J.E. Munby CMD DSO (ed.), *A History of the 38th (Welsh) Division, By the G.S.O.s I of the Division* (London, 1920), p. 3.

16　David A. Pretty, *Farmer, Soldier and Politician. The Life of Brigadier-General Sir Owen Thomas, MP Father of the 'Welsh Army Corps'* (Wrexham, 2011), p. 85.

17　A.J.P. Taylor (ed.), *Lloyd George: A Diary by Frances Stevenson* (London, 1971), p. 8.

18　See David A. Pretty, *Farmer, Soldier and Politician* previously cited.

19　*Welsh Outlook*, January 1916, p. 5.

20　Pretty, p. 86.

21　T.N.A. WO 95/2555/1, 14 R.W. Fus War Diary, 21 November 1914.

22　Diary of John Bradshaw for 1915 (Permission of Mr John Griffiths).

23　*Western Mail*, 13 November 1914.

24　Pretty, p. 94.

25　N.L.W. MS 3556E, Welsh Army Corps Draft Report.

26　*Western Mail*, 2 December 1914.

27　*Western Mail*, 1 January 1915.

28　Munby, pp. 3–4.

29　Emlyn Davies, *Taffy Went to War* (Privately printed, Knutsford, n.d.), p. 3.

30　<www.measuringworth.com> (Accessed 2 October 2017).

31　*Llandudno Advertiser*, 31 July 1915.

32　*Western Mail*, 18 December 1914.

33　Tucker, p. 13; see also the account by David Jones in Dilworth, pp. 42–43.

34　Pretty, p. 94.

35　Dilworth, pp. 49–50.

36　Chris Williams, 'A Question of "Legitimate Pride"? The 38th (Welsh) Division at the Battle of Mametz Wood, July 1916' in *Welsh History Review* 28/4 (2017), p. 741.

37　For a fuller analysis, see P.A. Crocker 'Some Thoughts on The Royal Welch Fusiliers in the Great War' in *Y Ddraig Goch – Journal of The Royal Welch Fusiliers*, September 2002, pp. 135–140 and Chris Williams, 'Taffs in the trenches: Welsh national identity and military service, 1914–1918' in Matthew Cragoe and Chris Williams (ed.), *Wales and War: Society, Politics and Religion in the Nineteenth and Twentieth Centuries* (Cardiff, 2007), pp. 126–164.

38　*Infantry Training, Vol. I, Training* (W.O./G.S.1914), p. 11.

39　Robert Graves, *Goodbye to All That* (London, 1929), p. 228.

40　Emlyn Davies, pp. 2–3.

41　*Western Mail*, 16 December 1914.

42　*London Gazette,* 13 June 1911.

43   Major General Sir Ivor Philipps' Obituary in *The Times*, 16 August 1940, p. 7, column E.
44   Munby, Order of Battle.
45   Munby, pp. xii-xiv.
46   *Field Service Regulations, Vol. I (Organisation and Administration) 1908*. p. 20.
47   *Field Service Pocket Book 1926*. WO 26/863, p. 3.
48   Munby, pp. 8–9.
49   N.L.W. MS 3556E, Welsh Army Corps Draft Report.
50   Wyn Griffith, p. 90.
51   Kenneth O. Morgan (ed.), *Lloyd George; Family Letters 1885–1936* (Cardiff and London, 1973), p. 175.
52   Chris Williams, p. 725, gives a full summary of the sources for their lack of confidence.
53   T.N.A. CAB 45/189, letter from Drake-Brockman.
54   Colin Hughes, *Mametz: Lloyd George's Welsh Army at the Battle of the Somme* (London, 1982), p. 31.
55   A.J.P. Taylor (ed.), p. 24.
56   N.L.W. MS 3556E, Welsh Army Corps Draft Report.
57   Pretty, p. 95.
58   *Daily Post and Mercury* (Liverpool), 2 March 1915.
59   *Caernarvon and Denbigh Herald,* 5 March 1915.
60   Dilworth, p. 46.
61   Munby, p. 6.
62   Munby, p. 9.
63   Tucker, p. 14.
64   38th Division *History*, pp. 5–10.
65   *Caernarvon and Denbigh Herald,* 14 May 1915.
66   Dilworth, p. 52.
67   Emlyn Davies, p. 4.
68   Colin Hughes, p. 32.
69   Colin Hughes, p. 38.
70   <www.1914–1918.net/rwf> (Accessed 1 October 2017); N.L.W. MS 3556E, Welsh Army Corps Draft Report.
71   N.L.W. MS 3556E, Welsh Army Corps Draft Report.
72   T.N.A., Records created by the Welsh Office and Wales Office, 1890–1914.
73   See, for example, *The Spectator*, 25 July 1914 pp. 13–14.

3

'England's best sword knocked out of her hand': German Strategy and Operational Plans for 1916

The Chief of Staff of the Imperial German Armies, Erich von Falkenhayn,[*] had a reputation as a cautious, but successful, strategist. Having been Prussian Minister of War since 1913, he had succeeded Helmut von Moltke the Younger following the latter's nervous breakdown and dismissal, on 14 September 1914, when Moltke's plan to deal with a war on two fronts, *Aufmarsch II West*, was already unravelling after the check on the Marne – the first reversal of German arms since 1860.[1] The commanders of Seven German Armies in the field answered to him, controlling between them 150 divisions – and he answered only to the Kaiser.

By the end of 1915 Falkenhayn had been in office for a year, and the Central Powers seemed very much in control of the war. Serbia had been defeated and was occupied by the Austrians and Bulgarians – the latter having joined the Central

General Erich von Falkenhayn.

Powers that year. Poland, Luxembourg, parts of France and most of Belgium were occupied by the Germans. Entente offensives on the Western Front had been halted in bloody ruin, while the Germans had introduced gas warfare, almost breaking the British line around Ypres. The Russian offensive in Galicia in December 1915 had failed, with the loss of 225,000 men, including 40,000 prisoners; and on 27 December the British had decided to evacuate Gallipoli, signalling yet another Entente failure. In Mesopotamia, a British force was besieged at Kut-el-Amara and was in grave danger of defeat. The Germans had the upper hand in East Africa, even though they had lost ground in South-West Africa. At sea, submarine warfare had caused heavy losses, including the liners *Lusitania* and *Persia*; and in the air, England had been bombed by Zeppelins for the first time. For the Entente it had been, in A.J.P. Taylor's words, a year that had no meaning other than to add names on a war memorial.[2]

---

[*] *General der Infanterie* Erich Georg Anton von Falkenhayn (1861–1922). After his removal as Chief of the Imperial General Staff in 1916 he held successful field commands in Romania, Palestine and Russia.

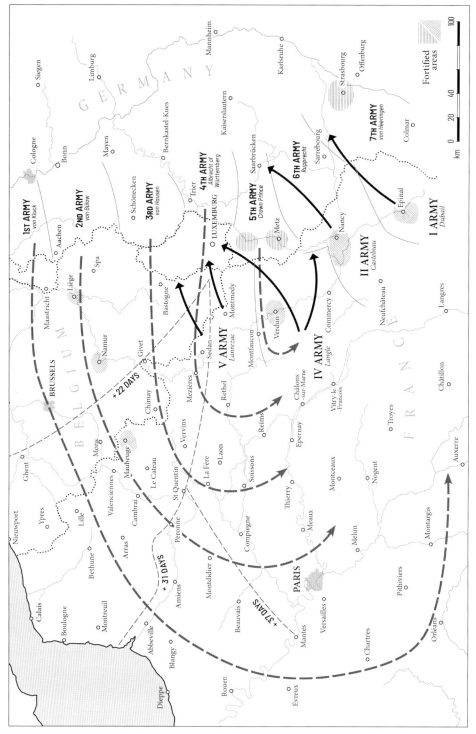

Map 3.i The German Plan for 1914 and French counter-moves.

Against this background, the Central Powers had every reason to expect victory during 1916. The strategic plans of the major protagonist, Germany, built on this position of strength. Submarine warfare was to become unlimited at sea (this was not implemented as the effect on the United States could not be managed); air attacks would be continued against England; and the Balkans would be totally subjugated.[3] In the occupied territories, the conscription of men as slave labour in Germany, in order to release German manpower for the Army, pre-figured future German behaviour.

However, the picture was not quite as rosy as might, at first glance, have seemed. In late 1914, Falkenhayn had pressed the manoeuvre which became known as 'the race for the sea' and after its frustration at the First Battle of Ypres in November 1914 he became convinced that victory could not be brought about by a single decisive battle like Sedan in 1870, for the simple reason that this was beyond the strength and capabilities of the German armies.[4] This was a dramatic reversal of his initial enthusiasm for a European war as the means of establishing Germany as the pre-eminent power in the western world. With the benefit of hindsight, he later wrote that the German declarations of war against Britain and France had been 'justifiable but overly-hasty and unnecessary.'[5] This in spite of the fact that he had been fully engaged in German deliberations over going to war, and was present at the meeting in July 1914 which gave full German endorsement to Austrian aims and actions in the Balkans, and their consequences.

Falkenhayn believed that he must develop a new approach if victory was to be gained. However, his uneasy relationship with the Imperial Chancellor, Theobald von Bethmann-Hollweg,*[7] in 1915, convinced him that he could not look for assistance from the political leadership of the Empire which was working feverishly in the diplomatic arena to try to detach Belgium and Russia from the Allied cause through separate peace treaties.[6] To Falkenhayn, these were mere distractions. A military solution would therefore have to be found to address Germany's strategic, political, objectives. It would be, in the words of one of Falkenhayn's subordinates, an operational approach with 'no analogue in history.'[7]

In pursuit of his revised belief he wrote to Bethmann-Hollweg, as early as November 1914, that Germany's enemies were too numerous and too powerful and that the German Army did not have the resources required to win the war in the manner described in pre-war Prussian military doctrine – that is, by the Napoleonic method of decisive battle in the open field and the destruction thereby of the enemy's army. Instead, therefore, Falkenhayn proposed using limited military successes as levers to achieve for a favourable political settlement, by convincing at least one of Germany's enemies to conclude a separate peace and thus undoing the *Entente*.[8]

Falkenhayn was right that Germany faced an increasingly challenging situation. In spite of how well things appeared at the end of 1915, she was gripped in that strategic vice of a war on several fronts: in the west, in Russia, in the Balkans and in support of the Ottoman Empire – not to mention in her rapidly diminishing colonial empire. Falkenhayn concluded that the most dangerous arena, where the war could certainly be won or lost, was not in Russia, but in the west. In France and Flanders, the Germans faced a large French army and a growing British Expeditionary Force. This front was densely manned by well-equipped enemies and the unsuccessful, bloody, failures of the Entente in trying to break through the front here during 1915 had

---

*   Theobald Theodor Friedrich Alfred von Bethmann-Hollweg (1856–1921) was Chancellor of the German Empire from 1909 to 1917.

proved just how difficult it would be to penetrate a defensive line. Then, once this first line had been broken *into*, and then *through*, it would be extremely difficult to break *out* and defeat the large Entente armies in the field. In spite of German successes in the east against the Russians in 1915, and the crushing of Serbia (of which Falkenhayn was also the architect), the Germans were able to muster only 25 uncommitted divisions out of the 117 in the western theatre as a true reserve. This figure would be nowhere near large enough to produce a decisive battlefield victory against the French Army, with its nearly two million men, plus six Belgian divisions and a British Army which had grown from seven to 38 divisions by the end of 1915 – and which could grow to 70 divisions even though these needed time to train and equip.

In theory, as Jack Sheldon has pointed out, Germany, with its almost 69 million people, mobilised 3.7 million men with another 5.5 million men of military age available for training. Around 10.5 million were liable for conscription but only just over a third of these were serving. If Germany called up the same percentages of conscripts as France, it could field an army of 6 million men – although equipping, housing and sustaining a force of this size was probably well beyond the resources of the Reich.[9] It is also important to understand that as well as the great Prussian Army, which included the regiments, divisions and corps from Berg, Hanover, Pfalz, Pomerania, Schleswig-Holstein, Silesia and Westphalia, the Kaiser's *Reichsheer* was made up of a number of national contingents from smaller German kingdoms which acknowledged the imperium of the Kaiser, but retained a degree of individual command and control. The largest of these was the Bavarian Army, with its three corps, but there were also corps from Saxony and Württemberg; and divisions or regiments from Anhalt, Baden, Brunswick, Hesse, Lippe, Mecklenburg and Oldenburg.

Falkenhayn had dismissed the idea of making the war against Russia the main effort of the Central Powers, mindful perhaps of Napoleon's downfall after 1812 in which Prussia had been a player, remarking even after the success at Gorlice in 1915 that victories in the east were achieved only at the expense of weakening German efforts in the critical, western, theatre of war. This approach certainly made him some enemies, among them the commander of the German army on the Eastern Front, Paul von Hindenburg[*] and his chief of staff, Erich Ludendorff.[†] This powerful combination believed that the German Army could win the war without diplomatic assistance. They felt that, with some reinforcement, they would be able to defeat the Russian armies in the field, and thus dictate peace in the east on highly favourable terms. The full force of the German and Austrian armies could then be turned westwards. Ludendorff had in fact developed a plan that, if successful, could have trapped and destroyed the main Russian field army while giving the German Army in the east time and space to pull back if things went wrong. Given their success in the battle of Tannenberg in August 1914, and Falkenhayn's failure

---

[*]   Paul Ludwig Hans Anton von Beneckendorff und von Hindenburg known generally as Paul von Hindenburg (1847–1934) largely controlled German policy in the second half of the Great War and served as the elected President of the Weimar Republic of Germany from 1925 until his death in 1934. He played the key role in the National Socialist Party's assumption of power January 1933 by appointing Hitler Chancellor of a 'Government of National Concentration'.

[†]   Erich Friedrich Wilhelm Ludendorff (1865–1937) was the victor of the battles of Liège and Tannenberg. From August 1916, his appointment as Quartermaster General (*Erster Generalquartiermeister*) made him the joint leader with Paul von Hindenburg of the German war efforts until his resignation in October 1918.

in the first battle of Ypres in October and November 1914, Hindenburg and Ludendorff had more influence within the Army than Falkenhayn: but Falkenhayn rejected Ludendorff's ideas.

This difference of opinion over both Germany's strategic direction, and the resulting changes required in the German army's so-far generally successful fighting doctrine, caused massive internal disputes in 1915. It was also the beginning of Hindenburg and Ludendorff's campaign, eventually successful, to have Falkenhayn removed from his post. To the German military mind, doctrine was essential and conventional thinking focused on the results achieved by the application of Clausewitzian principles during the three wars of the late 19th century against Austria, Denmark and France. In particular, the victory of Sedan was thought to embody the concept of *Schwerpunkt*, literally hard point, or more usually 'point of main effort'. This is a concept that endured through the Second World War and the Cold War and is still there today. This principle required the definition of the decisive point and the allocation of all available resources to a massive, crushing blow against the enemy's centre of gravity – the place, person or capability, the destruction of which would cause the enemy's collapse.[10]

In December 1915, Falkenhayn briefed Kaiser Wilhelm on his plans in principle for the conduct of the war during 1916 in the famous 'Christmas Memorandum'. In this briefing he used, for the first time, the now-infamous phrase 'bleed out' – often translated as 'bleed white' to describe how success would be achieved.[11] Generaloberst Hans von Plessen,* the Kaiser's Orderly Adjutant General and Commandant of the Imperial General Headquarters, recorded the meeting in his diary:

> General von Falkenhayn rolled out for His Majesty a serious picture of the situation with the conclusion that to carry the war to its end, an attack in the west, where all available strength has already been collected, must be conducted… It is to be then that the Entente will attack us in the west and thereby bleed themselves white [*sich dabei verblutet* – N.B. this actually translates literally as bleed themselves out, not white].[12]

Having agreed on the principle, the next question facing von Falkenhayn and the Kaiser was, which enemy on the Western Front to attack? At about this time, the Chief of the Imperial Austro-Hungarian General Staff, Field Marshal Conrad von Hötzendorf,† proposed to Falkenhayn that Italy should be the Central Powers' main effort for 1916. Knock out Italy, he said, and 400,000 Austrian troops could be transferred to the Western Front. Hötzendorf asked for nine German divisions in addition to the four he already controlled, to ensure success. Falkenhayn however disagreed, and two allies went their own ways – a clear example of the

---

*   Hans Georg Hermann von Plessen (1841–1929) was a Colonel-General (*Generaloberst*) and Canon of Brandenburg who held the honorary rank of *Generalfeldmarschall* as Commandant of the German General Staff. Von Plessen also held the office of His Majesty's Orderly Adjutant General (*SM diensttuender Generaladjutant*), thus making him one of the Emperor's closest confidants. By 1918 he was the oldest serving officer in the Imperial German Army. In 1918, von Plessen was awarded the *Pour le Mérite*, Germany's highest military honour. He remained close to the Kaiser until his abdication in November 1918.

†   Field Marshal Franz Xavier Joseph Conrad Graf von Hötzendorf (1852–1925), was the Austrian Empire's Chief of the General Staff during the July Crisis of 1914 that led to the outbreak of war. He argued for war against Serbia, on the ground that it was needed to hold together the polyglot Habsburg dominions, which seemed on the verge of breaking up.

difficulties of managing an alliance or coalition in which there is no single truly dominant partner; and perhaps also one of the great 'what-ifs' of history.

Falkenhayn, then, was not to be diverted by either Italy or by Russia, for he saw Britain as Germany's most dangerous enemy because of her imperial reach, naval power and industrial strength. However, Britain was also the most difficult enemy to defeat. German intelligence believed that the morale of the British Army was high, even though it was inexperienced and had suffered huge losses among its professional cadres during 1914 and 1915. As early as November 1914, Falkenhayn had written to Paul von Hindenburg that 'our most dangerous enemy is not in the east, but rather is England.'[13] Having been a member of the German Expeditionary Force and later the Occupation Force in China from 1900, Falkenhayn had first-hand experience of the British and their ability to project power across the globe. His memorandum of December 1915 stated that:

> Germany can expect no mercy from this enemy so long as he retains the slightest hope of achieving his object. England is obviously staking everything on a war of exhaustion. We have not been able to shatter her belief that it will bring Germany to her knees, and that belief has given the enemy the strength to fight on.

Comparatively, Britain was still weak on the Western Front and here, England's best sword, as Falkenhayn put it to the Kaiser his letter of 15 December, was the French Army. The French Army must therefore be destroyed as an effective instrument before British numbers could reach their peak.

The destruction of that best sword seemed eminently possible. Reports from agents and from field commanders seemed to indicate that the French Army was weakening. In November 1915, the Intelligence Section of the German High Command drew up an assessment of the French Army, which concluded that it was 400,000 men weaker than it had been in 1914, partly because of casualties and partly because of the long-term problem of a declining birth-rate. This conclusion held good although the 1916 class of recruits had been called up early. They may well have been right, given that the French had lost more men in the first four months of the war, than Britain was to lose throughout the entire war. Their losses at the end of 1915 had reached 50,355 officers and 1,911,332 men, of whom 1,001,271 had been killed or were missing.[14] German intelligence expected that the French would be forced to call up the 1917 and 1918 Classes of recruits by June 1916.[15] The situation seemed to be becoming worse because repeated failures by the French to break through the German defences appeared to be sapping the morale of the Army. The chief of intelligence in the Headquarters of the German Sixth Army reported from the interrogation of prisoners that: 'The morale of the troops, with few exceptions, can be characterized as bad. Some soldiers believe it will not get better, but only worse as a result of the failure in September and the high losses… It will be difficult to get the soldiers to attack.'[16]

Falkenhayn also believed that French political will was weakening. He based this view on the regular reports he received from a well-placed German agent in Paris, an Austrian named August Schluga, Freiherr von Rastenberg.* Schluga had been a German agent since 1866, first

---

*   August Freiherr Schluga von Rastenfeld (1841–1917) is accounted one of the most prominent men in the history of espionage.

in Austria and then in France. He had supplied German Intelligence with the war plans of the Austrian army in 1866 and of the French army in 1870; he repeated this feat once more in August 1914. Falkenhayn trusted Schluga's reports so completely that he read them himself as soon as they arrived in the Imperial Headquarters without waiting for any analysis by the Intelligence Section.

Having decided who to attack, the next question was, where? After several options had been considered, the city of Verdun and its ring of forts was chosen because Falkenhayn believed, rightly, that the French would commit every resource they had to stop a German break-through here. It was the scene of French humiliation at the hands of Prussia in 1792 and close to another, greater, debacle at Sedan in 1870. Its loss would open a road that would lead straight to Paris. Here, therefore, was to be the breaking-point of French willpower, hope and commitment. As Falkenhayn wrote: 'If we succeeded in opening the eyes of [the French] people to the fact that in a military sense they have nothing more to hope for, that breaking point would be reached, and England's best sword knocked out of her hand.'[17]

At the operational level, the fortress of Verdun was vulnerable to attack because it lay in the centre of a large bulge, or salient, in the French line which enabled the heavy German artillery to bombard it from three sides. Adolph Wild von Hohenborn, who had succeeded Falkenhayn as Prussian Minister of War, wrote of it that: 'the [French] positions will be so diminished [by German artillery] that not even a mouse can live in them.'[18] At the tactical level, the General Staff had concluded in an assessment in 1910 that a threat against Verdun would undermine the whole system of fortification in the area and force the French to make changes that would weaken the defence.[19] Finally, in logistical terms, the Germans had an advantage over the French here. The area behind the German front was well supported by railways, while German artillery could cut the rail lines easily on the French side, leaving only a narrow road along which French troops could be supplied. By attacking at Verdun, therefore, Falkenhayn believed that he could draw off his enemies' strategic and operational reserves into the mincing machine of German artillery and machine gun fire. Verdun was a place: 'for the retention of which the French command would be compelled to throw in every man they have.'[20]

The method that Falkenhayn chose was attrition – the wearing down of his opponent by bleeding him to death – and the time was early 1916, before the Entente powers had time to recover their strength. In response to a major German offensive which completely absorbed French fighting power, the British – Germany's most dangerous enemy – would be forced to launch an offensive of their own designed to relieve the French before their New Army was truly ready for battle. In doing so, like the French, they would wear themselves down and be 'punished'.[21] To Falkenhayn, it was irrelevant if the fortress of Verdun fell into German hands or not. The point was to force the French and British to commit their reserves to counter-offensives against the German attack. These counter-offensives would result in the wearing down – bleeding out – of the Allied armies to such an extent that the French government would be compelled to come to the negotiating table, bringing the British with them.

Although in its conception, the assault on Verdun was still in the classic tradition of seeking decisive victory on the battlefield as the means of reaching strategic goals, it was arguably the first time that such a calculated blood-letting was deliberately engineered to achieve it. As Alistair Horne observed: 'The macabreness, the unpleasantness of its very imagery could only have emerged from, and was symptomatic of, that Great War, where, in their callousness, leaders could regard human lives as mere corpuscles.'[22] This was a complete departure from the

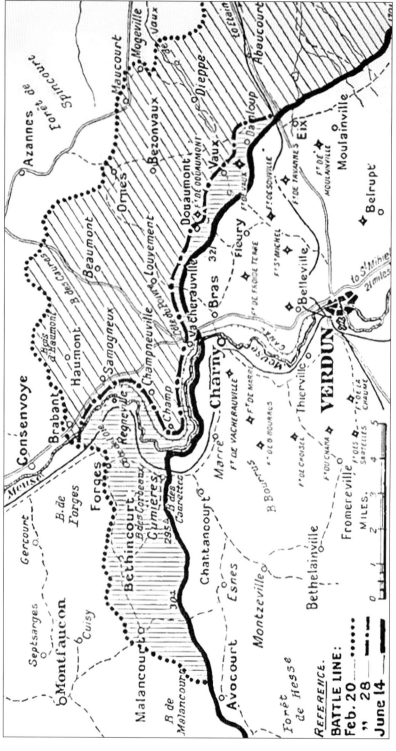

Map 3.ii Verdun, February to June 1916.

concept of the decisive action, achieved rapidly, at the point of main effort; but at the same time, Verdun *was* the *schwerpunkt*. Almost every modern, heavy, artillery piece was moved there in support of the offensive,[23] leaving German corps and divisions elsewhere with old German howitzers or captured Russian 200 mm guns. However, Falkenhayn was inconsistent. He allocated only six German divisions, 108,000 men, for the initial attack; four more, bringing the total to 180,000 men, were allocated in March.

Verdun and its forts were defended by 30,000 men; the attack, Operation *Gericht* ('Judgement'), opened on 21 February with a massive artillery barrage by 850 heavy and 350 medium guns along an eight-mile (13 kilometres) front lasting nine hours, thickened with a fog of gas shells. German aircraft controlled the skies. Flame throwers (*'flammenwerfer'*) were used for the first time on 22 February. The attack was, however, greatly hindered by French counter-battery fire, which largely destroyed the available German 17-inch howitzers and which also destroyed the artillery park near Spincourt with its stock of 450,000 shells.[24]

Ferocious fighting continued throughout February and March and, as Falkenhayn had predicted, the French committed every available resource. 6,000 lorries rolled up the single road, *la Voie Sacrée*, every day, bringing 50,000 tons of stores and ammunition and 90,000 men every week.[25] By the end of April, 89,000 Frenchmen had been killed – but attrition was not working entirely in favour of the Germans, for by the same date they had lost more than 81,000 men themselves. German gains, made on a very narrow attack frontage because of the small number of assault divisions allocated to the operation, were thus rightly described as being at an exorbitant price.[26] General Philippe Pétain,[*] commanding the army on the Verdun front, kept French divisions in the line for only short periods, rotating them every few days. As a result, a great deal of the French Army was drawn into the mincing machine to service this rotation, and its reserves were heavily depleted. This drew away many of the French divisions which had been earmarked for the planned Somme offensive, of which more in Chapter Four. Things were made worse when the French Commander-in-Chief, Marshal Joseph Joffre,[†] promoted Pétain to command the Army Group and placed the aggressive General Robert Nivelle[‡] in command at Verdun. Thus restraint was abandoned and Nivelle played into Falkenhayn's hands.

Falkenhayn knew that France would appeal to its allies to take measures that would divert the Germans and take the heat off them during this major offensive; but he had little regard for the ability of the Russians to do this effectively, partly because of their continued inability to match the Central Powers on the battlefield; and partly because he was sure that internal strife would bring about collapse: '… we are entitled to believe that Russia's internal troubles will compel her to give in within a comparatively short period.'[27] To make sure of this, the Germans handed a million roubles to the Jewish Marxist Alexander Parvus in order to fund and spread anti-war propaganda in Russia. However, the major Russian offensive under General Aleksei Brusilov on

---

*   Later Marshal Henri Philippe Benoni Omer Joseph Pétain (1856–1951), Head of State during the Vichy government from 1940–1943.
†   Marshal Joseph Jacques Césaire ('Papa') Joffre (1852–1931).
‡   Robert Georges Nivelle (1856–1924) was an artillery officer who like Falkenhayn had served in the Boxer Rebellion. Following the successes at Verdun, Nivelle was promoted to be Commander-in-Chief of the French armies on the Western Front in December 1916. He was responsible for the Nivelle Offensive at the *Chemin des Dames*, which failed to achieve a breakthrough on the Western Front and led to a major mutiny affecting half the French Army. Nivelle was replaced as Commander-in-Chief by Philippe Pétain in May 1917.

5 June took the Austrians by surprise, capturing over 190,000 Austrian troops along with 416 guns and howitzers in two weeks. Another 160,000 were taken in the weeks that followed. The Russians occupied Czernowitz in Hungary on 17 June.[28] Only German intervention prevented a worse disaster and checked a further offensive in July. This attack forced Falkenhayn to withdraw seven divisions of his 25 in reserve on the Western Front, and send these divisions to the east, disproving his own thesis. This meant the loss of almost one-third of his manoeuvre forces, which might either have fed the attack at Verdun or been used for an effective counter-attack against the British in response to the Somme offensive. It also led to the decision by Romania to enter the war on the side of the Entente – to her undoing.[29] However this was the last effective offensive move made by Russia and it cost the Tsar almost 1,000,000 men, leading to Russia's moral collapse, revolution and defeat.

What, however, was the German view of matters closer to home, on the Somme, where lay the junction of the French and British Armies and where there were indications of a large Allied operation building? In January 1915, von Falkenhayn had issued instructions for the improvement of the German fortifications on the Western Front. On the Somme, these instructions had been largely, if not completely, fulfilled. Barbed wire obstacles had been deepened and heightened – a subject discussed elsewhere. The front line had been increased from one trench to three, 150–200 yards apart. The first trench was to be occupied by sentries; the second (*Wohngraben*) held the bulk of the front-line trench garrisons; and the third trench contained the immediate reserve and was as well built and heavily wired as the main position. The trenches were traversed to prevent an attacker firing along the length of a trench if he gained entry; and had sentry-posts in concrete recesses built into the parapet. Dugouts had been deepened from six to nine feet (1.8–2.7 metres) to at least 20 feet (6.1 metres), 50 yards apart and large enough for 25 men. These dugouts were believed to be strong enough to resist the heaviest artillery fire. An intermediate line of strong points (*Stützpunktlinie*) had also been constructed about 1,000 yards behind the front line. Communication trenches then ran back from the front line to a reserve, or second, line. This lay beyond the range of Allied field artillery, forcing any attacker to pause while his artillery was brought forward before mounting another assault. After the Autumn battles of 1915, a third defence line another 3,000 yards back from the *Stützpunktlinie* was begun in February 1916 and was almost complete on the Somme when the battle began; most civilians had also been evacuated from the area close to the front. An operation order issued by the 28th Reserve Infantry Division stressed some measures to strengthen and deepen the defensive line:

> Of particular importance for the defence is the quick building in of machine-guns behind the front defence line, which command the ground behind and which, with flank fire, can support each other, so that enemy forces which may at any point have temporarily broken through, may be held up by machine-gun fire from further advance. Furthermore, behind the front line the conversion of villages into strong points is of the greatest importance. Such villages are: Pozières, Contalmaison, Bazentin le Petit, Bazentin le Grand, and Longeval.[30]

This reliance on the defence was another marked departure from previous German doctrine, which stressed the primacy of the offensive and regarded the defence only as a temporary phase of war, from which new offensives could be launched.[31]

Two German photographs of civilians being evacuated from the frontline area on the Somme.
(163 I.R. Regimental History)

The supporting German artillery located behind these lines of fortification was organised in a series of *Sperrfeuerstreifen*, or barrage sectors. Every infantry officer was expected to know the batteries covering his section of the front line. An extensive telephone system had been built to connect the trench garrisons with their supporting guns, with lines buried six feet deep (1.7 metres) for five miles (8 kilometres) behind the first line. When not in action, guns were automatically laid onto the immediate front of the German first line in a series of defensive fire tasks, which could be activated by telephone or by rocket-fired flares. On the first day of the Somme, when the British barrage lifted and the attacking troops were crossing no-man's land, survivors

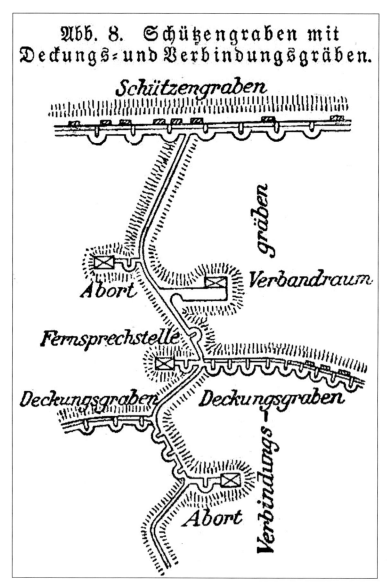

A contemporary diagram of German trench systems on the Western Front.

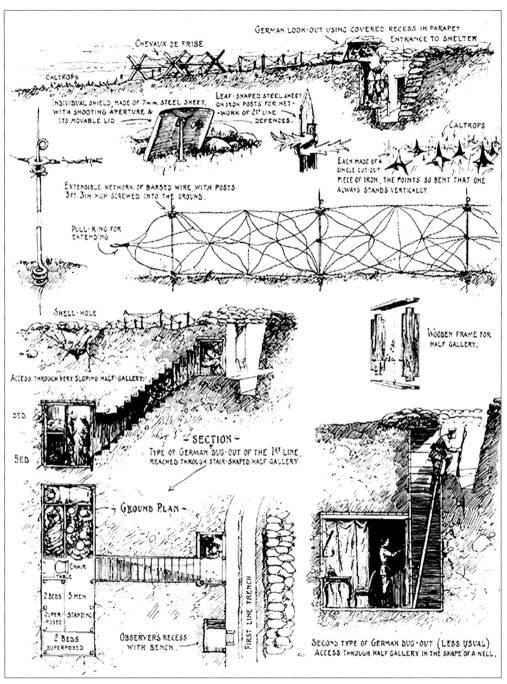

British diagrams showing the layout of German defences.

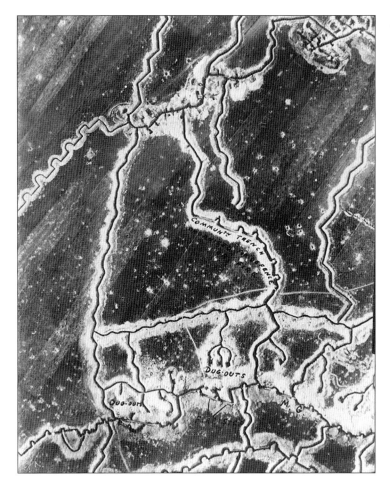

An Allied air photograph
of German trenches in
early 1916.

spoke of a short, silent, interval after which the German signal rockets went up, looking like a
line of poplar trees.[32]

Recorded targets for the guns had been carefully defined, linked to batteries and identified by
a simple matrix of map squares. For example, in the 26th Reserve Infantry Division sector, the
various sub-sectors were identified by letters:

Beaumont	B
Courcellette	C
Heidenkopf	H
Ovillers	O
Pozières	P
Serre	S

Artillery squares within these sub-sectors were then assigned numbers which greatly simplified
the business of calling for fire and reporting corrections, since an artillery observation officer

A German trench in late 1915.

German artillery preparing to move up to the front. (James Payne collections)

had only to order the map square by letter and name and the number of rounds in order that immediate fire would be brought down.

However, the Somme defences had two weaknesses that the rebuilding had not solved. Because the Germans held the high ground, their first line trenches were almost always on a forward slope, marked by white chalk from the subsoil which had been thrown up during construction, and easily seen by enemy observers. The defences were often crowded, with a regiment having two battalions near the front-line trench systems and the reserve battalion divided between the *Stützpunktlinie* and the second line. All troops were placed within 2,000 yards of the first line, accommodated in the new deep dugouts. The concentration of troops close to a forward slope guaranteed, therefore, that they would face the bulk of an Allied artillery bombardment.

These preparations were not unique to the Somme and the question must be asked, and answered, to what degree did the Germans expect an attack on the Somme? Certainly, it was part of Falkenhayn's intention, as we have already discussed, that the British should launch an attack in order to relieve the French. The British preparations on the Somme, which will be examined in the next chapter, were impossible to hide from German agents and from aerial reconnaissance: this latter was considerable, for by 30 June, the German air strength on the Second Army front stood at six *Feldflieger Abteilungen* (reconnaissance flights) with 42 aircraft; four *Artillerieflieger Abteilungen* (artillery observation flights) with 17 aircraft; *Kampfgeschwader 1* (Bomber-Fighter Squadron 1) with 43 aircraft; *Kampfstaffel 32* (Bomber-Fighter Flight 32) with eight aircraft; and a *Kampfeinsitzer Kommando* (single-seat fighter detachment) with 19 machines: a total of 129 aircraft.[33] Information from prisoners captured in trench raids provided yet more information on the detailed tactics, the likely date and place, and even the numbers and calibre of the British artillery committed to the attack.

As early as February, the Army High Command – *Oberste Heeresleitung (O.H.L.)* – signalled General Fritz von Below,* Commanding the German Second Army, and Crown Prince Rupprecht of Bavaria,† Commanding the Sixth

A German Pfalz E-1 aircraft.

Crown Prince Rupprecht of Bavaria.

---

*   Fritz Theodor Carl von Below (1853–1918).

†   Rupprecht (1869–1955) was the last Bavarian crown prince. During the first half of the Great War he commanded the German Sixth Army. From August 1916 he commanded Army Group

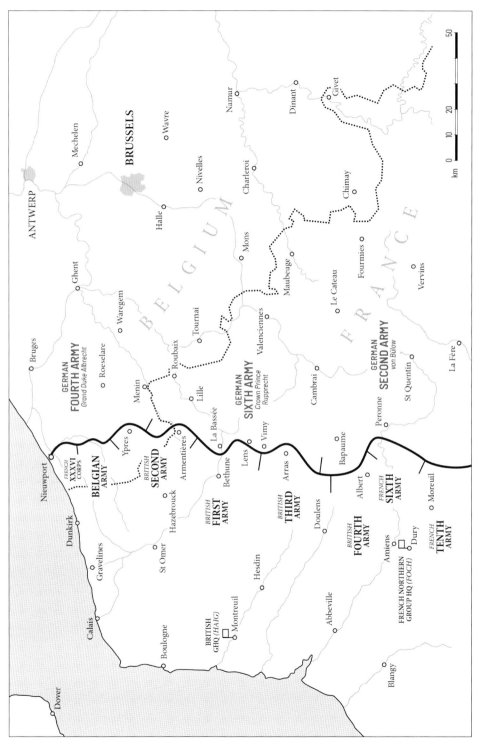

Map 3.iii   German and Allied Armies on the Western Front, 1916.

Army, to the effect that a British attack north of the Somme was likely once the Verdun operation was fully under way, stating the opinion that: 'The British cannot leave the French to struggle.'[34] At first, von Below and Prince Rupprecht were dubious, however soon after the British and French had reached agreement on the Somme offensive, the Germans began picking up indications and by early March they expected an attack on the Second Army which held the front from north of Gommecourt southwards to Noyon. Prince Rupprecht was described by his Chief of Staff, *General der Infanterie* Hermann von Kuhl,[*] as:

> … extremely industrious, [he] maintained battle maps in his office that showed the exact situation, worked his way systematically through all signals, letters, reports and orders and was constantly superbly informed…. he was always quick to appreciate the situation and personally weighed up the options for decision.[35]

This was not a man who was going to be easily misled. On the Second Army front, the German defence of the south bank of the Somme was the responsibility of XVII Corps (General Paul Fleck). On the north bank the XIV Reserve Corps (*Generalleutnant* Hermann von Stein[†]) held the line from the Somme to the Ancre. The Guard Corps (General Karl von Plettenberg[‡]) held the ground north of the Ancre opposite Serre and Gommecourt.[36] A breakdown of German divisions, eight of which were in the front line at any one time, is contained in the Appendix to this chapter.

In January, von Below launched a diversionary attack in support of the Verdun main effort, south of the Somme. At a cost of one officer and four men killed, this operation captured 1,300 prisoners and large quantities of weapons and equipment. Crown Prince Rupprecht also launched similar moves, *Rupprecht Operations I – IV*, which were more costly and of less value.[37] Falkenhayn believed nonetheless that these operations were useful: 'Extensive preparations for feint attacks had been made according to instructions… in this way we succeeded in keeping the enemy for a long time in uncertainty as to the sector to be chosen for attack.'[38] From early March, von Below pressed for further diversionary attacks to spoil the forthcoming Allied offensive, rather than hand them the initiative. Such moves would have required a diversion of reserves and other resources, especially artillery, from the German main effort at Verdun and were refused by Falkenhayn.

Falkenhayn, however, was more concerned with reports of a possible French counter-offensive in Alsace-Lorraine and an attack on the Sixth Army between Gommecourt to Ypres, in Flanders. In spite of the fact that Falkenhayn had set out, by attacking at Verdun, to bleed not only the French but also, and more significantly for the long term, the British, this is odd. A stated aim of the Verdun offensive was that the British should mount a large-scale offensive

---

'Rupprecht of Bavaria', which faced the British Expeditionary Force.

[*]   Generalleutnant Hermann Josef von Kuhl (1856–1958) was one of the most competent field commanders and General Staff officers in the German Army, He was one of only five recipients of both the 'military class' and 'peace class' of the *Pour le Mérite*.

[†]   Hermann Christlieb Matthäus von Stein, (1854 –1927) was a General of the Artillery and Minister of War later in the war. He was a recipient of *Pour le Mérite*.

[‡]   Karl Freiherr von Plettenberg (1852–1938) was Commandant-General of the Guard Corps, Adjutant General to the Kaiser and a recipient of *Pour le Mérite*.

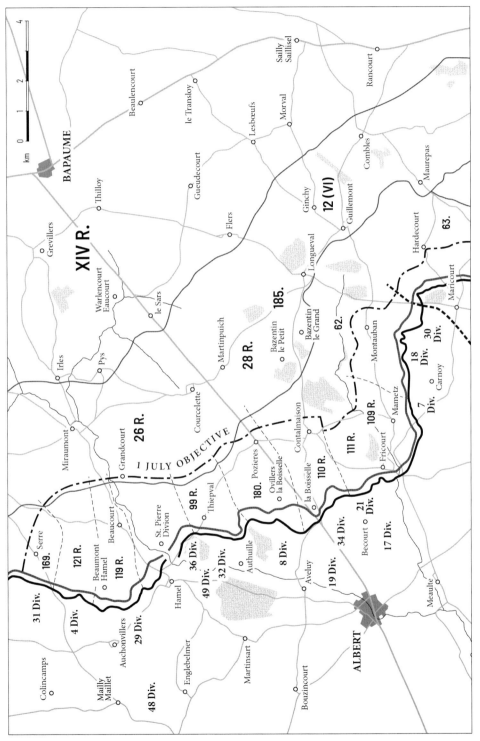

Map 3.iv The Layout of the German Second Army on the Somme, 1916.

to take pressure off the French, and thereby exhaust themselves. Here, on the Somme, was the evidence that Falkenhayn had in part succeeded in his aims and yet he refused to believe the truths that multiple sources of intelligence were telling him. His later account, *General Headquarters 1914–1916*, suggests that he viewed the likelihood of a British attack on the Somme as: 'long-expected and hoped-for';[39] however this does not accord with his approach at the time as recorded by his subordinate commanders. It must be concluded therefore that either this is as clear a case of cognitive dissonance as has ever been seen in the history of war; or else, as some authors have suggested, that the Christmas Memorandum was a fabrication, dreamed up later to justify Falkenhayn's actions.

In April, Falkenhayn had suggested a spoiling attack by the Sixth Army in northern France and southern Flanders, but again the demands of operations at Verdun ruled this out. In May, von Below, following on from his suggestions in March, once more proposed a pre-emptive attack to disrupt Allied preparations astride the Somme which would have required 13 divisions and 250 heavy artillery batteries.[40] Again because of resource constraints, especially in ammunition, this was scaled down in June to an operation from Ovillers to St-Pierre Divion. Von Below was however only assigned one additional artillery regiment and a few support units for the purpose. On 6 June, von Below reported that aerial reconnaissance showed that attacks at Fricourt and Gommecourt were possible, and that French troops south of the Somme had been reinforced in front of the German XIV and XVII Corps; further north the Guard Corps was felt to be especially vulnerable as it had only 12 regiments to hold 20 miles (36 kilometres) of front, and no reserves.[41]

As late as the middle of June, Falkenhayn was still dubious about the possibility of an Allied offensive on the Somme, largely because at the operational level, an offensive in Alsace-Lorraine would, if successful, threaten Germany itself. However, railway building, increased train movement, trench digging and the erection of camps around Albert opposite the Second Army continued to be seen by German air observers, and agents reported an imminent offensive. A British prisoner captured from the 46th Division told his captors that the British bombardment would start on 26 June and an attack on a 30-mile mile front would follow;[42] another un-named prisoner, identified only as a Polish Jew, captured by No 10 Company of the 119th Reserve Infantry Regiment, stated that the attack would begin at 05.00 hrs on 29 June.[43]

Throughout early and mid-June, von Kuhl at Sixth Army sent repeated assessments to *O.H.L.* in which his increasing alarm can clearly be observed:

> The British are now prepared for battle [3 June] … it is noticeable that the French have… established fresh reserves behind the left flank of the Somme.
>
> Aerial observers had spotted an increase in digging and new battery positions north of the Somme [7 June]. Something is clearly happening here.
>
> … large tented areas south of Albert, but north of the Somme [11 June] … networks of trenches have appeared in several places… It appears that an attack on both sides of the Somme is ever more probable.[44]

On 15 June, the Kaiser and Falkenhayn arrived at Crown Prince Rupprecht's headquarters. Rupprecht recorded the exchange in which Falkenhayn refused to believe that Second Army would be attacked, rather than an offensive mounted in Alsace-Lorraine.[45] The visitors then moved on to von Below's headquarters where they were briefed in detail. However apart from the 2nd Guards Reserve Division, no German reinforcements were sent to the area until the Allied attack was subsequently launched on 1 July and only then to the Sixth Army, which was given command of three divisions in reserve behind it. Between 20 and 23 June, further reports were made, making it clear that the British attack would take place from Gommecourt to the Somme on the Second Army front; Falkenhayn however continued to be fixed on the Sixth Army's area further north, blocking all attempts by Rupprecht to pass reserves or guns to von Below.[46]

Falkenhayn appears in hindsight to have been trying to command the Western Front personally, rather than trusting his subordinates. This was again a contravention of German doctrine, which stressed (and still stresses, although it no longer practices it), the devolution of authority to subordinates using *Auftragstaktik*, or mission-type orders. In this concept, subordinates are told their superior's intentions, and their part in them; given resources; and then required to devise the ways to achieve success. Obedience to orders is critical, but so to is disobedience if circumstances require it – such as when local knowledge trumps that of a superior remote from the area of operations. As any field commander knows, situational awareness is everything. Technology had, however, even at this point in history, delivered the long screwdriver. By the use of the telephone and the signal service, Falkenhayn could make decisions affecting the tactical level of command from *O.H.L.* in Berlin – and he did so. In this he was greatly assisted by Oberst (Colonel) Fritz von Lossberg* of the Operations branch who, although only a Colonel and therefore junior in rank to the commanders of German armies, had, under German doctrine, the authority of his chief.

These feverish Allied preparations seen by the Germans were the result of the request made on 11 June, when Pétain asked Joffre to bring forward the Somme offensive if possible.[47] Prince Rupprecht recorded that:

> … the French have not expanded their frontage… Headquarters XIV Reserve Corps, deployed on the right flank of Second Army, expects an attack in the very near future. It is striking that recently the enemy has increased the amount of fire directed at the normally quiet right flank of the Army. Perhaps this increase in battle activity is merely intended as deception and to disguise from us the fact that strong enemy forces and reserves have been withdrawn.
>
> … the British have actually withdrawn four divisions that were opposite the northern flank of Sixth Army and redeployed them on the Second Army front. In addition to the French XX Corps that is deployed along the Somme and apparently is tasked with maintaining contact with the British, the French XXX Corps, which was previously deployed in the area of Belfort, has appeared opposite Second Army south of the Somme, near to Lihons… In view of all this there can no longer be any doubt that a major offensive against Second Army is imminent.[48]

---

*   Friedrich Karl 'Fritz' von Loßberg (1868–1942) was later a General. He was a strategic planner and was Chief of Staff for the Second, Third and Fourth armies. He was present at the Battle of the Somme, the Battle of Arras and the Battle of Verdun, being the man always sent by *O.H.L.* to any area of crisis. In *Military Operations France and Belgium* 1917, Vol. I, Cyril Falls, the British official historian, referred to him as: 'a very remarkable soldier'. Loßberg was awarded the *Pour le Mérite* on 9 September 1916 and oak leaves on 24 April 1917.

Rupprecht's view was reinforced by reports from Second Army to *O.H.L.* and from General von Stein, commanding XIV Reserve Corps while at the same time, von Kuhl felt that any threat to Sixth Army had receded.[49] Second Army, in accordance with German doctrine, had therefore to identify and resource its point of main effort. This was to be north of the Somme and was formed by the redeployment of guns and by the movement of the 10th Bavarian Infantry Division from XVII Corps south of the Somme, into reserve behind XIV Reserve Corps. This meant that these divisions and regiments left in the line had to extend their frontages, usually at the cost of maintaining no second echelon or reserve behind the first line.[50] Stretching the defenders this thinly is a clear indication of the hard choices facing von Below and the risks he was prepared to take, combined with his confidence in the quality of the intelligence available to him regarding the limits of the attack zone.

XIV Reserve Corps had also to determine its main effort and this it did, identifying the 26th Reserve Division which was permitted to maintain four regiments in two brigades. The division was supported by 28½ field batteries and 10½ heavy batteries – a great increase on the standard allocation of two 6-battey regiments equipped with 10.5 cm howitzers and one 9-battery regiment with 7.7 cm guns. Many of these were, however, old or captured and included Belgian 57 mm, 87 mm and 120 mm guns; French 75 mm and 120 mm pieces; and even a few Russian guns. Some of these dated from before the introduction of recoil mechanisms and relied on horse transport – which was also in short supply.[51] Further south, around Mametz and Fricourt, the 28th Reserve Division was supported by 40 field guns, 20 light howitzers, 20 heavy howitzers, 16 obsolescent field guns and 12 captured heavy pieces.[52] In terms of direct fire support, the 26th divisional sector was covered by 90 heavy machine-guns of various types and calibres. Within their powers, therefore, the Army, Corps and Divisional commanders had done all they could to prepare for battle.

On 20 June, the Germans had used their new diphosgene gas shells with great effect, leading to a deep advance almost to the last outwork of Verdun on the heights of Bellevue on the 23rd. The next day, the British bombardment on the Somme commenced and from that date, no further German reinforcements and no more ammunition went to Verdun.[53] Thus a combination of a desperate French defence, an over-costly German attack on too narrow a front, the Russian effort under Brusilov, and the beginning of the Somme offensive saved Verdun and therefore the French Army. Falkenhayn's intentions had indeed played out by 1 July 1916 – but perhaps not quite as he had intended. Although the retrospective view is of a bloody reverse for British arms, the German perspective was summed up by Generalleutnant Otto von Moser, commander of 27th Infantry Division:

> If the German Chief of the General Staff and the Prussian Minister of War actually believed from their perspective that they had done everything possible and necessary to equip the German Army, then the first few weeks of battle on the Somme shattered this belief completely. This was certainly the way every man who commanded either a higher formation or a junior unit remembered it. They were all truly horrified at the appalling German inferiority and serious lack of combat supplies with which their troops had to struggle and from which they suffered.[54]

Appendix

German Second Army Order of Battle, 1 July 1916

Corps[a]	Divisions	Brigades/Regiments/other Troops	Where Placed
Prussian Guards (*General Karl von Plettenberg*)	1st Guards (*Oberst Eitel Friedrich, Prinz von Preussen*)	1 Guards Brigade • 1st Guards Infantry Regiment • 3rd Guards Infantry Regiment 2 Guards Brigade • 2nd Guards Infantry Regiment • 4th Guards Infantry Regiment 1st Guards Field Artillery Brigade (9 batteries of 10.5 cm guns, 12 batteries 7.7 cm guns) Three squadrons Guards Hussar Regiment 1st Company, Guards Pioneer Battalion 1st and 3rd Section, Guards Field Ambulance Company 1st Guards Pontoon Engineer Train	Warlencourt
	2nd Guards (*Generalmajor Friedrich von Friedeburg*)	3 Guards Brigade • 1st and 2nd Grenadier Regiments 4 Guards Brigade • 3rd and 4th Grenadier Regiments Schlotheim Cavalry Regiment Two squadrons Guard Uhlan Regiment Squadron 9th Dragoons Ersatz squadron 2nd Uhlans Ersatz Squadron 1st Horse Jaeger Regiment 2 Guards Artillery brigade (9 batteries of 10.5 cm guns) 2nd and 4th Guards Artillery battalions (each 6 batteries of 7.7 cm guns) 1st Guards Engineer Battalion Three companies pioneers Pontoon engineer detachment Signal detachment Trench mortar company	Barleux
Prussian Guards Reserve (*General der Kavallerie Wolf Freiherr Marschall von Altengotten*)	3rd Guards (*Generalmajor Oskar von Lindequist*)	6 Guards Brigade • Guards Fusilier Regiment • *Lehr* Infantry Regiment • 9th Colberg (Graf Gneisenau) (2nd Pomeranian) Grenadier Regiment Guard Reserve Uhlan Regiment 5th Guards Field Artillery Regiment (6 batteries of 7.7 cm guns) II Battalion 6th Guards Reserve Foot Artillery (3 batteries of 10.5 cm guns) I Company 28 (2nd Brandenburg) Pioneer Battalion Pioneer Company Nr 274 Garde-Minenwerfer-Co Nr 3 Signal detachment 3rd Guards Trench Mortar Company 75th Anti-Aircraft Section	Bazentin

Corps[a]	Divisions	Brigades/Regiments/other Troops	Where Placed
	1st Guards Reserve (*Generalleutnant Viktor Albrecht*)	1 Reserve Brigade • 1st Guards Reserve Regiment • 2nd Guards Reserve Regiment • 64th Reserve Infantry Regiment Three squadrons Uhlans Three squadrons dragoons 2nd Reserve Artillery Regiment 1st and 3rd Guards Artillery Battalions (each 6 batteries of 7.7 cm guns) Engineer battalion Pontoon engineer detachment Signal detachment Trench mortar company	Warlencourt
	111th (*Generalmajor Leo Sonntag*)	221 Infantry Brigade • Fusilier Regiment Feldmarschall *Prinz Albrecht von Preußen* (Hanover) No 73 • Infantry Regiment Hamburg (2nd Hanseatic) No 76 • 4th Hanoverian Infantry Regiment No 164 3rd and 4th Squadrons 3rd Baden Dragoon Regiment *Prinz Karl* No 22 Field Artillery Regiment No 221 (6 batteries of 7.7 cm guns) Foot Artillery Battery No 111(9 batteries of 10.5 cm guns) Pioneer Company No 221	Moislains
X Reserve *(Generalleutnant* **Robert Kosch)**	2nd Guards Reserve (*General der Infanterie Hugo Freiherr von Süßkind*)	26 Reserve Brigade • Two battalions 77 Westphalian infantry 38 Reserve Brigade • Two battalions 91 Hanoverian infantry • One battalion 55 Reserve Infantry Regiment 2nd Reserve Uhlan Regiment 20th Reserve Artillery Regiment (9 batteries of 10.5 cm guns) 10th Hanoverian Pioneers	Gommecourt
	10th Bavarian (*Generalleutnant Hermann Ritter von Burkhardt*)	20 Bavarian Infantry Brigade • R. Bavarian Reserve Infantry Regiment No. 6 • R. Bavarian Reserve Infantry Regiment No. 8 • R. Bavarian 16th Infantry Regiment *Großherzog Ferdinand von Toskana* • R. Bavarian Cyclist Company No. 10 3rd Squadron R. Bavarian 5th Light Horse Regiment Erzherzog *Friedrich von Österreich* 10th Bavarian Field Artillery Brigade (9 batteries of 10.5 cm guns, 12 batteries 7.7 cm guns) R. Bavarian Pioneer Company No. 18 R. Bavarian Pioneer Company No. 19 Signal Detachment Trench Mortar Company	in reserve Martinpuich

Corps[a]	Divisions	Brigades/Regiments/other Troops	Where Placed
XIV Reserve *(Generalleutnant Hermann von Stein)*	26th Württemberg Reserve *(Generalleutnant Friedrich von Hahn)*	51 Brigade • 119th (1st Württemberg) Reserve Infantry Regiment "Queen Olga" • 121st (3rd Württemberg) Reserve Infantry Regiment 52 Brigade • 99th Reserve Infantry Regiment • 180th Infantry Regiment Bavarian Reserve Infantry Regiment 8 4th and 6th Companies 13th Württemberg Pioneer Regiment Bavarian Pioneer Regiment 5 Württemberg Artillery Regiment[b] Württemberg Trench Mortar Regiment 226 Bavarian Trench Mortar Regiment 10	La Boisselle – Contalmaison – Fricourt – Mametz
	183rd Reserve (Prussia, Saxony and Württemberg (from 5 July 1916) *(Generalmajor Wilhelm von Schüssler)*	183 Saxon Infantry Brigade • 122nd (4th Württemberg) Fusiliers Reserve Infantry Regiment (incl M.G. Coy No 93 and Trench Mortar Coy No 93) • 183rd Reserve Infantry Regiment (incl M.G. Coy and Trench Mortar Coy No 91) • 184th Reserve Infantry Regiment (incl M.G. Coy and Trench Mortar Coy No 9) Reserve Field Artillery Regiment Saxon Pioneer Regiment No 183 Signal Company	
	28th Baden Reserve *(Generalleutnant Freiherr Franz von Soden)*	55 Reserve Brigade • 40th Reserve Infantry Regiment • 109th Baden Reserve Infantry Regiment • Reserve Jaeger Battalion No 8 56 Reserve Brigade • 110th Baden Reserve Infantry Regiment • 111th Baden Reserve Infantry Regiment • Reserve Jaeger Battalion No 14 Reserve Dragoon Regiment No 8 Reserve Field Artillery Regiment No 29 (composition unknown) 1st and 2nd Companies Reserve Pioneer Battalion No 13 1st and 2nd Companies Bavarian Pioneer Regiment Bavarian Pioneer Regiment 20 Saxon Pioneer Regiment 323	Beaumont Hamel – Thiepval – Pozières
	52nd Jäger *(Generalleutnant Karl von Borries)*	104 Infantry Brigade • Baden Infantry Regiment 170 • Infantry Regiment 66 • Baden Infantry Regiment 169 Reserve Infantry Regiment 15 Pioneer Regiments 103, 104 1st Battalion Bavarian Pioneer Regiment Field Artillery Regiment 52 (composition unknown) Trench Mortar Regiment 52	Bihucourt

Corps[a]	Divisions	Brigades/Regiments/other Troops	Where Placed
VI *(General de Kavallerie Georg von der Marwitz)*	11th *(Generalleutnant Theodor von Webern)*	21 Infantry Brigade • Silesian Grenadier Regiment *König Friedrich Wilhelm II* No.10 • Silesian Fusilier Regiment *General-Feldmarschall Graf Moltke* (Schlesisches) No. 38 22 Infantry Brigade • Silesian Grenadier Regiment *König Friedrich III* No. 11 • 4th Lower Silesia Infantry Regiment No. 51 Horse Jaeger Regiment No. 11 11 Field Artillery Brigade (9 batteries 10.5 cm guns, 12 batteries 7.7 cm guns) One company Silesian Pioneer Battalion No. 6 Signal Detachment Trench mortar company	Clery – Frise
	12th Infantry *(Generalleutnant Walter Charles de Beaulieu)*	24 Infantry Brigade • Infantry Regiment *von Winterfeldt* No. 23 • 3rd Silesian Infantry Regiment No. 62 78 Infantry Brigade: • Silesian Infantry Regiment No.63 • Silesian Infantry Regiment No. 157 Silesian Uhlan Regiment *von Katzler* 12 Field Artillery Brigade (9 batteries 10.5 cm guns, 12 batteries 7.7 cm guns) Two companies Silesian Pioneer Battalion No. 6	Astride the Somme, Hardecourt – Maurepas
	12th Reserve *(Generalmajor Kurt von Kehler)*	22 Reserve Infantry Brigade • Reserve Infantry Regiment *von Winterfeldt* (2nd Upper Schleswig) No 23 • Reserve Infantry Regiment No 38 • Reserve Jäger Battalion No 6 23 Reserve Infantry Brigade • Reserve Infantry Regiment No 22 • Reserve Infantry Regiment No 51 Reserve Uhlan Regiment No 4 Reserve Field Artillery Regiment No 12 (composition unknown) • 1st and 2nd Reserve Companies, Pioneer Battalion No 6	Guillemont
XVII *(General der Infanterie Günther von Pannewitz)*	35th *(Generalmajor Bruno von Uthmann)*	70 Infantry Brigade • Pommeranian Infantry Regiment *von Borcke* No. 21 • Pommeranian Infantry Regiment *von der Marwitz* No. 61 87 Infantry Brigade • Infantry Regiment No. 141 • West Prussian Infantry Regiment No. 176 • Horse Jaeger Regiment No.4 35 Field Artillery Brigade (9 batteries 10.5 cm guns, 12 batteries 7.7 cm guns) Company West Prussian Pioneer Battalion No. 17 Signal Detachment Trench mortar company	Ablancourt

Corps[a]	Divisions	Brigades/Regiments/other Troops	Where Placed
	36th (*Generalmajor Konstanz von Heineccius*)	69 Infantry Brigade • West Prussian Infantry Regiment No. 129 • West Prussian Infantry Regiment No. 175 71 Infantry Brigade • East Prussian Grenadier Regiment *König Friedrich I* (4. Danzig Infantry Regiment No. 128 (9 batteries 10.5 cm guns, 12 batteries 7.7 cm guns) Pommeranian Hussar Regiment *Fürst Blücher von Wahlstatt* 36 Field Artillery Brigade Two companies West Prussian Pioneer Battalion No. 17	Chaulnes
Army Troops		25 Mixed Landwehr Brigade 29 Mixed Landwehr Brigade Four mortar battalions 10.5 cm artillery battalion Two heavy mortar batteries Two pioneer regiments Signal battalion Medical regiment	

Notes to Appendix

a   The Corps troops in all cases included only a supply train, ammunition train, signal company and field hospital.

b   The artillery of the 26th and 28th Divisions, as previously noted, consisted of old or captured and included Belgian 57 mm, 87 mm and 120 mm guns; French 75 mm and 120 mm pieces; and even a few Russian guns.

Notes

1   T.M. Holmes, 'Absolute Numbers: The Schlieffen Plan as a Critique of German Strategy in 1914'. *War in History* No. 21 (April 2014).

2   A.J.P. Taylor, *Illustrated History of the First World War* (London, 1974), pp. 62–63. Martin Gilbert, *First World War* (London, 1994), p. 221.

3   Sir J.E. Edmonds, *History of the Great War based on Official Documents, by direction of the Historical Section of the Committee of Imperial Defence. Military Operations France and Belgium, 1916* (London, 1932), p. 52.

4   Robert T. Foley, *German Strategy and the Path to Verdun: Erich von Falkenhayn and the Development of Attrition* (Cambridge University Press, 2005) pp. 56–81.

5   Erich von Falkenhayn, *General Headquarters, 1914–1916 and its Critical Decisions* (London, 2009), p. 96

6   See Fritz Fischer, *Germany's Aims in the First World War* (English translation of *Griff nach der Weltmacht*, Düsseldorf, 1967), p. 215 et seq.

7   Wilhelm Groener to the Deutsche Reichsarchiv, 5 March 1934, DBA/MA, W10/51523.

8   Bethmann Hollweg's précis of Falkenhayn's position is set out in a letter to Arthur Zimmermann, dated 18 November 1914, T.N.A. GFM 34/215, *Der Weltkrieg (geheim) Bd. 2.*

9   Jack Sheldon, *Fighting the Somme. German Challenges, Dilemmas and Solutions* (Barnsley, 2017), p. 3.

10 Karl-Maria von Clausewitz (ed. and tr. Michael Howard and Peter Paret), *On War* (Princeton, New Jersey, 1976), pp. 194, 204–205, 248, 258, 617 et seq.

11 There is now some considerable doubt about this briefing and the accompanying memorandum that Falkenhayn cites in his memoirs. See Robert T. Foley, p. 1.

12   Hans von Plessen, *Tagebuch* [Daybook], 3 December 1915 cited in Robert T. Foley, 'A New Form of Warfare? Erich von Falkenhayn's Plan for Victory in 1916' on-line article accessed 18 August 2017.

13   Falkenhayn to Hindenburg, 18 November 1914, in Robert T. Foley, accessed 18 August 2017.

14   Edmonds, p. 26.

15   *Nachrichtenabteilung West*, Report dated 14 November 1915, printed in "Die Beurteilung der Kampfkraft der französischen Armee durch die deutsche OHL zwischen dem 1.1. und 29.8.16," Deutsche Bundesarchiv/Militärarchiv, DBA/MA, W10/51521, p. 4.

16   Nachrichten Offizier, Armeeoberkommando 6, Nachrichten von der Französischen Front im Abschnitt Angres-Ransart,' 23 December 1915, DBA/MA, PH3/607.

17   Falkenhayn to Kaiser Wilhelm II, 15 February 1915, in Martin Gilbert, p. 221.

18   Adolf Wild von Hohenborn, '*Kriegstagebuch*,' 11 December 1915, in DBA/MA, Wild Nachlass, N44/2.

19   Grosser Generalstab, 4.Abteilung, 'Denkschrift über die Festung Verdun,' 1910, Bayerisches Hauptstaatsarchiv — Kriegsarchiv, Munich, Generalstab 181.

20   Liddell Hart, p. 271.

21   Hermann von Kuhl to the Deutsche Reichsarchiv, 28 October 1932, DBA/MA, W10/51318; Falkenhayn, p. 63.

22   Alistair Horne, *The Price of Glory: Verdun 1916* (London, 1962), p. 36.

23   Sheldon, p. 20.

24   Liddell Hart, p. 294.

25   Martin Gilbert, p. 235.

26   Liddell Hart, p. 295.

27   Falkenhayn to Kaiser Wilhelm II, 15 February 1915, in Martin Gilbert, p. 221.

28   Martin Gilbert, p. 254; Liddell Hart, pp. 298–300. See also Timothy C. Dowling, *The Brusilov Offensive* (Bloomington USA, 2008).

29   Liddell Hart, p. 301.

30   Edward Hancock, *Bazentin Ridge* (Barnsley, 2001), p. 29.

31   This remained the case throughout the War. See especially Timothy J. Lupfer, *The Dynamics of Doctrine: The Changes in German Tactical Doctrine During the First World War* (Leavenworth Papers No. 4, U.S. Command and General Staff College, July 1981). See also *The Assault. War Experiences of a front-line Officer (Hauptmann v. Brandis of 24 Infantry Regiment)*, Published by the Chief of the General Staff of the Field Army, 15 September 1917.

32   'The Other Side of the Hill, No 1', in *Army Quarterly*, Volume VII No 2, January 1924, pp. 248, 251.

33   H.A. Jones, *The War in the Air, Being the Story of the Part Played in the Great War by the Royal Air Force*, Volume II London, 1928) p. 201.

34   Sheldon, p. 22.

35   Hermann von Kuhl, *Persönliches Kriegstagebuch*, 30 May 1917, cited in Sheldon, p. 13.

36   D. Rogers (ed.), *Landrecies to Cambrai: Case Studies of German Offensive and Defensive Operations on the Western Front 1914–17* (Solihull, 2010) p. 57–58.

37   Sheldon, p. 21.

38   Falkenhayn, p. 233.

39   Falkenhayn, p. 262.

40   Sheldon, p. 25.

41   Hermann Wendt, *Verdun 1916* (Berlin, 1931) pp. 172–173.

42   Edmonds, p. 317.

43   'The Other Side of the Hill No 1', p. 253.

44   Bundesarchiv Breisgau RH61/50652, *Persönliches Kreigstagebuch des Generals der Infanterie a.D. von Kuhl*, pp. 14–15.

45   Kronprinz Rupprecht, *In Treue Fest: Mein Kreigstagebuch Volumes I and II* (Munich, 1929), p. 482.

46   Sheldon, p. 31.

47   Liddell Hart, p. 296.

48   Rupprecht, p. 482.

49   RH61/50652, pp. 15–16; see also Generalleutnant a.D. Ernst Kabisch, *Somme 1916* (Berlin, 1937), p. 42.

50   Sheldon, p. 31.
51   Sheldon, p. 36.
52   Sheldon, p. 37.
53   Edmonds, p. 319.
54   Generalleutnant z.D. Otto von Moser, *Ernsthafte Plaudereien über den Weltkrieg* (Stuttgart, 1925), p. 159.

4

'Ending the war by fighting': Allied Strategy and Operational Plans for 1916

While the Germans were looking hard for a way to bring the war to an end on their terms during 1916, the Entente powers were also engaged in a very similar exercise; however for them, there were the issues of a coalition to be managed, partners and allies to consult, national red cards to be played – all of which the Germans could ignore. Allied war strategy for 1916 was formulated during a major conference at Chantilly, the headquarters of the French Commander-in-Chief, General Joseph Joffre, from 6 to 8 December 1915, where the War Ministers of France, Britain, Belgium and Italy, with their Military Chiefs, assembled. Representatives from Japan and Russia also attended – but not Serbia. This was the second Inter-Allied Military Conference and it followed a meeting at Prime Ministerial level in Paris on 17 November.

There was general agreement that the war would only be ended by fighting, not by negotiation; but Russia needed time to re-equip and the British Army, after the destruction of much of its Regular component during 1914 and 1915, needed time to train and gain experience. British casualties up to the end of 1915 totalled 21,747 officers and 490,673 men, of whom two-fifths were killed or missing.[1] This figure should be compared against the 1913 establishment of the Army, which was 223,000 in the field Army, 145,000 in the Regular Reserve and 64,000 in the Special Reserve – a total of 432,000. A figure greater than this had already been killed, wounded, been captured, or gone missing.

The outcome of the Chantilly conference was an agreement that co-ordinated, simultaneous attacks would be delivered by France, Britain, Italy and Russia with their maximum available forces on their respective fronts as soon as the circumstances were favourable. Until then, preliminary attacks would be made by the Russians, the Italians in the Alps, and the British and French in the west to wear down the Germans and Austrians – thus fixing the Central Powers around the whole perimeter of the war, but not becoming decisively engaged until the right time.[2] It was also agreed that all powers would accumulate material and equipment, that the Russians and Serbs would be given help to re-arm and re-equip, and that in the secondary theatres of the war – Salonika, the Balkans and Africa – only the minimum necessary resources would be committed. Interestingly, however, the French refused to consider the withdrawal of their own or British divisions from Salonika even when pressure mounted during the Verdun offensive.[3]

Shortly after the Chantilly conference, on 19 December 1915, General Sir Douglas Haig[*] replaced Sir John French as Commander-in-Chief of the British Expeditionary Force.[4] The B.E.F. now stood at 38 Regular, Imperial, Territorial and New Army divisions organised into three Armies – a fourth was formed in early 1916 and a fifth later that year.[5] Nine more divisions were sent from Egypt after the close of operations at Gallipoli.[6] It was clear that the Western Front would, for the British as well as the French, be the undisputed main effort. Not only had Sir John French been replaced by a convinced exponent of the Western Front approach, but Kitchener had lost the confidence of his colleagues in Cabinet after the munitions crisis of 1915 and his role as the adviser on strategy had been taken by the new Chief of the Imperial General Staff (C.I.G.S.), General Sir William Robertson.[†] Robertson had been French's Chief of Staff and there is some evidence that he dictated his own terms of reference before taking up the post of C.I.G.S.[7] Kitchener was reduced to being responsible for recruiting, clothing and feeding the armies.

Robertson, like Haig, believed that victory would only come in the west and that as many divisions as possible should be released from Britain, the Middle East and garrisons elsewhere, for France and Belgium. Second-line Territorial Force battalions and Indian Army units therefore relieved British Regulars in Imperial garrisons; a complete evacuation of the Dardanelles was accomplished in January 1916 and the troops taken to Egypt. From there, the 29th Infantry Division, a regular formation which had been formed for the Gallipoli campaign from troops in the Imperial garrisons, was moved to France along with two more divisions, the 27th and 28th, formed from troops in Egypt.

These divisions joined the steady stream of New Army and Territorial Force formations from Britain. In addition to the nine divisions from Egypt, another 10 divisions and the South African Brigade were sent to the B.E.F. between January and July 1916, a breakdown of which is in the Appendices to this chapter.[8] By the middle of the year, Haig thus had at his disposal 60 and two-thirds of the 112 British and Imperial divisions eventually raised for service in all theatres of war, less those in Britain for home defence, reserve and training;[‡] plus two cavalry divisions of the 21 divisions of the Indian Army – a total therefore of 62 and two-thirds divisions – now organised into 21 army corps and four armies,[§] a total of more than 1.2 million men. As these new divisions arrived, new corps headquarters were also formed: the XIII, XIV, XV, XVIII, I and II Anzac were formed in France and the VIII and XI Corps reconstituted after Gallipoli. The new formations joined the 95 French and six Belgian divisions on the Western Front, making a total of 163 Allied divisions facing 117 German divisions.

All the officers and men in the B.E.F. were still enlisted under the voluntary principle, but the method of enlistment had been systematized and a national register created under the control

---

[*]   Later Field Marshal Sir Douglas Haig, 1st Earl Haig, KT GCB OM GCVO KCIE (1861–1928).

[†]   General (later Field Marshal) Sir William Robertson, 1st Baronet, GCB GCMG GCVO DSO (1860–1933) served as Chief of the Imperial General Staff (C.I.G.S.) – the professional head of the British Army – from 1916 to 1918. He was the first and only man to rise from Private to Field Marshal in the British Army.

[‡]   This figure of 112 does not include the 10 divisions at home, or the Corps and Army level artillery, R.F.C., engineer and tank brigades (the equivalent of another 10 divisions) or the five division-equivalents of the Labour Corps. The figures have been compiled from the various annexes in Edmonds's official history cited in the bibliography.

[§]   See appendices I and II of this chapter.

of the Director-General of Recruiting, Lord Derby.* This was meant to reconcile the demands of the Army for manpower with those of the Royal Navy, the Merchant Marine and the war industries, calling up men as they were wanted and taking single men first. However, the supply of single men was inadequate and in January 1916, the Government was forced to introduce conscription under the Military Service Act;[9] an act that was applied to England, Scotland and Wales, but not at this time to Ireland.

Haig returned to Chantilly to meet Joffre on 29 December 1915,[10] where German preparations for an attack were noted, and where it appears that Haig received direction from Joffre to prepare plans for preliminary offensive operations. These were passed on by Haig to his, at this point, three Army Commanders – Generals Sir Charles Monro,† Herbert Plumer‡ and Edmund Allenby§ on 9 January.[11] On 18 January, Haig recorded the general principles for making such plans, which were to:

1   Employ sufficient force to wear down the Enemy and cause him to use up his reserves
2   Then, and not till then, throw in a mass of troops (at some point where the enemy has shown himself to be weak) to break through and win victory.[12]

Haig thought that to be most effective, attacks must start straight away – but he recognised that the Russians were in no position to play their part in the overall strategic plan. He therefore envisaged that on the Western Front the first principle would be fulfilled in two phases: first, the winter's activity would develop into a series of larger attacks; and secondly, a more general, co-ordinated series of attacks would be organised to draw in German operational and strategic reserves.[13] Haig also ordered Sir Herbert Plumer to draw up a plan for a subsidiary attack on the Messines ridge in Belgium; he also had a secret plan developed for an attack along the Belgian coast from Nieuwpoort towards Ostende, in conjunction with an amphibious landing.[14]

Joffre's initial concept on the other hand was that of 'bras dessus bras dessus', the attacking line of one ally extending that of the other; thus his fixation on an offensive on the Somme, where the junction of the French and British Armies lay. Joffre saw the French attacking on a front of 25 miles (40 kilometres), from Lassigny to the Somme, with 40 divisions; while the British attacked from the Somme north to Hébuterne, a distance of 14 miles (22 kilometres),

---

*   Edward George Villiers Stanley, 17th Earl of Derby KG GCB GCVO TD KStJ PC JP (1865–1948). Derby had served in the Militia and in 1914 directed an enormously successful recruiting campaign in Liverpool. He had sat as M.P. for Westhoughton but lost his seat in the 1906 general election. In 1908 he succeeded his father in the earldom and took his seat in the House of Lords. In July 1916 Derby returned to the government when he was appointed Under-Secretary of State for War by Prime Minister Herbert Asquith, and in December 1916 he was promoted to Secretary of State for War by David Lloyd George.

†   Later General Sir Charles Carmichael Monro, 1st Baronet GCB GCSI GCMG (1860 –1929). He commanded the evacuation from Gallipoli.

‡   Later Field Marshal Sir Herbert Charles Onslow ('Daddy') Plumer, 1st Viscount Plumer, GCB GCMG GCVO GBE (1857–1932), a cavalry officer and arguably the most consistently successful British General of the War on the Western Front and in Italy. He commanded the Army of Occupation in Germany in 1918–1919.

§   Later Field Marshal Sir Edmund Henry Hynman Allenby, 1st Viscount Allenby, GCB GCMG GCVO (1861–1936). He was also a cavalry officer and best known for his successes against the Turks in the Middle East.

with 25 divisions if possible, or as close to that number as could be mustered.[15] Joffre also asked for some preliminary moves in April and May, to draw off German reserves.

The area of the offensive had therefore been chosen for reasons of alliance solidarity rather than the practicality of the terrain or the weakness of the enemy. The British official history comments that Joffre suggested an attack on what could be seen as the strongest sector in the German defences, because the British would be obliged to take part. He was also insistent that an attack should be mounted as early as April, with another effort in May. This, he believed, would draw in German reserves and prepare the way for a decisive Franco-British assault elsewhere.

As to the ground, the River Somme makes a pronounced right-angled turn to the south at Péronne and from there, a range of chalk hills runs north-west, forming the watershed of the Somme, the Scharpe and the Scheldt. This ridge had been held by the Germans since the front had solidified during the Race to the Sea in late 1914. Everywhere, the Germans held the high ground. They covered the Allied lines with observed fire and looked deep into their rear areas. Thus everywhere that the attack was to take place, British troops would have to assault uphill in an area where their preparations would have been studied by the enemy for weeks; on the other hand, looking uphill, the German trenches were more clearly open to observation by British artillery spotters. It had been a quiet sector while held by the French, in contrast to the constant rumble of the Ypres salient. The country behind the line was largely undisturbed agricultural land with intact villages providing comfortble billets.

In spite of his earlier tendency to agree on operations in April and May, Haig refused the preliminaries, preferring a single main stroke; he accepted the attack plan on 14 February, on which date Joffre also agreed to abandon his ideas of preliminary offensives in April and May.[16] As the German attack developed at Verdun, Joffre asked Haig, on 22 February, to take over more of the line in the north so as to release French troops. Haig therefore accepted a section of the line from the French Tenth Army, around Arras, between the British First and Third Armies. Haig had in fact decided to take over the whole Tenth Army sector, not just part of it, to give the British an uninterrupted section of the front.[17] He created a new Fourth Army under General Sir Henry Rawlinson* for this purpose on 1 March 1916, with its Headquarters at Querrieu, five miles (eight kilometres) east of Amiens. This new Army

General Sir Henry Rawlinson.

---

*   General Sir Henry Seymour Rawlinson, 2nd Baronet and 1st Baron Rawlinson, GCB GCSI GCVO KCMG (1864–1925).

held the front from Maricourt to Hébuterne and extending the British front to 85 miles (136 kilometres).[18] The arrival of the British and their policy of active raiding and strafing upset what had been a comfortable backwater when held by the French. As well as wearing out British troops in minor skirmishes, this also had the effect of encouraging the Germans to strengthen their positions and improve their artillery.

The War Committee of the Cabinet in Britain had accepted on 28 December 1915, as a principle, that the B.E.F. would take part in major offensive operations in with the Allies. There was, however, reluctance on the part of some unless the French were wholly committed and in January, Robertson had been obliged to go into bat to support that principle, writing to Haig afterwards that:

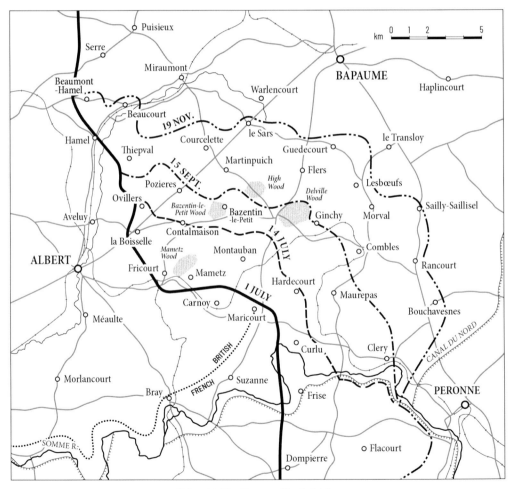

Map 4.i The Somme Battlefield.

One [Committee member] wants to go to the Balkans, another to Baghdad, and another to allow the Germans to attack us. I have used all the arguments you or any other soldier would use, but not with complete success… we are to make every effort "to prepare" for offensive operations in the Spring… "but without committing ourselves definitely to them."[19]

Joffre had made it clear to Haig that he wished the British to begin operations in April. But at 07.15 hrs on 21 February 1916, the German attack at Verdun began. From then until 24 March, the Germans advanced inexorably on the east bank of the River Meuse; command of the 52 French divisions in Army Group Centre was then given to General Philippe Pétain, commander of the Second Army. From 6 March to 7 June, when Fort Vaux fell, the German assault slowed but continued to gain ground.

The German attack succeeded in drawing in ever-increasing numbers of French troops, just as Falkenhayn had predicted: the French Army suffered 133,000 casualties by late April, and 360,000 by the end of the operation. Every French unit might therefore expect to lose its entire strength four times over during the course of the battle. Unsurprisingly, the French called loudly on their allies to help take the pressure from them: the Italians also called for help as they absorbed the Austrian attack at Trentino in May: thus the Russians made their last major effort of the war, the Brusilov offensive as outlined in Chapter 3.

Not surprisingly, Joffre was increasingly anxious that the British should take their part in relieving the strain on the French effort.[20] Haig discussed this at G.H.Q. on 25 February, with General Robertson:

After dinner, we discussed whether the British Army should comply with the French Generalissimo's request to attack in the month of July or wait till August 15th when we would be much stronger.

I had gone fully into the various aspects of the question and what might be the results if we did not support the French. I came to the conclusion that we must march to the support of the French. Robertson entirely agreed and took my notes away to study.[21]

All this had to pass the approval of the War Committee, a potentially difficult piece of navigation given its previously noted position. However, Verdun had changed the view in London as well as in France and on 31 March, Robertson submitted a paper to the Committee which tipped the balance of opinion in favour of the offensive.[22] He telegraphed Haig to this effect on 7 April and on 14 April, Haig went to the War Office to see Kitchener and Robertson:

I asked them definitely, "Did His Majesty's Government approve of my combining with the French in a general offensive during the summer?" They both agreed that the Cabinet had come to the conclusion that the war could only be ended by fighting, and several were most anxious for a definite victory over German arms… I explained to Lord K my general plan…[23]

Given that the French, Italians and Russians were now all committed to the offensive, it would have been impossible for the British to refuse their full participation.[24]

With this endorsement, there followed a series of meetings with Joffre over the date of the offensive. The first of these, on 26 May, was a heated affair:

General Joffre explained the general situation. The French had supported for three months alone the whole weight of the German attack at Verdun… if this went on, the French army would be ruined! He therefore was of the opinion that 1 July was the latest date for the combined offensive of the British and French.

 I said that before fixing the date I would like to indicate the state of preparedness of the British army on certain dates and compare its condition. I took 1 and 15 July, and 1 and 15 August. The moment I mentioned 15 August, Joffre got very excited and shouted that "the French army would cease to exist, if we did nothing till then!"… I pointed out that, in spite of the 15th August being the most favourable date for the British Army to take action, yet, in view of what he had said… I was prepared to commence operations on the 1st July or thereabouts.[25]

Joffre followed this meeting by sending a letter via his Liaison Officer at G.H.Q., giving notice that he expected the offensive to begin on 1 July and for the artillery bombardment to precede this.[26] Subsequently, Joffre demanded that the operation be brought forward to 25 June, to which Haig agreed, but once the situation at Verdun stabilised, the date was put back to 29 June.[27]

The last meeting between Joffre and Haig took place on 17 June

Then we discussed the date for starting our offensive. He wished it to be 1 July. I pointed out that we had arranged to be ready on the 25th [June] to please him. The 29th ought to be the latest starting date; in my opinion it was unwise to run the risk of the Enemy discovering our area of concentration and then attacking where our lines were thin and ill provided with artillery. Finally, we agreed that the attack should be fixed for 29th but Rawlinson and Foch will be given power if the day is bad to postpone the attack from day to day till the weather is fine.[28]

In fact, the weather was not fine. There was heavy rain on 28 and 29 June, enough to flood trenches and gun-pits, so that the start of the attack had to be delayed to 1 July.

As the French commitment to Verdun increased, so their resources for the Somme battle diminished. In the end, the French contribution shrank to 16 divisions on a front of eight miles (13 kilometres). On 1 July, only five of these divisions went into the attack, their task being only to support the British.[29] From late February, therefore, the planning and execution of the Somme battle became overwhelmingly a British and Imperial project. In spite of this, Haig made no adjustment to his objectives beyond preparing a subsidiary plan for an attack at Messines in Flanders: no contingency was made in the case of either partial success or failure on the Somme.

Haig's objectives remained, first, to break in to the German line between Maricourt and Serre; secondly, to seize and hold the high chalk down-land between Bapaume and Rancourt; thirdly to wheel to the left and roll up the whole German front as far as Arras, in order to create a breach large enough for this break-through to be turned into a break-out using all available troops, including the cavalry, advancing northwards, in combination with a subsidiary attack against the Germans south-west of Arras. The fourth phase envisaged a general advance towards Cambrai and Douai.[30] This was enunciated at a conference of his Army Commanders on 15 June:

.... I explained the scope of the offensive by the Fourth and two divisions of the Third Armies and enunciated certain principles.

The length of each bound forward by the infantry depends on the area which has been prepared by the artillery. The infantry must for their part, capture and hold all the ground which the artillery has prepared with as little delay as possible.

The effect of the artillery depends on (a) '"Accuracy of fire" and (b) "concentration", Commanders must insist on these points

The advance of isolated detachments [except for reconnoitring purposes] should be avoided. They lead to loss of the boldest and best without result: Enemy can concentrate on these detachments. Advance should be uniform ...

As regards the objective of the Fourth Army attack, it was:

Firstly, to gain the line of the Pozières heights, organise good observation posts, and consolidate a strong position. Then *secondly*, (a) If Enemy's defence broke down, occupy the Enemy's third line (on line Flers-Miraumont), push detachment of cavalry to hold Bapaume and work northwards with bulk of cavalry and other arms so as to widen the breach in the Enemy's line, and capture the Enemy's forces in the re-entrant south of Arras. The hill at Monchy le Preux (5 miles south of Arras) with intermediate points between it and Bapaume seems a suitable line for the cavalry to hold as a flank guard for covering the operations of the other arms.

(b) *If the Enemy's defence is strong* and fighting continues for many days, as soon as Pozières heights are gained, the position should be consolidated, and improved, while arrangements will be made to start an attack on the Second Army front.[31]

The main attack was to be made in the 14 miles (22 kilometres) between Serre, a fortified village incorporated into the German first line, and Maricourt to the south. The vital ground here, which the attack had to secure, was the long ridge running south-east from Thiepval to Guillemont. Once on this ridge, the Army could make the Germans' positions on either flank untenable. Since the ridge also carried both the German first and second lines, and the third line was still not fully completed, their entire position would be penetrated.

Rawlinson's Fourth Army of 18 divisions was given this task. Rawlinson's planning had begun as early as 6 March, only five days after the Fourth Army headquarters had been formed, at a conference with his three corps commanders – Lieutenant Generals Walter Congreve of XIII Corps,[*] Thomas Morland of X Corps[†] and Aylmer Hunter-Weston of VIII Corps.[‡] On 8 March, Rawlinson went down with 'flu and did not return from convalescence until the 29th.[32] While

---

[*]   Later General Sir Walter Norris Congreve VC KCB MVO DL (1862–1927). He was awarded the
      VC during the Second Anglo-Boer War and was Governor of Malta from 1924 to1927.
[†]   Later General Sir Thomas Lethbridge Napier Morland KCB KCMG DSO (1865–1925).
[‡]   Lieutenant General Sir Aylmer Gould Hunter-Weston KCB DSO GStJ (1864–1940) was a Scottish
      Unionist M.P. Nicknamed 'Hunter-Bunter', he was a supreme example of the worst sort of Great
      War General; he was described by Haig as a 'rank amateur', and his stupidity is well portrayed in
      Llewelyn Wyn Griffith's *Up to Mametz ... and Beyond.*

as at Loos; or rather, should the attack be made in stages. The second discussion addressed the question of whether the preliminary bombardment should be a short, intense fire-storm; or a longer more methodical hammering.[33]

Addressing the first question, Rawlinson recommended that the attack should be made in two stages, the first objective being the area from Mametz to Serre, including Fricourt, La Boisselle, Ovilliers, Thiepval and Beaumont Hamel; and the second about 1,000 yards deeper between Fricourt and Serre, including the German second line at Pozières Ridge. This was largely arrived at because of the strength of the German second line, the need to move the artillery, and the opinion expressed in private that the alternative approach 'frequently exhausts the attacker first'.[34] Addressing the second question, Rawlinson thought that there would be considerable trouble in cutting the German wire even with a long bombardment; and a short bombardment would have to be carried out in daylight, the troops moved up and assembled in daylight, with all the risks that attended such a move. He therefore came down to a long bombardment and the use of darkness to cover the assembly of the troops prior to a dawn attack.[35]

On 5 April, Haig summoned Rawlinson to G.H.Q. to discuss the plan. Haig's criticisms, which were serious, identified a lack of operational purpose, the want of emphasis on achieving surprise and the even distribution of troops along the line. Haig also, importantly, insisted on increasing the size of the initial objective, for which an additional corps, XV, under Henry Horne,[*] was allocated on 22 April; and including a subsidiary attack around Gommecourt. In the end the objective was not expanded to the extent that Haig had determined, but Rawlinson kept the additional corps. The Fourth Army staff went back to the drawing board and concluded that the artillery allocated for the attack was not sufficient for the task, a calculation that Haig rejected.[36] Rawlinson, although unhappy, agreed to carry out Haig's wishes and went off to make the arrangements as well as to tie matters down with the French on hs right.

In the plan as drawn up, in the south, XIII Corps would attack Montauban with the 18th (Eastern) and 30th (New Army) Divisions in its first echelon, with the 9th (Scottish) Division in the second echelon. Next, moving northwards, XV Corps would attack Mametz and Fricourt with the 7th, 17th and 21st Divisions in a single echelon. To their north, III Corps would attack La Boisselle and Ovillers with the 8th and 34th Divisions in the first echelon and the 19th Division in the second echelon. Extending the line still further north, X Corps with the 32nd and 36th (Ulster) Divisions in the first echelon and the 49th Division in the second echelon would attack towards Theipval, Leipzig Redoubt, Schwaben Redoubt and Stuff Redoubt. Finally, VIII Corps would attack Beaumont Hamel and Serre with the 4th, 29th and 31st (New Army) Divisions in the first echelon and the 48th Division in the second echelon. Three cavalry divisions – the 1st, 3rd and 2nd Indian – were held as an Army-level second echelon for exploitation along with the 12th and 25th Infantry Divisions. II Corps Headquarters with the 23rd and 38th (Welsh) Infantry Divisions were held as a true reserve.[37]

On 16 April, Rawlinson outlined the revised scheme of manoeuvre to his corps commanders. On the 19th, he wrote to Haig stating that he had modified the tactical plan to conform with his chief's wishes. The aim would be, as Haig had envisaged, to reach the Pozières – Grandcourt – Serre ridge on the first day, and the guns would not be moved up during this time. However,

---

[*]   General Henry Sinclair Horne, 1st Baron Horne GCB KCMG (1861–1929) was the only British artillery officer to command an Army in the war. He was the architect of the 'creeping barrage'.

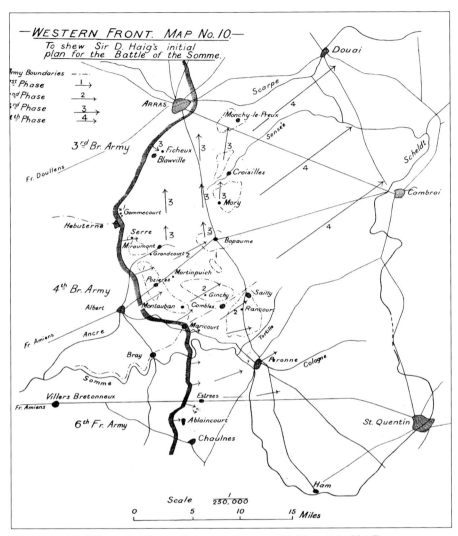

(Edmonds, *Military Operations France and Belgium 1916*, Vol. I)

he was away, on the 24th, the Army was reinforced by III Corps under William Pulteney.[*]
Rawlinson's plan was delivered to Haig on 3 April. Rawlinson obviously saw no chance of the
attack achieving an operational or strategic decision and he therefore seemed less concerned
about break-through, than about killing Germans during the assault, and then killing more
of them as they counter-attacked. Accordingly, there were two major areas of discussion in the
plan. The first of these was, whether a general attack across the whole front should be made,

---

[*]   Lieutenant General Sir William Pulteney GCVO KCB KCMG DSO (1861–1941). He was later
      Black Rod.

he expressed his concerns under five headings.[38] First, he thought the expanded first objective was a gamble given the strength of the German second line, the deficiency in artillery support and the difficulties if the German wire remained uncut – but that no doubt the Commander-in-Chief was in a position to know if this was a risk worth taking. Secondly, the inclusion of Montauban and the requirements of flank protection demanded an additional division. Thirdly, the attack on Gommecourt was beyond the capabilities of the Army – to solve this problem, three divisions of the Third Army – the 37th (New Army), 46th (North Midland) and 56th (London) divisions, under Headquarters VII Corps – were ordered by G.H.Q. to make a subsidiary, diversionary, attack around Gommecourt. Fourthly, Rawlinson stated that he would need further to consider the length of the bombardment; and last, consideration must be given to what subsequent operations should be mounted if the initial attack succeeded. On 6 May, Haig responded, saying he had considered the question of the bombardment and was now supportive of the long bombardment before the opening assault, having previously been in favour of a short bombardment – not exactly an answer to the question posed – and essentially telling Rawlinson to get on with the task.

Haig was right in one respect: that there seems to have been little emphasis in the planning on identifying the weaknesses in the German line and concentrating against them (a principle of war), making breaches in the line and exploiting these with second echelon or reserve forces. Indeed, the distribution of assault divisions appears to have been fairly uniform all along the line. As both Basil Liddell Hart and Edmonds, the official historian point out, this was probably because an attack of this kind was in reality a form of siege warfare, and siege warfare was not much studied in the British Army. During the Boer War, it had *withstood* several sieges, but these had really been encirclements; Sevastopol was its only experience of conducting a siege in the century that separated the Somme from Waterloo. During the Napoleonic wars, only a few major siege operations had been carried out – at Ciudad Rodrigo, San Sebastian and Badajoz; and in the century before that there had been only three others: Havana, Belle Isle and Louisburg. This form of warfare had, therefore, no intellectual respectability in the British Army and no real tradition of study.[*]

The artillery provided to support the operation totalled 1,537 guns,[39] that is, one gun per 20 yards of front, a density which had never yet been equalled by the British in the history of war. However, these statistics belied a fundamental problem: of the guns committed, only 467 were heavy calibres – 9.2-inch, 12-inch or 60-pdr – the rest were for the most part light 18-pdrs or medium 4.7 and 6-inch pieces. This meant that there was only one heavy gun per 57 yards of front: the French deployed 900 heavy guns on a front of eight miles, one per 15 yards. Production of artillery pieces was in the hands of the Royal Ordnance Factory and the four large firms of Vickers, Armstrong, Beardmore and Coventry Ordnance. These factories simply had not kept pace with demand: Sir John French had asked for 560 6-inch guns by June 1916; only 67 were actually delivered.[40] Nor were the heavy units of the Royal Garrison Artillery fit for their task: the official history recorded the view of the Minister of Munitions that: 'The Garrison Artillery in France is entirely untrained, it cannot shoot and is quite unfitted to work the perfect weapons that I have provided.'[41]

---

[*]   'Fortification and Artillery' was a subject at both Woolwich and the Staff College, Camberley – but siegecraft was not.

   The tasks of the artillery were to force the German infantry into shelters; if possible to destroy or neutralise those shelters and the fighting positions they supported; to destroy German artillery and its ammunition through counter-battery fire; to harass or prevent German reinforcement and supply; to cut communications; to halt counter-attacks; and to cut barbed wire. This last was of considerable importance to the attacking infantry, for without cutting the German wire there would be no entry to their lines. The German first defensive belt of wire usually ran through No Man's Land, about 20 yards in front of the first-line fire trench. It was by this time 30 yards wide and three to five feet high, as explained in Chapter 3. A second parallel belt had also been erected at about 15 yards distance, and thus the whole depth of the wire would be 75 yards, sometimes 100 yards. The wire, which was two or three times the thickness of pre-war agricultural wire, was laid in concertina-type lengths, supported by iron pickets and strands of wire to hold the whole together, to form a complex entanglement that would trap an enemy soldier and hold him. Wire entanglements were then covered by the fire of machine-guns and pre-recorded artillery and mortar shoots which would kill the trapped enemy.

   The issue was devastatingly simple: to cut these extensive belts of German wire in front of their fortified line required heavy shell. Light and medium would simply not do the job – and the bulk of the artillery was light and medium – even though 1,732,873 shells were fired in the first eight days of the battle.[42] Nor were the fuzes available up to the job. In the summer of 1916, most British shells were fitted with fuzes that would either penetrate a fortification and then explode, or else explode over the heads of troops in the open. Neither of these techniques could cope with wire, which required a sensitive fuze that would explode on contact with the wire strands, burst the shell casing creating shrapnel, and thus cut the wire. It was not until the introduction of the *Newton* No. 106E Mark IV fuze, and subsequently the No. 107, in late 1916 that this became possible, even though this fuze had been developed before the start of the

A German MG 08 team.

offensive.[43] What must be said, however, and this matter will be highlighted in later chapters, that in those areas where a breakthrough *was* made into the German positions, the subsequent effects of British artillery on German dugouts and entrenchments, on rear areas and supply routes, and on morale, was enormous and inflicted probably the greatest number of casualties during the fighting for Mametz Wood.

There was a further issue with artillery support, which was its command and control. In 1916, wireless (radio) communication was in its infancy and usually only reached corps headquarters, sometimes divisional headquarters. As the official history records, 'During the Somme the use of wireless was the exception rather than the rule.'[44] The means of controlling artillery fire was usually therefore telephone. Telephone lines however were only really viable in static position warfare; reeling out the miles of cable needed to connect an observer with the guns while in action was a tricky business, even if enough cable could be carried. It was not therefore possible for artillery to be made to conform to an advance by infantry or cavalry; rather, the infantry and cavalry had to conform to the artillery. This was achieved by laying down timed barrages on set lines, which corresponded with the predicted rates of advance of troops. If the advance was delayed, therefore, the barrage would get ahead of the troops and the enemy would not be suppressed. If the troops advanced too rapidly on the other hand, they would be hammered by their own artillery fire. Then, once the infantry had advanced to the limit of the guns' range, there would have to be a pause while the guns and their ammunition were moved forward: a pause which could give an enemy respite or the chance to counter-attack.

Air operations were an integral part of the operational planning, possibly for the first time. The strength of the Royal Flying Corps on the Somme front was 185 aircraft; The French Sixth Army had an additional 201 aircraft.[45] Thus the Anglo-French air forces considerably outnumbered the Germans' Second Army effort until mid-July. As well as aerial reconnaissance and the suppression of the German air effort, bombing attacks were to be made on the railways behind the German front, with the main effort commencing on 1 July, to ensure that damage could not be repaired in the days following the start of the offensive. Troops, transport columns, dumps and headquarters behind the battlefront were also to be attacked and the German ammunition depots at Mons, Namur and Lille were a high priority.[46]

The 9th (Headquarters) Wing of the Royal Flying Corps (R.F.C.) was moved to the Somme front to command and control operations at Army level. Under its command were Numbers 21, 27 and 60 squadrons, part of 70 Squadron, and No 5 Kite Balloon Squadron. The Fourth Army was allocated the direct support of the R.F.C.'s IV Brigade, with two squadrons of the 14th Wing, Numbers 22 and 24; four squadrons of the 3rd Wing, Numbers 3, 4, 5 and 15, and No 1 Kite Balloon Squadron for observation; this squadron detached one section to each corps headquarters. Those R.F.C. aircraft squadrons which were subordinated directly to Corps headquarters – that is, Numbers 3, 4, 9 and 15 – had 30 aircraft for counter-battery work, 13 for contact patrols against enemy aircraft; 16 for front line reconnaissance and photography, or the direction of destructive artillery bombardment. There were only nine aircraft in reserve. VII Corps, which was to operate in support of the Fourth Army, was allocated No. 8 Squadron with 18 aircraft and a Kite Balloon section from No. 5 Squadron.

The growth of the Royal Flying Corps was but one example of the way in which the B.E.F. had changed shape considerably since the start of the war. At Force, Army and Corps levels, there were a mass of specialist units: gas companies, field survey companies; camouflage units; drainage companies; anti-aircraft and searchlight units; electrical and mechanical companies;

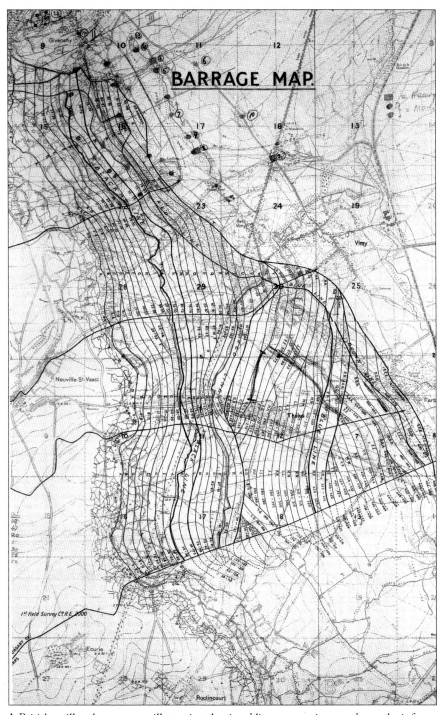

A British artillery barrage map illustrating the timed lines supporting an advance by infantry.

meteorological sections; kite balloon units; motor ambulance convoys; laboratories and schools; petroleum companies; and workshops of all kinds.

In spite of the fact that the date of the offensive had been brought forward from mid-August to the beginning of July, British logistic preparations the most extensive that had yet been undertaken in the entire history of the British Army in war.[47] A stock of 150,000 tons of ammunition, in particular artillery ammunition, of which 700,000 rounds of 18-pdr and 204,000 rounds of 6-inch ammunition was accumulated, using up to 90 trains per week.[48] Even these quantities were barely adequate: the expenditure of ammunition from 24 June to 23 July 1916 totalled 148,000 tons, and only 101,771 tons were landed in France during the same period to replenish stocks. Haig himself acknowledged in his final despatch of 21 March 1919 that in spite of the creation of the Ministry of Munitions to address the scandal of supply of 1915: 'Throughout the Somme battle the expenditure of artillery ammunition had to be watched with the greatest care.' Worse, the quality of shells was poor, with an increasing incidence of premature explosions, duds and faulty fuzes.[49]

There were massive tonnages of material to be carried forward to feed and equip the expanding force. Every day, each man – and each division had at least 18,000 men on its strength never mind the army and corps-level troops – consumed ¾ lb of tinned, fresh or frozen meat; 1¼ lbs of bread, biscuit or flour; 4 oz. bacon; 3 oz cheese; 8 oz. fresh vegetables or 2 oz. of dried; ⅝ oz. tea; 3 oz. jam; 3 oz sugar; ½ oz. salt; ¹⁄₁₆ of a tin of condensed milk; and mustard, pickles, pepper, oatmeal and butter all as extra.[50]

To move these enormous quantities, advanced supply depots collected and loaded trains of supplies for the front-line divisions which were despatched to exchange points. Here they were cross-loaded onto lorries and sent forward to divisional refilling points. At these points, horse drawn transport took supplies forward to refilling points for each brigade or divisional troops units; from there regimental transport and carrying parties completed the link to the men in the front line.[51]

Two million gallons of fuel per week were needed to service the fleet of motor lorries bringing supplies and men forward, a new problem in war and one which would soon surpass, for the first time, the requirements of forage for horses Tons of other stores of all kinds – including medical equipment, barbed wire, spare clothing and weapons – were accumulated behind the front, requiring more than 50 trains per week plus onward movement by road from the railhead, something that was very difficult to conceal from German air reconnaissance. Many miles of standard and narrow-gauge railway and tramway were laid to take the strain away from road transport right up to the front lines. All roads were also improved, however, and new causeways laid over marshy ground.

Three-and-a half miles (seven kilometres) of new trenches, along with additional dugouts to shelter troops were built by the Labour Corps Group allocated to the Fourth Army front; magazines and dumps were built, dressing stations and field hospitals erected and staffed. Gun emplacements and miles of communication trenches were dug. Telephone cables were deeply laid and mining operations undertaken beneath the German lines. In most places, water for men and horses was a serious problem so that many wells and boreholes had to be sunk, and more than 100 pumping stations built, with cans of water added to the growing mountains of supplies. All this is sometimes overlooked in the general recriminations about the level of casualties during the battle.

In spite of the scale of preparations, we must however ask ourselves, even though viewing matters in comfort from afar with the benefit of hindsight is dangerous, whether this plan was ever really realistic or viable? From the point of view of surprise, another principle of war, it was certainly not: the Germans had good intelligence on the matter, even if von Falkenhayn declined to believe it. In addition to which, the Germans' defensive preparations had been thorough, and it was well understood in the study of war that to succeed against a well-entrenched enemy, an attacking force should have a superiority of at least three to one, or preferably, five to one. The German Second and Sixth Armies, which faced the British (and Belgian) sector of the Western Front, totalled 53 divisions and five brigades.[52] Of these, eight divisions were in the line and three in the second echelon or immediate reserve in the British sector of the Somme offensive. A German infantry division consisted of two brigades, each with two regiments of four battalions and a machine gun company, plus artillery and divisional troops; it was thus about 25 percent smaller than its British equivalent. The British did not therefore have anything like a favourable force ratio for the attack, with only 11 divisions in the first echelon spread evenly against eight German divisions which, allowing for their smaller numbers, equated to six British divisions. In the second echelon there were five British and three German, divisions, the latter equating to 2¼ British divisions. The ratios were therefore barely two to one.

Next, it has to be understood that, as explained above, the available artillery was inadequate in quantity and quality for all its tasks. German defences were unlikely to be properly suppressed, nor avenues of approach opened through their wire, for the assaulting infantry.

Then there was the issue of the quality, rather than quantity, of the troops. Of the divisions committed to the operation, only four were pre-war Regular divisions, aside from the cavalry: these Regular divisions were depleted in quality by two years of war, certainly, but were still well led and well trained. Two were Territorial Force divisions. The remainder, the great bulk of the attacking force, was drawn from the New Armies, with all the issues of training and expertise already discussed. A G.H.Q. note, issued by the Chief of Staff, Lieutenant General Sir Launcelot Kiggell, on 8 May 1916, reminded all divisions that the officers and men of the New Armies were as yet untried, and that the general quality of the Army was not what it had been a year ago. The Army could now only operate according to detailed orders and could not be expected to take independent tactical actions at local level. Kitchener's aim had been to have the New Armies trained and prepared for major operations in 1917; and yet here, because of strategic considerations bearing on the war-time alliance, these men had to be committed a year earlier than had been planned. The overall quality of the assaulting troops was, therefore, barely equal to the task *had all other factors been favourably resolved.*

As to the question of a break-out, it has to be a matter of serious doubt as to whether the British Army of mid-1916 could have fought a war of mobility against the Germans. The majority of its fighting formations were infantry brigades and divisions, which would have to move on foot, supported by horse-drawn transport for their first line logistic lift, guns and heavy equipment. There were only three cavalry divisions available and these were as vulnerable to enemy artillery and machine gun fire as were the infantry. Motorised transport was still lacking and confined to supply and troop movement in the rear areas; thus the movement of large quantities of artillery ammunition, in particular, and fodder for horses was highly problematic; nor could fuel be moved easily. Railways could be laid, but this would take time. Air support could barely match the Germans, tanks and armoured cars were still experimental. Mobility was, therefore, limited and with it, the ability to supply an army moving away from its bases on an extended line of communications. Finally, command and control relied largely on telephones, which needed much manpower and time to lay lines. The issue of fighting quality and numbers aside, a quick glance at the four factors that determine logistic sustainability – demand, distance, destination and duration – should have been enough to tell anyone involved with the planning that this was an unrealistic plan, built on hope rather than experience.

It would, however, be wrong to characterize Haig's plan in the same light as Falkenhayn's deliberate butchery. Opinions on Haig are as polarized as ever and it is true that he often appeared cold and aloof, inflexible and ruled by time-tables.[53] However he was a man of strong religious convictions, who would not willingly or lightly send men to their deaths. He made the hard decisions that any officer in high command must do and maintained self-control and calm when the going got tough. He understood that frontal attacks were the only method of breaking into the enemy fortifications and that these would entail heavy losses. Such battles would inevitably be battles of attrition. He warned of this explicitly in a letter to the Press before the start of the Somme battle in May 1916.[54] However, as the official history records: 'As time went on Sir Douglas Haig became more and more affected by the optimism of Generals Joffre and Foch, which was supported by accounts given by the French General Staff of the tremendous effect of the German artillery at Verdun.'[55]

Was there an alternative? Rawlinson thought so. Rawlinson had commanded IV Corps at the first battle of Ypres and then throughout 1915. He was the only infantry officer among Haig's Army Commanders although the bulk of Haig's troops were infantrymen. Rawlinson's chief of staff, Major General Sir Archibald Montgomery, had been with him throughout the war to date. The German dispositions on the Somme were well known to Rawlinson's staff as the enemy had occupied their positions since 1914. The German units were known to be of good quality, but they had been in the area for a long time and were believed to be somewhat complacent. However even allowing for the difference in size, the force ratios between attackers and defenders were, as discussed, inadequate. Then the balance of the artillery, the inbuilt advantages of a positional defence and the quality of those defences had also to be considered.

Rawlinson believed that the most that could be expected on the first day of the attack was the penetration of the front line of German barbed wire and trenches. He knew, as an infantry officer, that to be sure of taking a trench system the artillery had to first cut the wire and neutralise the trenches and dugouts. It would be hard to accomplish this if the trench system targeted was too far away from the artillery – as was the case with the German's second line – particularly if it could not be observed from the British line. Therefore, Rawlinson advocated pausing after the capture of the first line to allow the artillery to be brought forward in order to support the next phase. Only then could another assault go in. Rawlinson famously referred to his approach as 'bite and hold', since it required the attacker to bite off one German trench system at a time and, when selecting the objective, not to be too greedy.[56] The objection to this, of course, is that any pause would allow the Germans to reinforce their line or counter-attack in accordance with their doctrine.

Rawlinson's acceptance of a plan that he clearly felt to be wrong must have haunted him forever afterwards. However, the root of the problem of the Somme was not the tactical plan, whatever its faults. The root of the problem was the fundamental shift in the aims, objectives and nature of the offensive. When first outlined, it formed part of an agreed, co-ordinated Allied operational and strategic plan that encompassed the entire perimeter of the war in Europe. It was part of an effort that would draw off German reserves, wear the enemy down, and then prepare the conditions for a more general attack leading to success. Unfortunately for the *Entente*, Falkenhayn was thinking along very similar lines. The Germans had to take far

Haig and Joffre at Chantilly, 23 December 1915.

less notice of alliance pressures than did either the French or the British, his decision-action cycle was always going to be faster, and Falkenhayn was thus able to pre-empt the Allies. This pre-emption succeeded in doing what it was meant to do – to draw the French Army into a battle of attrition. In doing so, it significantly reduced the French contribution to the battle and changed its nature from being part of a co-ordinated offensive plan, to taking the pressure off a beleaguered ally. Its results were therefore never going to be more than an amelioration of a bad situation rather than a decisive stroke.

Appendix I

British and Imperial Divisions, B.E.F. mid-1916

N.B., It should be noted that there was no permanent allocation of divisions to corps throughout the war, other than in the Australian and Canadian Corps; and that divisions were frequently moved from corps to corps, thus making the development of relationships between commanders and staffs impossible. The Portuguese, Italian and Labour Corps formations which served on the Western Front had not arrived by this date.

Regular Divisions	Guards, 1st, 2nd, 3rd, 4th, 5th, 6th, 7th, 8th, 27th, 28th, 29th
Cavalry Divisions	1st, 2nd, 3rd; 1st and 2nd Indian
New Army Divisions	9th, 12th, 14th, 15th, 16th, 16th, 17th, 18th, 19th, 20th, 21st, 23rd, 24th, 25th, 30th, 31st, 32nd, 33rd, 34th, 35th, 36th, 37th, 38th, 39th, 40th, 41st
Territorial Army Divisions	46th, 47th, 48th, 49th, 50th, 51st, 55th, 56th, 61st
Royal Naval Division	63rd
ANZAC Divisions (I and II ANZAC Corps)	1st Australian, 2nd Australian, 4th Australian, 5th Australian, New Zealand
Canadian Corps	1st Canadian, 2nd Canadian, 3rd Canadian, 4th Canadian, Canadian Cavalry Brigade
South Africa	Infantry Brigade

Appendix II

Reinforcements of the B.E.F., January–July 1916

Month	Total Moved	Divisions	Moved from
January	4	34th (New Army)	Britain
		35th (New Army)	Britain
		55th (West Lancs) (T.F.)	Re-assembled in France
		56th (London (T.F.)	Re-assembled in France
February	2	31st (East Midland)	Egypt (temporarily detached from France)
		46th (North Midland (T.F.)	Egypt (temporarily detached from France)
March	4	29th	Egypt
		39th (New Army)	Britain
		1st Australian	Egypt
		2nd Australian	Egypt
April	1⅓	New Zealand	Egypt
		South African Brigade	South Africa
May	3	41st (New Army	Britain
		61st (2nd South Midland) (T.F.)	Britain
		63rd (Royal Naval Division)	Mediterranean
June	5	11th (Northern)	Britain
		40th (New Army)	Britain
		60th (2/2nd London) (T.F.)	Britain
		4th Australian	Egypt
		5th Australian	Egypt
Total	19⅓		

Notes

1 Edmonds, p. 5
2 Edmonds, p. 27; B.H. Liddell Hart, *History of the First World War* (London, 1970), p. 270; Gary Sheffield and John Bourne (ed), *Douglas Haig: War Diaries and Letters 1914–1918* (London, 2005), p. 177.
3 Edmonds, p. 40.
4 Sheffield and Bourne, p. 173.
5 Liddell Hart, p. 269.
6 Victor Bonham-Carter, *Soldier True: The Life and Times of Field Marshal Sir William Robertson* (London, 1963), pp. 154–155.
7 See, for example, Paul Guinn, *British Strategy and Politics 1914 to 1918* (Oxford, 1965), p. 113.
8 Edmonds, p. 24.
9 *An Act to make provision with respect to Military Service in connexion with the present War.* 5 & 6 Geo. 5 c. 104. Received the Royal Assent 27 January 1916, introduced in March 1916 and not repealed until 1927.
10 T.N.A. PRO 30/57/53, Letter to Lord Kitchener.
11 Edmonds, p. 21.
12 Sheffield and Bourne, pp. 178–179.
13 Sheffield and Bourne, p. 179.
14 Edmonds, p. 32.
15 Liddell Hart, p. 304.
16 Edmonds, p. 29.
17 Edmonds, p. 37.
18 Edmonds, p. 27; Liddell Hart, p. 305.
19 Bonham-Carter, p. 154.

20   Liddell Hart, p. 304.
21   Sheffield and Bourne, p. 187.
22   Edmonds, p. 13.
23   Sheffield and Bourne, p. 186.
24   Lord Hankey, *The Supreme Command, Volume 2* (London, 1961), p. 444.
25   Sheffield and Bourne, p. 188.
26   Edmonds, p. 46.
27   Edmonds, p. 48.
28   Sheffield and Bourne, p. 191.
29   Edmonds, p. 46.
30   Edmonds, p. 41.
31   Sheffield and Bourne, p. 190–191.
32   A.H. Farrar-Hockley, *The Somme* (London, 1966), p. 62.
33   Edmonds, p. 248–250.
34   Farrar-Hockley, p. 64.
35   Edmonds, p. 251.
36   Edmonds, p. 252.
37   Liddell Hart, p. 306; Edmonds, pp. 254–256; John Ross, 'The Battle of the Somme' in *The First World War Battlefield Guide: The Western Front* [ed. Mungo Melvin], (British Army Headquarters, 2014), p. 65.
38   Edmonds, p. 256.
39   Liddell Hart, p. 306; Edmonds, p. 300.
40   Edmonds, p. 119.
41   Edmonds, p. 119.
42   Edmonds, p. 300,
43   *Official History of the Ministry of Munitions, Volume X : The Supply of Munitions* (H.M.S.O., 1922, Facsimile reprint by Imperial War Museum and Naval & Military Press), p. 56.
44   Edmonds, p. 71.
45   William Philpott, *Bloody Victory: The Sacrifice on the Somme and the Making of the Twentieth Century* (London, 2009), p. 269.
46   Edmonds, pp. 268–269.
47   Edmonds, pp. 270–287.
48   I.M. Brown, *The Evolution of the British Army's Logistical and Administrative Infrastructure and its Influence on GHQ's Operational and Strategic Decision-Making on the Western Front, 1914–1918* (University of London PhD thesis, 1996), pp. 159–162.
49   Edmonds, p. 122.
50   Edmonds, p. 101.
51   Edmonds, p. 101.
52   Peter Hart, *The Somme* (London, 2006), Appendix C.
53   See, for example, John Hussey, 'Portrait of a Commander-in-Chief', in Brian Bond and Nigel Cave (ed), *Haig: A Reappraisal 80 Years On* (London, 1998), p. 14 et seq.
54   T.N.A. WO 256/10.
55   Edmonds, p. 255.
56   See for example Ian Becket, 'Henry Rawlinson' in Ian Beckett and Steven Corvi (eds.), *Haig's Generals* (London, 2006), p. 171 et seq.

5

Christmas in France: The 38th (Welsh) Division's Deployment and Early Days at the front, December 1915–January 1916

While the final decision on the size and shape of the Welsh contribution to the war effort was being made, the 38th Division entered its final phase of preparations for the Front. During this period some of the older officers were replaced by younger, fitter men with more experience of modern war. Some of these came from India, others had recovered from wounds. R.C. Bell of the Central India Horse, for example, took command of 15 R.W. Fus in place of Fox-Pitt, while Dunn, in command of 114 Brigade, was replaced by Thomas Marden of the Welsh Regiment, who had commanded its 1st Battalion in France. Henry Lloyd-Mostyn of 17 R.W. Fus was replaced by J.A. Ballard, whom Emlyn Davies described as 'a Taffy-hater' and 'Colonel Bastard'.[1] The most controversial change was, however, the replacement of Owen Thomas in command of 113 Brigade, by the 37-year-old Victoria Cross winner, Llewellyn Alberic Emilius Price-Davies, on 24 November 1915.[2] Llewellyn Wyn Griffith described Price-Davies in *Up to Mametz* as the second most stupid soldier he ever met (Lieutenant General Aylmer Hunter-Weston won first prize). Price-Davies had done well in the small wars which preceded 1914 and had won his VC and a DSO in South Africa. He was, said Wyn Griffith, too dull to be frightened. His now-published letters fail to give us a kinder view of him.[3] Known as 'Jane' by his fellow regulars, he exemplified the thoughtless brutality that is many people's stereotype of the Great War General officer: certainly he was personally brave, but he was also unimaginative, slow, fascinated by the minor trivia of latrine buckets and polished brass. He was one of those officers who at the time had to be promoted to fill command appointments in a rapidly expanding army, promoted on the basis that bravery in

Brigadier General
Llewellyn Price-Davies.

combat signifies the ability to exercise high command – but for whom the demands of modern war turned out to be all too much.

Owen Thomas set about raising and organising the seven battalions of the new Reserve brigade in North Wales. Then, in early May 1916, Thomas was suddenly removed from command for no apparent reason. A groundswell of anger followed at this insult both in the country and in Parliament and a court of inquiry was convened. What this found was that he had been the unwitting victim of a social scandal – the celebrated affair of Mrs Mary Cornwallis-West and the wounded Sergeant Patrick Barrett of the Royal Welsh Fusiliers[4] – along with some unfavourable comments by Ivor Phillipps and doubts about his suitability to command expressed by Sir John French. These whisperings had damaged his reputation badly – with no cause. The court of inquiry restored his good name; he was granted the honorary rank of Brigadier General in perpetuity, a gratuity, and given a Knighthood in the New Years' Honours of 1917. He also received a letter from Lloyd George which, he said, would save him from being reviled by the many families whom he had influenced into sending their sons to the war while he now remained at home – forgetting perhaps that all three of Owen's sons were at the front on active service.[5]

The incidence of Welsh nationality and of the Welsh language, already discussed – although the latter was not universal by any means – certainly gave the 38th Division a strongly national character. Llewelyn Wyn Griffith, a native Welsh speaker, recorded an episode which exemplified this feeling in a later memoir, *The Pattern of One Man's Remembering*. Moving up to the line, the Welsh men of his company:

> … started singing in harmony… a fine old Welsh hymn in a minor key. The brigadier general [Price-Davies] asks me, "Why do they always sing these mournful hymns? Most depressing – bad for morale. Why can't they sing something cheerful, like other battalions?" I try to explain to him that what they are singing now is what they sang as children, as I did, in chapel, in the world to which they really belong. They are being themselves, not men in uniform. They are back at home, with their families, in their villages. But he does not understand. Nor can he, with his background.[6]

It is also of note that a number of the most notable writers, poets, artists and performers of this period also served in the 38th Division, nearly all of them in 15 R.W. Fus. They included Llewelyn Wyn Griffith, whose works have already been cited; the writer, painter, calligrapher and poet David Jones; the Welsh-speaking bard Ellis Humphrey Evans, or Hedd Wyn; Emlyn Davies and Bill Tucker, who have also been cited; and Harold Gladstone Lewis, author of *Crow on a Barbed Wire Fence*. The odd man out was Wynn Wheldon, in 14 R.W. Fus, who was later a prominent socialist writer and father of Sir Huw Wheldon. There is no evidence however that these men were aware of each other in the way that, in the Regular battalions, Siegfried Sassoon, Robert Graves, James Dunn and Frank Richards were;

Ellis Evans, 'Hedd Wyn' who joined 15 R.W. Fus in 1917.

or in the Territorial Force the author of *With Allenby's Crusaders,* J.N. More, and the artist Richard Lunt Roberts. In wartime it is unusual for a soldier to get to know another outside his own company; there was also the very clear divide, even in a New Army division, between officers and men; and finally, Ellis Evans and Emlyn Davies were to a degree separated from the others by the barrier of language.

On 5 November, orders were issued for the 38th Division to embark for service in France,[7] minus the field artillery which was yet to complete its training, and the motor ambulances and their workshop. Batches of men were sent home on seven days embarkation leave.[8] The War Diary makes it clear, however, that the entire division was not yet fully trained, and that further training would be required at the Front.

At this point it is necessary to compare the state of military training with that of the enemy that the division would face – the German *Reichsheer.* According to the constitution of April 16, 1871, every German male between the ages of 20 and 45 was liable for military service. A man would be called up for training with the class of the year in which he reached his 20th birthday and at the muster of each class, medical examinations and interviews were carried out, but few exemptions were permitted other than royalty, lunatics and convicted felons. Active military service was for three years in the cavalry or horse artillery, or two years in the infantry, artillery, engineers or supply services. This was followed by up to five years of liability for recall in the Regular Reserve; then home-defence liability in the *Landwehr* (Home Guard) for a further 11 years, the *Landwehr* was still liable for active service abroad. Moreover, from 1 January in the year that a class reached its 39th birthday, in the *Landsturm* (Home Guard Reserve) for seven years. This last body was not liable for combat duties but could release younger men for active duty by assuming duties in the rear areas. During his time with the Regular Reserve a man could be mobilised for two annual training periods, a liability that ceased only when a man was transferred into the *Landsturm.* Shorter periods of service were available for professional men and of course, there were many volunteers who filled the ranks of the Non-Commissioned Officers. All German commissioned officers were professionals.

In 1900 the idea of an Ersatz, or Supplementary, Reserve came into being. The Regiments thus created contained those men who for one reason or other had not been called up. They were required to serve for 12 years with up to three training sessions each year, although this rarely happened.

It was this system, which had originated after 1806, which permitted Germany could mobilize the four million trained men that it did between 1914 and 1917, even without considering the huge number of young men, who, like their counterparts in Britain, volunteered in the Summer of 1914. This system of conscription, originally devised by *Generalleutnant* Gneisenau after the Prussian defeat in 1806 as the *Krumpersystem,* offered two major advantages. First, it created a large pool of trained manpower that could quickly augment the regular army in an emergency. In August 1914, the German army needed just 12 days to expand from 808,280 to 3,502,700 men and from 1914 to 1917, four million men were called up but even so, the losses of the war meant that the class of 1918 class was called up early, between September 1916 and January 1917. Secondly, in a long war, the system offered a framework for the mobilisation of the entire manpower of the state, excepting the demands of the Navy and war industries.

Until January 1915, all recruits went to their regimental depot for three months' training before being posted to a field unit. After February 1915 recruits were then sent to depots close to the front lines for about three weeks for additional, specialized training in trench warfare techniques. All returning wounded also soldiers went to these depots for refresher training, which were staffed by convalescent officers and N.C.O.s whose experience would be passed on until they too were fit to return to front line service. A considerable contrast therefore to the hasty preparation of Kitchener's battalions.

On the 29 November 1915, the 38th (Welsh) Division was reviewed in pouring rain by Queen Mary – the King was unwell[9] – an event captured on a Pathé newsreel. Emlyn Davies recorded his memories of this event:

> The march across the windswept soggy Downs wearied the reluctant limbs and aching backs humped with full pack weighing 98 lbs. Nonetheless there were compensations. Taking a glance backwards we saw the long twisting mile-long procession of marching men, followed at the rear by a caravanserai of transport limbers, wagons and covered ambulances, all horse drawn by lively quadrupeds…. To see the khaki clad multitude with rifles at the order in vast array presented a picture to be admired. The Queen inspected in turn each battalion – Soldiers of the King.[10]

Lloyd George himself did not turn up to the review of the division and was represented by his daughter Olwyn.[11]

Between 1 and 4 December the brigades and divisional troops moved from Winchester to Southampton for embarkation and thence to Le Havre. David Jones recalled that on the outskirts of Southampton, an attempt was made to smarten the troops up and the division marched into town with its bands playing. However, Southampton was now immune to the sight of soldiers marching to the docks and no-one took much notice.[12] Llewelyn Wyn Griffith recalled that this march was:

> … in an even drive of wind and rain, into a late afternoon that found us on a wet quay-side, staring at a grey ship on a grey sea. Rain in England, rain in the Channel and rain in France; mud on the Hampshire Downs and mud in the unfinished horse-standings in Havre where we sheltered from the rain during the hours of waiting for a train.[13]

Wyn Griffith's memory is confirmed by the War Diary which remarked on the bad weather and rough crossing. Emlyn Davies recalled being up at 04.00 hrs for breakfast and waiting all day before embarking for the night crossing of 16 hours in the paddle steamer *La Marguerite*.[14] The phenomenon of 'rushing to wait' is one known to all armies, throughout history.

By 6 December, the whole division had moved into billets west of Aire, about 10 miles (16 kilometres) south of St Omer. Here it came under the direct orders of G.H.Q., but was attached to XI Corps for training.[15] Instruction was given in trench construction, maintenance and routine, sand-bagging, hygiene and drainage; wiring and the breaching of wire obstacles; bombing – i.e. the use of the new hand grenade; shooting, to get then up to firing 15 aimed shots per minute; the use of the new gas helmet; and live firing by the machine-gunners. Route marches and close-order drill also contined.[16]

It was not long before orders were received that this training behind the line was to be supplemented by training in the line. To that effect, infantry battalions and divisional troops units were to be placed under the instruction of brigades of the Guards and 19th Divisions, in the area between Givenchy and Picantin.[17] From 10 to 18 December, 13 and 16 R.W. Fus, with a

Llewelyn Wyn Griffith and his company in tents behind the line. (Family of John Bradshaw)

company of 19 Welsh, 129 Field Ambulance and specialist officers from 113 Brigade were to come under the Guards Division; while 10 and 15 Welsh plus specialists were to go to the 19th Division. From 18 to 26 December, 14 and 15 R.W. Fus, and specialists, would go the Guards while 14 and 15 Welsh went to the 19th; and from 26 December to 3 January 1916, 17 R.W. Fus, 10 S.W.B. and brigade staff would spend the New Year with the Guards while 11 S.W.B., 16 Welsh and attached specialists went to the 19th. Throughout the period the engineers, pioneers and trench mortar sections were to rotate separately under orders from the 19th Division.[18]

On 18 December, in preparation for these rotations, the division moved to new billets around St Venant, close to the Belgian border. Here, on 24 December, the divisional artillery began to arrive, replacing four London artillery brigades which had been temporarily attached to the division.* At the same time, each brigade was ordered to form a trench mortar battery, whose officers and men commenced training on Boxing Day at the Mortar School in St Venant. The War Diary also reported that the division had suffered its first fatal casualty, although without explaining how, on 11 December: an un-named private of 16 R.W. Fus.

Llewelyn Wyn Griffith recorded his memories of the prospect of moving into the line for the first time:

> Less than 24 hours stood between us and the trenches; there were two kinds of men in the world – those who had been in the trenches and the rest. We were to graduate from the

---

*   1/1, 1/4, 2 and 3 London Artillery Brigades T.F. and the 10th Divisional Ammunition Column.

one class to the other, to be reborn into the old age and experience of the front line, by the traversing of two miles over the fields of Flanders.[19]

David Jones had more explicit memories:

> … water gleamed between dilapidated breastworks, blue slime coated, ladling with wooden ladles… They speak low. Cold gurgling followed their labours… You step down between inward inclining, heavy bulged, walls of earth; you feel the lateral slats firm foothold. Squeaking, bead-eyed hastening, many footed hurrying, accompanying each going forward.[20]

This was the beginning of the division's apprenticeship as the officers and men learned the routine of trench life. Tours of trenches were not, as many people think, affairs lasting months. In the desperate days of late 1914 and early 1915 there were recorded instances of units holding the line for weeks at a time but by the spring of 1915, most divisions operated a rotation in

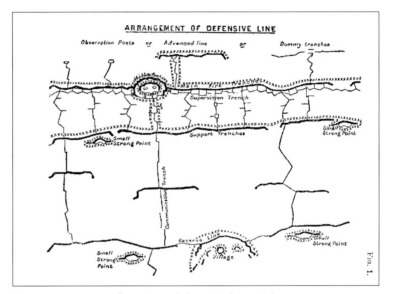

British trench layout in late 1915.

which each brigade spent a few days in the front, or firing, line; then a few days in the support line, then days in reserve – these last were often the worst period as the men would spend all night on duties like carrying supplies up to the line, or sand-bagging and wiring and other heavy work. This would be followed by a rest period and training, before the rotation began again. The official history described life in the line thus:

> Most of the daytime – invariably in the morning – the three lines, firing, support and reserve, were deserted except for a few sentries leaning against the parapet with periscopes handy, and for a sniper or two; everyone else was under cover, silent and, if possible, asleep. At dark a whole population suddenly appeared, literally out of the earth; working parties would set about draining, digging and wiring; from the rear, along the communication trenches, would come parties carrying rations, water, ammunition, sandbags, duck-boards, and everything imaginable. Behind these the roads were packed with horsed wagons and limbers… Then dawn would approach, the trench garrison would stand to arms and be dismissed to begin another similar day.[21]

Standing to arms, or stand-to, took place for 30 minutes either side of sunrise and sunset as these were considered the most likely times for enemy activity: either a dawn attack (even though the Germans would be silhouetted with the sunrise behind them), or a dusk raid. Every man had to be at his post in the line or in a forward listening post – a sap – alert, fully clothed and armed to be checked by the officers and sergeants. No lights could be shown after dark, so food was either cooked in dugouts during the day or brought up by company quartermaster sergeants in hayboxes – thermal containers. Breakfast was usually bread, bacon, tea and jam; lunch would be biscuits, jam and chocolate, or tinned bully beef; supper a hot mush of Maconochie's, a tinned stew of meat, sliced turnips and carrots in a thin gravy, named because of its manufacture by the Maconochie Company of Aberdeen. It became the standard fare of British troops in trenches, supplemented by potatoes or bread. The stew was tolerable when hot, but many hated it, some even calling it 'a man-killer' if eaten cold.[22]

Bernard Adams described the routine thus in his memoir *Nothing of Importance*:

Using a trench periscope in the line, a drawing by David Jones. (RWF Mus 2998b)

… it was usually "six days in and six days out." During these six days out we also invariably supplied four working-parties per company, which lasted nine hours from the time of falling in outside company headquarters to dismissing after marching back. Still, it was "billets." One slept uninterruptedly, and with equipment and boots off.[23]

It was during this period that the some of the men of the division became involved in the little-known second Christmas Truce. This occurred not far from Frelinghien on the Franco-Belgian border, where at Christmas 1914, Captain Clifton Stockwell of the 2nd Battalion, Royal Welsh Fusiliers, and Captain Friedrich *Freiherr* von Sinner of the 2nd (Silesian) *Jaeger* Battalion, had met in No-Man's Land to exchange compliments, beer and Christmas puddings.[24] At the time, although officially frowned upon, the truce was much covered in the Press – including *The Daily News*,[25] *Daily Mirror*,[26] *Manchester Guardian*[27] and the *Illustrated London News*[28] – and there was

British troops being fed hot rations in trenches. (IWM Q4843)

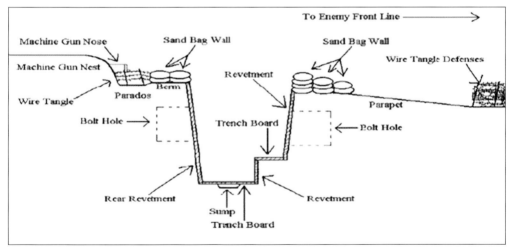

A cross-section of a British trench.

an understanding, even though anti-German feeling was running high at home, that where chance threw men together in war, even when they were on opposing sides, there was a companionship based on shared experience. The poet Siegfried Sassoon, another Royal Welch Fusilier, commented, as did others, that there was often more comradely feeling between the soldiers of the opposing armies, who shared the same dangers and privations, than between soldiers and civilians. Sassoon was in no doubt, for example, that troops would relish the opportunity to take on the pro-war Press, or politicians in safe billets, rather than the Germans.[29] Robert Graves, like Sassoon, served in the 1st and 2nd Battalions of the Royal Welsh Fusiliers and remarked that the men at the front loathed striking munitions workers at home far more than they hated the Germans, and would be 'only too glad of a chance to shoot a few'.[30]

On 19 December 1915, just as the division began its apprenticeship, Sir Douglas Haig had taken command of the British Expeditionary Force.[31] He was determined that there would be no repetition of the events of 1914. Firm instructions were issued right down the chain of command, reminding everyone of the 'unauthorized truce' of the previous year and ordering that 'nothing of the kind is to be allowed this year'.[32] Many divisional and brigade commanders issued orders that any German showing himself was to be shot.[33] On the German side, too, there were orders against fraternization, threatening the direst consequences: any visits, agreements not to fire on each other, exchanges of news or souvenirs were not only strictly forbidden, but would be counted as 'verging on high treason' – in other words, a capital crime.[34]

Most accounts of what happened come from 15 R.W. Fus., which had seen no serious action thus far and had no reason to feel animosity towards the Germans on a personal level – with the exception of those who had lost friends or brothers in other battalions. From 18 to 26 December the battalion was in the line at Laventie. Here, in the cold and wet of December, the line was described in the diary of an officer of a unit then holding the sector, Captain Carlos 'Pip' Blacker of the 1st Battalion Coldstream Guards:

> It consisted of a line of breastworks through which you could keep watch and shoot. The view through one of these loopholes was not inspiring. Across a stretch of no man's land and you beheld a conspicuous line of enemy breastworks which looked pale grey in the middle distance… At the foot of both lines ran narrow belts of rusty wire which looked dark against the grey sandbags beyond. And between those two belts lay a mostly featureless waste, patched with dead goosefoot and docks and pocked with shell-holes, the deeper ones half-filled with slimy water … A confrontation, winding away into seeming infinity on each side, alive with watchfulness.[35]

15 R.W. Fus. was not all together in the line, but each of its companies was under instruction from a different battalion of 2 Guards Brigade, and it was thus spread along a lengthy stretch of the line.[36] This dispersion solves the puzzle of why there are such differing versions of events among the witnesses. Llewelyn Wyn Griffith's company, C Company, was assigned to Blacker's battalion, 1st Coldstream Guards, and he recounted in *Up to Mametz* that Haig's orders had been received: 'We must confine our goodwill not only to fellow Christians', he wrote, 'but to Christians of allied nationality. We were to remain throughout possessed by the spirit of hate, answering any advances with lead.'[37]

On Christmas Eve, sounds of singing and merrymaking could be heard in the German trenches opposite C Company and the Coldstreamers, about 100 yards away, which were occupied by Catholic soldiers of the 13th Bavarian Reserve Infantry Regiment.[38] These men were reservists, dragged, probably unwillingly, from their civilian lives; they were also more easy-going as a people than the stern, Protestant Prussians. Soon, shouts of 'Merry Christmas, Tommy' were heard. These were answered with shouts of 'Merry Christmas, Fritz'.[39] Blacker confirms this account, saying that:

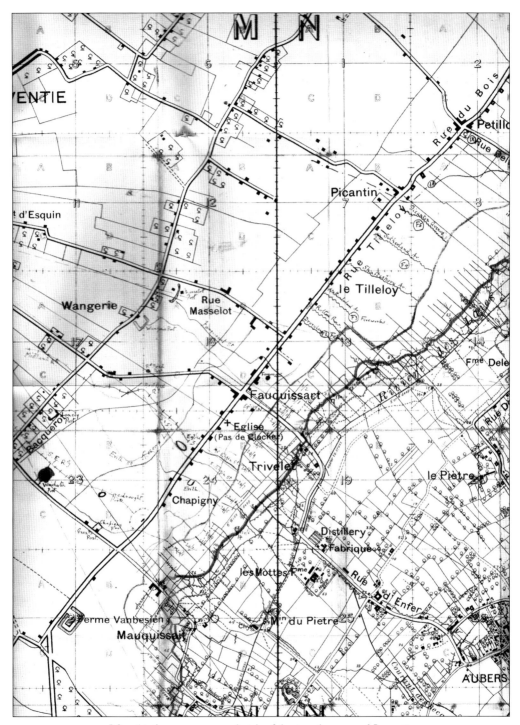

Map 5.i A contemporary sketch of the trenches around Laventie.

Laventie trenches Christmas 1915 where the second Christmas Truce occurred. (RWF Mus)

… the German breastworks were near enough for verbal exchange to be possible between the two sides…. I recall someone shouting across 'What have you got for dinner today Fritz?' The reply sounded like 'a fat goose' (more Germans spoke English than our people spoke German). Fritz was invited to come over, but at this stage there was no movement.[40]

Another witness to the exchanges on Christmas Eve in 15 R.W. Fus., but further up the line, was Private Bertie Felstead. Felstead died at the age of 106, in 2001, the oldest man alive in Britain and the last witness of these events.[41] Felstead was in D Company, attached to the 2nd Battalion Irish Guards. In later life, Felstead remembered how the German soldiers oppo-site sang, in German, a hymn which shared the same tune with the Welsh hymn 'Ar Hyd y Nos'. This was probably the German version of the hymn 'Go my Children with my Blessing' ('*Gehen meine Kinder mit meinem Segen*'). Their choice – probably a lucky chance – was taken as a much-appreciated acknowledgment of the nationality of the opposing company, and the Fusiliers responded by singing 'Good King Wenceslas'. After the night's carol singing, Felstead recalled that feelings of goodwill had so swelled up that at dawn, Bavarian and British soldiers clambered spontaneously out of their trenches. Shouting such greetings as 'Hello Tommy' and 'Hello Fritz', they at first shook hands in no-man's-land, and then presented one another with gifts. German beer, sausages and spiked helmets were given, or bartered, in return for bully beef, biscuits and tunic buttons. A similar account is provided in the diary of the Company Sergeant Major of D Company, John Bradshaw, a native of Lampeter in Cardiganshire,[42] which has only recently come to light.

In C Company's area, Wyn Griffith recounted his memories of a very similar scene:

As soon as it was light, we saw hands and bottles being waved at us, with encouraging shouts that we could neither understand nor misunderstand A drunken German stumbled

A field kitchen being enjoyed by British soldiers in a dugout. (IWM E1219)

The scene in a German dugout at Christmas 1915. (James Payne collections)

over his parapet and advanced through the barbed wire, followed by several others, and in a few moments there was a rush of men from both sides, carrying tins of meat, biscuits and other odd commodities for barter… this was the first time I had seen No Man's Land, and it was now Every Man's Land, or nearly so. Some of our men would not go and gave terse and bitter reasons for their refusal. The officers called our men back to the line, and in a few minutes No Man's Land was once more empty and desolate. There had been a feverish exchange of souvenirs, a suggestion for peace all day and a football match in the afternoon, and a promise of no rifle fire at night. All this came to naught.[43]

Blacker also recounted the events in this part of the line in his diary:

Loudening noises of shouts and singing came across no-man's-land, and when there was enough daylight figures could be seen moving about between their breastworks and wire. Our people followed suit. The Germans then came out in front of their wire. Our people did the same. No shooting anywhere. Both sides then gained in boldness until there was quite a crowd in no-man's-land… The two sides exchanged cigarettes and other souvenirs, including buttons and badges …The conversation, which was amiable, went on for about five minutes. It was brought to an end by a burst of shrapnel overhead.[44]

Felstead, whose company was removed from those of Wyn Griffith, remembered that there was a soccer match of sorts:

It wasn't a game as such, more a kick-around and a free-for-all. There could have been 50 on each side for all I know. I played because I really liked football. I don't know how long it lasted, probably half an hour.[45]

David Jones of B Company was attached to the 3rd Battalion Grenadier Guards. He recalled that on Christmas morning he heard the Germans singing Christmas carols and the cockneys of 15 R.W. Fus. singing louder, to drown them out. The London Welsh sang 'Casey Jones', a song he particularly liked.[46] Later that morning, however, the 3rd Grenadiers went into reserve and so Jones saw no more – but he did hear of the meetings in no-man's land and wrote of it in his epic poem, 'Anathemata':

I saw and heard their cockney song salute the happy morning; and later, this same morning… walking in daylight, upright, through the lanes of the war-net to outside and beyond the rusted trip-belt, some with gifts, none with ported weapons, embraced him between his fossa and ours, exchanging tokns.[47]

Recently, another previously unknown account has surfaced. This is the personal diary of Private Robert Keating, an under-age fusilier of about 16 years old in 15 R.W. Fus., who later transferred to the Royal Engineers, and survived the war. He died in 1967. In 1915, Keating was in A Company, assigned to the 1st Battalion Scots Guards who were opposite No. 246 Württemberg Reserve Infantry Regiment – Catholic soldiers again, but from the Rhineland, not Bavaria, and also reservists.[48] Keating recorded what had happened after the morning stand-to and breakfast were over on Christmas Day:

Had breakfast after which we shouted greetings to the Germans over the way. We shouted come over – they shouted come over. We stood up and saw them walking on their parapets then some of the Jocks ran across & Gordon [unidentified] and I. The officer was shouting come back! – come back! But we took no heed & went on.

The Germans who turned out to be the Württemberg Reserves crowded round us & chatted about old England – one fellow we were talking to was born in Northampton & was longing for the day when he could return. They said the war would end in a few months in our favour & that they were absolutely fed up with everything generally. Just as we were exchanging souvenirs the blooming artillery started and you should have seen us run: – Heaps of fellows we[re] caught in the barbed wire, but really there was no danger to us as the shells were dropping on the German trenches. The reason why we rushed back was

Robert Keating: Witness to the 1915 Christmas Truce. (RWF Mus)

because our artillery firing on the Allerman [i.e. Allemands, or Germans] might entice their snipers to fire on us. However, this was not so. Before leaving the Germans one of their officers told one of ours that they would not fire another shot for two days if we did the same, and believe me or believe me not, on our part of the line not a single shot was fired until we were relieved by the Irish Guards on Sunday evening [26 December]. Well, to revert, at 12 noon I was told off for fatigue duty with about two dozen other Scots, we had to… get a thousand sand-bags… Arriving back in the trench at 2.30 p.m. I dumped my load and joined a party who were burying a dead Scot in 'no-man's-land'. We intended burying a lot of fellows but owing to our artillery fire we had to abandon the attempt.[49]

The personal diary of Captain Sir Iain Colquhoun, a company commander with the Scots Guards, supports this account:

Stand to at 6.30. Germans very quiet. Remained in Firing Trenches until 8.30. No sign of anything unusual. When having breakfast about 9 a.m. a sentry reported to me that the Germans were standing up on their parapets and walking towards our barbed wire. I ran out to our firing trenches and saw our men looking over the parapet and the Germans outside our barbed wire.

A German officer came forward and asked me for a truce for Xmas. I replied that this was impossible. He then asked for ¾ hour [three-quarters of an hour] to bury his dead. I agreed. The Germans then started burying their dead and we did the same. This was finished in ½ hrs time. Our men and the Germans then talked and exchanged cigars, cigarettes etc for ¼ of an hour and when the time was up, I blew a whistle and both sides returned to their trenches.

For the rest of the day the Germans walked about and sat on their parapets. Our men did much the same but remained in their trenches. Not a shot was fired. At night the Germans put up Fairy lights on their parapets and their trenches were outlined for miles on either side. It was a mild looking night with clouds and a full moon and the prettiest sight I have ever seen. Our machine guns played on them and the lights were removed. Our guns shelled heavily all night at intervals of half an hour and the Germans retaliated on Sunken Road. I had to leave my dug-out five times during the night owing to shells.[50]

Further attempts at peace-making were quickly stamped out. Wyn Griffith recalled an irate brigadier, spluttering up the line, throwing out threats of courts-martial and ordering an extra dose of military action that night.[51] This was very likely to have been Brigadier General Lord Henry Seymour, the Commander of 2 Guards Brigade. Private Harold Diffey, another soldier of C Company 15 R.W. Fus., who survived the war and who also remembered the truce, recounted the same episode in a letter home:

After about 20 to 30 minutes a Staff Officer with red tabs… and a vociferous sergeant-major appeared yelling, 'You came out to fight the Huns, not to make friends with them.' So our lads reluctantly returned followed by a salvo from our 18-pounders which ended the episode.[52]

Keating also recorded Seymour's arrival:

The remainder of the day we spent in shouting to the Germans. Meanwhile the Brigadier General came round the trenches and told every fellow to shoot any German he saw… no one took any notice of this order and carried on as usual…[53]

Keating went on to record what had happened on Christmas Night:

[That evening] we were roused out by the Scots and dragged on to the parapet where we found all the Welsh fellows gathered. Here we were, Welsh and Scots all, clustered round the burning brazier which was placed on the outer parapet. The Germans were sending up star lights and singing – they stopped, so we cheered them & we began singing Land of Hope and Glory – Men of Harlech et cetera – we stopped, and they cheered us. So we went on till the early hours of the morning.[54]

Firmer measures were clearly needed to enforce the approved martial spirit, and Keating's diary of Boxing Day recorded that after the morning routine,

… The Germans were not firing but no-one got on the parapet although many heads were above. Orders were issued out that if any man was seen waving or heard shouting, they would be put to the wall at once [i.e. shot] – this order put an end to our fun…
… at 5.30 p.m. the Irish Guards relieved us but before going we were told not to mention anything of what happened in the trenches yesterday and today.[55]

Colquhoun's dairy recorded what happened to him on Boxing Day:

Fine day. No rifle firing, but no Germans showing. I went at 10 a.m. to Winchester House to explain to a Court of Inquiry my conduct on Christmas Day. The Brigadier (who came round my trenches 10 mins after my truce was over) didn't mind a bit but the Major General [Lord Cavan] is furious about it. The Coldstreams and our 2nd Batt are also implicated. Relieved by the 1st Irish Guards. Marched out by platoons down Sunken Road and Sign Post line to Rouge Choistre. Dropped the R.W.F. and marched via Rouge Bailleul to La Gorgue at 7 p.m. and billeted there.[56]

Later, both Colquhoun and the acting Commanding Officer of 1 Scots Guards, Captain Miles Barne, were tried by court-martial. Barne was acquitted of all charges, while Colquhoun received a reprimand, but this was not confirmed by Sir Douglas Haig – possibly because Colquhoun was related by marriage to the Prime Minister, Herbert Asquith.[57]

So ended the Christmas Truce of 1915. It did not receive the extensive coverage of 1914 but soldiers' letters home, at least those that escaped the censor's pencil, certainly recorded it. One such letter was published in the *Wrexham Advertiser* in January 1916:

It was a memorable Christmas Day in our trench as we had a truce with the enemy from Christmas Eve until Boxing Day morning. Not a shot was fired – quite a change with no lead flying around. The truce came about in this way. The Germans started singing and lighting candles at 7.30 on Christmas Eve, and one of them challenged any one of us to go across for a bottle of wine. One of our fellows accepted the challenge and took a big cake to exchange. That started the ball rolling. We then met half way to shake hands and exchange greetings with them. The Germans seem to be very nice chaps, and said they were awfully sick of the war. We were out of the trenches all day Christmas Day collecting souvenirs.[58]

It was, however, the last such event of the war, other than the sort of informal truces to bury the dead and recover the wounded which had been a feature of warfare for centuries and which lingered on in the Great War. There was little, if any, attempt at a truce over Christmas 1916 and none whatsoever in 1917. Fellow-feeling there might be – a degree of chivalry even – but by the end of the second year of war there was no hope of fraternization.

Neither the 38th Division nor 113 Brigade War Diaries make any mention of these events. The period of training under instruction was completed on 5 January 1916 and a new phase begun in which the whole of 113 and 114 Brigades were committed to holding a sector of the line in the Guards and the 19th Divisions' areas, followed on 10 January by 115 Brigade which relieved 113 Brigade. A week later, the divisional artillery began a period of attachments to units in the line.[59] During this time, 113 Brigade made a demonstration with plywood dummies, simulating an assault over the trench parapet, covered by an artillery barrage. This rather naive deception seems to have been designed to draw the Germans from their dugouts – at least according to the Corps War Diary.[60]

This sort of prank was in keeping with the spirit of dominating No-Man's Land and denying freedom of action to the Germans, which was enthusiastically followed by many brigade, divisional and corps commanders – Price-Davies of 113 Brigade was typical of many. It was also true of many battalion commanding officers, as Robert Graves described in *Goodbye to all That*, speaking of the same sector of the line as was now occupied by the 38th Division:

… both [Regular] battalions of the Royal Welch Fusiliers had made it a point of honour to dominate No Man's Land from dusk to dawn. There was never a night at Laventie when a message did not come down the line from sentry to sentry: "Pass the word; officer's patrol going out".[61]

113 Brigade also undertook its first trench raid, near the Boar's Head, on 10 January 1916, supported by artillery and trench mortar fire. This raid was carried out by a central party of one officer, six riflemen, four bombers, two carriers and two stretcher bearers; and two blocking or flank protection parties each of two riflemen, two bombers and two carriers.[62] 115 Brigade was also active, having taken casualties of three men killed and 19 wounded during its limited spell of trench duty in December.[63]

Lieutenant General Sir Richard Haking, the G.O.C.-in-C. XI Corps,* was a noted exponent of this approach. On 20 January 1916, Haking felt sufficiently confident in the progress made by the 38th Division to order the whole division into the line in place of the 19th Division. As he did so, he sent a memorandum to Philips which was to be read to all troops:

> Now that the 38th Division has completed its training in the trenches and is about to take over half the front occupied by XI Corps, I wish to convey to all ranks my appreciation of the manner in which they have set to work to make themselves efficient.
>
> Although, of course, a good deal remains yet to be done, this division has made more rapid strides towards efficiency than any of the several new formations that I have had under my command during the campaign.
>
> Now that you are about to take over part of oor line I anticipate with confidence that you will dominate the enemy in front of you; that your offensive spirit will be far superior to his; that your patrolling, sniping, trench mortar, bombing, infantry, artillery and engineer work will be better than his, and that with careful reconnaissance work and preparation you will shortly be able to continue the raids on his trenches which have already been carried out with such success by other divisions of the corps.[64]

The division was assigned a number of specialist engineer units to support its work in the line: a bridging section, a siege company, an additional field company and a tunnelling company; and two additional medium trench mortar batteries. With this move into the line, the division's introduction to the war – what Llewelyn Wyn Griffith called 'Prentice Days', can be said to have been completed.

---

*   Later General Sir Richard Cyril Byrne Haking GBE KCB KCMG (1862–1945) is remembered chiefly for the high casualties suffered by his forces, including Australian troops, at the Second Battle of Fromelles (19–20 July 1916), launched as a subsidiary diversion whilst the Somme battle was under way 50 miles (80 kilometres) to the south. He continued to command XI Corps in France and Flanders and in Italy until the end of the war.

Appendix

38th Division's Strength as at 30 November 1915[65]

Note the almost-total dominance of horse-drawn over motorized transport.

Offrs	O.R.s	Horses				Mules	Wagons				MG	Bicycle	Car	m/c	lorry	
		Riding	Draught	Hy Draught	Pack		limber	GS	4 wheel	2 wheel					<3 ton	>3 ton
521	15,212	648	597	188	147	454	165	109	149	102	53	515	34	21	3	3

Notes

1   Emlyn Davies, p. 7.
2   T.N.A. WO 95/2551/1, 113 Brigade War Diary 1–30 November 1915.
3   Peter Robinson, *The Letters of Major General Price-Davies VC CB CMG DSO* (London, 2013).
4   Tim Coates, *Patsy: The Story of Mary Cornwallis-West* (London, 2003).
5   Hughes, p. 38. See also Thomas's biography by David Pretty already cited.
6   Llewelyn Wyn Griffith, 'The Pattern of One Man's Remembering' in *Promise of Greatness* [ed. George A. Panichas], (London, 1968), p. 288.
7   38D/3/1123 No 1723 dated 5 November 1915 in T.N.A. WO 95/2539, 38th Division War Diary 1–30 November 1915.
8   Emlyn Davies, p. 7.
9   Munby, p. 14.
10   Emlyn Davies, p. 6.
11   *Manchester Guardian*, 30 November 1915.
12   David Jones, *In Parenthesis* (London, 1937), p. 7.
13   Llewelyn Wyn Griffith [ed Jonathon Riley], *Up to Mametz … And Beyond* (Barnsley, 2010), p. 4.
14   Emlyn Davies, p. 8.
15   T.N.A. WO 95/881, XI Corps War Diary 1–31 December 1915.
16   T.N.A. WO 95/2539, 38th Division War Diary 1–31 December 1915; Hughes, pp. 46–47; Jones, p. 7.
17   Munby, p. 15.
18   T.N.A. WO 95/2539, 38th Division War Diary 1–31 December 1915.
19   Wyn Griffith, p. 8.
20   Jones, p. 43.
21   Edmonds, Vol I, p. 157–158. See also Bernard Adams, *Nothing of Importance. A Record of Eight Months at the Front with a Welsh Battalion, October 1915 to June 1916* (London, 1917), pp. 107–108.
22   Wyn Griffith, p. 6 fn.
23   Adams, pp. 100–101.
24   Frank Richards, *Old Soldiers Never Die*, annotated by H. J. Krijnen and D. E. Langley, (Peterborough, 2004), p. 45–47, and voice recording in the Royal Welch Fusiliers' Museum (RWF Mus.); Captain J. C. Dunn, *The War the Infantry Knew 1914–1919* (London, 1994), pp. 101–103; C. I. Stockwell's diary and letters, cited in Major C. H. Dudley Ward, *Regimental Records of the Royal Welch Fusiliers*, Vol. III, *1914–1918: France and Flanders* (London, 1928), p. 112–113 and in RWF Mus. 2708; account by Lieutenant M. S. Richardson, dated 31 December 1914, in T.N.A. WO 95/1365, 2 R.W. Fus. War Diary, August-December 1914.
25   'Foes in trenches swap pies for wine', *Daily News*, 1 January 1915.
26   'An historic group', *Daily Mirror*, 1 January 1915, and Leader, 2 January 1915.
27   'Christmas truce at the Front', *Manchester Guardian*, 31 December 1914; 'The amazing truce', *Manchester Guardian*, 4 January 1916; and 'Christmas Day in the trenches', *Manchester Guardian*, 6 January 1915.
28   *Illustrated London News*, 9 January 1915.

29   See, for example, Siegfried Sassoon, 'Fight to a finish', *Cambridge Magazine,* 27 October 1917.

30   Robert Graves, *Goodbye to All That* (London, 1929), p. 296.

31   Sheffield and Bourne, p. 173.

32   See, for example, the signal issued by Major General Sir Charles Barter, GOC 47th Division, cited in Malcolm Brown and Shirley Seaton, *Christmas Truce* (London, 1994), p. 198.

33   Brigadier W. Thwaites, Commander 140 Infantry Brigade, for example, passed on his G.O.C.'s instructions in this way: Brown and Seaton, *Christmas Truce*, p. 198.

34   General Order from G.H.Q. Spa, dated 12 December 1915.

35   John Blacker (ed.), *Have You Forgotten Yet? The First World War Memoirs of C. p. Blacker* (Barnsley, 2000), p. 68.

36   T.N.A. WO 95/2556/1, 15 R.W. Fus. War Diary, 1 December 1915–28 February 1918.

37   Wyn Griffith, p. 13.

38   Hermann Cron, *Imperial German Army 1914–18: Organisation, Structure, Orders-of-Battle* [first published 1937] (Solihull, 2006), pp. 111–116.

39   Wyn Griffith, p. 14.

40   Blacker, p. 75.

41   'Bertie Felstead: the last known survivor of no man's land football died on July 22, 2001 aged 106', *The Economist,* 2 August 2001; 'Last soldier recalls the Christmas truce', *Sunday Telegraph,* 22 December 1996; 'Match of the century', *Daily Mail,* 9 November 1999; Felstead's obituaries in *The Times,* 26, 28 July 2001; *Daily Telegraph,* 26 July 2001.

42   Diary of WO II (C.S.M.) John Bradshaw, held by his grandson, Mr John Griffiths.

43   Wyn Griffith, pp. 14–15.

44   Blacker, pp. 75, 76.

45   Richard Alleyne, 'Veteran of 1915 soccer game dies', *Daily Telegraph,* 26 July 2001; Bertie Felstead, 'Football made us friends for a day', *Western Mail,* 12 November 1999.

46   Dilworth, p. 71–72.

47   David Jones, *The Anathemata* (London, 1951), p. 216.

48   *Reichsarchiv Militär-Verlag* (Berlin, 1927), S. 71, p. 146–147.

49   Robert Keating's Diary, vol. 1, 1 December 1915–6 July 1916, RWF Mus. 9203.

50   Sir Iain Colquhoun's diary has been made available on open source through his local historical society, the Vale of Leven: Sir Iain Colquhoun's Diary <www.valeofleven.org.uk> (Accessed 20 November 2015).

51   Wyn Griffith, p. 14.

52   Letter from Harold Diffey in RWF Mus. 7133f.

53   Keating's Diary, vol. 1.

54   Keating's Diary, vol. 1.

55   Keating's Diary, vol. 1.

56   Colquhoun's Diary.

57   Brown and Seaton, p. 205.

58   'Letter to Friends in North Wales', in *Wrexham Advertiser,* 9 January 1915. See also 'Nadoligyn y ffosydd', *Y Dinesydd Cymreig,* 13 January 1915.

59   T.N.A. WO 95/2539, 38th Division War Diary 1–31 January 1916.

60   T.N.A. WO 95/881, XI Corps War Diary 1–31 January 1916.

61   Graves, p. 114.

62   T.N.A. WO 95/2551/1, 113 Brigade War Diary 1–31 January 1916.

63   T.N.A. WO 95/2560/1, 115 Brigade War Diary 31 December 1915.

64   T.N.A. WO 95/2539, 38th Division War Diary 1–31 January 1916.

65   T.N.A. WO 95/2539, 38th Division War Diary 1–30 November 1915, Appendix II.

6

In the Line: The 38th (Welsh) Division from February to July 1916

On 7 January 1916, the 38th (Welsh) Division took over the Neuve Chapelle sector of the line from the 19th Division and from this time until the beginning of June it was continually in the line holding, in turn, every portion of the XI Corps' line from Givenchy in the south to Picantin in the north.[1] The War Diary of 14 R.W. Fus gives a taste of the rotation between units in and out of the line:

> Feb. 8. Relieved by 10th Welsh Regiment. Billets La Croix Marmuse.
> Feb 17. Marched to Gorre via Vielle Chapelle and Lacouture.
> Feb 21. Relieved 13th Bn. R.W.F. in front line, Givenchy
> Mar. 7. Marched to billets in Les Harrisoirs.
> Mar. 16. Took over trenches and islands at Festubert from 11th Bn. S.W.B.[2]

During the winter there was nothing in the way of major operations and for the most part, life in the trenches was one of boring, hard, uncomfortable drudgery interspersed with periods behind the line in billets. Llewelyn Wyn Griffith, now a Captain commanding a company, recalled that:

> There was always something to be done, involving a movement and a standing about. Digging, filling sandbags, building, carrying stores and ammunition, repairing the walls damaged by shell fire, scheming against the insidious attack of water, strengthening the barbed wire, resetting the duckboards…
>
> Across No Man's Land there were men sharing trouble with us, fighting the same losing battle against water, powerless before the sudden storm of bursting metal, and longing to be home again with their children.[3]

Wyn Griffith also recalled, like many others, the fact that the British lines seemed always to be below those of the Germans, as noted in Chapter 3: 'Wherever we stood in a trench, the Germans were above us, looking down from some ridge upon our amateurish struggles on the plain.'[4] The results of this were that all movement could be seen, as he noted when his battalion moved into the Richebourg St Vaast sector:

The enemy had in all probability observed our march. Or our entry into the village, and for an hour we were heavily shelled. A shell-burst, even in the soft mud of the trenches, seemed the greatest noise on earth, but when I heard a succession of "five-nines" hitting these houses I plumbed depths of terror hitherto undiscovered by me. I found it hard to maintain an appearance of unconcern while these monsters were stealing out of the silence into a hiss and a burst, reverberating in a rumble that lingered for some time as if it were loath to cease its echoing.[5]

One long entry in the Divisional War Diary recorded observations made of the Germans, who were believed to be from the 55th Guards Reserve Regiment – in fact they belonged to the 55th Westphalian Reserve Infantry Regiment, one of the regiments of the 2nd Guards Reserve Division (hence the confusion) and assigned to X Corps. German soldiers called out several times in good English asking who was opposite them. One German officer:

Was observed through a telescope to come up and speak to a man near point 95 [not identified but close to the area known as the Boar's Head, immediately south of Richebourg l'Avoué]. This officer wore a coat closed up at the throat and had a high straight collar. His cap was shaped like ours and was blue in colour with a red band round it.* His face was very pale, but he looked particularly clean.[6]

A German officer in the sort of uniform described in the scene at Richebourg l'Avoué.
(James Payne collections)

---

*   The standard *schirmmütze*, or cap, and uniform of the German Army officer at the time.

Map 6.i A contemporary trench map of the Neuve Chapelle sector.

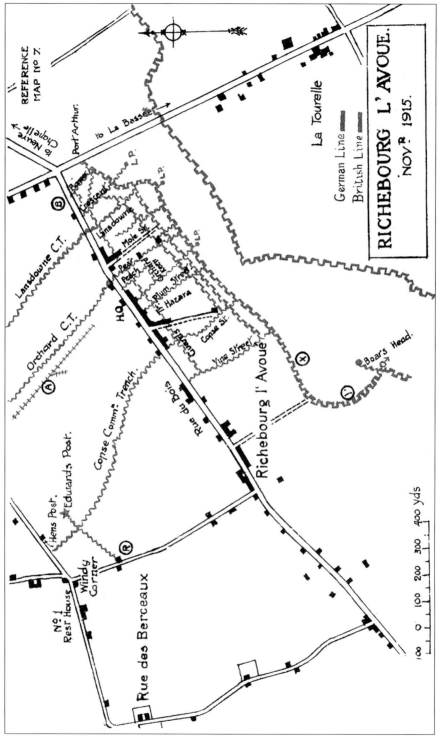

Map 6.ii A sketch showing the area around Richebourg l'Avoué, described in the report above.

In February, the British Guards Division was transferred to the Second Army. The 19th Division replaced it in the line and the 35th, another New Army Division, joined XI Corps. At the same time, as part of the extension of the British sector, the whole corps moved south and the 38th Division took over the line around Festubert. Here in March there was a great deal of flooding, which even the laconic letters of Brigadier General Price-Davies describe.[7] The front line consisted not of a trench, but a series of fortified posts known as 'islands', held by one or two sections. Dug-outs and shelters did not exist, communication trenches were flooded and as the German line was no more than 200 yards away, any movement in daylight was suicidal. Further back was a support line and further back again, the old British front line of 1915. Wyn Griffith described this in detail:

> This trench was wet and ill-built; there were but few fire-bays where the water was not ankle-deep above the duckboards, and in most parts, it was knee-deep... Our artillery bombarded the enemy's wire, his artillery shelled our trenches in retaliation: our guns, regarding this as an insult, doubled their fury, and the enemy responded to the challenge. The infantry sat and suffered, cursing all artillery, allied or enemy.[8]

These conditions meant a steady stream of casualties. The 14 R.W. Fus War Diary, for example, records on 9 April that casualties to date had been 27 killed or died of wounds and disease; 73 wounded and sick evacuated to Britain – that is, around 10% of the battalion's strength without any sort of major action.[9] 14 Welsh received drafts of 100 officers and men in both April and May,[10] which if transposed across the whole division would have amounted to a turn-over of 1,000 men per month for the whole division – underlining why the War Office had been so insistent on the creation of reserve units.

Four drawings by David Jones of front-line trench conditions in the early months of 1916. (RWF Mus 2998b)

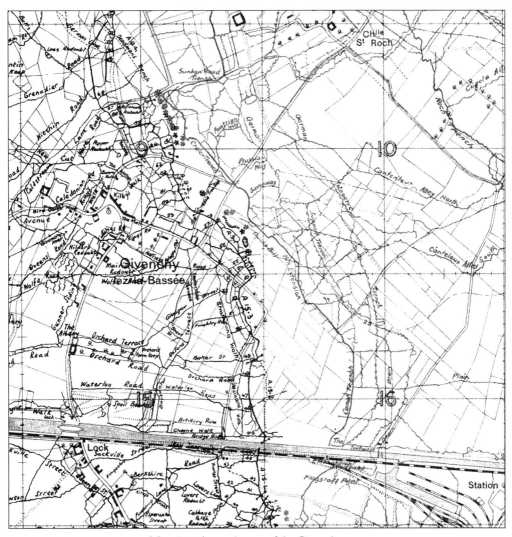

Map 6.iii A trench map of the Givenchy area.

Wyn Griffith recorded how one night a heavy trench mortar was set up and at dawn fired its bomb. 'A stutter of terrific detonations seemed to shake the air and the ground, sandbags and bits of timber sailed up slowly and fell in a calm deliberate way. In the silence that followed the explosions, an angry voice called out in English, across No Man's Land, "YOU BLOODY WELSH MURDERERS."'[11]

Some weeks later, the corps absorbed 33rd Division, again extending its frontage southwards to Auchy. The 38th Division therefore moved south. In this sector, which was extremely wet and low-lying, Givenchy had a particularly bad reputation, recalled by many commentators including not only Wyn Griffith, but also Robert Graves, Siegfried Sassoon, James Dunn and Emlyn Davies. There was constant mining, mortaring and sniping and the place seemed under a curse as there were casualties on every tour of frontline duty. Bill Tucker described the frequency of mines:

> … with unnerving suddenness, a square mile of earth would rock and convulse, followed by a deafening and prolonged roar. If it were night time – and because of its more shat-tering effects on the senses, it usually was – that roar was accompanied by vivid red flashed and stabs. In their glare scores of sandbags could be seen hurtling upwards and returning earthwards; bodies as well![12]

The divisional history records little note to record during the period except for the constant demands of the divisional and corps commanders to gain and maintain ascendency over the Germans and domination of No Man's Land by patrols and raids. David Jones famously recorded his impression of meeting a German patrol at night in No Man's Land in *In Parenthesis:*

> The thudding and breath to breath you don't know which way, what way, you count eight of him in a flare-space, you can't find the lane – the one way – you rabbit to and fro, you could cry… We maintain ascendency in no-man's-land.[13]

16 Welsh recorded a typical raid on 8 April near Givenchy:

> A raid was attempted against a hostile Machine Gun Emplacement… The wire cutting party completed its task and succeeding in planting a 'torpedo' [i.e. a Bangalore Torpedo] in position. Unfortunately, at the last moment the raiding party was discovered. Machine gun and rifle fire being turned upon them making it necessary to retire. 2nd Lieutenant O.M. Williams* missing and wounded. 1 man wounded and missing, believed dead, 3 men wounded.[14]

The Divisional H.Q. recorded the most successful of these raids as being mounted by 15 R.W. Fus on the night of 7/8 May and it was mentioned in G.H.Q. despatches as the third best raid yet carried out by any unit in the B.E.F.[15] This raid took place at Laventie, where only a few months before, the Second Christmas Truce had taken place. The raiding party was under the command of Captain Goronwy Owen and while in No Man's Land, it encountered a German wiring party just finishing their work. According to the official account, Owen changed his plan

---

* Oswald Morgan Williams (1897–1916) has no known grave. He had, however, discarded his identity disks and assumed the uniform of an enlisted man for the raid.

and followed the Germans back to their lines, attacking them as they entered their trenches and killing 'about 60' of them.[16] The War Diary's account says that:

> The Germans stood sandwiched together, some without equipment and arms, which seems to show that they did not constitute the ordinary garrison of the trench… some bombers on the parapet started to bomb successive bays to right and left from the ditch, outside the parapet… At one point a general rush was made by the occupants of a bay to a bomb store but before they could secure any bombs… they were put out of action by our leading bobers.[17]

Price-Davies recorded that: 'Raiding party gets into German trenches at 1.30 a.m. & inflicts much loss on the Germans. They unfortunately lose 2 officers, Osbourne Jones & Taggart otherwise the casualties were slight.' There were in fact four killed and 10 wounded. Herbert Taggart, aged 22, came from the Isle of Man and was killed as the raiding party withdrew. Noel Osborne-Jones was only 21 and from a Cardigan family. For many years, the bodies of the two officers and Private L. Grove were missing, however in December 2017, the researcher Lars Ahlkvist identified them as having been buried in Fournes-de-Weppes German Cemetery and subsequently relocated to Cabaret Rouge British Cemetery. Owen was awarded the DSO for this exploit; Corporal D.W. Bloor and Privates P.F. Witten and J. Heeson received the DCM; Sergeant G.P. Jones, Corporal F.T. Rosser and Privates F. Langdon and I. Downes were decorated with the MM, Downes' award being posthumous.[18]

Second Lieutenant Noel Osbourne-Jones, killed on the night of 7/8 May 1916.

A personal view of the story, recounted by Llewelyn Wyn Griffith who was on the spot, is rather different:

> It grew dark, and it was time to begin cutting lanes in our wire in front of the point of departure of the raiding party. Our artillery had been engaged during the day in cutting the enemy's wire, lest he should have any doubt about where we proposed to attack him … Soon there began a trickle of men into the trench, with blackened faces and hands, carrying weird weapons… They formed a line in No Man's Land, crawling slowly towards the gaps in the enemy wire. Last of all, the officer in command took with him a field telephone on which he could buzz signals back to the artillery liaison officer in the front line. After an eternity of waiting, a buzz announced that the reconnaissance of the wire proved it to be passable, another buzz told us that the party was assembled and ready for the assault …
>
> Zero, a buzz, and then a wild tornado of shellfire. They were off on their journey, inside this three-walled screen of flame. We knew that before many seconds the enemy would add a fourth wall of fire to this screen, and that his wall would rest with its foundation on our trench … We could, however, hear the bursting of bombs thrown by our own men, and we took heart at the sound; they must now be in conflict hand-to-hand … our men began

to trickle back to our line – some of them, for many never came back. We could get no coherent account of what had happened, but it was clear that their visit was not unexpected. Two officers did not return … we had paid dearly for the assault – no prisoner, dead, or alive, came into our hands… In the evening we heard a shout from No Man's Land, and I sent out a patrol to investigate: they brought back one of our men, slightly wounded…[19]

If this was the third most successful raid to be carried out up to this point by the B.E.F., one dreads to think what the less successful ones had been like. A few days later, on 16 May, Lieutenant Colonel Frank Gaskell, who had raised 16 Welsh in Cardiff, was badly wounded while going out to a forward post in a shell-crater in No Man's Land; he died the following day.[20] Smith was succeeded in command by his Second-in-Command, Frank Smith. Smith was an Inspector in the Glamorgan Constabulary, a trooper in the Glamorgan Yeomanry, a noted rugby player for Cardiff, and a veteran of the Matabele campaign and the South African War, where he had won the DCM. Around the same time, 10 Welsh managed in a single night to dig a sap half-way across No Man's Land, known as the Rhondda sap, which was used a month later by the Australians as the launch point for an attack during the battle of Fromelles, which resulted in bloody failure.[21]

The Corps Commander then made plans for a series of simultaneous raids on 3/4 June but was told by First Army Headquarters that he should not stir up the German line too much but could mount raids as he 'considered desirable from time to time.'[22] Three raids were mounted in quick succession. The raid by 14 R.W. Fus on 4 June in the Moated Grange sector near Neuve Chapelle was successful but the War Dairy records only that 'The late Capt. H.P. Williams and 60 others attacked enemy trenches. Casualties: three officers and 31 other ranks.'[23] Hugh Powell Williams was 33 years old and a native of Criccieth. His brother Hywel was also killed. A raid by 14 Welsh was also successful, but the third, by 10 Welsh, was stopped on the German wire with three men killed, and all the remaining four officers and 10 men wounded for no result.[24]

Another hazard with which the men became familiar was lice, as Bill Tucker reconted:

Our heads were never free, because hair harboured its own specie of lice which laughed at hot water, brushes or any other supposed onslaught… All places where men gathered were infected. the trench dugouts were particularly lousy … The old farm barns just behind the lines that served as billets for the troops during "rest" periods were equally lousy. Men would sit on the straw covered barn floor, with their backs to the wall, playing lighted candles around the lice-clusters in the seams of their tunic collars. At first it seemed that the misery of having to tolerate these pests was limited to the perpetual biting, itching and scratching. But it later became painfully evident that lice were the cause of more sinister effects… For want of better identification they called it Trench Fever… It lasted just five days – in fact the Germans called it the "Five Day fever."[25]

Mites, fleas, rats, mice and flies were also ever-present and to these was added the dangers of trench foot, caused by standing for days at a time in cold wet conditions; or stomach upsets. Bill Tucker also recounted the dangers of venereal disease: one whore-house in Béthune boasted that: 'The average lady on its staff was said to "service" a battalion of clients (about 1,000 men) before "retiring pale but proud."[26]

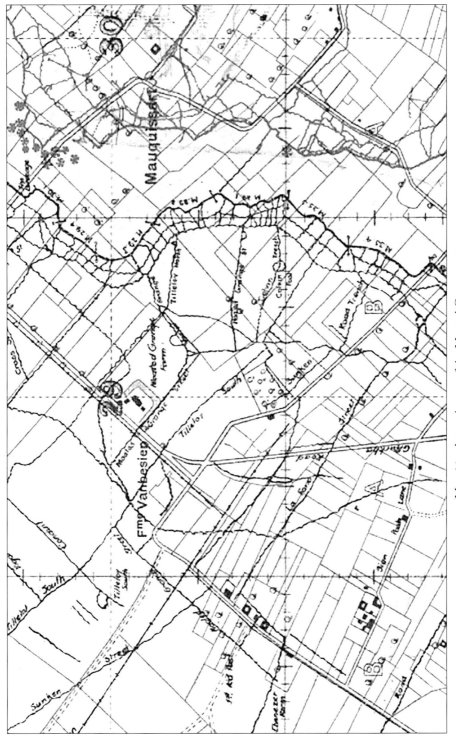

Map 6.iv A trench map of the Moated Grange sector.

The problem of rats was not confined to the British lines: a photograph of German soldiers dealing with the same problem.

David Jones recalled another feature of trench life: the stink: 'the unpleasant smell' of the 'bluish grey slime' covering the ground was worsened by the smell of latrines, mildew, damp, cordite, wood-smoke, the sweat of unwashed men, the whale oil used to dress the men's feet against trench foot and above all, the stench of rotting corpses – be they mules or men – hastily buried and often disinterred by the effects of shell fire.[27] At least from April onwards the weather improved. However, brigades in reserve did little in the way of training: time was spent on fatigues, working parties and drill apart from specialists, such as trench mortar, machine-gun or gas companies. It was not until the end of May that instructions came down for battalion and brigade training, and by that time the Somme offensive was close.[28]

Then, on 10 June while holding the line with two brigades and the divisional artillery near Neuve Chapelle, orders were received that the 38th Division should move south to prepare for the coming Somme battle. On 11 June the division handed over its duties to the newly-arrived 61st Division and began the move. Llewelyn Wyn Griffith recalled:

> For some reason unexplained to us, we marched through the heat of the June day, and after seven months of trench warfare we found the early stages troublesome until our feet were hardened… The marching in good air was leaving its mark on us all, and we were gaining a release from the humiliating burden of mud that had clogged our pores and had turned our thoughts into greyness.
>
> A month ago, the Company was a disintegrated body of men, tired and dull, dragging the day into the night and the night into the day, with a horizon bounded on all sides by that damnable, evil-smelling and unnatural soil. Now we were above ground, welded into a free-moving unit, handling its arms with its old vigour and precision, no longer "climbing up the rifle to the slope." It was strangely easy to forget that this revival would be of short duration to most of us.[29]

For two weeks a concentration area was occupied east of St Pol where training was carried out to prepare the officers and men for the great attack. Here, the division joined XVII Corps in Third Army. The training included a full trench-to-trench attack in various different permutations, since because the division was in reserve, the exact ground over which it might assault the enemy was not yet known.[30] Training in exploiting a break-through was also stressed:

> Divisions must, therefore, be practised in the passing of a fresh body of attacking troops through the troops which have carried out the first assault and have reached their objective. The second attack will be carried out on the same principles, the assaulting columns going straight through to the objective in successive lines.[31]

Training exercises were carefully planned with every unit given a defined objective and detailed orders. It was really the first time that brigade staffs had had the chance to control the movement of two or more battalions in concert with artillery, machine guns and trench mortars; and in effecting a passage of lines of one battalion through another. As exercises progressed, elements of the unexpected were introduced without warning and until the problem was solved, units concerned would be held up and awarded casualties by the umpires. Many valuable lessons were learned, not least the importance of maintaining communications with the artillery.[32]

The next move south, on 26 June, took the division to Rubempre where it joined II Corps in the Fifth Army, under the command of Lieutenant General Sir Claude Jacob.[*] The corps was in army reserve and verbal orders were received to the effect that the division was to be prepared to follow the cavalry in the event of a break-through and to take over Bapaume. The division was to be at six hours' notice to move.[33] Fusilier W.R. Thomas, a signaller with 14 R.W. Fus, recalled that the move took place by night:

> We would fall in ready for the off at dusk so that we would not be observed by aerial activity. We would move away arriving in billets or old barns, outhouses, hayricks etc, in the small hours of the dawn and be safely tucked away for the rest of the day so that no-one could see us. Thus did we move towards our final destination, the Somme, in about 10 days of night marching. Merry and cheerful lads but little did they think at the time that many of them… would be making the supreme sacrifice.[34]

The failure to make significant progress in the early period of the Somme battle changed these orders, however, and the division marched first north to Acheux and then back south to Treux where it joined XV Corps under Lieutenant General Sir Henry Horne. Price-Davies recorded that: 'Yesterday we motored across the old front line & the Bosche old front line & support then we walked into Mametz. Everything was perfectly quiet & though the Bosche should have been able to overlook everything, there was a great deal of traffic all over the country.'[35]

Immediately before the move, there were some rapid changes in command, most notably Lieutenant Colonel Davies in 14 R.W. Fus. According to Major G.P.L. Drake-Brockman's

---

[*]   Later Field Marshal Sir Claude William Jacob GCB GCSI KCMG (1863–1948). He remained in command of II Corps throughout the Somme and Third Ypres campaigns. After the War he commanded a corps of the British Army of the Rhine during the occupation and then served as Chief of the General Staff in India.

account, Davies (whom he mistakenly assigned to 16 R.W. Fus) was 'a politician pure and simple who knew nothing about soldiering before the war; his chief claim to fame was that he had subscribed much money to Mr Lloyd George's Liberal party fund.'[36] Davies had been recalled to England from his command at the urgent request of Lloyd George, just before going into action on the Somme. Drake-Brockman wrote that: 'There can only be one reason for the recall of [Davies and two other officers] and it was certainly a widespread impression in 38th Division at the time – namely that from a political point of view their lives were too valuable to be lost.'[37] Actually, Drake-Brockman is only half right, for Lloyd George had been appointed Secretary of State for War, following the death of Lord Kitchener; he was to take office on 7 July, coincidentally the day that the 38th Division was to go into action, and had chosen Davies as his Parliamentary Private Secretary.[38] Whether this was for the reasons Drake-Brockman stated, or in order to save Davies's life, remains unclear; however the impression on the officers and men of the division cannot have been a good one. He was succeeded by his Senior Major, Graham Gwyther, who had to take over command at short notice and on the eve of battle.

On 5 July, Philipps had a Special Order of the Day read to every soldier in the division on parade:

> You have worked hard for many months with an energy and zeal beyond praise to fit your-selves for the task you have voluntarily undertaken. You have undergone the hardships of a winter campaign with fortitude. You have earned the praise of your Corps Commanders for your courage, discipline and devotion to duty. You have now held for six months a section of the British line in France, during which time you have not allowed one of the enemy to enter your trenches except as a prisoner; and on several occasions you have entered the enemy's lines. 11 Officers and 44 N.C.O.s and men have already received awards from the King for gallant and distinguished conduct in the field. Your fellow countrymen at home are following your career with interest and admiration. I always believed that a really Welsh Division would be second to none. You have more than justified that belief. I feel that whatever the future may have in store for us I can rely upon you, because you have already given ample proof of your worth. During the short period in the Training Area you worked hard to qualify yourselves for still further efforts. I thank you most sincerely for the loyal and wholehearted way in which each one of you has done his utmost to carry out the task allotted to him. With such a spirit animating all ranks we can one and all look forward with confidence to the future, whatever it may have in store for us.
>
> You are today relieving the 7th Division, which has attacked and captured German trenches on a front of a little less than one mile and for a depth of about one and a half miles. In this attack the village of Mametz was captured, the enemy suffered very heavy casualties, 1,500 German officers and men were taken prisoners and six field guns were captured.
>
> The 1st Battalion, Royal Welsh Fusiliers and the 1st Battalion, Welsh Regiment of the 7th Division have both distinguished themselves in this attack,[*] and I am confident that the young battalions of the famous Welsh regiments serving in the 38th (Welsh) Division

---

[*]   Why Philipps should have said that 1 Welsh was in the 7th Division remains unclear. This battalion, serving in Salonika at the time, was never in its order of battle.

will maintain the high standard for valour for which all three Welsh Regiments have been renowned throughout the war.[39]

That same day, the division relieved the 7th Division about the village of Mametz and was ordered to prepare for the capture of Mametz Wood. It is now necessary, therefore, to step back and recount what had happened to cause Lloyd George's men to go to Mametz and in particular, to look at the role of other Welsh battalions in those opening days.

Notes

1   Munby, p. 15.
2   14 R.W. Fus War Diary, printed by Gale and Polden, 1920, p. 4.
3   Wyn Griffith, p. 26.
4   Wyn Griffith, p. 28.
5   Wyn Griffith, pp. 18–19.
6   Tactical Progress Report No 7 in T.N.A. WO 95/2539, 38th (Welsh) Division War Diary, January 1916.
7   Price-Davies, pp. 91–92.
8   Wyn Griffith, pp. 20–21.
9   14 R.W. Fus War Diary, p. 4.
10   T.N.A. WO 95/2559, 14 Welsh War Diary 1916.
11   Wyn Griffith, p. 21.
12   Tucker, p. 27.
13   Jones, *In Parenthesis*, p. 71.
14   T.N.A. WO 95/2561/3, 16 Welsh War Diary, April 1916.
15   Munby, p. 15.
16   *A Concise History of the 15th R.W.F, (1st London Welsh)* (Privately published, 1925), p. 7.
17   T.N.A. WO 95/2539, 38th (Welsh) Division War Diary.
18   *Concise History of the 15th R.W.F*, p. 7.
19   Wyn Griffith, pp. 58–60.
20   T.N.A. WO 95/2561/3, 16 Welsh War Diary, May 1916.
21   Hughes, p. 59.
22   T.N.A. WO 95/881, XI Corps War Diary.
23   14 R.W. Fus War Diary, p. 4.
24   T.N.A. WO 95/2539, 38th (Welsh) Division War Diary.
25   Tucker, pp. 22–23.
26   Tucker, p. 26.
27   Dilworth, *David Jones in the Great War*, p. 69.
28   T.N.A. WO 95/2539, 38th (Welsh) Division War Diary; T.N.A. WO 95/881, XI Corps War Diary.
29   Wyn Griffith, pp. 85–87.
30   Munby, p. 16.
31   Edmonds, Appendices to Vol. I, p. 125, 'Training of Divisions for Offensive Operations'.
32   T.N.A. WO 95/2539, 38th (Welsh) Division War Diary.
33   T.N.A. WO 95/2539, 38th (Welsh) Division War Diary.
34   'Notes on the 1914–18 War by Regimental Signaller W.R. Thomas Reg. No. 20214 on active service with the 14th and 1st Bns. The Royal Welch Fusiliers (38th & 7th Divisions)' in RWF Mus/Archives, p. 50.
35   Price-Davies, p. 107.
36   T.N.A. CAB 45/189, letter from Major G.P.L. Drake-Brockman dated 7 February 1930 with attachments.
37   T.N.A. CAB 45/189, letter from Drake-Brockman.
38   *The Times*, 11 July 1916.
39   T.N.A. WO 95/2539, 38th (Welsh) Division War Diary.

7

'The place was a ruin before, now it is a dust-heap': The First Assault at Mametz: 1–5 July 1916

The area around Mametz, in the south of the Fourth Army sector, was assigned to XV Corps with two divisions, the 7th and 21st. It was given three successive tasks: on the first day, to capture the German defences as far as Mametz Wood in co-ordination with XIII Corps to the right at Montauban and III Corps to the left at Contalmaison; secondly and subsequently, to pivot on XIII Corps and take Bazentin-le-Grand; and thirdly to capture Ginchy, Longueval and Delville Wood. Each objective was to be consolidated when secured and preparations put in place for subsequent phases. The initial main effort of the corps was thus north and south of the village and wood of Fricourt, to secure the triangle formed by these features which would be cleared later by a subsidiary operation. The junction of the two divisions was to be at Willow Avenue with the 21st Division prolonging the line northwards towards Contalmaison.[1]

Within the 7th Division, its three brigades were 91, on the right; 22 in the centre; and 20 on the right. 91 Brigade was to be on the main effort and was to advance in three phases, or waves, through Mametz village while 20 Brigade formed a defensive flank from the north-eastern outskirts of Mametz, down Orchard Alley trench to its junction with Apple Alley and then on into the front line. 22 Brigade was to wait until ordered forward and then clear the German trenches north of the Bois Français in conjunction with 50 Infantry Brigade on its left, which was to clear Fricourt village and Fricourt Wood.[2]

The ground here was typical of the Somme battlefield generally: open chalk down-land inter-spersed with woods and villages; however, the Germans recognised that this part of the line running eastwards towards Montauban was geographically weaker than elsewhere, with fewer mutually supporting spurs.

The principal woods were Fricourt and Mametz, with smaller copses such as Bottom Wood, Shelter Wood, Railway Copse and Hidden Wood. Between the two villages of Fricourt and Mametz were several farms which had been developed into strong-points by the Germans, and a network of rough roads and light railway lines. The German defenders of the area were men of the 28th Reserve Infantry Division, part of the XIV Reserve Corps. On the German left, facing 91 Brigade, was the 109th Reserve Infantry Regiment (109 R.I.R.); in the centre, facing both 20 and 22 Brigades was the 111th Reserve Infantry Regiment (111 R.I.R.); and on the right, 110th Reserve Infantry Regiment (110 R.I.R.). In the Second Line was the 16th Bavarian Infantry Regiment.

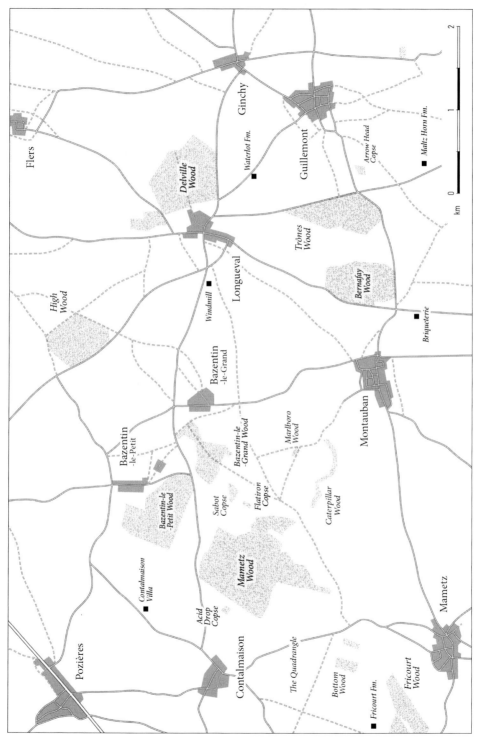

Map 7.i The area of assault between Mametz and Trônes Woods.

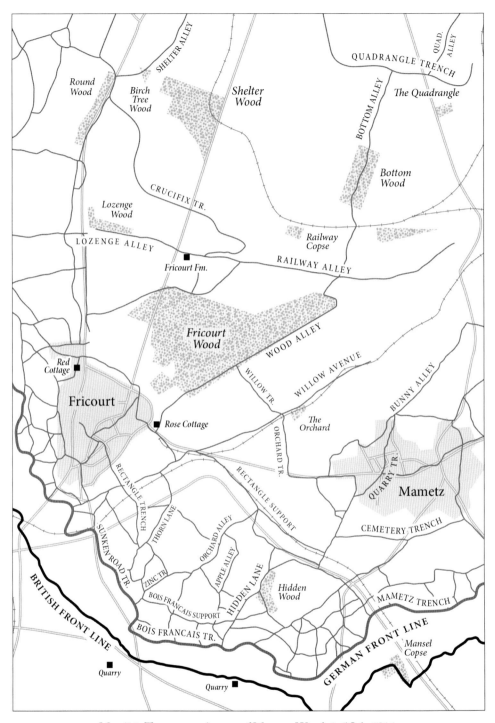

Map 7.ii The area south-west of Mametz Wood, 1–5 July 1916.

A German sketch of the positions of the 16th Bavarian Infantry Regiment in the Second Line and its failed counter-attack on 1 July 1916. (16th Bavarian Regimental History)

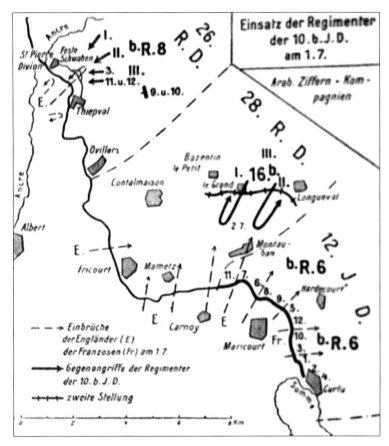

Bernard Adams, who served with 1 R.W. Fus in the area until he was wounded in June 1916, recorded his impressions in his memoir *Nothing of Importance*:

The high ground between the Ancre and the Somme forms a long tableland. There is no ridge, it is just a high flat country, from 330 to 340 feet [100 to 103 metres], cultivated and hedgeless ... from Thiepval down to Fricourt [the trenches] run almost due north and south; then they run up out of the valley onto the high ground at Bois Français (a small copse, I suppose, once; I have never discovered any vestige of a tree-stump among the shell-holes), and then abruptly run due east. It is as though someone had appeared suddenly on the corner of the shoulder... and pushed them off ... It is obvious that if you are at Bois Français, and you look north, you have an uninterrupted view not only of both front lines running down into Fricourt valley, but of both lines running on to the high ground north of Fricourt, and a very fine view indeed of Fricourt itself, and Fricourt wood. It is also quite clear that from their front lines running up onto the high ground north of Fricourt the Germans had a good view of *our* front lines and communications in the valley; but of Bois Français and our trenches east of it they had no enfilade view, as all our communications were on the reverse slope of this shoulder of high ground. So as regards observation

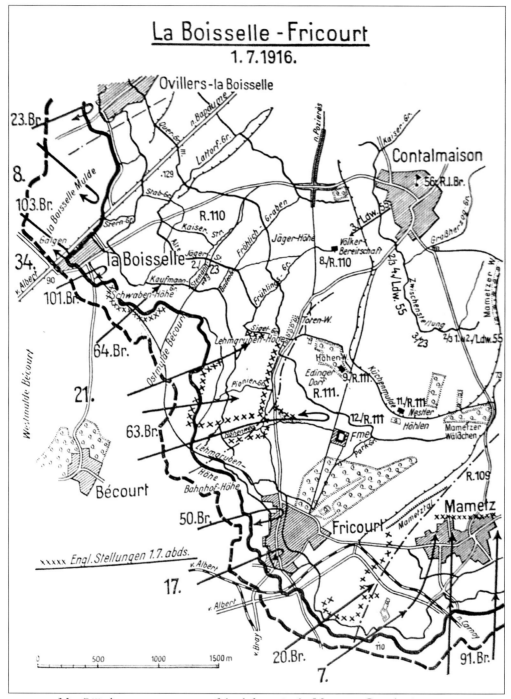

Map 7.iii A contemporary map of the defences in the Mametz – Contalmaison area.
(Source: *German Official History Somme–Nord*)

we were best off. Moreover, whereas they could not possibly see our support lines and communications at Bois Français, we could get a certain amount of enfilade observation of their trenches …[3]

Thus we come to the first Welsh involvement in the battles around Mametz: not the 38th Division, but a pre-war, Regular battalion – the 1st Royal Welsh Fusiliers (1 R.W. Fus). In the period immediately before the Somme offensive, the battalion – whose brutal experiences and losses in 1914 have already been mentioned – had been commanded by Lieutenant Colonel John Minshull Ford, known as 'Scatter'. Minshull Ford was 35 at the time of the Somme offensive. He had been in the Army since 1900 and before the War had served with the Regiment in China and at home. He spoke fluent French and at the outbreak of War had been a Captain serving with the 4th (Denbighshire) battalion as Adjutant; this was one of the first T.F. Battalions to serve in France. After the heavy casualties of 1914 there were many gaps to be filled in the rapidly expanding Army and Regular Officers were in great demand. In June 1915 he went to a staff appointment as Brigade Major and from there in October, as a temporary Lieutenant Colonel, to command 1 R.W. Fus. By the time he took command of the battalion he had already been wounded, awarded the Military Cross for bravery and been mentioned in despatches three times.[4]

Lieutenant Colonel (later Major General) John Minshull Ford. (NPG X154642)

The 1 R.W. Fus was one of the battalions of 22 Infantry Brigade in the 7th Division, along with 2 Royal Irish, 2 Royal Warwicks and 20 Manchesters – the first two being also Regular battalions and the last being a New Army unit. As a result of his experiences, Scatter had developed some firm ideas about how an infantry battalion should be organised, trained and equipped to deal with the problems of trench warfare. In place of the standard order of battle, 1 R.W. Fus was organised into a command post; four assault infantry companies; a bombing – or Grenadier – company of four platoons and the *Lewis* Gun section of four guns (the *Vickers* had been removed to brigade M.G. Companies); a Regimental Aid Post (R.A.P.); and the Quartermaster's stores and transport. To enter and capture German trenches, the assault companies were trained to find gaps in the enemy wire and, under covering fire, enter the position. Once a foothold, or footholds, had been established, the bombers would follow quickly and clear left and right along the enemy trenches, moving from traverse to traverse using these as cover, and paying special attention to dugouts: 'bombing along', in fact. Once the objective was clear, it would be secured by the assault companies who would establish blocks to prevent the Germans re-infiltrating, and the *Lewis* Guns would be brought up to reinforce them. Within each company there were

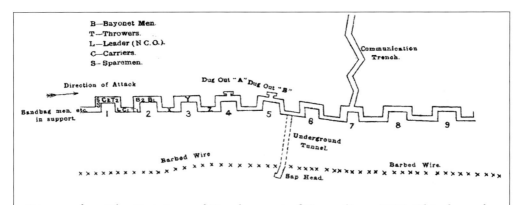

Diagram from The Training and Employment of Grenadiers, *1915. This shows the latest tactics by means of which a 'grenadier party' worked its way down a trench throwing grenades ahead of them. 'Bayonet men' in the lead were followed by dedicated 'throwers' and 'carriers'.*

A diagram showing the method of training and organising bombers for trench clearance.

dedicated carriers who did nothing but bring up fresh supplies of ammunition, and stretcher bearers from the R.A.P. Intensive tactical training and instruction on the use of the *Lewis* gun, the rifle grenade and the *Mills* bomb went on whenever the battalion was out of the line, for co-operation in the use of these weapons was essential.[5] This scheme of organisation and tactics was to prove highly successful and, widely adopted, would be the basis of the 1917 revision of organisation and tactics throughout the whole Army.

In February 1916, after only five months in command of the battalion, Scatter was promoted to the temporary rank of Brigadier General and took command of 91 Infantry Brigade, also in the 7th Division, where he began to introduce his ideas on organisation and tactics more widely with the approval of the Divisional Commander, Major General Herbert Watts.[*] He was succeeded in command of 1 R.W. Fus

Major General Herbert Watts, G.O.C. 7th Infantry Division, 1916.

---

[*]   Later Lieutenant–General Sir Herbert Edward Watts KCB KCMG (1858–1934), a veteran of the South African War 1899–1902. He later commanded XIX Corps in France.

by Lieutenant Colonel Clifton Stockwell, who had been born in 1879 and was commissioned in 1899; he was, as it happened, a fluent German speaker and as has already been mentioned, had been a company commander in 2 R.W. Fus at the time of the 1914 Christmas Truce. He ended the war as a Brigadier General and was by all accounts tough, at times unpleasant to deal with, brave but very fair. He was given the nickname 'Buffalo Bill' as reported by Robert Graves and referred to as 'Kinjack' in Siegfried Sassoon's *Memoirs of an Infantry Officer*.[6]

Stockwell recorded the events leading up to the attack on 1 July in his diary:

Lieutenant Colonel Clifton Stockwell.
(Major Miles Stockwell)

> *28th June.* – A filthy wet morning. Saw General Watts... Everyone full of beans. 11.30 a.m. – A last conference of officers. 1 p.m. – Order for the brigade to stand fast. 2 p.m. – Ordered up to the trenches to relieve the Manchesters and Borderers [*N.B.* the 20th Manchesters on the left of 22 Brigade and the 2nd Border Regiment on the right of 20 Brigade]. Everyone very bored – show off for 48 hours – no one quite knows why. [*N.B.*, this was the postponement agreed at high level due to bad weather as discussed in Chapter 4]. Relief completed at 1 a.m. Devil's own bombardment going on.
>
> *29th June.* – We move to our battle positions this morning, everyone in his proper place by about 3 p.m. All the officers in reserve under [Captain William] Holmes* have gone back... Our battle headquarters are good and safe. The 20th Manchesters, who are to assault, are in front of us; we are to support them... The bombardment has been terrific – a huge expenditure of ammunition. If all goes well we ought to break the Hun line to a depth of a mile or more the first day, taking the first two lines of defence.[7]

On 1 July, Stockwell recorded that unlike the bad weather of the previous days, it was 'a heavenly morning'. The battalion was awake, fed and standing-to soon after 05.00 hrs. At 06.45 hrs, the bombardment rose to a colossal intensity of noise and concussion: 'a continuous soughing of shells overhead'. 580 guns were firing in support of XV Corps along with several hundred trench mortars on a front of about two miles. The sensation in the British front line must have been seismic – never mind what the Germans were feeling even in their deep dugouts.

German feelings were in fact mixed depending on where the recipients of the bombardment were located. 110 and 111 R.I.R. both suffered badly from the bombardment, to the extent that

---

*   Later Lieutenant General Sir William Holmes KBE DSO• (1892–1969), G.O.C.-in-C Ninth Army during the Second World War. A certain percentage of officers was deliberately left out of battle during major offensive operations, in case of the need to reconstitute a unit after heavy losses.

A British mine being
blown before the
assault on 1 July 1916.

The ground in front of Mametz before the attack on 1 July 1916.

German prisoners from the 28th Reserve Infantry Division being escorted to the rear by British troops.

Oberst Freiherr Heinrich von Vietinghoff* had to pull his headquarters back to Contalmaison.[8] *Unteroffizier* Felix Kirchner, a forward observer of the 26th Reserve Field Artillery Regiment, recorded that: 'On 24 June thousands of guns opened fire on our trenches, dugouts, communication trenches, artillery positions and roads. We could not get any supplies from behind, no ammunition, no food, no water. The bearers of such things had to carry them from three to five kilometres and had to jump from shell hole to shell hole.' The effects of aerial torpedoes were especially terrifying.[9] Two German deserters, Arnold Fuchs and Ernst Girndt from an un-named battalion of 109 R.I.R. appeared in front of the British line on 27 June, followed by Oswald Lakemaker of 1./109 R.I.R. on 29 June. The interrogation reports of all three were similar; Lakemaker's reads that:

> He describes the front line trench as consisting of a line of shell holes. Four dug-outs of his platoon have collapsed… there was one good dug-out in his Zug [platoon] in which about 45 of them crowded during the bombardment. The entrance was twice blown in – they dug their way out… He said he had heard it was even worse behind than in the front line… Prisoner states morale is badly shaken… Prisoner says most of the men are longing for the attack to come. They remained in their dug-outs during the gas attack in the hope that if we attacked they would be captured.[10]

On the other hand, *Grenadier* Walter, of 119 R.I.R. at Beaumont Hamel remembered that:

> The seven day bombardment by the English did not cause us any losses. Our battalion occupied a three-line trench system and had built very strong and deep shelters. Our dugouts were eight to 10 meters deep and had been strengthened with heavy wooden beams and railroad ties. Luckily for us this provided quite adequate shelter. But several days before 1 July we had heard underground digging and knew a mine was being prepare.[11]
>
> At 07.25 hrs, British mines *were* blown and Stockwell could see 'our men going over the top for a mile on each side.' One of the biggest mines at Schwabenhöhe killed almost every man in No 5 Company of the German 2nd Battalion, 110 Reserve Infantry Regiment (II./110); only a rapid counter-attack by No 4 Company of the 1st Battalion (I./110) stopped a British penetration here.[12] Siegfried Sassoon, who was serving in C Company of 1 R.W. Fus, recorded the day's events in his diary:
>
> 7.45 a.m. The artillery barrage is now working to the right of Fricourt and beyond. I have seen the 21st Division advancing on the left of Fricourt; and some Huns apparently surrendering – about three-quarters of a mile away. Our men advancing steadily to the first line.[13]

Confused and contradictory messages came back from time to time. At 09.00 hrs Stockwell heard that all was going well on the flanks and he ordered the first two assault companies, A under Captain John Morgan and B under Lieutenant Howard Williams, to move up to their forward assembly area. An hour later however he was told to postpone any action.

What had happened was that 20 Brigade's front line had been badly damaged by German artillery fire and the brigade had had to shift its start line an hour before the assault back to

---

*   Later *Generaloberst* Heinrich von Vietinghoff (1887–1952). He was a recipient of the Knight's Cross of the Iron Cross with Oak Leaves. He commanded the German troops in Italy in 1945.

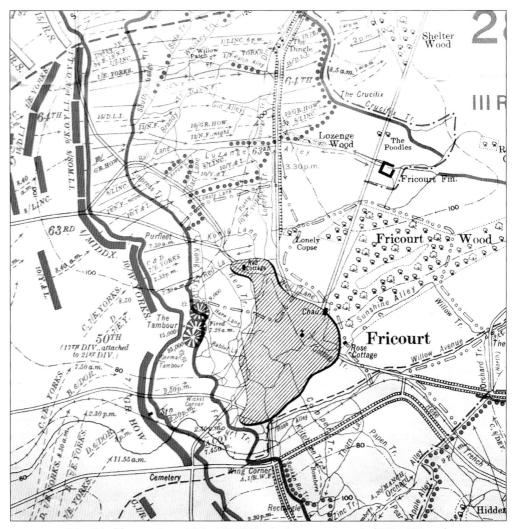

Map 7.iv The assault on 1 July, 1 R.W. Fus in the extreme south. (*Official History*)

the support line, causing some disruption. 2 Gordon Highlanders, on the right of 20 Brigade, crossed No Man's Land but the delay had given the Germans time to get out of their dugouts, man their machine guns, and open fire. Next to them, 9 Devons came under effective fire even before reaching the evacuated front line near Mansell Copse. In spite of the bombardment, the enemy was very much alive and throughout the attack the British suffered casualties from machine gun fire from the two villages of Fricourt and Mametz. In 91 Brigade the first two battalions, 22 Manchesters and 1 South Staffords, had a much easier time and quickly passed the German front line. In spite of casualties therefore, the first wave of the assault had crossed No Man's Land and entered the German first line but both leading brigades were engaged in hand-to-hand fighting in Mametz village, Danzig Alley trench, and on the left flank. It was not until 16.00 hrs that 91 Brigade reported Mametz village clear, at which time 20 Brigade was still fighting hard.

On the German side, *Oberst* Richard Schwarz of 121 R.I.R. recounted that:

> The principal work of the doctors and other medical personnel began in the morning of 1 July, soon after the English infantry's great frontal attack. At 08.30 the first lightly wounded streamed in. Not until the afternoon and evening were the stretcher bearers able to bring in the heavily wounded, some of them with horrible head, lung and abdomen injuries, in addition to smashed bones of every conceivable type.[14]

At 14.30 hrs, 20 Manchesters, in 22 Brigade, were ordered forward under a rolling barrage.[15] The first wave crossed No Man's Land without opposition but lost their way and swung to the right, meeting the Germans of the 109th Reserve Regiment in the Bois Français and bombing them out. The second wave was not so fortunate. 50 Brigade, which had been to attack on their left at the same time, had been badly cut up by German artillery earlier in the day and had failed to advance. Thus German machine-gunners around Fricourt were able to concentrate on the Manchesters: the bombing sections crossing with this wave were all killed or wounded and half the assault companies were also lost. Therefore, the bombers who were to have cleared Sunken Road trench, Rectangle Support, Zinc trench and Orchard Alley were not there. The Germans were holding all these in strength and the first wave of the Manchesters found themselves confined to the Bois Français.

At 15.45 hrs, Stockwell was briefed on the situation, which he described as 'not quite nice.' The high ground south of Fricourt, centred on the Rectangle which was a fortified keep in the midst of a complicated trench system, had to be cleared. 20 Manchesters were still stuck in the Bois Français and their own reserves, plus the brigade mobile reserve under Captain Edmund Dadd, had gone over to support them and to link up with the rest of the brigade in Apple Alley. Soon afterwards, Stockwell was ordered to support the Manchesters, and also to capture the Rectangle.[16]

To cross No Man's Land directly would have been suicidal, and Stockwell therefore ordered A Company and his bombers under Captain Robert Stevens to work round behind 91 Brigade using shell craters to infiltrate forward. This took time, but it worked. The special training and organisation put in place by Minshull Ford were now put to the test. Stevens was ordered to bomb westwards from the portions of captured enemy trenches into the roughly parallel tracks of Sunken Road and Rectangle trenches – which ran north-south from Fricourt. Morgan with A Company was to act in immediate support of the bombers, while Williams with B Company was to follow up and be ready to defeat any German counter-attack.

At 17.00 hrs Stockwell heard that Morgan was in position but not pressing ahead. He therefore sent his adjutant, Captain Brian Reeves, to 'ginger him up'. Reeves had to go over twice as things turned out and 'has done splendidly'. Two hours later, large numbers of German prisoners began to pass through, heading for the British rear. At 22.00 hrs – it was still light of course – Morgan and A Company had still not reached the rectangle and a German counterattack was developing through Fricourt. Half an hour later, A Company and the bombers were in the Rectangle and were consolidating the position finding that the Commanding Officer of the Manchesters had been killed;[17] Stevens and his bombers then pushed on and seized Sunken Road trench as far as Wing Corner, which was strongly held.[18]

20 Brigade had at last managed to secure its objectives on the right of 1 R.W. Fus. Stockwell was told that he should not push on into Fricourt as this would be bombarded and taken by assault the next morning, 2 July. However, Stockwell, who had caught up with the forward companies at 23.00 hrs, sensed that the Germans were shaken, and he therefore sent parties of bombers to try to get into the village. The bombers met little resistance and managed to secure the village; the report of this got through to the divisional headquarters just in time to prevent an unnecessary, and probably costly, bombardment.[19] Far from being congratulated, Stockwell was admonished for 'exceeding orders and upsetting the programme – an example of the rigidity of our operations'.[20]

Stockwell went on to record that the captured German line was of great strength. Each line was supplied with a double tier of dugouts connected by tunnels; canteens and a quartermaster's stores were captured:

> The principal feature of the operations had been the success of the Grenadier Company and the tactics they employed. The dreaded German bomber proved entirely futile when opposed to them, and thanks to them the battalion was able to capture five lines of strong trenches on a front of 800 yards, also Fricourt itself, with exceedingly small casualties (4 other ranks killed and 35 wounded) … Everyone very pleased with the battalion as they saved the situation on this front.[21]

Sassoon recollected that:

> Over two thousand prisoners taken by Seventh Division alone. First R.W.F. took over 200. Germans have gone back to their second line… Fricourt is full of British soldiers seeking souvenirs. The place was a ruin before; now it is a dust-heap.[22]

The following day, 3 July, 22 Brigade was relieved and concentrated in a valley close to Mametz village; here they rested throughout the day: '… battalions piled arms and lay down in an open grassy hollow south of the Carnoy-Mametz road, with a fine view of the British and (late) Bosche lines… Weather still, warm, sky rather cloudy.'[23] Siegfried Sassoon recalled the scene here in his poem *At Carnoy*, composed on 3 July:

> *Down in the hollow there's a whole Brigade*
> *Camped in four groups …*
> *To-morrow we must go*
> *To take some cursed Wood … O world God made![24]*

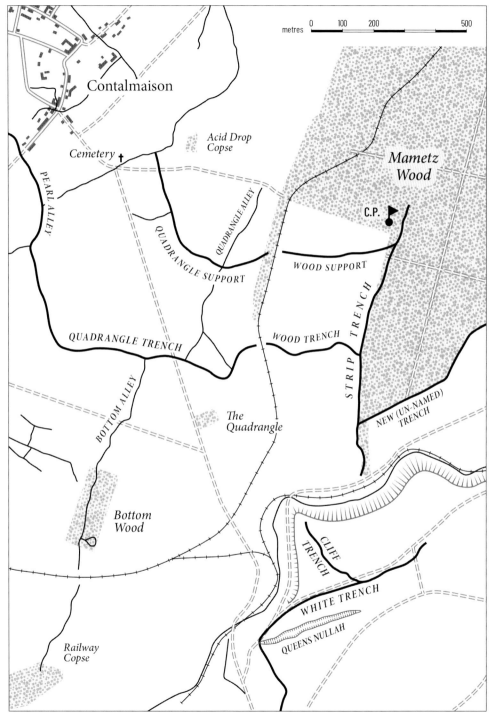

Map 7.v The action at the Quadrangle.

Despite the success around Mametz and Fricourt where in particular the casualty roll of 1 R.W. Fus was very different from the usual tale of woe on 1 July 1916, it was clear that further north, the attack had failed. Haig decided that he would not press matters there but reinforce what success he had. Further operations on 3 and 4 July were mounted to seize Bernafray Wood, east of Montauban, and Caterpillar Copse, close to Mametz Wood along with the line of the disused railway to its north and west. At 22.00 hrs on the night of 3 July, therefore, Stockwell recorded in his diary that:

> I got some mysterious orders to go and dig a trench. Apparently, the edge of Mametz Wood is not occupied, and we and the Royal Irish have to go and make a position there, but I can't make out on what authority. They say these places are unoccupied – it is pretty sketchy. Orders say if opposed we are to come back.[25]

A guide arrived from 91 Brigade at midnight and an hour later was still trying to find the right route through a maze of shell-holes and trenches. Stockwell refused to move the battalion until he had a clear route and at about 02.00 hrs the guide found a way through the communication trenches. It was not until 03.00 hrs, with the men worn out, that they reached their destination: 'an impossible place, on a bluff, within 50 yards of the forest. A bombing fight broke out at the end of the wood and we had to do a guy! [*i.e.,* to withdraw hastily]'[26]

Things were almost as confused over on the German side, as *Feldwebel* Robert Hauscheld of 111 R.I.R. recounted on 3 July:

> From battalion I received the order: "The position will be held to the last man!" To my inquiry and request for reinforcements came the answer: "Reinforcements and relief under way, perhaps tonight." The night, however, passed slowly under artillery fire with nothing to eat and only a little soda water to drink. I began to think we would not live to see morning.[27]

The intention of the orders that had puzzled Stockwell was that the two battalions should consolidate a position from the southern tip of Mametz Wood to Strip trench, Wood trench and Quadrangle trench as far as its junction with Bottom Alley (see map) as an unconfirmed report that the Wood was unoccupied had been accepted by the divisional and brigade staffs.[28] However 2 R. Irish had run into the Germans, killed some, and brought back the breach blocks of two field guns. Their experience, along with that of 1 R.W. Fus, made it clear that the Germans were within a few yards of the position that the battalions were to entrench. Stockwell, in accordance with his orders, withdrew the battalion back to its bivouacs.[29] Sassoon noted that 'We were out 11 hours and got back to our field about 8.30 a.m. Mametz is as badly smashed as Fricort.'[30]

The following morning, 4 July, orders were issued again to the effect that the line which the two battalions had been ordered to consolidate was to be attacked during the night of 4/5 July.[31] Stockwell sent his four company commanders to view the ground from a vantage point 2,000 yards to the rear – the only place from which the German position could be properly observed – but because the weather had closed in and it was raining hard, they saw little. The attack was to be co-ordinated with an assault by the 17th Division on the left. It appears that German troops driven from their front line on 1 July had fallen back here: *Leutnant* Ballheimer, of No 12 Company, III./186, recalled assembling men at a destroyed battery position by Mametz Wood:

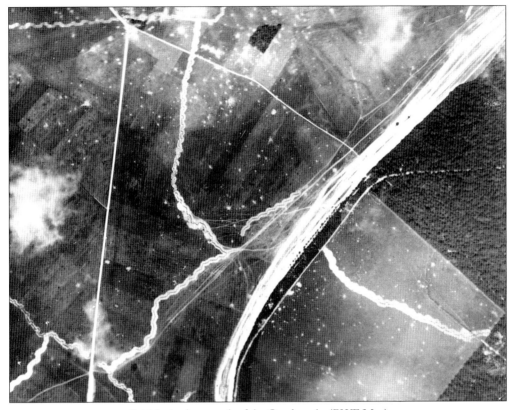

British air photograph of the Quadrangle. (RWF Mus)

'British artillery fire was coming down everywhere, the trench simply ended. It was not much more than 30 centimetres deep.'[32]

At 00.30 hrs 1 R.W. Fus was in position on the forward edge of Bottom Wood; 2 R. Irish was on the battalion's right and 7 Northumberland Fusiliers (7 N.F.), from the 17th Division, on its left.[33] The night was dark and the ground well sodden after the rain and the arrangements for the attack were later described as "casual":

> The wire in front of the German trenches was to have been cut during the afternoon, but the light was not good, and the artillery did not fire. The uncut state of the wire was not reported to Divisional Headquarters (7th) until 8 p.m. and "the 35th Artillery Brigade were hurriedly turned on to this work."[34]

It was then reported that the wire in front of Quadrangle trench was well gapped, but that in front of Wood trench there was only a single gap. Under these confused circumstances the attack went in at 00.45 hrs with two companies of 1 R.W. Fus, B on the right and D on the left, in the first wave. With no wireless, and an unreliable telephone line, the assaulting troops disappeared into the darkness and no news reached Stockwell, who was in a communication trench below Bottom Wood, for some time. First came news that B Company had lost its way (in fact the company had been held up by uncut wire), then that casualties were heavy, then that 2 R. Irish had been forced out of their objective. Finally, Williams, commanding B Company came back wounded; Stockwell therefore sent A Company forward behind B and at 2.10 hrs heard that A and D were on their objectives but were being fiercely counter-attacked. He therefore sent what remained of C Company under Captain Edward Greaves with the bombers under Stevens and the mobile reserve led by Edmund Dadd. As Sassoon recalled, C Company had been split up to provide carrying parties for the other companies and mustered only 26 men.[35] After a short pause Dadd re-appeared to explain that more bombs were needed but no more men were required, except for bombers. Stevens and Dadd then cleared the position and the objective was secured. 'Stevens and Dadd did splendidly, as did [Lieutenant Siegfried] Sassoon', wrote Stockwell.[36] 2 R. Irish tried to get through the one gap into Wood trench, but failed. Quadrangle trench ended close to the disused railway line and there was a gap of 200 yards between it and Wood trench, a gap swept by machine-gun fire, and this effectively prevented any help being sent to the R. Irish.

It had once more been a bombers' fight using the new organisation and tactics. As soon as the assault companies gained a lodgement in the German line, the bombers fanned out, clearing the trench from traverse to traverse, left and right. A block and bombing post were put up where Quadrangle trench came to a sudden end close to the disused railway line;[37] and another in Quadrangle Alley; and contact made with 7 N.F. on the left. 2 R. Irish was soon withdrawn and the whole of Quadrangle garrisoned by 1 R.W. Fus; the bombers and all surplus men were sent back to Bottom Alley.[38]

At 06.00 hrs on 5 July the Germans put in a counter-attack down Quadrangle Alley and Pearl Alley, from their second Line – now the front line. Although the second line trench could not be overlooked, Quadrangle Alley was shallow and, as Bernard Adams pointed out, it *could* be seen – the heads of the German bombers could be clearly made out: they were allowed to get close to the block and then bombed and fired at in enfilade by *Lewis* guns. A platoon of the battalion's bombers then went into the attack and drove the Germans right back to their second

Major Wölfl   Major Killermann   Major von Reitz

The Battalion Commanders of the 16th Bavarian Infantry Regiment who held the Second Line on 1 July 1916. (16th Bavarian Regimental History)

line; a second block was then put in 300 yards further north and close to the Germans' line. Two further German counter-attacks were defeated from this position throughout the day.

Leutnant Ballheimer, on the German side, observed that:

> Towards 8.30 a.m. the enemy started to bring down shrapnel and high explosive on the hollow behind us. Gradually the fire was adjusted onto the trenches. About 9.00 a.m. we saw dense lines of British infantry move through Mametz Wood…. Soon the British had disappeared into the Wood and over the hill to our left rear… the British advanced, throwing grenades left and right of the trench. All the time we still had grenades we kept them at bay. Then these began to run out and we also lacked machine gun ammunition… gradually our situation became hopeless.[39]

Ballheimer was obviously mistaken about the location of the British, since they did not enter Mametz Wood for another week.

Siegfried Sassoon was at the block on the eastern end of Quadrangle Trench; here, with several bombers and a *Lewis* gun team, he exchanged sniping with the Germans in Wood trench until one of the men, whom Sassoon calls 'Lance-Corporal Kendle' (actually Lance-Corporal James Gibson,[40] a favourite of his),[41] was shot in the head and killed. This made Sassoon lose his temper and with his revolver and a bag of grenades he ran across the open ground to Wood trench and threw two bombs into it:

> … quite unexpectedly, I found myself looking down into a well-conducted trench with a great many Germans in it. Fortunately for me, they were already retreating. It had not occurred to them that they were being attacked by a single fool… I slung a few more bombs… while a crowd of jostling helmets vanished along the trench[42]

He said rather more to his friend Edward Marsh: 'I chased 40 Bosches out of a trench by Mametz Wood all by myself. Wasn't that a joyous moment for me? They ran like hell and I chucked bombs and made hunting noises.'[43] Matters then degenerated into farce, as Robert Graves recounts in *Goodbye to All That:*

> Siegfried had then distinguished himself by taking single-handedly a battalion frontage that the Royal Irish Regiment had failed to take… He had gone over with bombs in daylight, under covering fire from a couple of rifles, and scared the occupants out. It was a pointless feat; instead of reporting or signalling for reinforcements he sat down in the German trench and began dozing over a book of poems which he had brought with him. The colonel [Stockwell] was furious. The attack on Mametz had been delayed for two hours because it was reported that British patrols were still out. "British patrols" were Siegfried and his book of poems.[44]

It was not until 14.00 hrs that Sassoon had decided to evacuate Wood trench and return to Battalion Headquarters where, as Graves reports, a 'glowering' Stockwell was quite understandably furious that Sassoon had neither properly consolidated the trench nor sent back any reports.[45] Stockwell had good cause – and if Sassoon had done his duty then the trench would have been consolidated, Mametz Wood entered and cleared, and many thousands of deaths prevented.

Siegfried Sassoon with
a group of bombers.
(Burntwood family)

That night, 1 R.W. Fus was relieved by 14 R.W. Fus.[46] With 1,200 men in the line, the trenches were for a time seriously overcrowded until 1 R.W. Fus withdrew and marched back to rest at Heilly. Sassoon recalled the arrival of the 14th Battalion of his Regiment:

> Our little trench under the trees was inundated by a jostling company of exclamatory Welshmen. Kinjack [i.e. Stockwell] would have called them a panicky rabble. They were mostly undersized men, and as I watched them arriving at the first stage of their battle experience, I had a sense of victimization. A little platoon officer was settling his men down with a valiant show of self-assurance… He spoke sharply to some of them, and I felt that they were like a lot of children.[47]

Out of a fighting strength of about 400, 1 R.W. Fus had suffered eight men killed, and two officers and 55 men wounded during the fighting on 4 and 5 July:[48] a very moderate butcher's bill indeed in the context of the Battle of the Somme. 14 R.W. Fus was one of the battalions of the 38th Division, and thus a Regular Welsh battalion had set the stage for the great assault by the New Army battalions.

But what had been the German experience of, and reaction to, the opening days of the Somme battle? Some veterans have already been quoted, but the assault north of the Bois Français had been mounted against the 28th Reserve Infantry Division, which was not on the corps or army main effort: this lay further north with the 26th Reserve Division and may thus partly explain why the British were successful here; the French even more so south of the Somme. The British penetration around Fricourt appears to have been made at the boundary between No 2 Company of the I./110 and No 4 Company of the I./111.

Mametz Village after the attack.
(*Illustrated London News*, 22 July 1916)

1 R.W. Fus in its bivouac field before operations on 3 and 4 July. (RWF Mus)

1 R.W. Fus' German opponents enjoying a similar rest behind the lines. (James Payne collections)

The War Illustrated, 29th July, 1916. Page 560

Royal Welsh Fusiliers Along the Somme

A heap of trench-mortar ammunition behind the lines ready for transport to the firing front.

First-aid for heroes of the Somme. Looking after the wounded in the trenches during the great advance.

Remarkable photograph of the Royal Welsh Fusiliers in bivouac. On July 6th these gallant fighters made a successful raid into the German trenches south of the La Bassee Canal. Inset: The East Yorks on the march through a French village to the front line. (Official Photographs.)

1st RWF on the Somme. (The *Illustrated London News*)

Boundaries are always vulnerable spots, chiefly because they require close co-ordination and they are restricted fire lines, and the British had been lucky enough to hit an inter-company, inter-battalion and inter-regimental boundary.[49]

The 109 R.I.R. had also suffered badly when their wire was cut by the British artillery: the 1st and 2nd Battalions suffered heavy losses during the attack and a counter-attack by the 3rd Battalion was stopped. They described their positions in front of the British 7th Division as 'in shell holes', with their telephone communications cut, although many of their dugouts were undamaged.[50] The Regiment's losses amounted to 14 officers and 94 men killed, 26 men wounded, and 24 officers and 1,749 who had simply disappeared.[51]

Von Below and the Commander of the XVII Corps, von Pannewitz, starved of men and resources, had had no choice but to stiffen the position north of the Somme at the expense of formations further south, and indeed to give ground, even though von Below had issued an order on 3 July which stated that: 'The outcome of the war depends on Second Army being victorious on the Somme. The large areas of ground that we have lost in some places will be attacked and wrested back.'[52] There were no means immediately available to make such an attack, however. The only reserves available to the 28th Reserve Division were the 55th *Landwehr* Regiment and two battalions of 23 I.R. – coincidentally the same number in the infantry of the line as that of The Royal Welsh Fusiliers – which were sent along with any troops that could be saved from 109 R.I.R., to occupy the second line and Mametz Wood.[53]

When Falkenhayn heard the news, he was furious, believing that any penetration should be immediately snuffed out by counter-attack.[54] He immediately drove to the Second Army Headquarters and after a brief but stormy conference, sacked the Chief of Staff, *Generalmajor* Paul Grünert. This was a blow aimed at von Below, who valued Grünert; he was replaced by Oberst Fritz von Loßberg (see Chapter 3). To replace a senior officer in the midst of a battle is a risky business, especially a chief of staff in the German system, charged with so much of his commander's authority. Crown Prince Rupprecht noted this in his diary:

> … such a measure also amounts to lack of confidence in the relevant commander, who does in fact bear the responsibility for any decisions taken. This, in turn, diminishes the commander in the eyes of his subordinates… the blame for what happened lies at the door of *OHL* itself, which did not arrange in time for reinforcements to be allocated to Second Army.[55]

Loßberg met Falkenhayn on 3 July and presented a long list of demands, including that all offensive action at Verdun should be halted – which did not happen. He then went on to St Quentin and threw himself into mastering the situation and bringing the staff into his confidence and way of doing business: 'The key man for the remainder of the German defensive effort until the battle died away was now in post.'[56] Loßberg, who never spared himself, was at full stretch along with all the staff throughout July, pushing reinforcement units into the line as they arrived, issuing orders right down to battalion level if required.

Once it was clear that the village of Fricourt had been outflanked, Loßberg ordered it to be evacuated by 111 R.I.R. on 2 July. The Regiment was relieved at 10.00 hrs the next morning by III./186 I.R., although most of the survivors remained in place to assist the new defenders.[57] This however put great pressure on 110 R.I.R. defending La Boisselle and this village too was lost on 3 July. This was a serious situation, because the southern flank of the Serre – Thiepval

Royal Garrison Artillery gunners shifting ammunition, Somme 1916.

plateau was in danger and if more of what was in effect vital ground was lost, the *Schwerpunkt* further north could be rolled up from the south.

Generalleutnant Franz von Soden, commanding the 26th Division, ordered 180 I.R. to hold its position around Ovillers at all costs to cover the evacuation of 110 R.I.R.[58] Within XIV Reserve Corps, 10th Bavarian Division, the only uncommitted formation, was ordered to reinforce the 28th Reserve Division and on the night of 1 July they were ordered to mount a counter-attack; the bulk of this took place to the north of the Fricourt-Mametz area, and was a costly failure.[59] In the wake of this, various redeployments were ordered, including that III./16 Bavarian I.R. was moved to the command of 185 Infantry Brigade and occupied Mametz Wood. General von Stein, the corps commander, recalled that:

> In order to prevent a breakthrough on the left flank [i.e. in the Fricourt area] I had to pull out of the line battalion after battalion which had just beaten off a major attack, transfer them by truck to the left and throw them into battle. When I gave the senior General Staff Officer, Major von Löwenfeld, the same order for the last available battalion, he said to me in a deadly serious voice, "Excellency, that is the last one!" I then replied, "Never forget this moment all your life. It is essential to be able to decide to deploy the very last of your resources, because the enemy my also be at the end of his."[60]

Loßberg also, with von Below's approval, reorganised the command organisation of Second Army. The corps became Groups named after their commanders, and XIV Reserve Corps became Group von Stein, responsible for all forces from the northern boundary of Second Army to the boundary between XIV Reserve and XVII Corps. Orders were issued to the defenders of Mametz Wood that they were to hold the second line and the northern edge of the wood, and that patrols were to be strengthened in the wood.[61]

Loßberg in fact took a huge risk at this point in accepting a British penetration around Fricourt and Mametz and rather than try to pug the gap, instead reinforced the main effort with the 3rd Guards Division. Despite casualties, the position was held. This adherence to doctrine and indeed logic was in marked contrast to the British approach, with its even spread of divisions across the front. Joffre saw the German point of view at once and advised – indeed tried to order – Haig to attack the area of Thiepval on 3 July; Haig however refused and put his resources into what he perceived as success around Fricourt and Mametz, thus perhaps letting the Germans off the hook.[62]

What made this error even worse was that the opportunity to occupy some of the key positions north of Mametz was lost by the failure to push forward at corps and divisional level. It is clear from the German sources cited, that some of the trenches around Mametz Wood were no more than scrapes, but that the delay gave the Germans time to dig deeper. *Regimental Records of The Royal Welch Fusiliers* notes that: 'The wood [i.e. Mametz] seems to have been a puzzle. There was still, for some reason, a belief that the enemy would relinquish it, though why he should do so with such easy access to it is not clear.'[63] The Official History is even more blunt:

> It would appear that if XV Corps had encouraged more vigorous action on the afternoon of the 3rd a hold on Mametz Wood could have been secured and Wood Trench and Quadrangle Trench occupied. The last-named objective was taken on the morning of the 5th, but others were to cost many lives and much precious time.[64]

Notes

1   T.N.A. WO 95/921, XV Corps War Diary.
2   T.N.A. WO 95/1631, 7th Division War Diary.
3   Adams, p. 97–98.
4   E.L. Kirby, *Officers of The Royal Welch Fusiliers 1689–1914* (Privately published, 1997), p. 47.
5   C.H. Dudley Ward, pp. 157–158. See also the Dairy of Clifton Inglis Stockwell in RWF Mus/ Archives.
6   Siegfried Sassoon, *Memoirs of an Infantry Officer* (London, 1930), p. 22 et seq.
7   Stockwell's Diary for 28 and 29 June 1916. See also his letter to the official historian, Edmonds, in T.N.A. CAB 45/189.
8   *Deutsche Reichsarchiv, Schlaten des Weltkrieges* (*Taschenbuch*, Berlin, 1930), '*Anlage zu Band 20, Pt I, Somme-Nord*', p. 53.
9   'The Other Side of the Hill No 1', pp. 251–252.
10   Cited in Hugh Sebag-Montefiore, *Somme: Into the Breach* (London, 2016), p. 196.
11   See <http://roadstothegreatwar-ww1.blogspot.co.uk/2013/07/the-german-experience-at-battle-of-somme.html> (Accessed 16 January 2018).
12   Jack Sheldon, *The German Army on the Somme, 1916–1918* (Barnsley, 2005), p. 158.
13   Siegfried Sassoon (ed Rupert Hart-Davis), *Diaries 1915–1918* (London, 1983), p. 82.
14   See <http://roadstothegreatwar-ww1.blogspot.co.uk/2013/07/the-german-experience-at-battle-of-somme.html> (Accessed 16 January 2018).
15   Sassoon, *Diaries*, p. 84.
16   Stockwell's Diary for 1 July 1916; T.N.A. WO 95/1660/5, 22 Infantry Brigade War Dairy 1 July 1916.
17   T.N.A. WO 95/1665/1, 1 R.W. Fus War Dairy; Sassoon, *Diaries*, p. 84.

18   Dudley Ward, p. 196.
19   T.N.A. WO 95/1665/1, 1 R.W. Fus War Dairy.
20   Stockwell's Diary for 2 July 1916.
21   Stockwell's Diary for 2 July 1916.
22   Sassoon, *Diaries,* p. 85.
23   Sassoon, *Diaries,* p. 86.
24   Siegfried Sassoon, 'At Carnoy', 3 July 1916, in *Collected Poems 1908–1956* (London 1986), p. 22.
25   Stockwell's Diary for 3 July 1916.
26   Stockwell's Diary for 4 July 1916. See also Sassoon, *Diaries,* p. 87.
27   See<http://roadstothegreatwar-ww1.blogspot.co.uk/2013/07/the-german-experience-at-battle-of-somme.html> (Accessed 16 January 2018).
28   T.N.A. WO 95/1660/5, 22 Infantry Brigade War Dairy 3 July 1916.
29   Dudley Ward, p. 200.
30   Sassoon, *Diaries,* p. 88.
31   T.N.A. WO 95/1631, 7th Division War Diary.
32   Sheldon, *German Army on the Somme,* p. 182.
33   See the account in Michael Renshaw, *The Welsh on the Somme: Mametz Wood* (Barnsley, 2015), pp. 35–38.
34   Dudley Ward, p. 201.
35   Sassoon, *Diaries,* p. 88.
36   Stockwell's Diary for 5 July 1916.
38   Sassoon, *Diaries,* p. 89.
38   Dudley Ward, p. 202.
39   Sheldon, *German Army on the Somme,* p. 182.
40   No 24460 Lance-Corporal James Gibson, *Soldiers Died in the Great War,* <www.forces-war-records.co.uk> (Accessed 22 January 2018).
41   Jean Moorcroft Wilson, *Siegfried Sassoon. The Making of a War Poet. A Biography 1886–1918* (London, 1998), p. 269.
42   Sassoon, *Memoirs of an Infantry Officer,* p. 91; Sassoon, *Diaries,* p. 89.
43   Moorcroft Wilson, p. 269.
44   Graves, p. 251.
45   Sassoon, *Memoirs of an Infantry Officer,* p. 95.
46   T.N.A. WO 95/2551/2, 14 R.W. Fus War Dairy, p. 5.
47   Sassoon, *Memoirs of an Infantry Officer,* p. 97.
48   Dudley Ward, p. 202.
49   Sheldon, *German Army on the Somme,* p. 159.
50   Sheldon, *German Army on the Somme,* p. 369.
51   Sheldon, *German Army on the Somme,* p. 162.
52   Sheldon, *German Army on the Somme,* p. 176.
53   Sheldon, *German Army on the Somme,* p. 369.
54   Falkenhayn, p. 36.
55   Crown Prince Rupprecht of Bavaria, *In Treue Fest: Mein Kriegstagebuch, Vols. I & II* (Munich, 1929), p. 495.
56   Sheldon, p. 65.
57   Sheldon, *German Army on the Somme,* p. 183.
58   Franz *Freiherr* von Soden, *Die 26. (Württembergische) Reserve-Division im Weltkrieg 1914–1918, I. Teil* (Stuttgart, 1939), p. 113.
59   Sheldon, p. 74.
60   Sheldon, p. 75.
61   3rd Battalion 16th Bavarian Infantry Regiment, *Garde-Infanterie-Division I* order dated 12 July 1916 in *Kriegsarchiv* Munich.
62   Sheldon, p. 66.
63   Dudley Ward, p. 204.
64   Edmonds, p. 9.

8

'They want butchers, not brigadiers': Mametz Wood, 5–7 July 1916

With the German first line taken in the Fricourt – Mametz area, Haig's next objective was their second line on the next ridge, Bazentin. In order to achieve this, preliminary operations were required by three corps: III, XV and XIII, which were to attack respectively Contalmaison on the left; Mametz Wood and Acid Drop Copse in the centre; and the small wood of Bernafay and the larger feature of Trônes Wood on the right. When successfully completed, these operations would place the Fourth Army within striking distance of the German second line. Haig visited Rawlinson on 2 and 4 July to impress on him the importance of Trônes and Mametz Woods, which would secure the right and left flanks of the attack.[1] Kiggell, Haig's Chief of Staff, underlined the importance of these two features, especially Mametz Wood, writing that:

> Mametz Wood is of great tactical importance. Unless it is in our possession the left flank of the main attack [i.e. on the German second line] would be very insecure… Furthermore, with Mametz in our possession Bazentin le Petit Wood and the enemy trenches to the south of it will be seriously threatened by us, and it may prove possible to assault them… For these reasons it is considered that only such a state of demoralisation on the enemy's side as would justify great risks being taken to profit by it immediately would justify the launching of the main attack before Mametz Wood had been captured.[2]

Rawlinson, although in general agreement, was not entirely convinced of the Wood's importance as vital ground and recorded in his diary the following day that: 'I am doubtful about whether we are wise to wait for the capture of Mametz Wood before launching our attack against Longueval.'[3] It seems that Haig had a different concept for the main assault on the German second line from Rawlinson's ideas, but he failed to explain or communicate this to his subordinate. Rawlinson felt that he had no option but to assault the German position frontally between Bazentin le Grand Wood and Longueval and to do so as soon as possible – Mametz was certainly an important consideration but could have been screened by artillery fire and smoke and thus outflanked. Haig, on the other hand, had formed a view that, by securing the northern edge of Mametz Wood and with it the ability to attack the German line by observed, enfilade, artillery fire, the German positions could be taken by a flank attack launched from Mametz Wood, passing between Bazentin le Petit and Bazentin le Grand Woods and approaching Longueval over relatively flat ground and through the German trench system from the west.[4] It was some days before the two men finally understood each other's views.

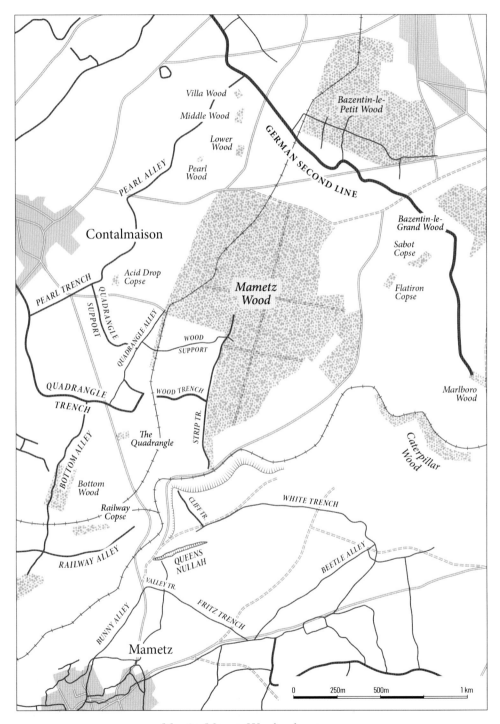

Map 8.i Mametz Wood and environs.

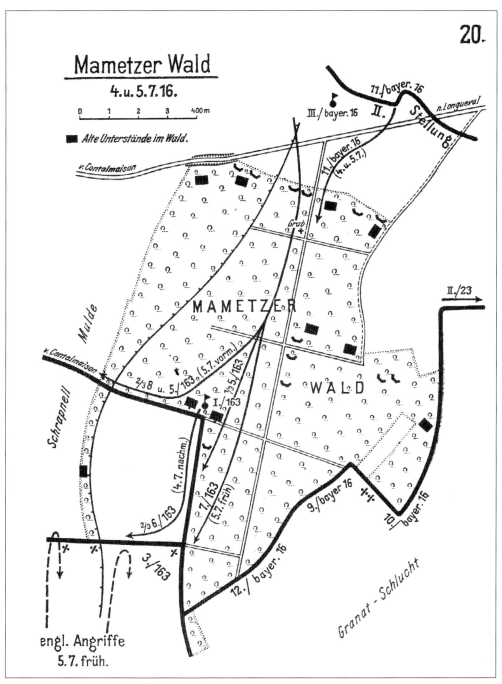

Map 8.ii The German Dispositions in Mametz Wood, 5 July 1916.
(Source: *German Official History Somme–Nord*)

On 5 July, the 38th (Welsh) Division, now attached to Sir Henry Horne's XV Corps, moved into the line from Bottom Wood to Caterpillar Copse, along the southern edge of Mametz Wood, with the 17th (Northern) Division on their left.[5] Caterpillar, which was on a steep bank, had been made into a strong redoubt by the Germans to protect the flanks of what was sometimes called 'Happy Valley', between it and Mametz Wood. Caterpillar had been taken on 3 July along with the also-fortified Marlborough Copse to its north-east.[6]

The orders from Fourth Army to the corps commanders were explicit: capture the two woods of Trônes and Mametz as quickly as possible. XIII Corps was given the task of capturing Trônes Wood as far north as the railway line; and XV Corps the mission to secure Mametz Wood and Acid Drop Copse by the morning of 7 July. III Corps meanwhile was to secure Contalmaison

British air photograph
of Mametz Wood.
(RWF Mus)

An oblique British air photograph of Mametz Wood. (RWF Mus)

Mametz   Bois de Foureaux Bois de Mametz   Bazentin le Petit   Contalmaifon
(Granatfchlucht)

An oblique German air photograph of Mametz Wood and Bazentin Ridge.
(16th Bavarian Regimental History)

village, Bailliff Wood and the railway cutting north of the village.[7] 'They have', Rawlinson wrote in his diary, 'fresh divisions and I hope all will go well.'[8]

Mametz Wood was, at this point, still relatively undamaged and described by Siegfried Sassoon as 'a menacing wall of gloom'.[9] It was a large, mature wood of oak, hornbeam, lime, willow, hazel, beech and ash trees of the sort common on chalk down-land in England as well as northern France. The trees were around 30 to 40 feet (9 to 12 metres) high and beneath them, the floor was a thick undergrowth of brambles and saplings, the result of a lack of woodland management over the two years of the war to date. It measured about one mile (1,600 metres) from north to south and about three quarters of a mile (1,200 metres) from east to west at its widest point, making it about 220 acres (90 hectares) in area, and thus the biggest wood in the Somme battlefield area.[10] The wood however tapered to a point at its most southern extremity, leaving a wide open space on its south-eastern face. On its eastern side, an oddly shaped projection, known as 'the Hammerhead', protruded somewhat between Flatiron Copse and Caterpillar Copse. Internally the wood was divided into blocks by a series of rides: one central ride ran from north to south and there were two lateral rides at right angles to the centre.

In the context of the geography and geomorphology of the whole objective area, when viewed from the captured German first line which roughly followed the road from Mametz village to Montauban, the ground fell away northwards, in a gentle convex slope for just over half a mile (800 metres) but then suddenly changed to a steep chalk bank, almost a cliff, which varied from 30 to 50 feet in height (9 to 14 metres). This bank

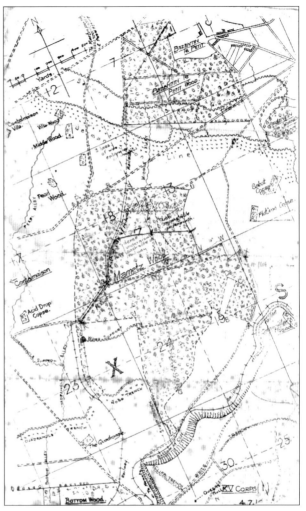

The sketch map of Mametz Wood issued to all units as an Annex to the Divisional Operation Order. (T.N.A. WO 95//2539/4, 38th Division War Diary (G.S.)

had been formed by the erosive forces of the Willow Stream, a winterbourne which was usually dry in summer but which ran strongly in wet weather. From the base of the cliff, the ground then rose steadily for more than a mile (1600 metres) northwards towards the next ridge which ran through Bazentin to Longueval. Mametz Wood lay on a low spur flanked by two shallow re-entrants: that to the east was called the *Granatshluct*, or grenade canyon, by the Germans and that to the west, the *Shrapnelmulde*, or shrapnel valley. From its southern edge it was just 300 yards to the Willow Stream; to its south-west lay Bottom Wood and to its north-east, Bazentin le Petit and Bazentin le Grand Woods. Smaller copses flanked it: Acid Drop on the western side between the Wood and Contalmaison; Flatiron and Sabot on the eastern side between the Wood and Bazentin le Grand; and on the south-eastern side, the small block of Marlborough Wood and the long hanger of Caterpillar Copse which picked up the end of the cliff and ran on roughly towards Montauban for three-quarters of a mile (1,200 metres).

Any assault from the south would, therefore, have to descend the slope from the new British front line, in full view of the Germans; then negotiate the cliff with the troops wearing full equipment and struggling to keep any formation; then cross the rising open ground from the Willow Stream to the Wood. An assault from the east, coming out of Caterpillar Copse, would be in dead ground as it began but would soon descend into the eastern re-entrant, the *Granatshluct*, and then be in full view of the Wood as the attackers climbed the slope towards it. At the same time, an assault from the east would be enfiladed by fire from Flatiron and Sabot Copses.[11] All these features, including the internal structure of Mametz Wood, had

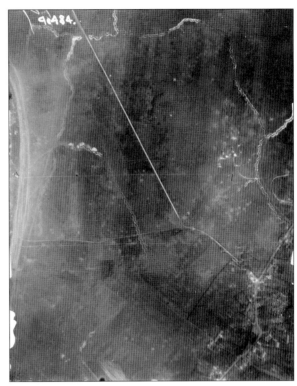

British air photograph of Acid Drop Copse and Contalmaison. (RWF Mus)

been well mapped and code letters assigned to various points around the perimeter of the Wood – these are shown on the map at the beginning of this chapter; there was also good quality aerial photography taken on or about 29 June which clearly showed the trenches and other features, but which very much flattened the rise and fall of the ground. The final feature of interest was Queen's Nullah, a prominent gully behind the British line, which served as cover for an advanced dressing station, brigade and battalion headquarters and trench mortars throughout the battle.

The German second line trench (*II Stellung*) lay about 300 yards north of the top of Mametz Wood and behind it was a secondary, switch, trench. In front of it, running from Contalmaison to the western edge of Mametz Wood, was a strongly built trench with 20 foot (6 metre) dugouts known as *Kaisergraben* ('Emperor's ditch') but which after its capture by the 17th Division on the night of 4 July, was renamed Quadrangle. It was described as being well wired, with deep dugouts and connected to Ovillers by Fourth Street trench and its left joined to Mametz Wood by Wood trench.[12] Between Quadrangle, the Wood and the German second line lay a network of trenches shown on the map. Wood Trench (*Tote Stellung* to the Germans) and Wood Support (*Weissgraben*), in spite of Siegfried Sassoon's antics, remained held by the Germans, as did Pearl Alley. Wood trench and Strip trench were seen by the 2 R. Irish patrol already cited in Chapter 7 and described as being strongly wired and well-traversed, with collapsed trees making the going more difficult still.[13]

A contemporary photograph
of Mametz Wood from
Marlborough Wood on 7 July 1916.
(greatwarphotos.com)

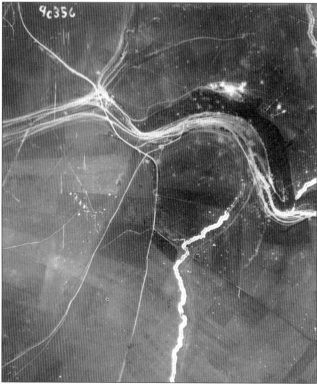

British air photograph
of Caterpillar Copse.
(RWF Mus)

Modern photograph of the
trench at the northern edge
of Caterpillar Copse.
(A.M. Goulden)

Modern photograph
of a section of narrow-
gauge railway track now
doing duty as a fence-
post outside Caterpillar
Copse. (A.M. Goulden)

Modern photograph of the forming-up place on the northern side of Caterpillar Copse and the axis of advance on 7 July, from Marlborough Wood. (A.M. Goulden)

Modern photograph of Flatiron and Sabot Copses (to the right) and the southern edge of the Hammerhead, from Marlborough Wood. (A.M. Goulden)

Modern photograph of the defenders' view from the Hammerhead towards the direction of attack on 7 July. (A.M. Goulden)

Modern photograph of Queen's Nullah from the south, which can be made out by the line of bushes. (A.M. Goulden)

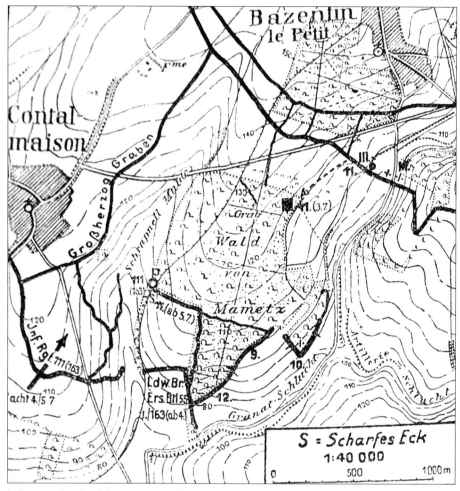

A German sketch of the positions held around Mametz Wood on 4/5 July, before the relief by the *Lehr* Regiment, showing the new entrenchments. (16th Bavarian Regimental History, p. 186)

East of Mametz Wood, the second line commanded the whole of the open slopes. The forward positions could thus be easily and quickly evacuated or reinforced from the second line. The various woods and copses were not heavily entrenched, probably in part because digging trenches among mature tree roots is very difficult; and partly because no observation was possible from within the woods; however, all these woods, large and small, were occupied by the Germans and connected to the trench system. From their edges, the open ground between could be dominated by machine gun and observed artillery fire and it is clear from various accounts in the war diaries and from survivors that in the pause between the initial British assault and the first attack by the 17th and 38th Divisions, the Germans had dug more trenches around the edges of the Wood than were indicated on maps and in intelligence reports. This has been documented in the archaeological report of 2015 already cited in the introductory section of this book,[14] and will be examined further.

Two photographs of the
Regimental and 2nd
Battalion headquarters
staffs of the 163rd I.R.
(163 I.R. Regimental
History)

Lieutenant Colonel (later Brigadier General) J.R. Gaussen recorded how the Royal Flying Corps was engaged in limiting German observation of the pending attack: '6 July. A brilliant piece of work by the R.F.C. not recorded. Behind the German lines six observation balloons were clearly visible: 12 British planes, in six pairs, simultaneously swept overhead and attacked them and all six… were brought down in flames.[15]

The German troops defending the area had been relieved on 3 July and were then drawn from the 16th Bavarian Regiment, part of 20 Infantry Brigade of the 10th Bavarian Division,

and elements of the 28th Reserve Infantry Division.[16] The
Bavarians had been reinforced with two Machine-Gun
Sniper Companies – *M.G. Scharffshutzen Truppen* Nr.
44 under *Oberleutnant* Heinrich Stroh and Nr. 87 under
Oberleutnant Thomas Scherer.[17] The eastern and northern
parts of the Wood itself was garrisoned by the Bavarians
and supported from what was now the German main line.
They had, according to their own records, found digging
inside the Wood difficult and so had left most of the
Wood alone. They had however dug an entrenchment on
the southern and eastern edges of Mametz Wood which
was linked to their positions in Flatiron and Sabot Copses
and from there to their main line; the supporting positions in the open ground on the sides of the Wood were
Wood trench and Wood Support to the west, and Flatiron
Copse to the east. This trench system was so new that it
had no name in either the German or the British records
and it had no deep dugouts and does not seem to have
been wired. It was, however, known about, for the 38th

The Regimental Colour of the
Lehr Infantry Regiment.
(Lehr Regimental History)

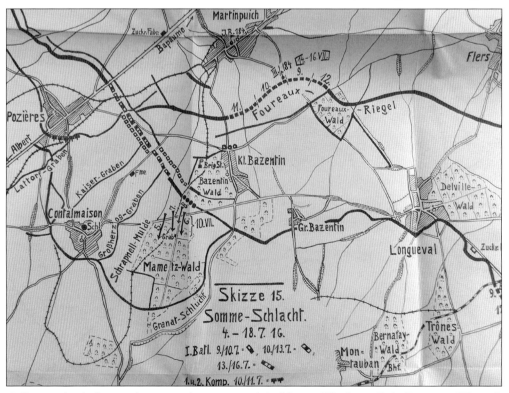

A German sketch showing their entrenchments around the Mametz Wood area. (Lehr Regimental History)

Division's War Diary notes that: 'the enemy were reported to be holding a trench from S.20. a.1 1/2 to S.20.a.0.0. strongly'.[18] Fusilier W.R. Thomas even drew a sketch of part of it, around the Hammerhead, in his personal memoir.[19] It is surprising that no previous accounts have acknowledged or described this entrenchment. To the right of the Bavarians, II./163 I.R., originally of the 111th Division but now detached to the 28th Division, held the open ground between Quadrangle trench and the western edge of the Wood and the edges of it, and Contalmaison, with I./163 I.R. in Contalmaison itsef.

The regimental history of the 163rd is sketchy, and provides only a few glimpses of their experience as they moved from Martinpuich into the line:

> Some of the men were able to catch a fat pig in the village. With great joy the wildly resisting animal was led through the trenches to the slaughtering block.
>
> At 12.15 midnight the battalion was ready to move. The departure proved to be quite difficult as it was very dark, and the first vehicle got lost in the village. There was great confusion; only with a lot of effort, as we could not use our lights, were we able to redirect the convoy onto the right road. It was bitingly cold that night; the troops huddled closely together and were rattled around for hours on the roads shot to pieces.[20]

At some point after 5 July, however, another redeployment took place and this can be traced in the German accounts cited later in this chapter. The Bavarians had been pulled back to the second line,[21] leaving only one-and-a-half companies as a reserve in the centre of the Wood. The 3rd Guards Division, with the Guards Fusilier Regiment, the 9th Colberg Grenadier Regiment (2nd Pommeranians) and the *Lehr* [i.e. Training] Infantry Regiment, had been hurried forward from Valenciennes and relieved the 28th Reserve Division and the Bavarians between the Bapaume – Albert Road on the German right, as far as Flat Iron Copse, with the whole of Mametz Wood inclusive to it.[22] The 3rd Guards Division had served on the Eastern Front and in the Carpathians and had taken heavy casualties there. It had been re-organised in May 1915 and in April 1916 transferred to the Western Front where it had served in Champagne before being move to the Somme.[23] The *Lehr* Infantry Battalion – the infantry instruction battalion – was raised in 1819 for the Prussian Army. In 1914 it was part of the Prussian Guards Corps and stationed

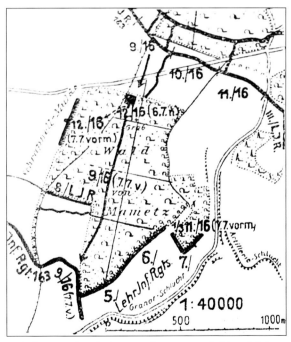

A German sketch showing the positions held on 7 July. (16th Bavarian Regimental History, p. 187)

The Kaiser reviews the Guards Fusilier Regiment before the opening of the Somme battles. (Guard Fusiliers Regimental History)

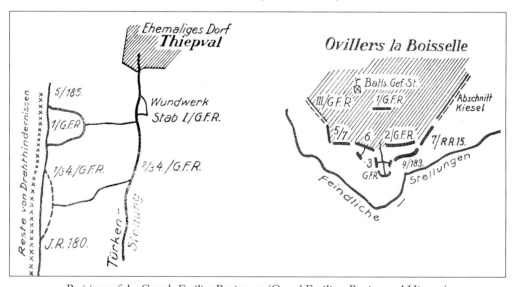

Positions of the Guards Fusilier Regiment. (Guard Fusiliers Regimental History)

in Potsdam. On mobilisation on 2 August 1914, the *Lehr* Battalion was expanded to regimental strength as the *Lehr* Infantry Regiment, with three battalions each of four companies. It was formed as follows:

Company	Origin
1st, 3rd, 6th, 11th	*Lehr* Infantry Battalion
5th, 7th, 8th	Infantry Small Arms School
	N.C.O.'s School, Potsdam
	Weapons Trials Centre
2nd, 4th, 9th, 10th	Guards reservists from the Guards Fusiliers, 9th Grenadiers and other Regiments.
12th	All the above
M.G. Coys	All the above

A further re-adjustment occurred on 7/8 July when the 3rd Guards were relieved by the 183rd Division, from the Cambrai sector. The Guards Fusiliers moved to the Ovilliers area and the 3rd or Fusilier Battalion of the 9th Grenadiers (not to be confused with the Guards Fusilier Regiment), with the M.G. Battalion, had been sent to Flers, but were hurriedly recalled and redeployed with Regimental H.Q. at Pozières along with No 3 Company as a reserve; I./9 with three companies, the Fusiliers (III./9) with four companies and the M.G. Battalion in the line from Fricourt to Ovillers; and II./9 in Contalmaison.[24] II./163 I.R. was still in place in Wood and Wood Support; it was relieved by III./122 I.R.[25]

On the eastern side,[26] II./*Lehr* remained with the 5th, 6th and 7th Companies in the line and the 8th Company was in immediate support. The 3rd Battalion of the same Regiment, comprising the 9th, 10th, 11th and 12th Companies, was in and around Flatiron and Sabot Copses. In the second line, I./*Lehr*, the Guards Fusiliers and the 9th Grenadiers continued the line north-eastwards and remained until they were partly relieved in turn for a rest period by the 183rd I.R, whose 2nd Battalion was in the line 400 metres south-west of Martinpuich towards Contalmaison, the 3rd Battalion was south-west of Bazentin le Petit, and the 1st Battalion north and west of Pozières.[27] Behind the *Lehr* Regiment were the Bavarians and the II./184 I.R.[28] The inter-regimental boundary in the Wood seems to have been the central north-south ride – the same boundary as was to be chosen by the British attackers.[29] The conditions were found to be difficult and British artillery fire relentless. III./122 lost five officers and 220 men in two days, for example.

Many of the officers and men of the *Lehr* Regiment had been specially selected as instructors to train the Prussian Guards and were for the most part professional soldiers, *Freiwilliger*, rather than conscripts. This professional core had then been augmented by Guards reservists in order to expand to Regimental strength. After mobilisation the Regiment, as part of the 3rd Guards Division, had taken part in the invasion of Belgium and France; it took part in the capture of Namur and was then transferred to the Eastern Front to join the Eighth Army in time to participate in the First Battle of the Masurian Lakes. It then fought in the Battle of Łódź. It continued fighting in the Carpathians and Galicia and then participated in the Gorlice-Tarnów Offensive before returning, as described above, to the Western Front with the 3rd Guards Division in April 1916. The *Lehr* were among the best trained, best motivated, most experienced and best equipped Regular troops available – and they were to be opposed

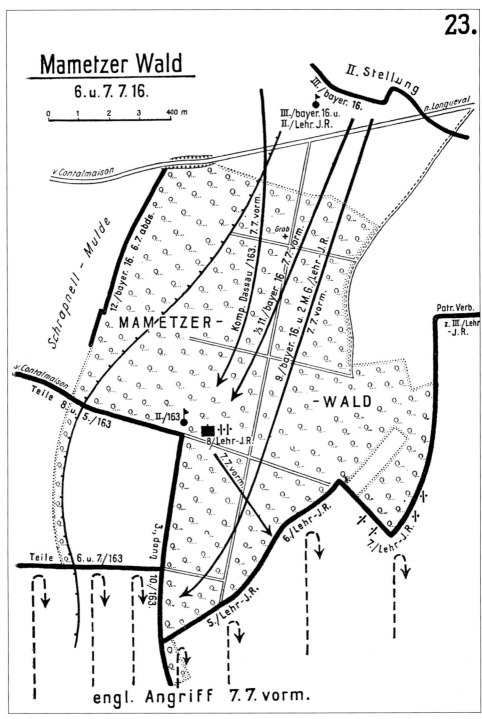

Map 8.iii German dispositions in Mametz Wood, 7 July 1916.
(Source: *German Official History Somme–Nord*)[30]

by a relatively untested New Army brigade – a wholly imperfect instrument for their defeat. The other two Regiments of the 3rd Guards were also largely professional and officered by the Prussian aristocracy.

This accentuated the imbalance of force ratios within the attack zone. On paper, these looked good for the British, with the 17th, 23rd and 38th Divisions, each with 12 battalions, against three German Regiments – 122, 183 and the *Lehr*, each with four battalions. At first glance this looks like 4:1 in favour of the attackers. However, it ignores the presence of other German units of the 9th Grenadiers, the 163rd and the 16th Bavarians, as well as not making allowance for the advantages of the defence in fighting from prepared positions, with prepared artillery support – and of course the quality of the troops engaged. The actual ratio was at best 2:1.

Having received the orders from Headquarters XV Corps, the 38th (Welsh) Division prepared for the assault. On the night of 5 July, the division, with two brigades in the first echelon – 113 and 115 – moved into the line. 113 Brigade held Fritz trench and Danzig Alley with 13 R.W. Fus; Quadrangle and Railway Alley with 14 R.W. Fus; Bottom Wood and Cliff trench with 15 R.W. Fus; and Railway Copse and Bunny Alley with 16 R.W. Fus.[31] 115 Brigade garrisoned Caterpillar Copse, Loop and most of White trench; 114 Brigade was held back in reserve. Emlyn Davies of 17 R.W. Fus described the trenches, the old German first line support, as:

> … studded with dugouts dug deep into the chalky sub-soil… the 40 to 50 feet deep dugouts, making in toto a vast catacomb joined as in a labyrinth. Every convenience had been fitted, including electric lighting, cooking apparatus, and an electric alarm system.[32]

On the division's left was the 17th (Northern) Division which held Quadrangle trench up to its junction with Quadrangle Alley and to the right was the 18th Division, part of XIII Corps, which held Caterpillar Copse. The divisional frontage was therefore around 900 yards. The two assault divisions were supported by the artillery of the divisions which they had relieved in the line – the 21st and 7th respectively; this being because the guns of these divisions had already registered a great many targets and the forward observation officers were well acquainted with the area. During the 5th, what the Army called 'battle procedure' took its course. The orders from the divisional headquarters were framed by the G.S.O. 1, Lieutenant Colonel Henry ap Rhys Pryce, and sent down to the brigades. The commanders and their brigade majors in turn digested the orders, extracted their parts in the plan, framed and issued orders to their battalions – and so on down the line until, it was hoped, every Private soldier knew his task.

On 6 July there was some re-adjustment of positions resulting in a side-step to the right: the 17th Division took over Bottom Wood and the 38th Division assumed responsibility for the western half of Caterpillar Copse and for the advanced post of Marlborough Wood; the latter was held by a platoon of the divisional cyclist company and a section of XV Corps Motor Machine Gun Company, which came under command 115 Infantry Brigade for the operation.[33] The assault was planned for the morning of 7 July. First, a heavy artillery bombardment would be directed onto the German second line and all the support trenches and strong-points in and around the Wood. The timetable for this was firmly laid down by the C.C.R.A. XV Corps and would begin at 07.20 hrs and last for 40 minutes.[34] The 21st Divisional artillery group was reinforced with 121 Brigade of the 38th Division; the whole Wood was to be 'searched' using every available gun with fire especially concentrated on the edges of the Wood in front of the attacking infantry. Acid Drop, Flatiron and Sabot Copses were also targeted, as they were known to harbour German machine-gun posts. Overlaid on the divisional artillery with its 18-pdr and 4.5-inch howitzers would be the corps artillery with its 9.2-inch guns; these would be primarily directed onto the German second line and the various cross-roads and railways in their rear area.[35]

At zero hour, 17th Division was to attack and capture Acid Drop Copse and the small protruding strip L-M-N-K on the south-western corner of Mametz Wood with its disused section of railway line, from the south-west. Simultaneously, the 38th Division would attack and seize the Hammerhead (A-X-C-B) on the eastern side, from the east, but using only one brigade.[36] Both divisions were to work towards the central ride, which was the inter-divisional boundary, and then swing north. 17th Division was to hold the northern edge of the Wood from T to P and to send special parties to clear Wood trench, Wood Support and the remainder of Mametz Wood west of the central ride. 38th Division was also ordered to clear the southern edge of Mametz Wood, and the strip of wood at H, and from it to attack and clear Strip trench from the rear; the northern and eastern edges V-U-T, and to 'join hands' with the 17th Division at the northern edge of the Wood, at Y.[37]

Moreover, a preliminary operation by 52 Infantry Brigade of the 17th Division was required to secure the left flank of the attack. For this, the 17th Division had to attack and capture Quadrangle Support trench and the parts of Pearl Alley and Quadrangle Alley that connected it to the German main line. This would be carried out in darkness with Zero Hour set for 02.00 hrs after a heavy preliminary bombardment of the German positions. The G.O.C. 17th Division, Major General Thomas Pilcher, was not convinced that this operation could succeed. He argued, without success, that an operation not co-ordinated with other activity, and subject to enfilade fire from Contalmaison on the left and Mametz Wood on the right, would fail. He was over-ruled.[38]

The start of the main operation depended on this preliminary attack. If it was successful – and it was assumed that it would be – then Zero Hour would be 08.00 hrs. If Quadrangle Support was still in enemy hands ('failure' was not mentioned) then Zero Hour would be delayed by 30 minutes, a concession known as 'Scheme B'.[39] Quadrangle Support and Pearl trench would then be the first objective of the 17th Division in the main assault. As the attack progressed, the artillery fire would be lifted according to a timetable ahead of the advancing infantry until at 09.30 hrs, all guns would be firing beyond the Wood. In the event of Scheme B being called, the fire plan would commence at 08.00 hrs by firing on Quadrangle Support, before lifting to other targets at 08.30 hrs.[40]

There were several serious problems with the plan as issued. First, the issue of the preliminary operation in the dark, at a time when no night viewing devices were available other than artillery star-shell. Second, the two assaulting divisions would be essentially moving towards each other, and indeed firing into each other. Even in 1916, boundaries were restricted fire lines and were not to be fired over without careful co-ordination and de-confliction; the scheme of manoeuvre in this attack would however guarantee that both direct and indirect fire would meet friendly forces coming in the opposite direction. Third, if the German second line and the small copses were not properly suppressed by the artillery then the attacking troops of the 38th Division would be caught in the flank by enfilade fire from the north and suffer heavy losses. Last, if Scheme B were to be activated, the start of the artillery fire plan would be only 30 minutes before Zero Hour, not 40. None of this seems to have worried the planners at corps and divisional levels. Finally, by delaying until daylight and after a preliminary operation, all chance of surprise would be lost.

In the 38th Division, the task of assaulting the Wood fell to Brigadier General Horatio Evans and 115 Brigade, reinforced by 115 Field Company R.E., 19 Welsh, the troops in Marlborough Wood and with 13 Welsh also available in support and in reserve. At 08.00 hrs on 6 July, ap Rhys Pryce visited Evans and gave him an advance briefing on his mission and tasks. Evans was told to attack the south-east corner of the Wood from Caterpillar Copse at 08.00 hrs, but no mention was made – according to Evans's papers – of any advance to the central ride, nor of a move northward through the Wood.[41] The two men then set out to view the ground. Troops in the line reported that the Wood was held right to the forward edges, but not in great numbers, although it was admitted that there was no definite information on the strength and dispositions of the enemy inside the Wood. Evans made a detailed study of the ground north and east of Caterpillar Copse while Pryce went forward to Marlborough Wood.[42] Evans noted that his men could assemble out of sight of the enemy in dead ground north of Caterpillar Copse provided they did not push too far up towards Bazentin le Grand Wood. Evans also appreciated the problem of enfilade fire from the north and decided that he must confine the attack to a narrow front of a single battalion, with the brigade moving forward in echelon, keeping close to the northern edge of Caterpillar Copse. He also decided on supporting fire from his trench mortars and medium machine guns in Caterpillar Wood.[43]

Evans then met up with Pryce and explained his plan, asking that 'special provision' be made to protect his right flank.[44] The two men then parted, Pryce to work on the divisional operation order and Evans to get his battle procedure going. Evans reached his headquarters between 14.00 and 15.00 hrs that afternoon, 6 July, and issued a warning order to the Commanding Officers of 16 Welsh, whom he detailed to lead the attack, and 10 and 11 S.W.B. which were to be in support; the War Diary of 16 Welsh records that a party of eight officers went forward to reconnoitre the area of Queen's Nullah and beyond; two were wounded by shell fire during the task, while the battalion moved through Carnoy, Triangle Post, Loop, Loop trench, Montauban Alley and Caterpillar trench 'to a valley north of Caterpillar Copse. Between them and Mametz Wood there was a slope which hid them from the enemy's view.'[45] 17 R.W. Fus was to be in brigade reserve even though an additional battalion had been earmarked for this task. Lieutenant Colonels Smith, Greenwood, Porter and Lloyd Mostyn were to make their own reconnaissance and stand by for detailed orders. Evans also ordered Captain Job and Lieutenant Neville of the Trench Mortar and M.G. Companies to make a reconnaissance and report their findings back to him. No orders were, however, sent to the C.O.s of 13 or 19 Welsh; or the O.C. of 151 Field Company; or, it seems, the occupants of Marlborough Wood. Frank Smith of 16 Welsh immediately also realised the danger to his right flank and asked that the battalion form up in the dark, and assault at first light. He was told that as all plans were synchronised at corps level, it was too late to make any change.[46]

Supporting the attack was 113 Brigade under Price-Davies, which was to engage Mametz Wood with machine-gun, rifle and trench mortar fire.[47] At 23.00 hrs on 5 July the brigade was holding Caterpillar Copse with C Company 13 R.W. Fus, White trench with A Company, Danzig Alley and Fritz trench with B and D Companies; 14 R.W. Fus also had A and B Companies in Danzig Alley; 15 R.W. Fus was holding Cliff trench; and 16 R.W. Fus was in Caftet Wood close to Carnoy village, south of Mametz and on the old British front line. H.Q. XV Corps had allocated two *Flammenwerfer* (captured German flame-throwers) to the 38th Division and these arrived with the brigade to help provide support.[48] The brigade reported heavy German artillery fire from midnight onwards and requested counter-battery fire; the German artillery caused significant casualties even though the brigade was only acting in support: three officers and 84 men wounded and 32 men killed on 6 July alone.[49] At 18.00 hrs that evening the Germans made a bombing attack on 15 R.W. Fus which was repelled from Cliff Rrench.[50]

The third brigade of the 38th (Welsh) Division was 114, composed of 10 Welsh, 13 Welsh, 14 Welsh and 15 Welsh. 10 Welsh supplied working parties and carrying parties for casualties and supplies throughout the battles of 5–7 July. 13 Welsh remained in reserve, on call to 115 Brigade, but was never ordered forward. The 14 and 15 Welsh remained in divisional reserve, with 124 Field Company R.E. stayed behind Pommiers Redoubt.

During the afternoon, the G.O.C., Ivor Philipps, briefly called on Brigadier General Evans at H.Q 115 Brigade and made vague references to an objective greater than the Hammerhead and the edge of the Wood. When pressed for details, all he would say was that orders would be issued shortly – thus missing an opportunity for advance warning and preparation.[51] Shortly afterwards, orders were received to move 16 Welsh and 11 S.W.B. into preliminary positions in Loop trench (to the rear of White trench) by 21.00 hrs and then into Caterpillar Copse by 02.00 hrs on 7 July. Evans went off to sort out the move and left Charles Veal, the Brigade Major, to issue the formal orders which were ready in draft, but which might need to be corrected when the divisional operation order arrived.[52] As he did so it began to rain. It had been raining for three days according to the account of Private J.H. Hughes of 11 S.W.B.,[53] and this had turned the ground to clinging mud which made all movement from then on difficult.

The divisional orders were not issued until 20.30 hrs, leaving precious little time for the cascade of information down to the troops. The forming-up places for the four battalions of 115 Brigade were to be much as Evans had envisaged: 16 Welsh, followed by 11 S.W.B. in the valley in front of Caterpillar Copse; 10 S.W.B. in Caterpillar Copse itself, and 17 R.W. Fus further back towards Montauban Alley and Loop trench. 13 Welsh remained as described with 113 Brigade; 19 Welsh moved into Loop trench and both battalions spent all day waiting for orders that never came.[54] However when Lieutenant General Horne, the corps commander, was briefed on these dispositions he decided to interfere – not himself having seen the ground, nor being responsible for the direct conduct of the attack:

> The corps commander considers that it is dangerous to collect more than two battalions in the western end of Caterpillar Wood and valleys in the vicinity owing to the danger of hostile shell fire if the troops are overcrowded. Two battalions are sufficient for the attack on the eastern projection of the wood with a third in support in Montauban Alley and a fourth further back. Any reinforcements required in the wood should shelter by the southern tongue [marked H on the map] which the division should be able to capture without difficulty when the troops have entered the wood from the east, and assisted by those from the west, are clearing up the southern portion of the wood.[55]

The 38th Division's orders were changed accordingly and when Evans returned to his headquarters at 23.00 hrs he found Charles Veal, the Brigade Major, struggling to get amended brigade orders out in time to the battalions. Llewelyn Wyn Griffith had been posted to the brigade headquarters not long before as a staff learner and he recorded Evans's reaction in a conversation the following morning with the Brigade Signal Officer, Captain Andrew Taylor:

> The General was cursing last night at his orders. He said that only a madman could have
> issued them. He called the Divisional Staff a lot of plumbers, herring-gutted at that. He
> argued at the time and asked for some control over the artillery that is going to cover us,
> but he got nothing out of them. We are not allowed to attack at dawn, we must wait for the
> show at Contalmaison… [56]

Taylor replied that he was not surprised that Evans had cursed: 'The truth about the Brigadier
is that he's got too much sense. He was soldiering when some of the fellows above him were
still playing marbles.'[57] It is possible however that Evans misunderstood what he was being told
– probably through tiredness and worry. He appears to have believed that he was being told to
attack on a two-battalion frontage, when he had been at such pains to explain to ap Rhys Pryce
why the frontage had to be narrow. He wrote later that:

> It appears to me now that the dispositions were all cut and dried by divisional headquarters
> and that the reconnaissance was simply made to satisfy them and that I was a mere figure-
> head, I was given no discretion in the matter. These dispositions were the first intimation
> that the attack was to be made on a two-battalion frontage.[58]

However, in the orders as issued, he was not in fact being told to attack in this way at all, merely
being told – unhelpfully, unnecessarily and in a manner probably guaranteed to cause confusion
– where his troops should be positioned *before* the attack, but not *during* it. An addition to the
Divisional Operation Order read as follows:

For the first five lines [i.e. of Order No 36] substitute:

> The general plan of attack will be: 115th Infantry Brigade will have two battalions in posi-
> tion in Caterpillar Wood by 2 a.m. A third battalion will be in Montauban Alley, and a
> fourth battalion near the Loop. The last two should be in position by 6 a.m.[59]

It must also be said that the artillery plan and the preliminary operation were imposed on the
divisional staff from corps; and that some of the refinements, such as the smoke-screens south
of Flatiron and Sabot Copses, were helpful and in accordance with his own request even though
Evans did not himself have control over the guns.

Evans then went out again to speak to his Commanding Officers in Caterpillar Copse and
brief them on the changed plan. Nevertheless, there was little time for the small brigade staff
– the B.M., a staff captain and a learner – to produce detailed orders, different from those of
which Evans already warned his Commanding Officers, and get them into the hands of the
units in a timely manner. It was 02.00 hrs on 7 July, only six hours before Zero, before they
left the headquarters and some time later before the units received them, although the War
Diaries do not record the time of receipt. Under the revised plan of attack, the brigade would
assault Mametz Wood with two battalions leading: 11 S.W.B. on the left, with its left flank
hard up against Caterpillar Copse; and 16 Welsh on the right. Each battalion's frontage was
250 yards, with two companies in each of two waves, all companies with two platoons forward
and one in echelon.[60] The axis of advance was north-west. This alignment meant that the
right flank of 16 Welsh would be dangerously close to Flatiron Copse and its machine-guns
and would therefore form up 'as soon as the smoke barrage on the eastern edge of Mametz

Wood and around Flatiron Copse and Sabot Copse is formed', which was timed for 07.45 hrs.[61] Finally, a reconnaissance patrol was to be sent to the south-eastern tip of the Wood in the early morning, if assurances were forthcoming that the artillery was not firing on that area.[62]

At 02.00 hrs, just as the orders went out to the units of 115 Brigade, the preliminary operation by the 17th Division began.

Pommiers Redoubt, the headquarters of 115 Infantry Brigade.

As it happened, the Germans of 163 I.R. were preparing a counter-attack from Quadrangle Support at the same time and the trench was strongly held. The Germans spotted the attack developing immediately and put up star-shells; to make matters worse, the British artillery barrage fell short, among the attacking troops, and those of the leading wave who made it as far as the German wire found that this was still intact and uncut. The attack petered out. The Germans then counter-attacked at 04.00 hrs but were themselves thrown back – however fighting continued and this, as the official historian later put it: 'greatly interfered with preparations for the main attack.'[63] At 05.25 hrs, the 17th Division received further orders from H.Q. XV Corps to implement its part in Scheme B and to assault Quadrangle Support again at 08.00 hrs. This attack took place in full daylight, uphill, across open ground and through mud. Not surprisingly the German machine-gunners in Mametz Wood had a field day. The attackers pulled back having suffered heavy losses.

Meanwhile the reconnaissance to the southern edge of the Wood which had been ordered was mounted by A Company 15 R.W. Fus under Lieutenant Rees Jones. In the hours before the patrol, the battalion's positions had been heavily bombarded by German 5.9 cm guns. As the patrol moved forward it attracted German machine gun fire which wounded Lieutenant Henry Harris and 11 men. It was clear that the Germans held the edge of the Wood in strength.[64] 15 R.W. Fus held their positions throughout the day until relieved by 16 R.W. Fus which had come forward from reserve at Carnoy.

Soon after dawn, while the fighting around Quadrangle Support was in progress, Llewelyn Wyn Griffith recalled that the headquarters of 115 Brigade closed down in the old German front line and re-opened in Pommiers Redoubt, a captured German position on the road from Mametz to Montauban; it had, as he said, a good view of the Wood although the valley beyond Caterpillar Copse where the battalions were forming up was dead ground.[65] Here, telephone lines were laid to keep Evans in contact with the divisional headquarters, the other brigades, the artillery and, as far as possible, his battalions – although the chief means of communication with the Commanding Officers would be written messages carried by runners. Here, at around 07.00 hrs, Evans returned after a night without sleep. Wyn Griffith reported that:

… standing in a trench, scanning the wood with our glasses, it seemed as thick as virgin forest. There was no sign of life in it, no one could see whether it concealed 10,000 men or 10 machine guns, its edges were clean cut, as far as the eye could see, and the ground between us and the wood was bare of any cover. Our men were assembled in trenches above a dip in the ground, and from these they were to advance, descend into a hollow, and cross the bare slope in the teeth of the machine gunners in the wood. On their right, as they advanced across the bullet-swept zone, they would be exposed to enfilade fire, for the direction of their advance was nearly parallel to the German trenches towards Bazentin, and it would be folly to suppose that the German machine guns were not sited to sweep that slope leading to the wood.[66]

Shortly afterwards, news came in of the failure of the 17th Division's attack and the re-timing of Zero Hour to 08.30 hrs under Scheme B; the information was sent on to the battalions. Evans also recounted later that he had been instructed to make contact with the officer appointed by the corps headquarters to arrange the smoke barrage, but as there was no information as to who or where this officer might be, no contact was made.[67] In the event, no smoke was laid down. Some authorities have suggested that this was because the wind was not favourable, however the answer becomes clear when one makes a detailed comparison of the Corps and Divisional Operation Orders. The requirement for a smoke barrage is laid down in the 38th Division's order, however there is no mention of it at all in the XV Corps order or the accompanying artillery operation order. Therefore, the smoke barrage was merely an aspiration by the divisional staff, which they had neglected to co-ordinate and demand from the corps level of command. At the time, this failure contributed hugely to the loss of life on 7 July and as with the German entrenchments on the edges of Mametz Wood, it is surprising that previous researchers have not uncovered it. The most likely explanation is that those same researchers had no military experience and did not, therefore, understand what they were looking *for* in terms of military-technical information, nor when they saw it, what they were looking at.

At 08.00 hrs, as ordered, the artillery barrage began. Emlyn Davies recalled that the: 'Preliminary bombardment seemed to set the wood on fire, smoke pouring forth in quantity and density almost obscuring all vision.'[68] The German accounts describe it as '*Trommelfeuer*', or drumfire.[69] However it must be recalled that Davies was in 17 R.W. Fus, and was at least a mile from the start line of the attack. His description is therefore suspect and probably drawn from a different occasion. There were in fact problems, as Wyn Griffith recalled:

A few minutes after eight, all our telephone wires to the battalions were cut by the enemy's reply to our fire. There was no smoke screen, for some reason never explained – perhaps someone forgot about it. [N.B., see above] This was the first departure from the simplicity of the printed word [i.e. of the Operation Order as issued]. Messages came through, a steady trickle of runners bringing evil news; our fire had not masked the German machine guns in Mametz Wood, nor in the wood near Bazentin …[70]

The two leading battalions had formed up as already described.[71] They began the assault as planned at 08.30 hrs as soon as the barrage lifted, but because of the disruption of the communications, the news did not reach Evans until 09.20 hrs.[72] At about the same time, the Machine Gun Company was ordered to send two additional guns to the west of Caterpillar Copse to enfilade German trenches on the eastern end of Mametz Wood. As soon as the main advance began, 11 S.W.B. and 16 Welsh came under heavy flanking fire from the Prussian Guards in Flatiron and Sabot copses. The attack got no closer than 300 yards from the edge of Mametz Wood and the survivors took cover in shell holes; following waves in turn came under the same heavy fire and had to be pulled back into dead ground. According to Thomas Marden, 'machine guns smote them hip and thigh… the enemy concentrated their fire on the successive waves, as they came over the crest, and annihilated them in turn.'[73] Private William Joshua, a Lewis gunner in the leading wave of 16 Welsh, later recalled in a letter to the author Colin Hughes, that:

> We advanced about 50 yards when the German machine guns opened up. Sergeant Harries [*sic*] shouted out they are yards high and it appeared so, then going down a gentle slope to the wood the enemy got range with deadly effect.
>
> One of my gun team gave me the signal to take a casualty's place in the team, and as I struggled on, I felt a severe shock in my thigh and I was looking down for my leg, thinking I had lost it. Another platoon came along and rested for a breather leaving about 10 casualties behind including a sergeant from the cycle company of which a number had joined us to bring us up to strength. Each wave passing me left its quota of dead behind.
>
> Our company runner came along and asked me where Capt. Hardman [the Company Commander] was, as the order was to retire. I replied that he was somewhere ahead. A large number of our planes were flying low.
>
> Now the German artillery started up, and to add to the horror rain started to fall heavily making the churned-up ground into clinging mud. I dumped my equipment and started to crawl back, hugging the ground. Some stretcher bearers found me and took me to a large shell hole. They were members of the Tylerstown Silver Band who had enlisted en bloc in our early recruiting days…
>
> My two sergeants, Harries[*] and Thomas[†] were killed also my closest pals G. Leyshon and Reg Davies.[‡] Two brothers Trevaskis [*sic*] died.[§] They were always first on parade when we formed in Porthcawl; made corporals the same day; officers the same day and die together.[74]

Major James Angus, the Second-in-Command of 16 Welsh, showed great leadership and personal courage in exposing himself to enemy fire while directing the advance. Thirty-four year old Captain John Williams of C Company was also prominent and was badly wounded; he died of his wounds on 12 July. Williams was a noted rugby player, who played club rugby for Cardiff. A three times Triple Crown winner, out of 17 appearances for Wales, usually on the wing, he was on the losing side only twice. He also spoke fluent French. Company Sergeant Major Richard Thomas, mentioned by Joshua, was lying beside Captain Williams; he attempted

---

*   Charles Harris, b. 1883 See <http://glamarchives.gov.uk> (Accessed 25 January 2018).
†   Company Sergeant Major Richard Thomas, b. 1881 <http://glamarchives.gov.uk> (Accessed 25 January 2018).
‡   Privates Ernest Alfred Leyshon and Reginald Davies <http://glamarchives.gov.uk> (Accessed 25 January 2018).
§   Leonard and Arthur Tregaskis, b 1883 and 1884 respectively <http://glamarchives.gov.uk> (Accessed 25 January 2018).

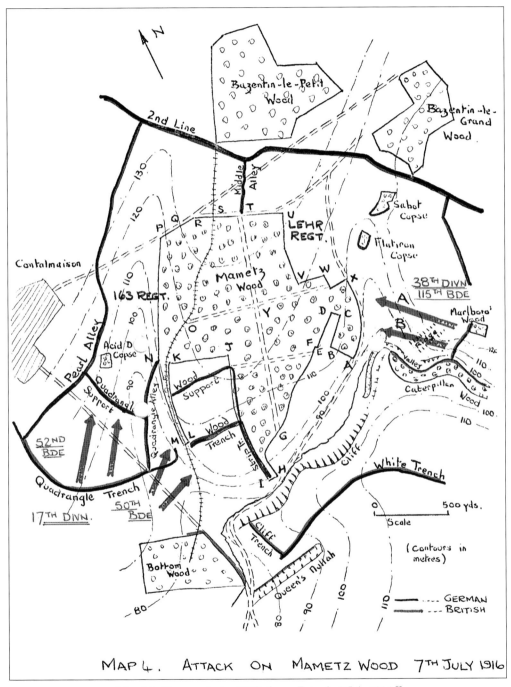

Map 8.iv The assaults by 115 Infantry Brigade, 7 July 1916.[75]

Note: All letters noted in the text hereafter refer to this map.

Modern photograph of the culminating point of the attack on 7 July. (A.M. Goulden)

to move forward and while raising himself up was shot through the head. Thomas, a member of the Glamorgan Constabulary in peace-time, was also a Welsh rugby international. The Tregaskis brothers were not the only siblings in 16 Welsh to die at Mametz: Privates Henry and Charles Morgan, from Cardiff, were both killed on 7 July; and Privates Albert and Ernest Oliver were killed on 7 and 10 July respectively. Jonathan Hicks gives detailed biographies and accounts of many of the casualties in 16 Welsh, in his book *The Welsh at Mametz.*

11 S.W.B., meanwhile, tried to approach Mametz Wood through the gulley running between Caterpillar Copse and the slope leading up towards Flatiron Copse, in dead ground, with B Company leading, but machine gun fire from the edge of Mametz Wood drove the battalion back. The Adjutant of the battalion, Lieutenant Thomas Pryce Hamer, another amateur rugby international, was killed by fire from the Hammerhead.[76] Private J.H. Hughes, a survivor, recalled:

> The Germans had seen what our intentions were, for they came running from … Bazentin le Petit up to the Wood, having machine-guns and snipers already there, our lads rushed to get over the top of the ridge, but they fell as quickly as they appeared… about two platoons got over, and from there, did not move.[77]

Because communications were so bad, Charles Veal sent his Staff Captain, Harold Hinton,* to Caterpillar Copse. Hinton sent back a written note which arrived at 10.10 hrs, telling Evans and

---

*   Captain Harold Virgo Hinton, late of the Welsh now General List [T.N.A. WO 95/2560, 115 Brigade War Diary]

Veal that the attack had stalled and that the troops were digging in about 300 yards from the Wood having taken casualties amounting to one officer and 60 men in 16 Welsh; five officers and 30 men in 11 S.W.B.[78] He suggested another artillery bombardment and this suggestion was immediately sent to the C.R.A. at divisional headquarters. Evans also gave orders that the Brigade Machine Gun Company under Captain Edward Job was to push another two guns into Caterpillar Copse and engage Sabot and Flatiron Copses in order to neutralise the German fire. But in the meantime, the situation was deteriorating beyond Evans's ability to control it. German fire was intensifying, as Joshua's and Hughes's accounts testify, and casualties were mounting. Hughes also recalled that the German gunners deliberately targeted wounded men trying to get back, and stretcher bearers: 'I many times murmured what curs they were.'[79] This was not the only recorded incident of German soldiers murdering the wounded: Sergeant Tom Price of 13 Welsh also reported that 'I saw the Germans that had come out of the wood bayoneting our wounded – I saw the downward motion of their rifles which indicated to me what they were doing – bayoneting our wounded boys.'[80] 10 S.W.B. was ordered to reinforce the two leading battalions but the battalion's progress was slow through the muddy, congested trenches and it was 13.30 hrs before the leading company arrived in the area[81] – further proof that Evans's original dispositions had been more correct than those imposed from above.

On receipt of Evans's message, the C.R.A. 38th Division, Brigadier General William Thompson, was in communication with the corps headquarters by wireless – the 7th Division had been ordered to hand over two wireless stations to the 38th[82] – and initially the request was not well received: 38th Division was told to 'continue the fight keeping the situation in their own hands,' and not to commit more than two battalions.[83] However, for some reason there was a change of heart and soon the two were preparing the new bombardment fire plan. At 10.20 hrs, Thompson was informed that the corps artillery would bombard the eastern side of Mametz Wood from 10.45 hrs to 11.15 hrs and, ignoring the omission of earlier, the C.C.R.A. added that if he 'wanted more smoke barrage they could employ the special party which was with them.' It is not clear whether this was a gunner fire control party or Royal Engineer special company. Thompson was also told to use the fire from his own batteries which could, unlike the heavy guns' fire, be observed and corrected.[84] This information was passed to Evans – the War Diary says that he received it at 10.25 hrs – but there was no chance that he would be able to get word down to the battalions in time:

> We were a thousand yards away from the battalions, with no telephone communication; there were maps at divisional headquarters, they knew where we were, they knew where the battalions were, and they knew that our lines were cut. A simple sum in arithmetic… Our operation was isolated; no one was attacking on either flank of our Brigade, so there was complete freedom of choice as to time. With all the hours of the clock to choose from, some mastermind must needs select the only hour to be avoided. He did not ask himself whether the order could reach its ultimate destination in time… the answer to that sum in arithmetic.[85]

As it happened, by 11.00 hrs, Taylor and his signallers had restored the telephone lines. Frank Smith of 16 Welsh called in to report that the artillery fire was dropping on his men in spite of the flares that had been issued to mark the forward edge of the advance and which were lit at 11.00, 15.00 and 19.00 hrs.[86] Even so, he was using the barrage to advance slowly. However,

Officers of 16 Welsh before the battle. (RWF Mus)

inaccurate high explosive fire and lack of smoke again failed to neutralise the Germans' enfilade shoot from the north and the attack ground to a halt once more. At 14.15 hrs, the leading companies of 10 S.W.B. took up the attack for a third time but the Commanding Officer, Lieutenant Colonel Sidney Wilkinson,[*] was killed and the advance again petered out.[87] It must be remembered that the *Lehr* Regiment contained many former instructors from the Small Arms School, who were excellent shots and were effectively snipers. These men would have identified priority targets, especially officers, and killed them without compunction.

Throughout the day, casualties had been collected by stretcher bearers and dealt with by the field ambulances. 130th Field Ambulance had set up an advanced dressing station at the Citadel and a main dressing station in the church at Morlancourt; here it dealt with the less seriously wounded – 'sitting cases' – all those more seriously wounded were to be sent to 131st Field Ambulance and those who were sick to 129th. There were also advanced collecting sections at Minden and Triangle Posts, on the Mametz – Montauban Road, of four officers and 108 men with six motor and three horse-drawn ambulances. Four abandoned German dugouts within Caterpillar Copse were also found, cleaned out, and taken into use for collecting wounded. Bivouacs were constructed nearby from waterproof sheets and walking wounded collected and sent back to the Loop through Caterpillar trench, which was too narrow for stretchers.[88] The sodden ground and the heavy fire of the enemy made it impossible to get casualties back quickly from Caterpillar Copse and so stretcher cases were carried across the open ground between trenches in order to reach the dressing stations at

[*]   Lieutenant Colonel Charles Darley Harvey DSO, *Foresters*, took command on 9 July. His diary is in the archives of the Royal Welsh in Brecon, 1.88 Box 17.

Triangle or Minden Posts – stretcher bearers were at times carrying their wounded burdens for up to three miles through the mud at the cost of casualties to the stretcher bearers, medical orderlies and doctors.

A fourth attack was ordered by Headquarters XV Corps over the wireless link to H.Q. 38th Division for 17.00 hrs, preceded by another heavy bombardment of 30 minutes; the corps commander was insistent that the troops must get into the eastern edge of Mametz Wood.[89] The orders for this were not in Evans's hands until after 16.00 hrs and the telephone lines forward were again cut. Evans decided that he must go himself into Caterpillar Copse to organise the new attack and bring up the last available battalion, 17 R.W. Fus. Llewelyn Wyn Griffith went with him:

> … we set out for Caterpillar Wood and to reach the battalions. Although the day was fine, the heavy rains of the preceding days had turned the chalky soil into a stiff glue. The hurry in our minds accentuated the slowness of our progress, and I felt as if some physical force was dragging me back. Haste meant a fall into a shell hole, for we had abandoned the attempt to move along the trench. Shrapnel was bursting overhead, and a patter of machine-gun bullets spat through the air. We passed through Caterpillar Wood, and in a disused trench on our left I saw an Artillery officer. I turned off to ask him whether his telephone was working and learned that he was in communication with a Heavy Artillery Group somewhere beyond Pommiers Redoubt [i.e. the corps heavy artillery]. I ran down the trench to re-join the General, and we dropped down the bank into the nullah between Caterpillar Wood and Mametz Wood, passing a stream of "walking wounded" making their way out. There was a dug-out in the bank, with scores of stretchers down on the ground in front, each stretcher occupied by a fellow creature, maimed and in pain. This was the Advance Dressing Station; 20 rounds of shrapnel would have made stretchers unnecessary. Along the bare ridge rising up to Mametz Wood our men were burrowing into the ground with their entrenching tools, seeking whatever cover they might make. A few shells were falling, surprisingly few. Wounded men were crawling back from the ridge, men were crawling forward with ammunition. No attack could succeed over such ground as this, swept from front and side by machine-guns at short range. Down in the nullah we were out of sight of the enemy, but 15 minutes of shrapnel would have reduced the brigade to a battalion, and every minute that passed seemed to bring nearer the hour of our inevitable annihilation. We were caught in a trap, unable to advance, unable to withdraw without being observed. It must ever remain one of the many mysteries of the War why the enemy did not pound us with shell fire, for this was so obviously the only place of assembly.[90]

It was now 16.40 hrs, only 20 minutes before the laid-down Zero Hour. The leading battalions of 115 Brigade were exhausted and casualties, especially among the officers, were high. 16 Welsh, the battalion most heavily engaged, had lost six officers dead, another six wounded, and 268 men killed, wounded and missing:[91] that is around a third of its fighting strength and enough to render it ineffective. Evans called the Commanding Officers together and ordered them to prepare to assault the Wood again, with 17 R.W. Fus and 10 S.W.B. in the first wave. By the time this had been sorted out – in particular it took time for 17 R.W. Fus to get forward, the artillery bombardment had come and gone – and gone too deeply into the Wood to have any effect on the defences at the Wood's edge. The Germans were fully alert. Evans was not prepared to launch an assault under these conditions and knew that it would take more time to co-ordinate a fresh attack. He was determined therefore to postpone the operation until later that evening or even the following morning. Wyn Griffith recalled that:

> "This is sheer lunacy," said the General. "I've tried all day to stop it. We could creep up to the edge of the Wood by night and rush it in the morning, but they won't listen to me…. It breaks my heart to see all this." "If I could get you through on the telephone, would you talk to them again?" I asked. "Of course, I would, but all the wires are cut, and there is no time to go back." "I know of a telephone to an Artillery Group, and they might get you through to the Division," I answered. "Find out at once whether I can get through," he replied.
>
> I hurried up to the trench where I had seen the Artillery officer and found that his wires were still uncut, and as I ran back to the General, I prayed in my heart that they would hold; the lives of some hundreds of men depended upon it… When I came back to the hollow, I could not find the General. I ran from one group of men to another, working my way up the ridge, until I found him organizing the defence of the position against any possible counter-attack… 10 minutes later I sat in the trench while the General spoke on the telephone, tersely describing the utter folly of any course of action other than a gradual withdrawal under cover of outposts, and quoting figures of our casualties. He was arguing with determination. There was opposition, but he won.[92]

Wyn Griffith persuaded Evans to rest for a while and as he had eaten nothing all day, brewed tea in a signallers' dugout and gave it to the General along with some cheese and a ration biscuit from his haversack. Evans, close to exhaustion, unburdened himself to Wyn Griffith, who felt that Evans had saved the lives of many hundreds of his officers and men:

> I spoke my mind about the whole business … you heard me. They wanted us to press on at all costs, talked about determination, and suggested that I didn't realize the importance of the operation. As good as told me that I was tired and didn't want to tackle the job. Difficult to judge on the spot, they said! As if the whole trouble hadn't arisen because someone found it so easy to judge when he was six miles away and had never seen the country and couldn't read a map. You mark my words, they'll send me home for this: they want butchers, not brigadiers. They'll remember now that I told them, before we began, that the attack could not succeed unless the machine guns were masked. I shall be in England in a month.[93]

Evans was indeed relieved of his command, but not for another six weeks. There is no evidence that he was dismissed because of his outspoken views, or for want of zeal; there were plenty of examples of this happening and in such cases, removal was immediate. Evans in fact left command in August at the age of 56, having commanded the brigade in the field since November 1915, at a time when the brigade was employed in a quiet sector of the line near Serre.[94] Changing command and passing it to a younger man was not, in these circumstances, out of the ordinary. Moreover, his opinion was shared by Philipps, the G.O.C., who is reported to have given instructions that if 115 Brigade experienced heavy machine gun fire it should withdraw and request a further bombardment.[95]

German accounts of the fighting on 7 July are sketchy. The regimental history of the 163rd Regiment described the trenches around Mametz Wood during the rain that fell as 'filled with water and mud so that working and moving around was made very difficult. The shelters turned into water holes and thus, lost their purpose of protection; some of them collapsed altogether.'[96] However it is also clear that as well as entrenching the southern and eastern edges of Mametz Wood, although they had not been able to put up barbed wire, the Germans had connected these trenches to Flatiron and Sabot Copses by a hidden communication trench. They had also developed the trench known as *Mittelallee* – Middle Alley – from the second line to the central ride of Mametz Wood on its northern edge. This was remarked on by many veterans at the time,[97] but seems not have been give weight – or even noticed – by historians of the battle.

An account by the *Lehr* Regiment stated:

> On 7 July, the enemy artillery increased fire until it became a barrage and in the evening, their artillery tried to penetrate the 5./L.I.R [i.e. the 5th Company of the 2nd Battalion *Lehr* Infantry Regiment] and parts of Infantry Regiment 122. They did not succeed.
>
> West of Mametz Woods, the English infantry tried to advance towards the Bavarian Infantry Regiment 16. Here, too, they did not manage to gain a foothold. The platoon *Setzermann* of the Machine Gun Company *Ludwig* was able to counter these attempts of attack from their position at the South-West edge of Mametz Woods with great success and supported Infantry Regiment 16 effectively in their defence.
>
> However, what sacrifices were made to obtain this defence! *Leutnant* R. Posse of the 11th Company Lehr Infantry Regiment was wounded, the *Unteroffiziere* Josesofski, Marburg, von Schmeling, Tacke and 22 fusiliers of the Guards fell, 134 wounded, seven missing.[98]

A British air observer concurred with this assessment, dropping a note at 17.30 hrs to say that Quadrangle Support trench was still strongly held and that he could plainly see the field grey uniforms from 800 feet up; and that throughout the assaults to the west of the Wood, German signal rockets could be observed, followed by heavy artillery fire being brought down on the attackers.[99]

The official German account of the Somme in the *Schlachten des Weltkrieges* series has this to say, although it must be observed that the text does not accord with the dispositions noted on the accompanying maps:

> At about 10 am [on 7 July 1916], a severe English attack against the positions between Contalmaison and Mametz Woods as well as against its south-eastern edge began. 9 West Riding Battalion and 12 Manchester Battalion (52 Brigade) attacked 2./Lehr-Infanterie-Regiment, 12., 9. and 11./163 while 16 Welsh and 20 South Wales Borders (114 and 115 Brigade, 38 Division [*sic*] attacked 10./163 and 11/Lehr-Infanterie regiment. These strong English [*sic*] forces emerged mainly through the *Schrapnellmulde* in order to attack 11./163 from behind [i.e., the re-entrant to the west of Mametz Wood]. *Leutnant* of Reserve Boss took the left wing platoon and rushed forward; he bombarded the English who advanced in a single phalanx formation and subsequently retreated suffering substantial losses due to their confusion by the surprise attack.[100]

The supporting fire of the artillery and of 113 Brigade, the trench mortars and the M.M.G.s was not therefore completely ineffective. However, even if troops had managed on 7 July to get into the Hammerhead after crossing the open ground, swept as it was by German fire, they would have faced huge problems. 115 Brigade War Diary tells us that: 'Owing to the dense nature of the undergrowth it would have been impracticable to have carried out the programme for the attack as laid down by the time given even had no opposition been encountered.'[101]

Reasons for the failure on 7 July are not hard to find. Aside from the rain, mud and contrary wind, the assaulting troops were subjected to heavy, unsuppressed flanking fire from Flatiron and Sabot Copses, and frontal fire from the edge of Mametz Wood; artillery preparation was poorly co-ordinated with the advancing infantry and badly delivered; the lack of the smoke screen was a disaster; timings were hopelessly over-ambitious; communications by telephone and runner were shaky and inadequate to stitch together a complex plan. The assault took place in daylight, when either a surprise attack at dawn or a night attack in darkness would have been better timed. Any attack should have been simultaneous with the assault of the 17th Division, thus preventing the Germans from concentrating all available artillery on each attack in turn. Only a single brigade of the 38th Division had been committed, and in that brigade only three of six available battalions had been put into action. At corps level, the various assaults and barrages were poorly orchestrated and did not deliver concentration or surprise – principles of war and of the attack – onto the enemy, who was therefore allowed time continually to recover, re-group and counter-attack either by fire or by manoeuvre.

It is the duty of every level of command to de-conflict and co-ordinate its subordinate forma-tions, allocating resources and priorities. In this case, H.Q. XV Corps seems to have acted simply as a post-box for messages, when not actively interfering with the tasks allocated to its subordinates; nor had H.Q. 38th Division covered itself with glory. Only one of its brigades was in action and rather than allowing Evans to conduct the battle, with control over the artillery, it had tried to manage matters by remote control. Even worse, there had been no calculation of the time required to prepare for the various attacks. Evans later wrote that this was:

> … a deliberate operation which required careful preparation and personal reconnaissance of the whole area by me with the COs. This was physically impossible to do. The position of Brigade Headquarters was such that no personal observation could be obtained of the progress of the attack.[102]

It is clear that the 38th Division Headquarters was being very heavily directed from XV Corps and it may therefore be going too far to place all the blame for piecemeal attacks on Philipps; it was after all Horne who had directed the attack from two opposing directions on 7 July from positions over a mile apart. That said, Philipps had certainly failed to organise supporting fire (see below 113 Brigade) even though 113 Brigade's objective, as ordered by Horne, was to be ready to enter the Wood via the southern strip.

Going up a level of command, Headquarters XV Corps seems to have been far more ready to interfere with, and proscribe, the work of its divisions, than to command, control and co-ordi-nate their actions – possibly because Horne did not trust either Philipps or Pilcher. Pilcher himself, who was like Philipps later removed from command, disputed the orders he had been given and did his best to mitigate the casualties which he knew would follow: 'It is very easy', he wrote, 'to sit a few miles in the rear, and get credit for allowing men to be killed in an undertaking foredoomed to failure…'[103] The Corps Headquarters also failed to allow sufficient time for the passage of orders and made no allowance for any breakdown in communications or for the operation of Murphy's Law – that anything that can go wrong, will go wrong.

However, Evans must come in for at least part of the blame, having hitherto been regarded as the hero of the piece for, rightly, having got the final assault cancelled. He was very hard on himself in his personal notes written after the event:

> I cannot be held blameless in the conduct of the attack in the following points. I should have impressed more strongly on C.O.s when I saw them in the nullah the absolute necessity of going straight for the wood at all costs. Had more determination been shown by them at the outset it is possible that the edge of the wood might have been gained though with very heavy casualties.
>
> I should have followed my inclinations and have gone down to Caterpillar Wood when I could get no information. I should then have obtained a better grasp of the situation and my personal order that a direct advance be made … would have had more weight than such an order from a staff captain.
>
> Again, I should at a later stage have gone down with 10 S.W.B. I should have been there sufficiently early to draft definite suggestions for a further attack in the event of success not being gained …
>
> I did not make clear what was in my mind that with a modification of the artillery programme, bringing up the few remaining available reserves, replenishing the T.M. [trench mortar] ammunition and thoroughly reorganising units and explaining in detail on the ground I should be prepared to again attack in two or three hours.[104]

All the above may or may not be true and in his defence, Evans was in the pinch so often felt by formation commanders before the advent of radio – that once away from the headquarters and the telephone lines, the closer he got to the front line, the smaller his span of command would become and the less, therefore, he would be able to control.

However, Evans also misinterpreted his orders concerning the attack frontage and did not contest them with the G.O.C.; nor was he, it seems, ever going to commit more than two battalions to the Wood, when in fact he had six battalions available to him – his original four plus 19 Welsh which, although a pioneer unit, was capable of combat; and also 13 Welsh which was in reserve and available to him. Given that the Germans had four companies on the edge of the Wood – the 5th, 6th 7th and 8th Companies of the *Lehr* Regiment – Evans's plan to assault with only the four companies of 16 Welsh was hopelessly inadequate to break in to the German position and then roll it up; even with 11 S.W.B. following, the local force ratios were only 8:4, or 2:1, not taking into account the disparity of quality among the forces engaged which has been addressed in Chapter Five; as well as the advantage the defenders enjoyed in being entrenched and prepared. The minimum required would usually be at least 3:1, or better still, as previously discussed, 5:1. With anything less, casualties would rapidly have eroded the attackers' combat power and brought them to a halt. This is underlined by the quality of the assaulting troops – these were not the men of the 7th Division who had penetrated the German first line, but far less experienced and far less well-trained troops. Evans had enough forces to attack, first, the two Copses and remove the threat of flanking fire using most of a full battalion on each if needed, and still retain 12 companies for the assault on the Wood. All assaults would, however, have needed heavy supporting fire from both artillery and trench mortars, and from machine guns to avoid what happened to 11 S.W.B. even when that battalion used the most covered approach to the Wood.

The need for suppressing fire is additionally vital when considering the perspective of individual soldiers, as Chris Williams and Colin Hughes both point out in their analyses of the battle. General Horne is on record as saying that: 'machine guns will not stop fresh troops if they mean to get in'. However, one can only surmise that Horne himself had never experienced machine gun fire and I, the author of this book, can assure his ghost from personal experience that he was talking nonsense. The technology of 1916, the German Army's *Maxim Maschinengewehr 08*, could deliver up to 600 rounds per minute, per gun, and keep firing almost indefinitely if supplied with enough ammunition. A single gun could therefore destroy an entire battalion in just over a minute, unless the gunners were made to take cover.[105] Rudolf Stadebacher, a German machine-gunner in 111 R.I.R. which was located close by, to the west, reported firing 22,000 rounds on 1 July and inflicting 'dreadful casualties' on the British.[106] As a result, some soldiers simply went to ground when they came under effective fire; others turned back. 'We just wilted', recalled one survivor who had been under this devastating fire.[107] The Germans' pre-planned artillery tasks, as described Chapter Three, was also deadly. Once the first assault had been halted and the troops brought to the ground by machine gun fire, it was artillery fire that killed most men. 'Our position became a living hell', wrote Sergeant Perriman of 11 S.W.B., who had been ordered to take a platoon back into Caterpillar Wood and then attack the machine gun posts that were causing the havoc. The attack was put in but Perriman and others were hit by shrapnel, bringing it to a halt.[108] To have followed Horne's principle would have led to enormous casualties, for no result.

It is easy to criticise the role and effectiveness of the artillery, but one must be mindful of the state of the available technology as previously explained in Chapter Four. Without radio, it was impossible to keep the barrage directly in front of the infantry and thus silence the German machine-gunners. Even so, the view of senior gunners was described in a report after the Somme battle by Colonel S.W.H. Rawlins, and cited by Colin Hughes: 'the full destructive power of the available artillery must not be sacrificed to, nor be impeded by, the whims of subordinate commanders.'[109] The principle that artillery would be commanded at the highest level but controlled at the lowest was still in the future, and dependent on the introduction of battlefield radio. On the other hand, Kiggell, Haig's Chief of Staff, wrote in a General Order to all armies – re-transmitted to all corps and then divisions – some important lessons on what later became known as the creeping barrage:

> It is beyond dispute that on several occasions where field artillery has made a considerable "lift", that is to say, has outstripped the infantry advance, the enemy has been able to man his parapets with rifle and machine gun. An infantry brigadier whose command has met with conspicuous success, ascribes it largely to the fact that his men have insisted on advancing close under the field artillery fire, even at the risk of an occasional casualty from our own guns. His men were thus enabled to gain an enemy's trench almost without loss and in time to meet the defenders' hand to hand as they emerged from their dugouts and before they could mount their machine guns.[110]

Evans's personal notes state, bitterly, that: 'The artillery had not previously registered on the points on which fire was directed and observation was very difficult consequently their fire was

British 4.7-inch gun in action, June 1916.

ineffective and did not attain the desired results.'[111] As the artillery was that of the in-place divisions, it *should* have been registered and therefore both accurate and observed; the orders from the C.C.R.A. XV Corps, tellingly, contain no instructions to register targets.

Things had gone badly for the 38th (Welsh) Division, but they had gone no better on the western side of the Wood. Renewed efforts by the 17th Division had failed to make progress and III Corps had been evicted from Contalmaison by a German counter-attack; a planned assault here at 20.00 hrs was also cancelled. The objective of the 17th Division in particular was a formidable challenge, as was laid out by Arthur Conan Doyle in his survey of the war in 1918.[112] 113 Brigade had lent supporting fire and was then ordered to support the 17th Division by making a reconnaissance of Strip trench and then a demonstration south of the trench to draw the Germans' attention away from Wood trench. 16 R.W. Fus had been tasked with this and, astonishingly, two patrols managed to get up to Strip trench via a communication trench, reporting it strongly held. They were followed by a party of 30 bombers under Lieutenant H.J. Cundall, the brigade bombing officer, and two companies of 15 R.W. Fus. However the Germans soon discovered the attackers and, with surprise gone, machine-gun fire drove them back with the loss of three officers wounded, four men killed and 63 wounded.[113] Writing after the war, Price-Davies commented on this episode, the lack of communication within his brigade, to other brigades and to the divisional headquarters, and to his dislocation from the brigade units on 7 July:

> I was visiting my forward posts and looked down on Mametz Wood at a few hundred yards' range. I was by a Lewis gun post when I became aware of an attack in progress by what I believe were the 6th Dorsets [in the 17th Division which was attacking the Wood from the west while 115 Brigade attacked from the east]. They were creeping forward and using rifle grenades against the strip of wood jutting out towards us. I had never heard of this attack and got covering fire to work as quickly as possible, but the Lewis gun jammed, and the

attack fizzled out… We occupied a position from which very heavy covering fire could have been brought to bear had this been organised.[114]

115 Brigade was pulled back leaving only two companies of 17 R.W. Fus, which had not been engaged, to hold Caterpillar Copse and Marlborough Wood. There had been some successes, as Jonathan Hicks rightly points out: the trench mortars had put two German guns in the southern part of Mametz Wood out of action, and the M.G. Company had reduced the enemy fire from Bazentin le Grand Wood, Flatiron and Sabot Copses.[115] However at the end of the day, as darkness fell, both III and XV Corps were back where they had started that morning.[116]

Notes

1   Sheffield and Bourne, pp. 196, 198
2   Kiggell to Rawlinson dated 8 July 1916, RWLN 1/6 f. 87d in the war journal of Lord Rawlinson of Trent (Rawlinson MS), Library of Churchill College Cambridge.
3   Rawlinson MS, 9 July 1916.
4   Sheffield and Bourne, p. 202.
5   Munby, p. 17.
6   Gerald Gliddon, *The Battle of the Somme: A Topographical History* (Stroud, 1996). The features are described alphabetically.
7   T.N.A. WO 95/431, Operation Order 32/2/23 (G) dated 5 July 1916 in Headquarters Fourth Army War Diary.
8   Rawlinson MS, 7 July 1916.
9   Sassoon, *Memoirs of an Infantry Officer,* p. 64.
10 *The Times,* 14 July 1916. The correspondent's article was written two days before.
11 The description was obtained from the author's personal reconnaissance of the ground in July 2016 and June 2018; see also the patrol report of 3/4 July 1916 from 2 R. Irish in Appendix II to WO 95/2539, 38th (Welsh) Division War Diary, July 1916.
12 'The German Defence during the Battle of the Somme: Mametz Wood and Contalmaisons, 9th-10th of July 1916', part of the series 'The Other Side of the Hill' in *Army Quarterly* Volume IX, No. 2, January 1925, p. 251.
13 Appendix IV to H.Q. XV Corps Operation Order No 14, dated 5 July 1916.
14 Archaeological Excavation Report Mametz Wood
15 T.N.A. CAB 45/189, Letter from Gaussen.
16 A. Stosch, *Deutsche Reichsarchiv, Schlaten des Weltkrieges* (*Taschenbuch,* Berlin, 1930), 'Anlage zu Band 20, Pt I, Somme–Nord',* maps 19 and 20; Josef Karl Brennslecht, *Das Königlich Bayerische 16. Infanerie-Regiment Großherzog Ferdinand von Totana im Weltkrieg 1914–1918* (München, 1931), p. 187.
17 Brennslecht, p. 194.
18 T.N.A. WO 95/2539, 38th Division War Diary, July 1916, entry on 7 July 1916. See also the account in 'The Other Side of the Hill No 2', p. 251.
19 W.R. Thomas, ‚Notes on the 1914–18 War', p. 68.
20 Holge Ritter, *Geschichte des Schleswig-Holsteinschen Infanterie-Regiment Nr. 163* (Oldenburg, 1926), p. 134.
21 Brennslecht, p. 187.
22 'The Other Side of the Hill No. 2', p. 246.
23 Generalmajor a.D. Carl Graf von der Schulenburg-Wolfsburg, *Geschichte des Garde-Fusilier-Regiments,* Preuß. Anteil, Band 157, Appendix (Berlin, 1926).
24 Schulenburg-Wolfsburg, p. 129; J. von Hansch & F. Weidling, *Das Colbergsche Grenadier-Regiment Graf Gneisenau (2. Pommersches) Nr. 9 im Weltkriege 1914–1918* (Oldenburg 1929), pp. 292–294.
25 Ritter, p. 138.
26 Ernst Mügge, *Das Württembergische Reserve-Infanterie-Regiment im Nr.122 im Weltkrieg 1914–1918* (Belserche Derlagsbuchhandlung, Stuttgart, 1922), p. 16.
27 Dr Armin Hase, *Das 17 Königleichten Sachsen Infanterie Regiment Nr 183* (Dresden, 1922), p. 24.

28 'The Other Side of the Hill No 2', p. 247; J. von Hansch & F. Weidling, pp. 299–301; Ernst Neumann, *Vierzig Monate Westfront : Geschichte des Infanterie-Regiments 184, Teil 1: 1915–1916* (Berlin, 1934), p. 253.
29 *Somme-Nord*, Map 23.
30 *Somme-Nord*, Map 23.
31 T.N.A. WO 95/2552, 113 Brigade War Diary, July 1916.
32 Emlyn Davies, p. 30.
33 Dudley Ward, p. 202; T.N.A. WO 95/2539, 38th Division War Diary, July 1916.
34 XV Corps Artillery Operation Order No 14, issued on 6 July 1916, in T.N.A. WO 95/921 (G.S.).
35 Appendix VI to T.N.A. WO 95/2539, 38th Division War Diary, July 1916 – XV Corps Artillery Operation order.
36 Renshaw, p. 50.
37 H.Q. XV Corps Operation Order No 15, issued at 10.00 hrs 6 July 1916, in T.N.A. WO 95/921 (G.S.)
38 Renshaw, p. 50.
39 T.N.A. WO 95/921 (G.S.), H.Q. XV Corps Operation Order No 15.
40 T.N.A. WO 95/921 (G.S.), Appendix V to H.Q. XV Corps Operation Order No 14, dated 5 July 1916.
41 RWF Mus/Archives 3684, *Personal notes on the operations about Mametz Wood as far as the 115th Brigade is concerned*, by Brigadier H.J. Evans.
42 Evans, p. 2; Renshaw, p. 58.
43 Evans, pp. 2–3; see also Hughes, p. 82.
44 Evans, p. 2.
45 T.N.A. WO 95/2561/3, 16 Welsh War Diary July 1916.
46 T.O. Marden, *History of the Welch Regiment, 1914–1918* (Cardiff, 1932), pp. 382–383.
47 T.N.A. WO 95/2551, 113 Brigade War Dairy.
48 T.N.A. WO 95/921 (G.S.), H.Q. XV Corps War Diary, Operation Order 14; WO 95/2552, 113 Brigade War Diary for 6 July 1916.
49 Jonathan Hicks, *The Welsh at Mametz Wood. The Somme 1916* (Talybont, 2016), p. 61.
50 T.N.A. WO 95/2555/1, 15 R.W. Fus War Diary 1916.
51 Evans, p. 4.
52 T.N.A. WO 95/2560, 115 Brigade War Diary.
53 'Story of the Attack on Mametz-Wood, July 1916' by J.H. Hughes 11 S.W.B. in the archives of the Royal Welsh, Brecon, 2014 252.1–3.
54 Operation Order No 36, issued at 20.30 hrs on 6 July 1916; Appendix VII to T.N.A. WO 95/2539/1, 38th Division (G.S.) War Diary, July 1916.
55 T.N.A. WO 95/921 (G.S.), H.Q. XV Corps War Diary entry for 19.40 hrs on 6 July 1916.
56 Wyn Griffith, p. 100.
57 Wyn Griffith, p. 101.
58 Evans p. 5.
59 Appendix VII to H.Q. 38th (Welsh) Division Operation Order No 36 is the additional order No G 260.
60 T.N.A. WO 95/2561/3, 16 Welsh War Diary July 1916.
61 H.Q. 115 Brigade Order No 62 in T.N.A. WO 95/2560.
62 H.Q. 115 Brigade Order No 62 in T.N.A. WO 95/2560.
63 Edmonds, p. 30; T.N.A. WO 95/1981, 17th (Northern) Division War Diary, July 1916.
64 T.N.A. WO 95/2555/1, 15 R.W. Fus War Diary 1916.
65 Wyn Griffith, p. 99.
66 Wyn Griffith, p. 101.
67 Evans, p. 7.
68 Emlyn Davies, p. 30.
69 J. von Hansch & F. Weidling, p. 299.
70 Wyn Griffith, pp. 102–103.
71 T.N.A. WO 95/2561/3, 16 Welsh War Diary July 1916.
72 T.N.A. WO 95/2560, 115 Brigade War Diary.

73   Marden, p. 383.
74   Letter from William Joshua to Colin Hughes, pp. 87–88.
75   T.N.A. WO 95/2539/1, H.Q. 38th Division (G.S.) War Diary, July 1916.
76   Hicks, pp. 56–58.
77   Account by J.H. Hughes.
78   WO 95/2560, 115 Brigade War Diary.
79   Account by J.H. Hughes.
80   P. Hart, *The Somme* (London,2006), p. 256
81   WO 95/2560, 115 Brigade War Diary; see also C.T. Atkinson, *History of the South Wales Borderers*
     (London, 1931), p. 244 and Hicks, p. 35.
82   T.N.A. WO 95/921 (G.S.), H.Q. XV Corps War Diary, Operation Order No. 15.
83   T.N.A. WO 95/921 (G.S.), H.Q. XV Corps War Diary entry for 10.10 hrs on 7 July 1916.
84   T.N.A. WO 95/921 (G.S.), H.Q. XV Corps War Diary entry for 10.20 hrs on 7 July 1916.
85   Wyn Griffith, p. 103.
86   WO 95/2560, 115 Brigade War Diary.
87   Hughes, p. 89.
88   T.N.A. WO 95/2549/2, 130 Field Ambulance War Diary 1916.
89   WO 95/2560, 115 Brigade War Diary Appendix XV, signal from H.Q. 38th (Welsh) Division timed
     at 14.18 hrs but not received until 16.04 hrs.
90   Wyn Griffith, pp. 103–104.
92   T.N.A. WO 95/2561/3, 16 Welsh War Diary.
93   Wyn Griffith, pp. 104–105.
94   Wyn Griffith, p. 106.
95   Wyn Griffith, p. 130; WO 95/2560 115 Brigade War Diary.
96   Renshaw, p. 68.
97   Holge Ritter, *Geschichte des Schleswig-Holsteinschen Infanterie-Regiment Nr. 163*, p. 143.
98   See, among others, the accounts by Private G.J. Jones in the Colin Hughes Archive, Cardiff
     University; John Daniels in Jonathan Hicks, p. 2,716; letter from David Jones in RWF Mus 3694.
99   Paul Muhlmann und Wilhelm Mohs, *Geschichte de Lehr-Infanterie-Regiment und seiner
     Stammformationen* (Stuttgart, 1931).
99   H.A. Jones, *The War in the Air, being the part played by the Royal Air Force in the Great War 1914–1918*,
     Vol. III, (Oxford, 1928), pp. 223–224.
100 *Somme-Nord I. Teil, Die Brennpunkte der Schlacht im Juli 1916*, p. 176.
101 T.N.A. WO 95/2560, 115 Infantry Brigade War Diary, July 1916
102 Evans, p. 11.
103 T.N.A. CAB 45/190, letter from Major General Pilcher, 1930.
104 Evans, pp. 6–7.
105 Williams, p. 747; Hughes, p. 92; Renshaw, p. 83.
106 Sheldon, *German Army on the Somme*, p. 160.
107 See the recorded interviews of, for example, Sergeant T.J. Price dated 15 and 16 January 1974 and
     Ronald T. Morgan dated 4 April 1974 in Colin Hughes' papers deposited with Cardiff University
     Special Collections and Archives (SCOLAR), 461/1/1 and 461/1/6.
108 Williams, p. 748 citing Perriman's papers in the Imperial War Museum.
109 Hughes, p. 93.
110 Army Order 256 dated 16 July 1916 in WO 95/2560, annexed to 115 Brigade War Diary, July 1916.
111 Evans, p. 4.
112 Arthur Conan Doyle, *The British Campaign in France and Flanders: 1916* (London, 1918), pp. 118,
     122, 123.
113 T.N.A. WO 95/2555/1, 15 R.W. Fus War Diary 1916; *Concise History of the 15th RWF*, p. 8.
114 T.N.A. CAB 45/190, letter from Price-Davies dated 6 March 1930.
115 Hicks, p. 36.
116 T.N.A. WO 95/1981, 17th (Northern) Division War diary, July 1916; T.N.A. WO 95/921 (G.S.),
     H.Q. XV Corps War Diary entry for 20.52 hrs on 7 July 1916; see also Edmonds, p. 31.

9

'We are stuck in the wood': Mametz, 8–9 July 1916

On the night of 7 July, Rawlinson had written to his wife that: 'We are stuck in the Wood. It is very difficult to find out what is going on, but I expect we shall make some progress… The Germans are fighting hard but reports and examination of prisoners show that they are hard put to it to hold on.'[1] When the news of the failure that day reached XV Corps Headquarters, he was highly unimpressed:

> A day of heavy fighting without much success. We took Contalmaison in the morning but failed to get into Mametz Wood. Prisoners tell us the Bosche are in a state of chaos, but their machine gunners seem to go on fighting all right. In the pm we lost Contalmaison without sufficient excuse I think as it is reported we were shelled out. I have ordered both attacks to be renewed. It is raining hard tonight. We must go on pressing the Bosche now they are getting tired as fresh troops may be brought up.[2]

Haig too was not impressed, writing in his diary on 8 July:

> The 38th Welsh Division, which had been ordered to attack Mametz Wood had not advanced with determination to the attack. General Horne, commanding XV Corps, is enquiring into General Philipps's conduct as divisional GOC. The artillery preparation was… reported as "highly satisfactory".[3]
>
> Sir H. Rawlinson stated that his plan was now to pierce the Enemy's second line near Bazentin le Grand. I pointed out the necessity for having possession of Mametz Wood before making any attempt of this kind. The moment for taking the Enemy by surprise here had passed, and the fighting in the Mametz Wood showed that the Enemy's "morale" was still good. I therefore gave Rawlinson an order to consolidate his right flank *strongly* in the south end of Trones Wood, and to capture Mametz Wood and Contalmaison before making any attempt to pierce the Enemy's second line. This was later confirmed in writing.[4]

Kiggell also wrote to Rawlinson to underline Haig's displeasure: '… the C in C did not consider the withdrawal from Contalmaison on the 7th and the failure to capture Mametz Wood were creditable performances.'[5] But on the 8th, Haig had also written in a letter to his wife, with misplaced confidence and a singular lack of situational awareness, that: 'The troops are fighting well and the battle is developing slowly but steadily in our favour. In another fortnight, with

Divine Help, I hope that some decisive results may be obtained. In the meantime, we must be patient and determined.[6]

During the night of 7/8 July, the 38th Division was ordered to make a raid, the object of which appears to have been to 'support and develop' an earlier patrol by 15 R.W. Fus; the divisional staff asked for clarification and received a terse reply, in contrast to the often detailed and over-proscriptive orders which had been handed down to date. The raid was to be on:

> ... something like a company front, not necessarily by the whole company ... The place must be chosen by the commander of the 113th Brigade now holding the line, who should carry out the raid and fix the exact point. Neither corps nor division, not being on the spot, could fix this.[7]

Price-Davies in turn passed on the instructions to 14 R.W. Fus under Lieutenant Colonel Graham Gwyther, who had been in command for only three weeks.

The original orders stated that after an artillery bombardment:

Lieutenant Colonel Graham Gwyther

> ... at 2 a.m., bombing parties will go down the cliff against the southern end of STRIP TRENCH and will move up it, keeping a party above ground as long as possible, and sending a party in the trench to bomb dug-outs.
>
> On reaching junction with WOOD TRENCH one party will proceed Northwards to make a block, and another will work along WOOD TRENCH to meet 17th Division.
>
> Another attack of 50 men, and 4 Lewis guns, will leave the road below the cliff, with their left near the junction with the railway, and will attack point G. This party will advance into the wood sufficiently to cover the construction of a strong point at G.

A company of 19 Welsh was detailed to dig a communication trench from Cliff to Strip trenches and 124 Field Company R.E. was ordered to accompany the raid in order to construct three strong points at point G, at the southern end of Strip trench and at its junction with Wood trench.[8] The orders were received in H.Q. 113 brigade at 15.00 hrs. However, it appears that Price-Davies decided to amplify the orders given and he had decided to attack Strip trench with an entire battalion. The War Diary notes that orders were sent out to 14 R.W. Fus, but no time is given for this. 14 R.W. Fus has only a single line entry for the whole day, noting that the battalion was in bivouacs at Minden Post. Fusilier W.R. Thomas recalled that:

From the morning of the 6th July until the eve of the final assault on Mametz Wood 9th July we did nothing else but consolidate by interminable carrying parties up and down Danzig Alley. We thought at the time they are first of all trying to kill us by sheer fatigue. We carried hundreds of rolls of barbed wire, iron pickets, sandbags, picks, shovels etc.[9]

Gwyther certainly received these orders and issued his own. Just after 21.00 hrs, the divisional headquarters reported to XV Corps that:

113 BDE (15th Royal Welsh Fusiliers) made a bombing attack yesterday evening up Strip Trench but was driven back. The 113 BDE now preparing to make an attack up Strip Trench with one battalion. Hour of attack not yet settled.[10]

At about 22.35 hrs, this information was given to Horne When he learned that Price-Davies planned a battalion attack rather than a raid, Horne telephoned Philipps to make it plain that all he required was a localised probing raid on the southern part of Mametz Wood, and not 'an isolated attack by one battalion on point H.'[11] The copy of the message in the Corps War Diary is endorsed in manuscript – possibly in Horne's own hand – 'Told to stop this attack' and 'Keep carefully'.

Gwyther was then very surprised to receive a call from Price-Davies ordering an entirely new operation which he had to organise in the dark and at short notice: 'fresh orders had to be issued at the 11th hour… I consider that with my whole battalion I could have got a firm foothold in the wood… I have never discovered why the bewildering and sudden change of orders on the night of 7 July were issued by divisional headquarters.'[12]

At 22.00 hrs on 7 July two patrols from 16 R.W. Fus went out towards the Wood, with inconclusive results. At 02.00 hrs on 8 July there was no sign of the raid being launched and a telephone conversation between Price-Davies and the C.O. of 16 R.W. Fus, Lieutenant Colonel Ronald Carden, that there was no sign of 14 R.W. Fus. Gwyther's own account describes what happened when the raiding party started its approach:

The party started off down the communication trench leading to the front line and our starting place in good time under normal conditions; as however the communication trench was full of other troops of our brigade, progress was so slow that I attempted to get to the position overground, but found that our advance was so impeded by barbed wire and other obstacles that I considered it advisable to resort to the communication trench again, and the result was that the party arrived very late at the point from which the attack was to be made. Daylight was commencing, the element of surprise was problematical, and I therefore decided not to risk men's lives unnecessarily and reported the situation to Brigade Headquarters.[13]

Gwyther had indeed sent a report by a runner to Brigade Headquarters at 03.00 hrs saying that the trenches were so congested that they had been unable to get forward.[14] This seems odd. H.Q. 113 Brigade's War Diary gives the lay-down of the two forward battalions, with 13 R.W. Fus spread between Fritz and White trenches; 16th in Queen's Nullah, Cliff, Valley and White trenches and Bunny Alley – eight companies spread over almost 4,000 yards of trenches and hardly a severe degree of congestion. It is more likely that because the orders had arrived very late,

Gwyther was searching for an excuse that would absolve both him and his brigade commander of blame for aborting the raid. Gwyther's account shows that he, like others, held the divisional headquarters responsible for causing chaos when in fact it was being directed from above.

In the early afternoon of 8 July, Horne arrived at Philipps's headquarters[15] to discuss the situation, since reports from prisoners seemed to indicate that the Germans might have evacuated the Wood. Patrols sent forward to check this by the 17th Division were, however, heavily fired on.[16] As a result, Horne ordered a night attack on Strip trench on 8/9 July which would then be exploited on the 9th. The attack was ordered for 02.00 hrs on 9 July and was given to 113 Brigade which was in the line opposite the southern edge of the Wood.

At 04.10 hrs, the divisional H.Q. reported the aborted raid to H.Q. XV Corps. Horne was briefed and demanded to know why no attack had taken place, as subsequently did Rawlinson, telling Major General A.A. Montgomery to telephone Horne, directing him to remove Philipps and Pilcher, which he did at 10.20 hrs. Meanwhile, Horne had ordered an investigation, at 06.30 hrs, and 10 minutes later sent an instruction to H.Q. 38th (Welsh) Division: 'Corps Commander desires to see Major General Phillips [sic] at Corps Headquarters at once.'[17]

Whatever it was, Philipps's explanation for the failure of 14 R.W. Fus, coming on top of the events of 7 July, was more than enough for Horne. When Haig and Rawlinson came to his headquarters on 9 July he said that: 'He was very disappointed with the work of the 17th Division (Pilcher) and 38th Welsh Division (Phillips) [sic].'[18] He had in fact already given orders for the removal from command of Philipps, which took effect at 11.00 hrs that morning.[19] In fact Philipps knew his fate by the time that Montgomery had phoned from Army headquarters at 10.20 hrs. It must be said that Price-Davies and Gwyther were probably very lucky not to go the same way. Price-Davies acknowledged this in a letter:

> … on the 8th/9th [N.B., this must mean 7th/8th] I was to have carried out an attack on a small scale. It was miscarried owing to a battalion taking too long to reach the starting point. The Divisional Commander has been degummed. I am sorry, as I fear I contributed but the plan I thought a bad one… [20]

Haig's Diary for 9 July 1916 recorded more details of the meeting:

> In the case of the [38th] division, although the wood had been most adequately bombarded the division never entered the wood, and in the whole division the total casualties for the 24 hours are under 150! A few bold men entered the wood and found little opposition. Deserters also stated Enemy was greatly demoralised and had very few troops on the ground.[21]

Haig was, of course, misinformed. No troops had entered the Wood, the Germans were there in strength and casualties amounted to 182 officers and men killed, 329 wounded and missing.

Major General Charles Blackader* had been commanding a Territorial Brigade in Ireland and had presided over many of the courts-martial of the Republican leaders, including Padraig

---

*   Major General Charles Guinand Blackader CB DSO (1869–1921) commanded the Gharwhal (Indian) Brigade on the Western Front in 1915, and 177 Infantry Brigade of the 59th Division,

Pearse whom he had sentenced to death.[22] Blackader obviously heartily disliked this duty and had made his feelings known. On 21 June he had been transferred to France, pending a new appointment. On the morning of 9 July, he was surprised to be ordered to H.Q. XV Corps and from there to take command of the 38th Division. However, when he arrived, at 10.55 hrs, he was sent back to H.Q. Fourth Army, because events had already moved on.

Haig had, it seems, intervened: Montgomery's telephone call had been to relay that information to Horne and tell him that Major General Herbert Watts, G.O.C. 7th Division which was then resting in reserve, should be appointed to the temporary command of the 38th Division. Watts knew the ground and the situation; he had achieved a significant run of success on and after 1 July; and it was felt that he might stiffen the Welsh division and repeat his victory. In due course Blackader would take command but for now, Watts was given the freedom to: 'dispose of [i.e. deploy] the 38th Division as he wished, keeping any brigades he wanted, or using them as required.'[23]

The removal of a formation commander at any level during a battle was a serious matter and indicates the degree to which the High Command's confidence in Philipps had broken down. As we know, his appointment had never been welcomed by the Regular Army and one senses that a handy excuse was gladly seized upon to remove him. That said, and as discussed in the previous chapter, Philipps had neither commanded the division on 7 July *as* a division, committing all his forces to achieve a decisive result; nor having handed the attack over to one subordinate had he given Evans all the freedom, control and resources required to carry out the task. Quite simply, Philipps was out of his depth. Because of this he had not challenged orders imposed from afar by the Corps Headquarters, orders which were the direct cause of the failed attacks on 7 July. His supine behaviour was in stark contrast to that of Pilcher, in command of the 17th Division, who repeatedly challenged what he saw as futile orders that would achieve nothing but senseless slaughter. Even so, this did not save Pilcher from the same fate as Philipps and he was also removed before the end of July.[24]

The news soon reached Lloyd George, who wrote to his brother William on 11 July that: '… the General has broken down in health and he returned home last night bringing with him his ADC Lieut. Gwilym Lloyd George.'[25] Philipps remained a Liberal M.P. and was re-elected in 1918; in 1917 he was made a Knight Commander of the Most Honourable Order of the Bath in 1917, no doubt a compensation prize engineered by his patron, Lloyd George, who was by then Prime Minister. Gwilym transferred into the anti-aircraft branch of the Royal Artillery, with which he remained for the rest of the war.

On 8 July, the 17th Division mounted two furious assaults on Quadrangle Support trench, again without success. The 38th Division by contrast had a quiet two days; even so, 113 Brigade had lost two officers and 33 men wounded, eight men killed and four missing on 8 July on top of four men killed and three officers and 63 men wounded on 7th.

Watts arrived at Headquarters 38th Division 10 minutes after Philipps left. He was quickly briefed and immediately afterwards, orders came for a renewed attack on Mametz Wood early in the afternoon of 9 July – an attack that was soon afterwards postponed to the morning of 10 July.

which was sent to Dublin during the Easter Rising of 1916. He held command of the division until retiring due to ill-health in May 1918.

Much of the enthusiasm for renewing the assault on Mametz Wood seems to have been based on the assumption that German morale was low – this in spite of the very determined and effective resistance that was everywhere obvious. Relying on uncorroborated interrogation reports from prisoners is never reliable, as a prisoner in the shock of capture will usually tell his questioner what he thinks the other wants to hear, and what will get him treated better. The Germans in fact were surprised at how easily they had repulsed the attacks of 7 July and were in no mood to withdraw. Indeed, on the night of 8 July, No. 9 Company of the Fusilier Battalion, 9th Grenadiers, made a raid with 50 men on the boundary of the 17th and 38th Divisions.[26]

By 9 July, 183 I.R. was deployed with now had II./ and III./183 under *Hauptmann* Röbler and Major Rahmann in trenches called by the Germans *Kabelgraben* and *Roedergraben* – north-west of Contalmaison – and I./183 under *Hauptmann* Hase in reserve at Pozières.[27] 122 I.R. was reinforced by 230 men from the Fusilier Battalion of the 9th Grenadiers and re-deployed on 9 July;[28] I./122 was in the village of Contalmaison with its Headquarters in the Chateau. III./122 was in Quadrangle Support with 10, 11 and 12 Companies, reinforced by part of No 5 Company of II./122; and No 9 Company III./122 – down to 50% strength – was in Wood Support.[29] 6 and 7 Companies II./122 were in reserve in the second line but were brought forward, as recounted by *Leutnant* Köstlin, commander of No 6 Company:

> In the afternoon of 9 July, I received the order to advance to Mametz Woods with the 6. Company and two machine guns in order to strengthen the III. Battalion. I was told to bring as many drinks, food, hand grenades and flares as possible… as dusk fell, I left R-Position along with my company in order to first go back to our field kitchen and then to the ammunition depot at Martinpuich.[30]

The *Lehr* Regiment history described their situation during 8 and 9 July thus:

> On 8 July, 7.30 a.m., the Machine Gun Company *Ludwig* relieved its two platoons in the Mametz Woods and replaced them with the platoons *Böcker* and *Behrend*, which had been held back in the II. Position, [i.e. the second line] without any losses. It had been raining the whole night again.
>
> Nothing of importance on 8 July! Thus the II./L.I.R. could reflect on the events of the day. *Feldwebelleutnant* Lehrmann, the *Unteroffiziere* Kallis, Manns and 6 men had fallen, 42 wounded, 2 missing.
>
> Nothing of importance happened for the II./L.I.R. on 9 July either. However, the enemy devastated the trenches with its Artillery fire once more, destroyed two machine guns in the Mametz Woods with a direct hit, wounded Gunners Graf and Gone and Private Klingstein, killed Gunner Fischer who had rushed forward with replacements guns from the II. Position; due to the collapse of the defensive power on the left wing, it was necessary to remove the 8./L.I.R. from covering the flanks and put them in with the 7./L.I.R.
>
> When the victims of the II./L.I.R. were counted on the evening of 9 July, 12 brave soldiers had fallen, 50 were wounded, 5 missing. Even the officers were decimated. The Lieutenants of the Regiment Handewerk, Bölk, Ferfer were wounded.
>
> The III./L.I.R. had suffered tremendously due to the enemy artillery during the days of 8 and 9 July. The artillery raged through the trenches and back terrain, clearly wanting to destroy all life after their unfavourable experience in Mametz Woods, before their infantry

set out for another attack. However, there were definite signs that decisive enemy attacks were imminent. We saw infantry movement in various places, saw entrenchments on the hills west of Montauban, observed constantly circling aircraft above us, saw travelling artillery and vehicle convoys and we had the impression that powerful forces gathered in the *Granat* and *Artillerieschlucht*.

A German photograph of the N.C.O.s of the *Lehr* Infantry Regiment who defended sections of Mametz Wood throughout the battle. (http://roadstothegreatwar-ww1.blogspot.co.uk/2013/07/the-german-experience-at-battle-of-somme.html)

A postcard sent by *Feldwebel* Hoffmann of the 3rd Battalion, *Lehr* Regiment. (http://roadstothegreatwar-ww1.blogspot.co.uk/2013/07/the-german-experience-at-battle-of-somme.html)

How many great targets they made for our artillery! But we were powerless due to our reduced arms and ammunition and had to make do by using curtain fire to keep the enemy attack at bay.

On 8 and 9 July, the casualties for the III./L.I.R. were *Unteroffizier* Könnicke and 8 Fusiliers of the Guards who fell,[*] 67 wounded and 1 missing. The Machine Gun Company also had 1 dead, many wouded or buried alive.[31]

The Germans, although suffering, were firmly in control of the Wood and were ready for what they saw as the inevitable renewal of the attack.

Notes

1   Rawlinson MS Vol 1, letter to Lady Horne on 7 July 1916.
2   Rawlinson MS Vol 1, diary entry for 7 July 1916.
3   National Library of Scotland Acc 3155, No. 97, Earl Haig of Bermersyde Papers, MS Diary entry for 8 July 1916.
4   Sheffield and Bourne, p. 201.
5   T.N.A. WO 95/5, G.H.Q. (G.S.) War Diary, 9 July 1916.
6   Sheffield and Bourne, p. 201.
7   T.N.A. WO 95/921, H.Q. XV Corps (G.S.) War Diary, entry at 21.10 hrs 7 July 1916.
8   T.N.A. WO 95/2552, 113 Infantry Brigade War Diary July 1916, Appendix 9, Operation Order No 56; Dudley Ward, p. 204.
9   Thomas, 'Notes on the 1914–18 War', p. 54.
10   T.N.A. WO 95/2552, 113 Infantry Brigade War Diary, entry at 21.05 hrs 7 July 1916
11   T.N.A. WO 95/921, H.Q. XV Corps (G.S.) War Diary, entry at 22.35 hrs 7 July 1916.
12   T.N.A. CAB 45/189, letter from Gwyther.
13   Renshaw, p. 76.
14   T.N.A. WO 95/2552, 113 Infantry Brigade War Diary, entry at 03.00 hrs 9 July 1916; WO 95/2539 38th (Welsh) Division War Diary, 9 July 1916.
15   T.N.A. WO 95/921, H.Q. XV Corps (G.S.) War Diary, entry at 13.40 hrs 8 July 1916.
16   T.N.A. WO 95/2539 38th (Welsh) Division War Diary, 8 July 1916; WO 95/2552, 113 Infantry Brigade War Diary, entry at 15.30 hrs 8 July 1916.
17   T.N.A. WO 95/921, H.Q. XV Corps (G.S.) War Diary, entries at 06.30 and 06.40 hrs 9 July 1916.
18   Sheffield and Bourne, p. 201.
19   Philipps's departure was noted in a brief entry in the War Diary, T.N.A. WO 95/2539.
20   Price-Davies, p. 108.
21   Sheffield and Bourne, p. 201.
22   See the accounts in Stephen Stratford, *The 1916 Easter Uprising* (London, 1998).
23   T.N.A. WO 95/921, H.Q. XV Corps (G.S.) War Diary, entry at 10.20 hrs hrs 9 July 1916.
24   Williams, pp. 749–750.
25   William George, *My Brother and I* (London, 1958), p. 255.
26   J. von Hansch & F. Weidling, p. 307.
27   Armin Hase, *Das 17 Königleichten Sachsen Infanterie Regiment Nr 183* (Dresden, 1922), p. 25.
28   Mügge, *Das Württembergische Reserve-Inf.-Regiment Nr. 122 im Weltkrieg*, p. 17; J. von Hansch & F. Weidling, p. 309.
29   'The Other Side of the Hill', No. 2, p. 248.
30   Mügge, *Das Württembergische Reserve-Inf.-Regiment Nr.122*, p. 20.
31   Muhlmann und Mohs, p. 320.

---

[*]   i.e., reservists of the Guards Fusilier Regiment who had been drafted into the Lehr to make up its strength.

10

'Another day of heavy fighting': Mametz Wood, The Attack of 10 July 1916

At 02.00 hrs on the morning of 9 July, Headquarters 38th Division, still under Philipps' command, issued orders for a new attack at 16.00 hrs that afternoon from White trench, against Strip Trench and the southern edge of Mametz Wood. The order gave two possible alternative methods of progressing through the Wood, depending on the outcome of the first phase of the attack, on Strip trench.[1] The method chosen by Philipps, at 04.00 hrs, was that two brigades were to be used simultaneously. On the left, 113 Brigade under Price-Davies was to attack and clear Strip trench as far as the first lateral ride, with its remaining three battalions in echelon. At the same time, 114 Brigade under Marden was to attack on the right, to the east of the central ride. Once both brigades had reached the first lateral ride, 113 Brigade would consolidate the south-western approaches to the Wood (I, J, K, L, M, N on the map), while 114 Brigade moved methodically northwards, clearing the rest of the Wood. By noon, however, Philipps had been removed and Horne decided to postpone the attack, telling the 38th Division staff that: 'the attack being prepared by you for 4 p.m. this afternoon will not take place. All preparations for making that attack are to be ready by early tomorrow morning.'[2]

The Corps Headquarters followed this message with more information indicating that piece-meal attacks should be avoided and that a series of heavy blows was more likely to achieve success:

> All prisoners captured in the last 24 hrs express astonishment that our infantry does not attack in greater strength instead of bombing up trenches in twos and threes. The enemy is much in confusion there being small groups here and there of every regiment. There are some stretches of country without any enemy in it at all. If our infantry attacked in strength they could sweep the whole of them back… all communication trenches to the rear are smashed. This information confirms that already received from aircraft and other sources. Corps Commander impresses on all commanders the necessity of utmost vigour and deter-mination in the attacks to be delivered today and great results which accrue therefrom. He looks to divisional commanders ensuring his directions on this point are carried out.[3]

It was all very well for Horne to slope his shoulders and demand efforts from his subordinates, but there seems no sense that it was his duty to direct, command and control an orchestrated series of attacks, properly resourced. This want of proper command by Horne will be addressed in the concluding chapter of this book. Instead, Horne continued to interfere in small-scale

Colonel Bonham-Carter, the GSO I of the 7th Division, who accompanied Major General Watts to the 38th Division. Seen here with his brother, Admiral Sir Stuart Bonham-Carter.

operations, proscribe the actions of his subordinates and dissipate their efforts in flagrant defiance of his own directive. The 17th Division was, for example, told to make one last attempt on Quadrangle Support – the seventh – before being relieved by the 21st Division, but there was no attempt to co-ordinate this with the attack by the 23rd Division on Contalmaison at 18.00 hrs, nor with the action by the 38th Division. 17th Division went in unsupported from either flank and unsurprisingly failed to achieve its objective.[4]

During the afternoon of 9 July, as we have seen, Major General Herbert Watts assumed command of the 38th Division and was given a free hand on the disposition of his subordinate units and formations. He decided, however, not to break up the existing structure of brigades – probably quite rightly – but to employ the whole division in the assault. Watts also brought with him several professional staff officers from the 7th Division to increase the horsepower of the headquarters. These included his G.S.O. I, Lieutenant Colonel Algernon Bonham Carter,[*] and Major Geoffrey Drake-Brockman, whose accounts of what followed are very detailed and will be cited in the analysis in the concluding chapter of this book. Orders, however, continued to be sent out under the imprimatur of Lieutenant Colonel ap Rhys Pryce, of whom Watts had a high opinion.

Watts' plan was similar to that laid down by Philipps, but in the first wave he decided to commit the whole of 113 Brigade on a narrow front west of the central ride, with 114 to the east. 115 Brigade and 123 Field Company R.E. were to be ready at Minden Post, less two companies in Caterpillar Copse, in reserve. In doing this he clearly sought to avoid the fragmented nature of the attack on 7 July and the potential fratricide of two formations assaulting towards each other. The whole of the Wood was to be the objective of one formation – his own – with the

---

[*]   Later Colonel Algernon Lothian Bonham Carter DSO (1881–1957).

central ride, marked with red flags as the leading battalions advanced, being used to de-conflict real estate. The attack would be timed to coincide with an assault by the 17th Division up Wood Support and Quadrangle Support trenches. Although there was little subtlety and no attempt at deception in the plan, an attack in this strength might establish favourable force ratios in the assault for the first time, taking note of the intelligence gained from German prisoners. The two leading assault brigades were also to establish depots of ammunition, water, rations and engineer stores in Queen's Nullah, Caterpillar Copse and White trench, with 115 Brigade providing the carrying parties needed to take the stores forward when called for.

The new orders were ready around 17.30 hrs on 9 July. Price-Davies and Marden, the commanders of 113 and 114 Brigades – but not, strangely, Evans of 115 Brigade – were called the six miles (9.6 kilometres) rearwards to the Divisional Main Headquarters at Meaulte, a location known to the British Army as Grove Town. There, as Marden later recalled in his *History of the Welsh Regiment,* they: 'were given orders by a GOC and staff, whom they had never seen before, to capture Mametz Wood at dawn on 10 July, zero hour being fixed for 4.15 am.'[5] By the time the brigade commanders had got back to their own headquarters and briefed their brigade majors and staff captains, it was nearly midnight. This gave them in reality no more than an hour to write orders and get them out to the Commanding Officers while simultaneously moving their battalions into position. This sort of contracted time-frame should have led to disaster; however, the units were already briefed on the earlier, Philipps, plan and the new orders were not too dissimilar. There had also been time for brigade, battalion and company commanders to familiarise themselves with the ground and the approaches to the objective, if not the conditions inside the Wood. Things were rushed, though. Captain John Glynn Jones recalled in later years that he and his fellow officers were:

> Crowded around the door of a dug-out with the CO inside and hardly audible we were given some very small prints of the wood and what appeared to be instructions. They were verbal, decidedly "sketchy" and to me appeared to be more like instructions for a ceremonial parade than an order for battle… When I look back at what was intended to be our general method of advance, I can well understand how it developed into what it did.[6]

As well as the orders, Headquarters XV Corps sent out a message which was to read to all troops at dawn, immediately before the assault:

> The Commander in Chief has just visited the corps commander and has impressed upon him the great importance of the occupation by us of Mametz Wood. The corps commander requests that the division and brigade commanders will point out to the troops of the Welsh division the opportunity offered them of serving their King and Country at a critical period and earning for themselves great glory and distinction.[7]

Even allowing for the more deferential nature of societies and armies at that time, one can hardly feel, down the passage of years, that Fusilier Thomas Atkins and his mates would have found this message either inspiring or helpful. A mug of hot tea and a ration of rum with the Corps Commander's compliments would probably have made much more of an impression.

In terms of the execution of the attack, it was to be in orthodox, wave, formation with four yards between each man and 100 yards between each line or wave, the troops carrying rifles

Modern photograph taken from the probable position of Cliff trench, the start line of the attack on 10 July, towards Mametz Wood. (A.M. Goulden)

Modern photograph taken of the line of the cliff, on the abandoned railway line at its base. (A.M. Goulden)

Modern photograph taken at the bottom of the cliff, looking upwards. (A.M. Goulden)

with fixed bayonets at the high port – a stark contrast to the flexible formations and specialised equipments used by the 7th Division on 1, 2 and 3 July. On leaving White trench, the troops would move first downhill on a convex slope for between 100 and 300 yards – the distance increasing from west to east – before having to scramble down the steep cliff and across the stream bed and railway line at its base. The final part of the approach was gently uphill on a concave slope to the edge of the Wood. As soon as the troops reached the top of the cliff they would be under observed direct and indirect fire from the Germans in their trenches on the edge of the Wood, unless the British artillery suppressed the enemy's ability to destroy the attack before the troops closed on the Wood. What the attack from the south did avoid, however, was the German enfilade fire from Flatiron and Sabot Copses – although flanking fire from the southern edge of the Hammerhead (A, B, E on the map) might well be a problem.

Modern photograph of the remains of Strip trench, just inside the current western edge of Mametz Wood. (A.M. Goulden)

Modern photograph of the defenders' view from the south-west corner of Mametz Wood.
(A.M. Goulden)

Modern photograph of the defenders' view from the Hammerhead, looking towards the Welsh Memorial
and the direction of attack on 10 July. (A.M. Goulden)

Once in the Wood, the first objective, which was the area to the south of the first lateral ride *and* the Hammerhead, was to be secured by 06.15 hrs. The second objective was the area between the first and second lateral rides; and the third objective the area from the second lateral to the northern edge of the Wood. At each lateral, strong-points were to be constructed; 124 Engineer Field Company and two companies of pioneers from 19 Welsh were attached to 113 Brigade; and 151 Field Company and the remainder of 19 Welsh were grouped with 114 Brigade to carry out this work.[8] There are some references to an attached unit from an Engineer Special Brigade; these units usually provided gas or smoke, but there is no evidence that this was employed.

As well as increasing the weight of the attack in terms of numbers of troops, Watts also directed a significant increase in the weight of artillery fire, along with the use of new techniques developed by both the British and French during the opening phases of the Somme battle. The first of these techniques was focused on deceiving the Germans as to the timing of an assault; the second was what became known as the 'Creeping Barrage', referred to in Chapter Four. The first technique involved a bombardment of the enemy's forward positions and then lifting the fire to the rear, as if an assault was about to commence. This would draw the defenders out of their dugouts. After a few minutes, fire would again descend on the forward line, catching the defenders on the parapets.

For the attack on 10 July, a combination of these techniques was to be tried. Every gun in the 7th and 38th Divisions would be brought to bear, although Lieutenant Colonel C.O. Head, commanding 120 Field Artillery Brigade, said later that: 'I don't remember we had any orders whatever for the attacks on Contalmaison or the Mametz Wood.'[9] From 03.30 hrs to 04.15 hrs, all guns would fire on the southern edge of the Wood (J, H, G, E, B, A, X) and at 03.55 hrs a smoke barrage would be fired for 30 minutes around Strip trench and at A, B, C, X – along the long southern side of the Wood – in order to screen the approach down the cliff and up to the Wood itself. At 04.15 hrs the barrage would then lift, or 'search', back to a new barrage line just north of the first lateral while maintaining fire on Wood Support. At 06.15 hrs the barrage would lift again to the second lateral allowing the two leading brigades to move forward and clear the area between the rides. This was expected to take no more than 45 minutes – hopelessly over-optimistic as events proved – and at 07.15 hrs the barrage would again lift to the northern edge of the Wood allowing the infantry to press forward and establish themselves 'inside the north edge of the wood, making strong points...'[10] Finally, at 08.30 hrs, the barrage would lift again to the German second line.

Fire support was to come from other means as well as artillery. Machine-gun fire from No 5 M.M.G Company in Marlborough Wood and Caterpillar Copse was to fire north-west towards Middle Alley, to prevent the Germans reinforcing the Wood from their second line: 10 S.W.B. was ordered to send two Lewis guns and 40 men to carry out this task,[11] which was to be supported by the corps artillery's medium howitzers. Three heavy trench mortars in Queen's Nullah and all available medium mortars in Cliff trench were also to fire on Strip trench. Price-Davies was ordered to take eight guns forward to support the attack and to establish liaison with the 17th Division on his left in order to de-conflict fire. Four of these would be positioned along the road in the area of White trench to support the beginning of the attack; the remainder would be brought up with the third wave to consolidate the western edge of the Wood. 114 Brigade was also to take eight guns, four to cover the centre of the Wood and four the eastern edge. An additional heavy mortar was to fire on the Hammerhead in support of 114 Brigade's light mortars.

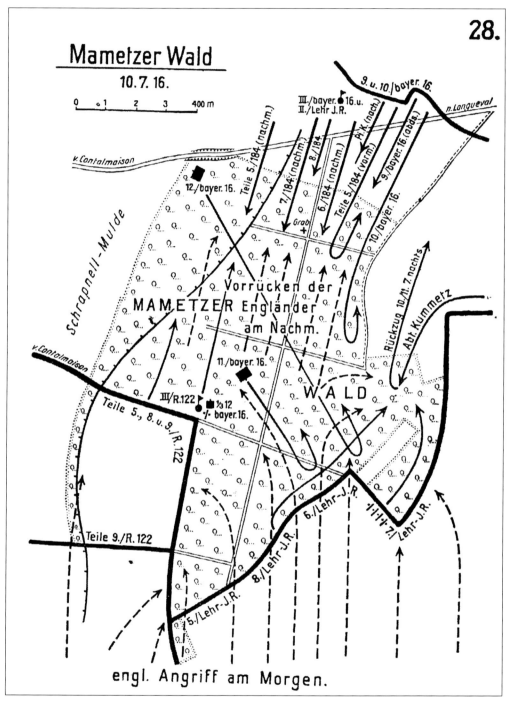

Map 10.i The German Dispositions in Mametz Wood, 10 July 1916.
(Source: *German Official History Somme-Nord*)

It was recognised that communication with supporting fires, as well as between units and formations, would be a challenge and all brigade and battalion commanders, as well as the Divisional Signal Company, were ordered to lay telephone wire, use flags or semaphore signals, and employ runners to provide as much information as quickly as possible up the chain of command. The Divisional Signal Company was ordered to set up a visual receiving station [i.e. for flag or semaphore] in Queen's Nullah but given the close nature of the Wood, this was not a measure that was likely to be successful. If all else failed, then hourly reports were to be made even if these were negative in nature.[12] In the end, with wires being frequently cut as the Signal Company's War Diary makes plain, runners carrying written or verbal messages were the only reliable method of maintaining communication.

What of the Germans in Mametz Wood on the night of 9/10 July? The southern edge of the Wood was still held by the four companies (5, 6, 7 and 8) of II./*Lehr*. Behind them were 11 and 12 Companies III./16 Bavarian I.R.;[13] 5, 7 and 8 Companies of II./184 I.R. (183rd Reserve Infantry Division) had also been brought forward from the second line with the 183rd I.R. of the same division.[14] The 183rd Division had in fact been reported detraining and boarding lorries at Vélu, east of Bapaume, on 6 July by air reconnaissance.[15]

The 16th Bavarians had been actively patrolling in order to gather intelligence and to exploit any opportunities. One patrol from No 7 Company II./16th Bavarians on the night of 9/10 July had brought in a badly wounded British officer and a more lightly wounded soldier, both of whom helped to confirm the identity of units. Another patrol from No 8 Company recovered

German troops detraining, as described in the British air reconnaissance report quoted.
(James Payne collections)

two grenade launchers. As a reward, those involved were given cash rewards and liquid refreshment of the sort generally appreciated by infantry soldiers of all nations by the Regimental Commander, *Oberstleutnant* Bedall. One hopes they lived to enjoy their rewards:

> I grant the participants of this patrol the following cash rewards: Gefreiter Redlhammer, as leader, 10 Marks; Gefreiters Seidl and Grashuber, 5 Marks apiece… To the men involved [in recovering the grenade launchers] I award 25 litres of beer (to be received from the canteen at the next opportunity![16]

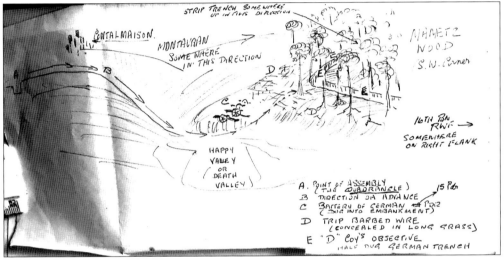

A sketch of the German entrenchment on the edge of Mametz Wood by W.R. Thomas.
(RWF Mus)

A German trench on the edge of a wood; the hasty defences constructed around Mametz Wood between 3 and 7 July 1916 would have looked like this. (James Payne collections)

A smashed German artillery limber outside Mametz Wood as described in the sketch by W.R. Thomas, possibly where Robert Graves later picked up his carved chalk memento (see Chapter 12).

Modern photograph of the trench line inside the southern edge of Mametz Wood, as shown in the sketch by W.R. Thomas. (A.M. Goulden)

Modern photograph looking towards Mametz Wood, matching the view in the sketch by W.R. Thomas. (A.M. Goulden)

A group of men of II./*Lehr-Infanterie-Regiment*. (http://roadstothegreatwar-ww1.blogspot.
co.uk/2013/07/the-german-experience-at-battle-of-somme.html)

Wood trench and Wood Support were held by a mixed bag of 5 Company, 2nd Battalion, and 8
and 9 Companies of the 3rd Battalion, 122nd Württemberg Reserve Infantry Regiment (183rd
Reserve Infantry Division) which had relieved the 163rd Infantry Regiment. The remainder
of 122 I.R. held Quadrangle Support, Contalmaison village and the *Kaisergraben* with two
companies of I./184 I.R.[17] East of the Wood, the German second line from Bazentin le Grand
to Bazentin le Petit was held by III./*Lehr* (9, 10, 11 and 12 Companies), which also held the
forward positions in Flatiron and Sabot Copses. Continuing to the north-west, a mixed force
of I./*Lehr* (1, 2, 3, 4 Companies) was in the second line along with No 9 Company of the
3rd, or Fusilier, Battalion, 9th Grenadier Regiment; Nos 2 and 3 Companies of I./Guards
Fusiliers; the headquarters, one M.G. company and two infantry companies of I./184 I.R.[18] The
Guards Fusiliers were now seriously under strength and badly shaken after the fighting around
Contalmaison.[19]

   Leutnant Köstlin, commanding No 6 Company of 122 I.R., recalled that on the night of
9/10 July he and his company had been ordered forward, but had been told he should not try
to get through Mametz Wood because it was being regularly shelled. He decided instead to
reach the frontline trenches via the *Shrapnelmulde*, the re-entrant to the west of the Wood.
Here, the company was fired on by a British machine gun to their right, on the eastern edge
of Contalmaison. This scattered the company, most of the men returning to the second line;
Köstlin, *Leutnant* Koch and 30 men made it to the line. Köstlin went on to describe the
position west of Mametz Wood, probably – from his description – in Quadrangle Support
trench:

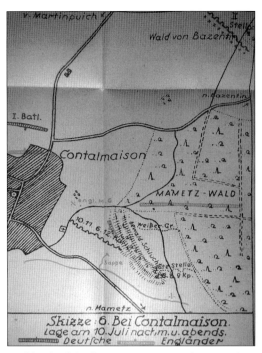

Sketch of the German positions to the west of Mametz Wood on 10 July. (Regimental History, 122nd R.I.R.)

… Our trench followed the slope between Contalmaison and Mametz Woods in a south-easterly direction towards the southern corner of the woods. It dropped off quite considerably to the north and east and ran parallel to and about 200 metres to the north of the road Contalmaison – Mametz… for the most part we were lying at a slope away from the enemy and thus, were quite protected..[20]

Various estimates have been made of the force ratios at this point and these are difficult to determine given the casualties sustained on both sides. At the corps level, there were three British divisions, 17th, 23rd and 38th, each with 12 infantry battalions but probably reduced by 10 percent from casualties, making a total effective strength of 32½ battalions. On the German side the 122nd, 183rd and *Lehr* Regiments numbered 12 battalions, probably reduced by 20 percent making nine and a half battalions; to which

Modern photograph taken at the bottom of the cliff, towards Mametz Wood. (A.M. Goulden)

must be added the 9th Grenadiers, another two battalions, making 11½ in all – a ratio of just less than 3:1 in favour of the attackers. However, this must be qualified by the advantage of the defenders in prepared positions with pre-planned fire support; and by the fact that with the attacking force coming on in waves, and with at least three battalions per division held back in reserve, more of the defenders would be engaged at any one time than would the attackers. The force ratios in terms of troops were therefore probably close to even and it would be the artillery and supporting mortar and machine-gun fire which would make the difference, by suppressing the defenders' ability to engage the attack until too late.

In spite of the rushed orders, the assault battalions of the two leading brigades were in position on their start lines at 03.00 hrs on 10 July, a morning which dawned fine but cloudy and overcast with no wind. Although cool at first, it grew very hot later in the day reaching the mid 80s Fahrenheit, high 20s Celsius.[21] On the left, in the narrowest part of the assault frontage, 16 R.W. Fus was to lead 113 Brigade's attack, followed by 14 R.W. Fus. On the right, 114 Brigade assaulted with two battalions in the first wave: 13 Welsh on the right, heading for the Hammerhead, and 14 Welsh on the left. Lieutenant Colonel Ronald Carden,* commanding 16 R.W. Fus and a charismatic leader, famously addressed the battalion: 'Boys, make your peace with God! We are going to take that position and some of us won't come back. But we are going to take it.' Tying a coloured handkerchief to his walking stick he added, 'This will show you where I am.'[22]

At 03.30 hrs the barrage opened as planned[23] and 20 minutes later the smoke screen was laid south of the Wood – there was very little drift given the lack of wind. 114 Trench Mortar Battery alone fired 125 bombs at the Hammerhead. One German soldier, *Unteroffizier* Gottfried Kreibohm of No 10 Company, III./*Lehr* Regiment, recorded his experience:

> The artillery fire was absolutely frantic. Nearly every shell landed in the trench. Some men were buried alive while others were blown into the air. *Unteroffizier* Wahlen's squad had dug the deepest hole into the side of the trench for protection. It was too deep, for two shells landed directly on top of them and six men were entombed inside. We immediately began tearing away at the earth and could hear someone shouting, but our rescue efforts did not save everyone.[24]

Leutnant Köstlin also reported the weight of fire coming down:

> From 4 a.m. onward, we had no longer been able to establish contact with the Battalion Commander, Major v. Zeppelin, whose battle station was approximately 600 metres from us at the southern edge of Mametz Woods, as the interjacent [*sic*] valley was covered with blanket fire by the enemy – The latest order for the Battalion had been that we were to act on our own without waiting for further orders…[25]

---

*   Ronald James Walter Carden (1875–1916) had been commissioned into the 17th Lancers and served extensively during the South African War. He was one of a number of Regular cavalry officers who were sent to New Army battalions to supply experience and expertise.

The start line for the attack was further from the objective on the right than on the left and at 04.05 hrs, the two leading battalions of 114 Brigade crossed it and headed for the Wood, so as to be close to the objective when the barrage lifted. The *Official History* described the scene:

> … 13th and 14th Welsh advanced in waves of platoons at 100 yards interval in accordance with tactical instructions issued by the Fourth Army. It is very doubtful if this was a suitable formation considering the strength of the enemy's machine guns, and it had already been abandoned by the French, who advanced as we did later in the war, by "packets".[26]

The Germans had not of course been able to wire their hasty trenches on the Wood's edge. It took four minutes to cross the deadly zone from the British line to the base of the cliff: '… a passage through a maelstrom of rifle and machine-gun bullets, shrapnel and shell-casing fragments flying at every angle.'[27]

This movement by 13 and 14 Welsh seems not to have been expected by 16 R.W. Fus and caused some confusion, exacerbated because Carden had gone across to Headquarters 114 Brigade to tie up coordination details (responsibility for liaison was always from left to right, and rear to front) and had not returned. The Second-in-Command, Major J.R.H. McLellan, assumed that Carden had become a casualty and, not knowing the full picture, ordered the battalion to advance:

> On reaching the brow of the hill [i.e. before negotiating the cliff], the leading lines saw the 114th Brigade, or part of it, retiring and they too wavered. Some went forward but almost all returned to their previous positions. This was not a headlong flight but was done slowly and was largely owing to someone who cannot be traced raising a shout of "Retire".[28]

What had happened was that 14 Welsh had attacked with two companies, C under Captain Dagge on the left and B under Captain L.G. Godfrey on the right, moving out of White trench; and two others, A under Captain Milbourne Williams and D under 2nd Lieutenant Wilson, from Beetle Alley. D was in reserve. White trench was only partially dug and had been finished by the battalion during the night of 8/9 July; it was described as being on the high ground overlooking Mametz Wood from the south.[29] The battalion negotiated the cliff and crossed the open ground in good order, arriving at the edge of the Wood just as the barrage lifted. Two German machine-guns inside the Wood were attacked and put out of action single-handedly by Lieutenant F.J. Hawkins. The scheme for the artillery had worked well and there were few casualties among the Swansea Pals; the following waves were less fortunate and there were more casualties, including the Second in Command, Major G. d'A. Edwards, and three of the four company commanders; Captain Johnson took command of the battalion.[30] On their right, however, 13 Welsh, with A and B Companies in the first echelon and C and D in the second, came under fire from machine-guns of the *Lehr* Regiment on the southern edge of the Hammerhead, which caught the assault in the flank. Sergeant T.J. Price remembered what happened in a letter years later to Colin Hughes:

> As the barrage started, we moved off in quite an orderly fashion… the tension and noise cannot be described, what with the traction of shells through the air and the noise of explosions all around us, and it was impossible to give verbal orders and we had to rely on hand

signals for directing any move. Men were falling in all directions due to intense machine gun fire coming against us. How we got into the wood I do not know; but we got there and entered it for a short distance before the Germans came at us – head on – and there was quite a lot of action before we got into shell holes or any other form of cover, we could get. The Germans followed us to the edge of the wood but as our lines were then able to fire on them, they quickly returned to the protection of the tree stumps.[31]

It was this repulse of the Rhondda men that had triggered the retreat of 16 R.W. Fus. Carden however had now returned to his battalion and the advance of 113 Brigade began once more:

Captain G.C. Westbrooke and Lieutenant A.V. Venables had shown great coolness in pulling their men together, and this time the movement was carried out in good order. All the officers state that the advance down the hillside under heavy artillery and machine gun fire was executed with perfect steadiness.[32]

Westbrooke had been a master at Ruthin School in North Wales before the war; he was twice mentioned in despatches and later won the Military Cross; Venables was also mentioned in despatches.

The delay, however, meant that the battalion had lost the protection of the barrage and as the War Diary indicates, II./*Lehr* directed heavy fire from the edge of the Wood, supported by fire from the 122nd Infantry Regiment in Quadrangle Alley and Wood trench, along with artillery and mortars. This fire soon broke up the attack formation. Carden, his stick held high and very conspicuous, was wounded but he picked himself up and struggled on to the edge of the Wood where he was killed.[33] The two leading companies of 14 R.W. Fus, A and B, in the second wave were following 100 yards behind and they too were caught in the interlocking German fire as the made the final approach. Fusilier W.R. Thomas recalled that the battalion had been ready to move two hours before Zero and the men were anxious to get started, hover as they descended into 'Happy Valley' – at the base of the cliff – they: 'met a withering German machine gun and rifle fire from our right flank. This is the spot where we lost most of our comrades, many being killed outright...'[34] There were shouts of 'Retire' from the leading companies, especially as there were heavy casualties among the officers and N.C.O.s including Major Graham Gwyther, in command of the battalion, who was wounded. Captain John Glynn Jones was in the third wave and described what he saw as he broke the crest above the cliff:

Machine guns and rifles began to rattle, and there was a general state of pandemonium, little of which I can remember except that I myself was moving down the slope at a rapid rate, with bullet-holes in my pocket and yelling a certain amount. I noticed also that there was no appearance whatsoever of waves about the movement at this time, and that the men in advance of us were thoroughly demoralised. Out of the most terrible "mix-up" I have ever seen I collected all the men I could see and ordered them into the cutting [at the base of the cliff]. There appeared to be no-one ahead of us, no-one following us, and by this time it was broad daylight and the ridge behind us was being subjected to a terrible artillery and machine gun fire.

I well remember thinking "Here comes the last stand of the old Carnarvon and Angleseys" as I ordered the men to get ready, and posted a Lewis gun on each of my flanks… Meanwhile, men were crawling in from shell-holes to our front, with reports of nothing less than a terrible massacre, and the names of most of our officers and NCOs lying dead in front.[35]

Gwyther had, as we know, only taken over command at short notice and on the eve of battle and this, with the rushed orders recounted earlier by Jones, may account the fact that through error, only two companies of 14 R.W. Fus had been committed to the attack and the other two left behind.[36] It was the remnants of only half a battalion, therefore, that Jones collected. At least some of the battalion had got into the Germans' trench on the edge of the Wood, as W.R. Thomas recorded:

> … we came up against further German resistance in the shape of a counter-attack from a party of bombing German infantry. We had managed to get into their trench, and they were probably some reserves that had to come to the rescue of their comrades in the trench… I caught a glimpse of them but was not able to fire rifle shots and they were not able to aim rifles at us. At the point of entry into the trench I recall vividly that it was full of dead and dying German infantry, casualties apparently inflicted by our artillery barrage…[37]

13 Welsh in the meantime on the far right made another attempt with C and D Companies to get into the Wood, which the *Lehr* Regiment repulsed, but a third effort succeeded in breaking in. Once inside the Wood, the men of 13 and 14 Welsh struggled with the dense undergrowth, which made movement all but impossible; even the rides were difficult to make out. Sergeant Richard Lyons reported later that only four officers were carrying compasses, which made it difficult to keep a sense of direction among the trees and the noise of battle:

> Many of the shells, probably from both sides, hit the trees above us, detonated and caused us more casualties. Progress through the wood was slow mainly due to German machine-gun fire but also to the density of the undergrowth in the wood. This also impeded visibility. It was difficult to maintain our sense of direction, but I was helped in this by being able to tell the difference between the sound of our guns and the Germans.[38]

Others, like Hayes commanding 14 Welsh and Captain J.S. Strange of the same battalion also recalled the difficulty of maintaining direction.[39] The leading companies of 16 R.W. Fus also entered the Wood, although with heavy casualties, and the bombers managed to make progress up Strip trench. The undergrowth was, it appears, not so thick here but the artillery barrage had blown trees into and across the trench, which was also flooding with water pouring in from a nearby pond whose banks had been breached by shells.

A Company of 10 Welsh was sent in to the Wood at about 04.30 hrs to support 13 Welsh, followed soon afterwards by the rest of the battalion. Many casualties, including Lieutenant Colonel Ricketts, the C.O., were taken as the troops negotiated the cliff. One platoon of A Company under 2nd Lieutenant Henry Cowie attacked the German machine-guns that were firing from the southern edge of the Wood and although Cowie was killed, one gun was silenced and several prisoners taken.[40] At about 06.15 hrs the battalion reached the first objective, and began to dig in.

The fighting with the guardsmen of the *Lehr* Regiment had been fierce around the southern edge of the Wood, as later observers reported. The writer Gerald Brennan visited the Wood in the aftermath of the battle and dscribed it thus:

Its trees were torn and shattered, its leaves had turned brown and there was a shell hole every three yards. This was a place where something almost unheard of in this war had taken place – fierce hand-to-hand fighting in the open with bombs and bayonets. What seemed extraordinary was that all the dead bodies there just lay as they had fallen in their original places as though they were being kept as an exhibit for a war museum. Germans in their field-grey uniforms, British in their khaki lying side by side, their faces and their hands a pale waxy green, the colour of rare marble. Heads covered with flat mushroom helmets next to heads in domed steel helmets that came down behind the ears. Some of these figures still sat with their backs against a tree and two of them – this had to be seen to be believed – stood locked together by their bayonets which had pierced one another's bodies and sustained in that position by the tree trunk against which they had fallen. I felt I was visiting a room in Madame Tussaud's Chamber of Horrors, for I could not imagine any of those bodies having ever been alive. Yet the effect in its morbid way was beautiful.[41]

Christopher Williams's painting *The Welsh at Mametz*. (National Museum and Galleries Wales)

Emlyn Davies reported that:

> After violent hand-to-hand fighting with bomb and bayonet the enemy was overcome and driven with similar weaponry further into the wood's expanses … Gory scenes met our gaze. Mangled corpses in khaki and field grey; dismembered bodies; severed heads and limbs; lumps of torn flesh half way up the tree trunks; a Welsh Fusilier reclining on a mound, a red trickle oozing from his bayoneted throat; a South Wales Borderer and a German locked in their deadliest embraces – they had simultaneously bayoneted each other. A German machine gunner with jaws blown off lay against his machine gun, hand still on the trigger.[42]

Frank Richards in *Old Soldier Sahib* spoke of 'the ground all around us being thick with dead of the troops who had been attacking Mametz Wood.'[43] Robert Graves described much the same scene in his autobiography:

> Mametz Wood was full of the dead of the Prussian Guards Reserve, big men, and dead Royal Welch and South Wales Borderers of the new-army battalions, little men. Not a single tree in the wood remained unbroken… I passed the bloated and stinking corpse of a German with his back propped against a tree. He had a green face, spectacles, close-shaven hair; black blood was dripping from the nose and beard. I came across two other unforgettable corpses; a man of the South Wales Borderers and one of the Lehr Regiment had succeeded in bayoneting each other simultaneously. A survivor of the fighting told me later that he had seen a young solder of the Fourteenth Royal Welch bayoneting a German in parade-ground style, automatically exclaiming as he had been taught: "in, out, on guard…"[44]

Lieutenant Glynn Jones, with what remained of 14 R.W. Fus, decided that he could not stay where he was all day, howevr:

> 2 Lt [C.H.] Stork, C.S.M. F. Thompson and Cpl. [T.] Pudner were sent out as a patrol to search the wood. They reported it clear for 200 yards except in the direction of Wood Support. This was reported back to the C.O. 15th R.W.F. and we received orders to dig in where we were. The line was very thick at this time and Battalion much mixed up.[45]

At about 05.30 hrs, in response first to appeals for support and then to a direct order, 15 R.W. Fus also entered the Wood through what remained of the 14th, with A Company leading and B, C and D behind; they were followed by the leading two companies of 13 R.W. Fus, the last of 113 Brigade's battalions. These three battalions, 13, 15 and 16 R.W. Fus, pushed out patrols and were able to move up to the first cross ride, linking up with the 6th Dorsets of 17th Division in Wood trench. A limited counter-attack by the Germans at this point was easily repulsed but 10 Welsh had to send a company across to help shore up 15 R.W. Fus' position, because Wood Support was still in German hands and the whole of the left of the advance was threatened.

The Commanding Officer of 15 R.W. Fus was a Regular officer, Lieutenant Colonel R.C. Bell. David Jones remembered him standing casually and beautifully dressed, as another officer called out to him, 'Well, Bell', a rhyme that found its way into *In Parenthesis*, as 'Well, Dell'.[46]

A fanciful picture of the fighting in Mametz Wood; the Germans are wearing uniforms that are at least a year out of date.

Captain Macdonald and RSM Jones, 15 R.W. Fus. (RWF Mus)

Bell did not help matters in the Wood by sending back a message to say that the second objective had been captured – not true, as only the initial objective was held and the source therefore of more confusion.[47]

After a time, German soldiers began to surrender in large numbers. Glynn Jones, with the survivors of 14 R.W. Fus in the gully below the cliff, saw about 40 Germans coming out of the Wood with their hands up:

> Suspecting a trick, I ordered my men to cover them, but allowed them to approach us. When they got about halfway, I went out to meet them, accompanied by a sergeant, and sent them back to our headquarters. As this appeared to point to the wood being unoccupied, I sent a small patrol to examine it; and then we all moved forward. Crossing the trench on the fringe of it, we entered the wood at the entrance of the main ride, and with two patrols in front advanced up the ride in file, as the undergrowth was very thick.[48]

Those surrendering were men of 5 Company, II./*Lehr*, who were trapped between 16 R.W. Fus in Wood trench and 14 Welsh in the centre. The German account of the battle noted that:

> 5. and 6./Lehr-Infanterie-Regiment were overrun at the southern and south-eastern front of the woods despite their brave resistance. Since then, all contact with 5./Lehr-Infanterie-Regiment, whose commander had fallen into enemy hands, was lost. Some men of 6./Lehr-Infanterie-Regiment had been able to retreat through the dense woods.[49]

David Jones recalled seeing German prisoners, officers among them, whose long field-grey coats 'with bits of red piping of exactly the right hue & proportion',[50] he could not but admire.

13 and 14 Welsh had also pushed forward to and beyond the first lateral, reaching it at around 05.00 hrs while the barrage was still falling just beyond it, although many rounds were falling short, as the 13 Welsh War Diary reported:

> We suffered many casualties from our own shell fire, Major [Charles] Bond being killed [he was the acting Commanding Officer]. When it was realised it was our own barrage we were in and not that of the Hun, the order to withdraw was given and the battalion withdrew for a time. During the interval we fell in with the 10th Welsh coming up to reinforce and we got in touch with the 14th Welsh. Lt. Col. Hayes [C.O. 14 Welsh] ordered the battalion to dig in along the ride at E.[51]

Hayes sent a runner back to Marden at the brigade headquarters asking for the artillery fire to be shifted forward, a request that Marden passed on, but the request was refused, and the fire plan continued as programmed.[52] Marden told Hayes to strengthen his position and be ready to advance as his original orders dictated. The official history says that this refusal, 'afforded the enemy such a respite that he thought better of evacuating the wood completely,' the commander of the 28th Reserve Division having given orders at 04.15 for the Wood to be evacuated.[53]

By 06.00 hrs therefore the southern end of the Wood had been captured, and there was pleasure at Corps, Army and G.H.Q. levels when the initial reports began to arrive, Haig writing in his diary of his satisfaction that two brigades had entered the Wood.[54] There had, however, been considerable casualties, including four of the battalion commanders killed or wounded: Gwyther

Modern photograph of the attack on
the Hammerhead. (A.M. Goulden)

A German sketch of the British
attack on 10 July and the German
retirement. (16th Bavarian
Regimental History, p. 189)

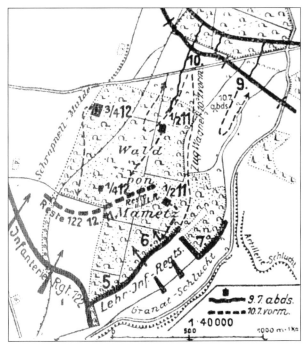

of 14 R.W. Fus; Carden of 16 R.W. Fus; Ricketts of 10 Welsh; and Bond of 13 Welsh. Ricketts had been wounded in the leg, his femoral artery cut, but he continued to direct battle whilst lying down until carried off the field. Many company officers had also been killed or wounded and in the thick undergrowth it was proving very difficult to maintain control over the companies and battalions. As Glynn Jones recalled, the attack was: 'A beautiful operation on paper, showing more text book knowledge than experience, but ridiculous for a wood full of the unknown, and bodies of men completely lost in thick undergrowth and without leaders.'[55]

This lack of control was exacerbated by the fact that the two brigade commanders were still well behind their commands, having been ordered to remain on the end of the telephone at their command posts by the G.O.C. They were therefore relying on runners to receive reports and issue instructions, but without any situational awareness or personal contact. This led to one of the Commanding Officers being given de facto command of the brigade in combat – and most of the Commanding Officers had no experience of commanding anything in combat, let alone a brigade. Price-Davies was disappointed in the performance of his brigade and after the action, his brigade major delivered the following summary of his views to the Commanding Officers:

> The initial advance against the wood appears to have been carried out with the utmost gallantry by all ranks in the face of heavy fire from artillery and small arms. After the wood was entered, however, and certainly by the time the first objective was reached the sting had gone from the attack and a certain degree of demoralisation set in. The desire to press on had vanished and it was only by the utmost strenuous efforts on the part of a few officers that it was possible to make progress.[56]

The Germans, moreover, still held the Hammerhead and Wood Support trench on the flanks of the attack. Some veterans remarked that the Germans had a trench running along the eastern edge of the Hammerhead – a continuation of the works on the southern edge of the Wood – and a concealed communication trench linking the Hammerhead with Flatiron Copse,[57] which would explain the way in which 7 and 8 Companies of II./*Lehr* under *Leutnant* Pfeiffer worked their way back towards the northern edge of the Hammerhead and there linked up with the 3rd Battalion in Flatiron Copse. No 2 M.G. Company also withdrew skilfully and although two guns were lost, the remaining three kept up a sustained and accurate fire as the crews leap-frogged from shell-hole to shell-hole back towards the second line. In the centre of the Wood, what remained of 6 Company of II./*Lehr* joined up with two platoons of the 16th Bavarians and held on until the early afternoon before withdrawing.[58]

At 06.15 hrs the British artillery lifted to the second lateral ride. In spite of the relative lack of heavy guns, British artillery *after* 1 July took a heavy toll on the German defenders in the relatively shallow trenches in front of Mametz Wood and within the Wood itself. The second line had deep dugouts, mostly being used as dressing stations, but these were vulnerable to the heavier calibres of the British artillery which broke up the trenches and caved in the dugouts, burying the men in them alive. *Gefreiter* Hetschold of No 2 M.G. Company (*Ludwig*) of the *Lehr* Regiment moved into the second line at Bazentin-le-Petit and recounted what happened when it was shelled:

> In the dugout in which I was, 100 comrades soon gathered. It was a strong dugout but after a short barrage it also gave way. First an entrance collapsed and many suffocated. Then a

shell landed in the middle and we were all thrown hither and thither … But then the next followed immediately. A fearful rending, all the candles were out, shouts and groans. I can still breathe, I hear my comrades calling … four metres of earth lie on them, I shudder. There is no escape here. As we make for the second entrance, the next shell smashes it in. We are buried alive… We scratch the earth down with our hands and feet. Dead comrades are unearthed. We press close to the steps. If the earth falls from above, we are lost. My hair stands on end. Then – a shout of joy! A small ray of light comes from above. We are saved… Only a few comrades are still with me from our company. We stick together like true brothers.[59]

As noted in the artillery orders cited in Chapter Seven, the British corps and army heavy artillery batteries bombarded the German rear areas, railways and roads, making re-supply all but impossible. Water was a particular problem on the Somme and it had been for this reason that the British had sunk so many new wells (see Chapter Four); the Germans could get neither enough food nor enough water to the front line; the wounded in particular suffered from thirst with men drinking dirty water brought to them from puddles or shell-holes. *Leutnant* Köstlin recalled, for example, that: 'The men … drank the yellow dirty rain water from the grenade holes as they were so painfully thirsty.' Soldiers leaving the Wood in search of water were frequently killed by shrapnl.

As the artillery fire shifted northwards, the infantry followed. 113 Brigade met stiff resistance around Point J, where 122 I.R. had its command post in a strong dugout, and from Wood Support trench; Lieutenant Colonel Oswald Flower* was therefore sent forward with the two uncommitted companies of 13 R.W. Fus, 'to find out the exact situation and reorganise the brigade.'[60] Soon afterwards, however, Price-Davies himself was given permission to go forward into the Wood with Lieutenant Colonel Edward Gossett of the Fourth Army staff. As he made his way up Strip trench, he saw some men running back in panic – no doubt the source of his reprimand afterwards cited above. David Jones of 15 R.W. Fus, who calls Price-Davies 'Aunty Bebbidge', also saw this incident and cited it in *In Parenthesis*:

The Assault on Mametz Wood, by David Jones.
(RWF Mus 2998b)

---

*   Lieutenant Colonel Oswald Swift Flower (1871–1916) had served with 2 R.W. Fus in Crete, China, Burma and India.

Jerry's through on the flank ... and: Beat it! –
That's what that one said as he ran past:
Bosches back in Strip Trench – it's a
Monumental bollocks every time ...[61]

Order was soon restored however and Flower with his two companies moved through the men of 16 R.W. Fus, with orders to drop one company, A Company, to hold the line of the first lateral cross ride, while the second, B Company, pushed on.[62] In reality, the two companies became caught up in the confused fighting among the trees and made little or no progress that morning. David Jones recalled hearing the men of 14 R.W. Fus singing *Jesu lover of my soul* – one of the hymns specified in Regimental Standing Orders for use by the Royal Welsh Fusiliers at church parades – and then seeing his platoon commander, Lieutenant R.G. (Robert) Rees move forward before being shot dead:

He sinks on one knee
and now on the other,
his upper body tilts in rigid inclination
this way and back...[63]

The Regimental Commander of the *Lehr, Oberstleutnant* Kumme (who was later captured with his staff by the 9th Leicesters) was meanwhile taking stock of the situation. Flatiron and Sabot Copses had been heavily bombarded by the British artillery, but no infantry assault had followed. He therefore sent a message to the C.O. of III./*Lehr*, Major von Kreigsheim, urging him to reinforce II./*Lehr* in the Wood. It was probably this which caused the British official historian, Edmonds, to make the judgement that the failure to lift the British artillery fire earlier had caused the Germans to re-think. Von Kriegsheim detached one platoon from each of 9, 10 and 12 Companies and added a platoon of 5 Company II./184 I.R. under *Leutnant* Krause.[64] This composite company, called *Gruppe* Kummetz after its commander, *Leutnant* Kummetz, the commander of No 1 M.G. Company of the *Lehr,* 65 arrived at the eastern edge of Mametz Wood, probably via the concealed communication trench, around 09.00 hrs and made contact with 7 and 8 Companies of II./*Lehr*.[66] Thus reinforced, the Germans made the Hammerhead a hell for the assaulting Welshmen. Kriegshiem later sent one more platoon, but reluctantly, as he feared an assault on the copses and would not risk weakening the second line.[67] As well as reinforcing from the east, the Germans also sent a considerable reinforcement into the Wood through Middle Alley at about 09.35 hrs, in spite of heavy British artillery fire on the Wood north of the second lateral and on the second line itself.[68] These reinforcements, as reported by *Gefrieter* Siegel of 184 I.R. and others, were 5, 6 and 7 Companies of II./184 R.I.R., and 9 and 10 Companies of III./16 Bavarias.[69]

13 Welsh could make no progress at all on the right of the Wood against this reinforced German position. The last of 114 Brigade's battalions, 15 Welsh, was therefore sent in just before 07.00 hrs, and together the two battalions were able to push through the Hammerhead to Point X – but they were then thrown back again by Kummetz's men at about 08.20 hrs. The Germans had got behind 15 Welsh with machine-guns and as a result, two platoons were almost annihilated with only four survivors out of 80. At some point in the action, although it is uncertain when, Major Christian Phillips, the acting Commanding Officer, was killed – so too

was Major Percy Anthony who took up the command. Following the report that the Germans were reinforcing the northern edge of the Wood from the second line through Middle Alley, an artillery bombardment was called for, but only 15 minutes' fire was available, and the effect was therefore minimal. 15 Welsh fell back to the line D – E around 10.30 hrs, maintaining contact with 13 Welsh to its left. The British line then ran on across the Wood to Point J and then southwards along the edge of the Wood.

Marden, the commander of 114 Brigade, was still not in the Wood and at 10.30 hrs, with his attack stalled, he placed Hayes, the C.O. of 14 Welsh, in command of all troops east of the central ride and ordered him to push on to the second lateral. This Hayes managed to do in the centre, moving forward with 14 Welsh about 200 yards, but being held up on the right. 10 Welsh War Diary recorded that:

> At 2.00 pm, the 10th had orders to advance to the 2nd objective which was done in 2 files of 2 companies each. One file was strongly opposed by machine gun fire and sniping and returned to the trench to reorganise. This file advanced again after about 20 minutes and went through to the second objective.[70]

Marden was clearly very anxious to get into the Wood himself and reorganise the brigade; Watts, however, would not do this but instead made matters more confused than ever by committing two battalions of 115 Brigade, again without their brigade commander. These were two battalions that had remained largely out of the action on 7 July: 17 R.W. Fus, under Lieutenant Colonel J.A. Ballard, was sent to support 113 Brigade on the left; and 10 S.W.B under Lieutenant Colonel J.N.R. Harvey went in behind 114 Brigade on the right. Orders were sent from Watts to Price-Davies on the left to try to work around Wood Support trench and advance without clearing it. Price-Davies had a telephone, but the noise of battle was so great that he could neither hear nor be heard. 15 and 16 R.W. Fus were meanwhile pulled out of the Wood, which was becoming severely congested with nine battalions and part of a tenth in the dense undergrowth.[71] These two new battalions arrived at about 14.40 hrs.

Brigadier General Thomas Marden.
(R. Welsh Museum Brecon)

The Germans on the left of the Wood, meanwhile, could see the British moving in the south-western part of the Wood and realised that the defences had been penetrated. *Leutnant* Köstlin wrote that:

> At midday, we observed for the first time that we still had manpower in our trenches situated to the left of us outside Mametz Woods close to the Battalion's command post…

Using my binoculars, I thought I recognised *Oberleutnant* Seidel...* Maybe an hour later, one of my guards drew my attention to the south-westerly corner of the woods which was situated about 400 metres behind us to the left... All of a sudden, it became clear to me what must have happened earlier that morning over there and at Montauban – The English must have broken through the area to the left of us without us noticing let alone preventing it. They must have penetrated the completely destroyed positions at the southern edge of Mametz Woods during the morning, and the only thing we had seen, had been the retreat of the last remainders of the companies who had been able to free themselves from the enemy after being overwhelmed... Our situation had become quite alarming: not only was the left flank threatened but the English had already by-passed us with the occupation of Mametz Woods which could only be a matter of a few hours now... We knew we had a restless enemy in front of us who tried to wear us down through continuous attacks.[7]

Köstlin also reported firing on a British patrol with devastating effect:

They emerged from their siege-trench brandishing their weapons. We duly welcomed them with well-executed rapid fire which was downright cataclysmic due to the short distance. Most of them fell immediately. A few who had managed to come close to our rampart collapsed there after being hit by our hand grenades. The rest rushed back to their trench suffering further losses. By midday, a considerable amount of dead and wounded English soldiers had piled up at the head of the siege-trench... we also lost a number of our brave men during our defence, mainly through an enfilade coming from behind us to the right... Soon *Leutnant* Koch was shot in the back.[73]

This was a forward patrol of 6 Dorsets, 17th Division, under Lieutenant Clarke moving up the strip of woodland in the re-entrant towards Wood Support. Major G.C. King of 7 East Yorks was watching the action and had seen German soldiers withdrawing from the western edge of the Wood, and also British troops behind Wood Support – almost certainly men of 113 Brigade. He ordered his company to fire on the Germans and, believing the Germans to be pulling out, sent two platoons under Lieutenant R.B. Cracroft to assault the junction of Quadrangle Alley and Quadrangle Support trenches, by rushing over the open ground. In conjunction with this, Captain Thomas Heathcock was to lead his men to the western end of Wood Support, with the south-western corner of Mametz Wood as their objective. The Germans had re-occupied Acid Drop Copse and as Cracroft charged forward, he was met with machine-gun fire from there and from Köstlin's troops. These attacks failed and both Heathcock and Cracroft were killed.[74]

Ballard, in command of 17 R.W. Fus, became the fifth casualty among the Commanding Officers and this caused a delay while the Second-in-Command, Major Cockburn, came up to

---

*   Seidel and the Battalion Commander, Major Hermann von Zeppelin (1870–1916), managed to get away but both were afterwards killed by artillery fire. Von Zeppelin was related to *Generalleutnant* Count Ferdinand von Zeppelin (1838–1917), the celebrated aeronautical pioneer and champion of the airship, and a member of the noble family of Zeppelin in Württemberg. He was buried at Bertincourt but his body was later removed to the *Waldfriedhof* in Stuttgart along with many other soldiers of the 122nd Reserve Infantry Regiment.

10-18 Inside a German command post in Mametz Wood, similar to that of Major von Zeppelin, 122nd Reserve Infantry Regiment. (James Payne collections)

A wrecked German bunker in Mametz Wood, possibly the command post of Major von Zeppelin. (James Payne collections)

Modern photograph of the remnants of Major von Zeppelin's H.Q. bunker; Professor David Austin (right) and Mr Nick Keyes (left). (A.M. Goulden)

The Funeral of Major von Zeppelin at Bertincourt on 12 July. (122 I.R. Regimental History)

take charge. However, the arrival of these two fresh British units gave an added boost to the attack. After a further artillery bombardment starting at 14.00 hrs, the two battalions began to move. 17 R.W. Fus by-passed the eastern end of Wood Support trench and the German strong-point there, as reported by *Leutnant* Matthaei of 8 Company II./184 I.R.[75] On their left, 13 R.W. Fus bombed down Wood Support, linking up with 6 Dorsets of the 17th Division coming in from the west. 10 S.W.B. also made progress on the right, reaching the line Y – V, with some patrols nosing forward to towards the north-eastern corner of the Wood until progress was halted by machine-gun fire from Kummetz's men on the northern fringe of the Hammerhead.[76] Two companies of pioneers from 19 Welsh had been tasked to dig a trench just south of second lateral, which they duly began; they should also have dug a communication trench, but one of the two companies was employed on carrying ammunition and the job was not therefore done.[77]

Marden, meanwhile, had at last been given permission to enter the Wood, and once inside he met Price-Davies and ap Rhys Pryce – the latter had come up with the two reserve units. He ordered the attack that had begun around 14.40 hrs to halt, although not all units received the instructions and 17 R.W. Fus, for example, continued to press forward, reaching their second objective at 15.50 hrs.[78] After a conference, it was decided to straighten the line and, at 16.30 hrs, to make a co-ordinated advance through the whole Wood. Lieutenant Colonel J.R. Gaussen, commanding 11 S.W.B., later recalled that he went forward with Marden to see where the line was. However, they missed the line and went right to the northern edge of the Wood and were not fired on, although German prisoners later said that reinforcements were slipping in then.[79]

Maintaining communications was a constant headache, as Emlyn Davies recalled:

> The communication system was set up in a chain made up of field telephones at intervals of a 100 yards or so, manned by three signallers in each. The arrangements made were that on a line being broken, a man from the rear went forward to the next station, repairing the line and remaining forward in the event of a casualty. A slender enamelled wire, Army, 01, provided the connections. On cutting the line was difficult to repair for the reason that the ends would fly away scores of yards and often unfound in the dense scrub. Consequently, the repairer carried with him a fresh roll from reserve stock until such time as the stock was exhausted, a happening which within two or three days became a act.[80]

However, the new attack was pressed forward, with 17 R.W. Fus supported by 14 and 15 Welsh making good progress in spite of casualties inflicted by German snipers in the trees – the *Lehr* Regiment, it will be remembered, contained many expert marksmen from the infantry small-arms school in Berlin. By 18.30, the attack was no more than 40 yards from the northern edge of the Wood, but at the cost of many casualties, including six officers. The War Diary recorded that:

> … a definite clearing of the enemy out of the centre of the wood and its complete occupation was carried out solely by the 17th R.W.F. Several Officers bear testimony to the splendid behaviour and courage of our men and to the brilliant and determined way in which they succeeded to advance in spite of the density of the undergrowth. During the latter part of the advance some of our men in their tremendous eagerness to get to close quarters with the enemy pushed so far forward that they reached our own barrage. Between 60 and 70 prisoners were taken…[81]

10 S.W.B., which had been tasked to clear the Hammerhead, managed to get between *Gruppe* Kummetz and the rest of the *Lehr* Regiment; von Kriegsheim therefore ordered Kummetz to withdraw, leaving 10 S.W.B. in possession of most off the Hammerhead, but not the northern edge which was still held by the Germans, and also still dominated by machine-gun fire from the trenches on the eastern side.

Things were not so good for the British on the far left. Here, 13 R.W. Fus had a wide frontage to cover and took longer to get forward than the other battalions. As they closed on the northern edge, they came under heavy German machine-gun fire and pulled back to a line 200 yards south of the Wood's edge with the left flank bent back along the old railway line.[82] The Commanding Officer, Lieutenant Colonel Oswald Flower, was wounded by a British shell and later died of his wounds. Command of the battalion devolved on Captain H.W. Hardwick. Here, tired and nervous, hungry and very thirsty,[83] the battalion dug in. To their right, 10 Welsh had been ordered to move up astride the centre ride in two columns as described earlier and they came up alongside 113 Brigade. 17 R.W. Fus had also been obliged to pull back somewhat, chiefly by the British barrage which was falling on them.

Once the northern edge was reached, all battalions came under heavy fire from machine-gun and rifle fire out of Middle Alley. The *Lewis* Gun teams of 113 M.G. Company were caught up in the general scramble to get clear of this, although 2nd Lieutenant Cullen remained at his post; he was shot by his comrades who mistook him, in his isolated position, for a German. Attempts by 14 Welsh and 17 R.W. Fus to counter-attack Middle Alley were frustrated by the

British patrol advancing into Mametz Wood.

thick undergrowth, in spite of valiant efforts to bomb the Germans out by Lieutenant John Strange, Lieutenant Yorke and Lieutenant Arthur Rosser.[84]

That evening, General von Stein, in command of the XIV Reserve Corps, ordered the 28th Reserve Division to hold the Wood at all costs – underestimating the numbers of British troops in the Wood and the degree of penetration achieved. At 19.00 hrs, II./184 I.R. (5, 6 and 7 Companies), supported by a company of pioneers from the 28th Pioneer Regiment and two companies (9 and 10) of III./16 Bavarians, were ordered into the Wood.[85] Fusilier W.R. Thomas, who had been wounded and then been moved to the rear, recalled taking cover in a shell hole from where he could see north of the Wood – he was probably somewhere close Queen's Nullah:

> Looking towards the furthest north-west corner of the wood some ¾ mile away I could see several hundreds of fully accoutred German reserves silhouetted on the skyline pouring into the wood from the north across our front from the direction of Contalmaison. When I say fully accoutred I could discern clearly from out of my [undamaged] left eye that they were wearing their full packs on their backs.[86]

Pushing down from the northern edge, the Germans reinforcements soon came upon the British digging in hard and halted. They too began to dig in. The appearance of the Germans caused a degree of panic among, in particular, 13 R.W.F., and there was a good deal of wild firing which aroused the ire of Price-Davies, until order was restored, and the men settled down for some much-needed rest. Price-Davies later wrote that:

> … demoralisation increased towards evening on the 10th and culminated in a disgraceful panic during which many left the wood whilst others seemed quite incapable of understanding, or [were] unwilling to carry out the simplest order. A few stout-hearted Germans would have stampeded the whole of the troops in the wood.
>
> Later in the night, rapid fire was opened on the slightest alarm and several of our men were hit and one officer killed by this undisciplined action.
>
> The brigadier general commanding wishes all credit given for the early success but thinks we should recognise and face our failures … [87]

The German attack was recorded rather differently in the 15 R.W. Fus War Diary:

> About 9.00 pm … a small counter-attack supported by enemy shelling was made from the north, and a few men panicked down the central drive carrying with them at the southern outskirts of the wood several score of others who, officerless, had lost their way. The sight of these men falling back had the unfortunate effect of making our own artillery shell the northern portion of the wood, inflicting many casualties on the men digging the front trenches 300 yards within the border.[88]

Emlyn Davies reported that Price-Davies himself was struck on the left side during this counter-attack by German shrapnel: '… picking it out, immediately flinging it away, exclaiming, "God! That was hot." His patch pocket had prevented further penetration.'[89] 10 S.W.B. also continued throughout the night to patrol against the most northerly part of the Hammerhead.

Leutnant Köstlin reported hearing the firing and hoping that it meant that the British had been pushed out of the Wood, a hope he soon gave up, however:

> In the evening, we had the satisfaction of watching the crash of an English aircraft above Mametz Woods. The plane spun slowly, revolving around its own axis, crashing from a considerable height down onto the canopy of the trees where we lost sight of it… At about 7 p.m., an intense barrage onto our trench and curtain fire onto the area behind us resumed and lasted the entire night.[90]

It was in this confused series of actions, going on messily towards midnight, that David Jones recorded in *In Parenthesis*, calling Mametz 'Queen of the Woods':

> When the shivered rowan fell
> you couldn't hear the fall of it.
> Barrage with counter-barrage shockt
> deprive all several sounds of their identity,
> what dark convulsed cacaphony
> conditions each disparity
> and the trembling woods are vortex for the storm;
> through which their bodies grope the mazy charnel-ways –
> seek to distinguish waling men from walking trees and branchy
> moving like a Birnam corpse.[91]

Soon afterwards, Jones was wounded and passed out of the Somme battle.[92]

Over to the division's left, Contalmaison fell to the 23rd Division at about 17.30 hrs and as a result, the 17th Division was finally able to clear Quadrangle Support trench. On the German side, *Leutnant* Köstlin managed to get what was left of his company away:

> … about midnight the fire ceased, and we decided to rush for it. The plan worked successfully, and although a number of men were wounded by shells and stray bullets we succeeded, a total of five officers and 120 men, in reaching the barbed wire entanglements in front of the second line position at 1.30 am. Here we were greeted by a machine gun which suddenly opened from the trench but throwing ourselves on the ground and shouting we soon convinced the gunner of his error and luckily with no cost to ourselves.[93]

At the Headquarters of the British Fourth Army, Rawlinson expressed satisfaction with the day's events, writing in his journal:

> Another day of heavy fighting. The 38th Division succeeded in capturing practically the whole of Mametz Wood and the III Corps also took Contalmaison. In these circumstances I have decided to begin the bombardment of their second line tomorrow and to attack it on the 13th at dawn, weather permitting.[94]

Haig also noted that:

I saw Gen. Horne, commanding XV Corps at Heilly. He reported that Gen. Watts (Comdg 7th Division) had temporarily taken command of the 38th Welsh Division and had nearly got the whole of Mametz Wood. What an effect on the division has a good commander![95]

Price-Davies of 113 Brigade however was not so pleased and pursued his earlier line of attaching adverse criticism to his Commanding Officers – even when he himself had not been in the Wood – In his after-action report on the battle. Commanding Officers were, moreover, later told that 'the word "retire" is not to be used and that any man using it is liable to be shot on the spot. Officers must deal with all cases of indiscipline of this nature which can only be stamped out by the most drastic action.'[96] In a letter to his wife he played up his own part during the course of events:

At 4.15 am I felt frightfully hungry & had a cup of tea & a sandwich. About 7 a.m. we were told that we had captured the whole wood & prisoners I went off to see the captured wood. There was a great number of dead Germans & we took some machine guns too. After that it became clear that we had not captured even half the wood, also things were not going well that's how I got tangled up in it. I thank God I have come through. Well I stayed and tried to do my level best as a commander … Harry Williams … says the men say I saved the situation!! So nice of them. What I lack is power of organisation & I don't suppose I will ever overcome it & I think I will put it to our HQ so as to give them the chance of getting rid of me if they want. Well we remained in the fighting in the thickest undergrowth all day. Machine guns bothered us a great deal & snipers… We had no water & I got so dry I had nothing to eat but an officer gave me some jam sandwiches and about 11 pm Marden gave me chocolate & biscuits but still no drink [except] two tiny sips from a water bottle.[97]

Possibly the fact that a company of 10 Welsh from 114 Brigade had had to support his own troops close to Wood Support made Price-Davies feel that his own brigade had not done all it should. He later back-pedalled – if somewhat meanly – in the light of new information saying that his first report:

… was made up after the receipt of the accounts furnished by battalion commanders and from my own personal experience. Since then, however, I have had the accounts of certain gallant actions performed by officers and other ranks, and I felt that possibly I may have not given my brigade full credit for what they did in Mametz Wood.

This is probably in great part due to the painful impression left on Lt. Col. Bell and myself by the discreditable behaviour of the men in the division who fled in panic at about 08.45 pm on 10 July. [N.B. Price-Davies and Bell were the only Regular officers of the brigade who saw what happened and did not become casualties].

The result has been that the initial success of entering the wood in the face of very heavy artillery and small arm fire has not been brought to notice sufficiently.

I feel that some brigadiers would have made a very readable story with the material available. They would, no doubt, have dwelt upon the capture of guns in the wood, and on the number of machine guns to our credit, as well as upon the difficulties of attacking through a thick wood in the face of snipers and machine guns.

Though I deprecate all forms of bragging and consider that when failure is disclosed it should be faced, I think it is possible that a certain amount of praise, in fact making the most of such successes as we obtain, is good for morale and improves the confidence and self-respect of the men.[98]

One wonders who the other brigadiers were, to whom Price-Davies rather cattily refers; it appears most likely that they were brigade commanders in the 3rd and 9th Divisions who were engaged in the fighting for Trônes Wood and High Wood after 14 July. A private letter, undated, gives a slightly more realistic view of things in the Wood, though:

Well tired as we were the Bosche was more tired & kept surrendering but it was a job to get hold of such a great wood with tired men. Well-trained fresh regulars would have found it hard on manoeuvres even!![99]

By contrast, Brigadier General Thomas Marden congratulated all ranks of 114 Infantry Brigade. Allowance must be made for the fact that Marden was himself a Regular officer of the Welsh Regiment, but he wrote in his message to the brigade that:

Wood fighting is recognised as the most difficult form of fighting [N.B., actually this was arguably not so as the accolade probably belonged to fighting in towns and built-up areas] and it reflects the greatest credit on all engaged that at the end of the day all units of the brigade were under their own commanders. The advance to the attack was carried out in perfect order by the 13th and 14th Welsh, to whom fell the majority of the wood fighting, the severity of which is shown by the casualty lists. The 10th and 15th Welsh showed equal steadiness in the advance when called on to support... With such a splendid start, the 114th Infantry Brigade can look with confidence to the future, and with pride to the past.[100]

In his report to the divisional commander, Marden said that all ranks had 'behaved with great dash and gallantry in the face of considerable fire.'[101] Certainly, 114 Brigade had lost 48 officers and 1,240 men killed, wounded and missing during the day, and had taken 190 prisoners. There was a mixed view of the success of operations on 10 July by those on the ground, therefore – but success there had been; and the penetration of the Wood on 10 July set the scene for the final phase of operations the following day.

The last word on the fighting of 10 July must go to the German defenders, whose assessment concurred with this view. A message from the Regimental Commander of 122 R.I.R. to his officers and men is couched in strikingly similar terms to those used by Marden. It also highlights, interestingly, that the problem of artillery firing on its own infantry was not a problem confined to the British Army:

Also, I must thank the men for their exemplary conduct during the strenuous days we have of late passed through. Nothing has affected that, not even the regrettable way in which the 2nd Battalion has been imperilled by the fire of our own artillery. This incident has been made by me the subject of rigorous and strict inquiry, especially the resulting loss of lives of faithful comrades.

A British reconnaissance aircraft prepares to take off.

God grant that the offensive power of our greatest enemies in this war may also in the future be stayed by our resistance.[102]

Oberstleutnant Bedall of the 16th Bavarians wrote in his diary that:

There was very heavy fighting in Mametz Wood in which No 1 Section of the Machine Gun Company suffered the exceptionally great loss… of 15 men and one platoon commander killed, 12 men wounded. Towards evening a furious struggle began in Mametz Wood. This lasted the entire night until morning. The 3rd Battalion of the 16th Regiment, and the 2nd Battalion of the *Lehr* Regiment, were effectively destroyed.[103]

A post-war account went further still:

Over 400 prisoners of five different [German] regiments had been captured [on 10 July], the defenders being reduced to 140 men of the II./Lehr Regiment, II./184th, and engineers [i.e. the company of the 28th Pioneers]. The various German headquarters had no clear knowledge of the situation: the 183rd Division felt sure that the British had reached the northern edge of the wood which the 3rd Guards Division thought was still in German possession. The 183rd Division, having no remaining reserve, begged for reinforcements to retake the wood, but only one battalion was available, and that not until the next morning. The only reinforcements received on the 10th were No 8 Company of the 2nd Battalion, 77th Reserve Infantry Regiment (from the 2nd Guards Reserve Division), 120 recruits and two machine guns.[104]

Appendix

German Regiments Order of Battle, Mametz Wood
3rd Guards Division

Guards Fusilier Regiment
Regimental Commander
Oberstleutnant Freiherr von Humboldt-Darhroeben
Adjutant
Oberleutnant von Koenig
I./G.F.R. Major Jachmann
      Adjutant – *Oberleutnant* von Ratzmer
II./G.F.R.   Major von Umann (to Jun 1916)
               Hauptmann von Tschirnhaus (kia Jul 1916)
      Adjutant – *Leutnant* Ridisch von Rosenegt
III./G.F.R. Major von Mühlman
      Adjutant – *Leutnant* Behr
1 M.G. Co   *Hauptmann* Franz
2 M.G. Co   *Hauptmann* Reithe

9th Colberg Grenadier Regiment *Graf Gneisenau* (2nd Pommeranian)
Regimental Commander
Major von Kleist
Adjutant
Leutnant von Kriger
I./9 Grenadiers   *Hauptmann* von Detten
      Adjutant – *Leutnant* Rede
II./9 Grenadiers   Major von Seelhorst
      Adjutant – *Leutnant* Ostermener
Fusiliers/9 G.R.   *Hauptmann* von Sebersen
      Adjutant – *Leutnant* Lenser
M.G. Battalion   *Hauptmann* Eid

Lehr Infantry Regiment
Regimental Commander
Oberst von Zippelskirchen
Oberleutnant Kumme (10 Jul 1916)
Adjutant
Oberleutnant von Ratzmer
Leutnant von Pfeiffer (May 1916)
Leutnant von Wittig (10 Jul 1916)
I./Lehr   Major Jachman
               Oberleutnant Kumme (4 Jul 1916)
               Hauptman von Schauroth (Jul 1916)
      Adjutant – *Leutnant* von Rohbeiter
               Leutnant R. von Rosenngt (7 Jul 1916)
No 2 M.G. Coy   *Hauptmann* von Reiche
               Hauptmann Ludwig (Jul 1916)
II./Lehr   Major von Umann
                Major *Freiherr* von Esebeck (1915)
      Adjutant – *Leutnant* von Hosang
III./Lehr   Major von Mühlmann
                Major von Kriegsheim (Jun 1916)
      Adjutant – *Leutnant* Behr

| | *Leutenant* Leffe (Jul 1916) |
| *No 1 M.G. Coy* | *Oberleutnant* Kummetz |

No 5 Guards Field Artillery Regiment
Commanding Officer – *Oberstleutnant* Dietz

3rd Infantry Division

77th Reserve Infantry Regiment
Regimental Commander
Oberstleutnant Voight
Adjutant
Oberleutnant Dreyer

I./77 I.R.	*Hauptmann* Reinhard
	Adjutant – *Leutnant* Niehoff
II./77 I.R.	*Hauptmann* von Frankenberg-Lütwitz
	Adjutant – *Leutnant* Weiterer
III./77 I.R.	Major von Lettow-Vorbecht
	Adjutant – *Leutnant* H.
Pioneer Coy	*Leutnant* Evers
1 M.G. Coy	*Leutnant* Borchers
2 M.G. Coy	*Leutnant* Fincht
3 M.G. Coy	*Leutnant* Wellhausen

111th Infantry Division

163rd Schleswig-Holstein Infantry Regiment
Regimental Commander
Oberstleutnant Sicht
Adjutant
Oberleutnant Hampe

I./163 I.R.	*Hauptmann* Weede
II./163 I.R.	*Hauptmann* Niemeyer
III./163 I.R.	*Hauptmann* Albrecht
No 1 M.G. Coy	not identified
No 2 M.G. Coy	not identified

183rd Reserve Division

122nd Württemberg Reserve- Infanterie-Regiment
Regimental Commander

Oberstleutnant Karl Gauter	1 Jul 1915 – 20 Oct 1915
Oberstleutnant Philipp Bowintel	21 Oct 1915 – 20 Nov 1915
Oberstleutnant Karl Gauter	21 Nov 1916 – 26 Feb 1916
Oberstleutnant Alfred Wald	26 Feb 1916 – 4 July 1918
I./122 R.I.R	Major Theodor Stern
II./122 R.I.R	Major *Freiherr* Alfred von Zukow
III./122 R.I.R	Major Hermann von Zeppelin	k.i.a. 11 Jul 1916
Hauptmann Herbert Müller	
M.G. Bn	not identified

17th Royal Saxon Infantry Regiment No 183
Regimental Commander
Oberstleutnant Schulze

I./183 I.R.	*Hauptmann* von Hase
II./183 I.R.	*Hauptmann* Köhler
III./183 I.R.	Major Rahmann
M.G. Bn	not identified

Infantry Regiment No 184
Regimental Commander
Oberstleutnant Wilhelm von Steinau-Steinrud

I./184	*Hauptmann* Weisse
	Major Otto (Jul 1916)
	Adjutant – *Leutnant* Werner
II./184	*Hauptman* von Gaja
	Major von Reiss (July 1916)
	Adjutant – *Leutnant* Greiner
III./184	*Hauptmann* G. Soldan
M.G. Bn	not identified

No 1 Company 28 Pioneer Regiment
Officer Commanding – *Leutnant* Zschimmer

10th Bavarian Infantry Division
16th Bavarian Infantry Regiment *Großherzog Ferdinand von Totana*

Regimental Commander	*Oberstleutnant* A. Bedall
Adjutant	*Hauptmann* Ernst *Freiherr* von Lutz
I./16th Bavarians	Major J. Wölsl
Adjutant –	Oberleutnant F. Marschall
II./16th Bavarians	Major O. Killermann
Adjutant –	*Leutnant* E. Soder
III./16th Bavarians	Major F. von Reitz
Adjutant –	*Leutnant* H. Thoma
No 1 M.G. Coy	*Leutnant* O. Kessler
No 2 M.G. Coy	*Leutnant* A. Psister
No 3 M.G. Coy	*Leutnant* M. Seitz
44 M.G.-Scharffschützen-Truppe	*Oberleutnant* H. Stroh
87 M.G.-Scharffschützen-Truppe	*Oberleutnant* T. Scherer

Notes

1   T.N.A. WO 95/921, XV Corps War Diary, Appendix 61A/13, 38th Division Operation Order No 38 issued at 02.00 hrs on 9 July.
2   T.N.A. WO 95/921, XV Corps War Diary, Appendix 61A/13.
3   T.N.A. WO 95/921, XV Corps War Diary, Appendix 61A/19.
4   T.N.A. WO 95/1981, 17th Division War Diary for 9/10 July 1916.
5   Marden, p. 384.
6   T.N.A. CAB 45/189, letter from Captain J. Glynn Jones dated 28 April 1930 with additional notes.
7   T.N.A. WO 95/921, XV Corps War Diary, Appendix 61A/23.
8   T.N.A. WO 95/2539, 38th (Welsh) Division War Diary, Operation Order No. 39 dated 9 July 1916.
9   T.N.A. CAB 45/189, letter from Lieutenant Colonel C.O. Head.
10   T.N.A. WO 95/2539, 38th (Welsh) Division War Diary, Operation Order No. 39 dated 9 July 1916.
11   T.N.A. CAB 45/189, letter from Lieutenant Colonel J.N.A. Harvey.
12   T.N.A. WO 95/2539, 38th (Welsh) Division War Diary, Operation Order No. 39 dated 9 July 1916.

13   Brennslecht, p. 189.

14   Armin Hase, p. 27; Neuman, p. 259.

15   Jones, *War in the Air*, II, pp. 224–225.

16   Sheldon, p. 79.

17   Mügge, *Das Württembergische Reserve-Infanterie-Regiment Nr. 122*, p. 22.

18   Schulenburg-Wolfsburg, p. 132; J. von Hansch & F. Weidling, p. 309; George Soldan, *Das Infanterie-Regiment Nr. 184* (Oldenburg, 1920), p. 33.

19   Muhlmann und Mohs, p. 278–302; *Somme-Nord,* Band 20 map 28.

20   Account by *Leutnant* Köstlin in *Das Württembergische Reserve-Infanterie-Regiment Nr. 122*, p. 23.

21   https//http://ww1weatherreports.wikifoundry.com/page/Somme accessed 28 February 2018.

22   Conan Doyle, p. 126.

23   J. von Hansch & F. Weidling, p. 310.

24   Hicks, p. 304.

25   Account by *Leutnant* Köstlin in *Das Württembergische Reserve-Infanterie-Regiment Nr. 122*, p. 24.

26   Edmonds, Vol II (1916), p. 9.

27   Thomas Dilworth, *David Jones in the Great War*, p. 111.

28   T.N.A. WO 95/ 2556, 16 R.W Fus War Diary, Appendix 1 to July 1916.

29   T.N.A. CAB 45/191, letter from Captain J.S. Strange.

30   T.N.A. WO 95/2551, 13 Welsh War Diary July 1916.

31   Letter from Sergeant T.J. Price dated 26 January 1974 in Hughes, p. 107.

32   T.N.A. WO 95/ 2556, 16 R.W Fus War Diary, Appendix 1 to July 1916.

33   Dudley Ward, p. 206.

34   W.R. Thomas, 'Notes on the 1914–18 War', p. 59–60.

35   Dudley Ward, p. 206. See also the account in T.N.A. WO 95/2555/2, 14 R.W. Fus War Diary.

36   T.N.A. CAB 45/189, letter from Lieutenant Colonel G.H. Gwyther dated 21 April 1930. He attributes the confusion to the orders from his brigade commander, Price-Davies.

37   W.R. Thomas, 'Notes on the 1914–18 War', p. 62.

38   Sergeant R. Lyons, August 1972, to Colin Hughes, p. 108.

39   T.N.A. CAB 45/189, letters from Hayes and Strange.

40   T.N.A. WO 95/2559/1, 10 Welsh War Diary.

41   Gerald Brennan, *A Life of One's Own* (London, 1962), pp. 205–206.

42   Emlyn Davies, p. 31–32.

43   Frank Richards, ed H.J. Krijnen and D.E. Langley, *Old Soldiers Never Die* (Peterborough, 2004), p. 130.

44   Graves, pp. 252–253.

45   T.N.A. WO 95/2555/2, 14 R.W. Fus War Diary.

46   David Jones, *In Parenthesis* p. 154; Dilworth, *David Jones in the Great War*, p. 110.

47   Hicks, p. 86.

48   Dudley Ward, p. 207.

49   *Somme-Nord I. Teil*, p. 197.

50   Thomas Dilworth, *David Jones in the Great War*, p. 115.

51   T.N.A. WO 95/2559/2, 13 Welsh War Diary, July 1916.

52   T.N.A. WO 95/1639, 7th Division Artillery War Diary 05.26 hrs, 10 July 1916.

53   Edmonds, Vol II (1916), p. 51.

54   Sheffield and Bourne, p. 201.

55   T.N.A. CAB 45/189, letter from Captain J. Glynn Jones.

56   T.N.A. WO 95/2552, 113 Infantry Brigade War Diary, July 1916 Appendix XX; a message dated 16 July 1916.

57   See especially the account by Lieutenant Colonel J.N.R. Harvey DSO, C.O. 10 S.W.B. in T.N.A. CAB 45/190.

58   Muhlmann und Mohs, pp. 296–299.

59   Muhlmann und Mohs, pp. 319–320.

60   T.N.A. WO 95/2552, 113 Infantry Brigade War Diary, Appendix XV dated 14 July 1916, Summary of the action at Mametz Wood by Brigadier General Price-Davies.

61 David Jones, *In Parenthesis* p. 180.
62 Dilworth, *David Jones in the Great War*, p. 110.
63 David Jones, *In Parenthesis*, p. 166.
64 Neumann, p. 259.
65 Muhlmann und Mohs, p. 298.
66 *Somme-Nord, I. Teil*, p. 199; Georg Soldan, p. 34.
67 Muhlmann und Mohs, p. 321.
68 T.N.A. WO 95/921, XV Corps War Diary, Appendices B62/6 and 6a.
69 *Somme-Nord*, Band 20 Map 28; Neumann, p. 259–260; Brennslecht, p. 189.
70 T.N.A. WO 95/2559/1, 10 Welsh War Diary.
71 T.N.A. WO 95/2556/1, 16 R.W. Fus War Diary; WO 95/2559/4, 15 R.W. Fus War Diary; WO 95/2561/2, 17 R.W. Fus War Diary; WO 95/2562/1, 10 S.W.B War Diary; WO 95/2562/2, 11 S.W.B. War Diary.
72 Account by *Leutnant* Köstlin in *Das Württembergische Reserve-Infanterie-Regiment Nr. 122*, pp. 24–26.
73 Account by *Leutnant* Köstlin in *Das Württembergische Reserve-Infanterie-Regiment Nr. 122*, pp. 26–27.
74 Renshaw, pp. 108–109.
75 Neumann, pp. 274–276.
76 *Somme-Nord, I. Teil*, p. 216.
77 T.N.A. CAB 45/189, letter from Major J.N.A. Kirkwood.
78 Renshaw, p. 106.
79 T.N.A. CAB 45/189, letter from Gaussen.
80 Emlyn Davies, p. 32.
81 T.N.A. WO 95/2561/2, 17 R.W. Fus War Diary.
82 T.N.A. WO 95/2555/1, 13 R.W. Fus War Diary.
83 Thomas Dilworth, *David Jones in the Great War*, p. 114.
84 *Cambrian Daily Leader*, 20 July 1916.
85 *Somme-Nord*, Band 20 Map 28; Neumann, p. 280; Brennslecht, pp. 189–190.
86 W.R. Thomas, 'Notes on the 1914–18 War', p. 64.
87 T.N.A. WO 95/2552, 113 Infantry Brigade War Diary, July 1916 Appendix XX; a message dated 16 July 1916.
88 Dudley Ward, p. 388.
89 Emlyn Davies, p. 33.
90 Account by *Leutnant* Köstlin in *Das Württembergische Reserve-Infanterie-Regiment Nr. 122*, p. 27.
91 Jones, *In Parenthesis*, p. 179.
92 Thomas Dilworth, *David Jones in the Great War*, p. 116.
93 'The Other Side of the Hill', in *Army Quarterly* Vol 9, No 2 (January, 1925), p. 257, citing historian of 122nd Reserve Infantry Regiment.
94 Rawlinson MS Vol 1, 10 July 1916.
95 Sheffield and Bourne, pp. 201–202.
96 T.N.A. WO 95/2552, 113 Infantry Brigade War Diary, July 1916 Appendix XVIII dated 23 July 1916.
97 Price-Davies, p. 108.
98 T.N.A. WO 95/2552, 113 Infantry Brigade War Diary, July 1916 Appendix XXVI, Report to H.Q. 38th (Welsh) Division by Brig.-Gen. Price-Davies dated 20 July 1916.
99 Robinson, p. 108.
100 T.N.A. WO 95/2557, 114 Infantry Brigade War Diary, July 1916.
101 T.N.A. WO 95/2557, 114 Infantry Brigade War Diary, Appendix C, 16 July 1916.
102 Regimental Order dated 9 July 1916 taken from a prisoner of No 5 Company, II./122 R.I.R. in *Edward Hancock*, Bazentin Ridge (Barnsley, 2001), p. 29.
103 T.N.A. WO 95/2541/1, A.A. & Q.M.G. 38th Division War Diary, July 1916.
104 Neumann, p. 283.

11

'Dead and mangled bodies were strewn everywhere': Final Acts, 11–12 July 1916

Only the truly exhausted could have slept in Mametz Wood on the night of 10/11 July 1916 – sporadic fighting and artillery fire from both sides continued until dawn, about 05.00 hrs on 11 July.[1] Matters were made even more uncomfortable by the fact that the German barrage contained a proportion of gas shells.[2] Food and water remained short, as Emlyn Davies recollected:

> During the battle we subsisted on iron rations, a bag of inch square biscuits and a larger biscuit of concrete confection.* On one occasion only did I espy the CQMS with his cooky assistants bring a trolley of food and steaming tea into the arena† … Water was in short supply and with a few companions we limped into Mametz village where stood a water cart. It involved a traipse of over two miles each way.[3]

The situation was no better for the Germans, as the regimental historian of 163rd I.R. recorded:

> A battle fought during a dark and rainy night with the use of so much ammunition and material is probably the most difficult task ever demanded of human nerves. On a bright day, the moment of weakness is easily overcome. The soldier sees his comrades, he sees his leader, the weak can feel uplifted by the strong. During the night, everyone is on their own as at night, every event has a profound effect on a human being; the approaching enemy suddenly appears in front of him, he does not see him coming, the enemy seems to be stronger than he actually is, he feels alone, his comrades and his leader seem out of reach.

---

*   The so-called 'Iron Ration' comprised an emergency ration of preserved meat, cheese, biscuit, tea, sugar and salt carried by all British soldiers in the field for use in the event of their being cut off from regular food supplies. The ration consisted of 1 lb (0.45 kg) preserved meat (usually corned beef), 3 ozs. (85 g.) cheese, 12 ozs. (340 g) biscuit, 5/8 oz. (15 g.) tea, 2 oz (56 g.) sugar, 1/2 oz (14 g salt), 1 oz. (28 g.) meat extract (usually Bovril). It could only be consumed if specific orders had been issued. This is what Llewelyn Wyn Griffith had reported giving Brigadier General Evans to eat.

†   Rations were brought forward on horse-drawn wagons using hay-boxes, metal containers immersed in an outer box which was then filled with boiling water to keep food hot. Once these wagons had got as far as they could, the hayboxes were carried forward by teams of men sent back from the companies in the line. This would have been a very difficult and dangerous procedure during the fight for Mametz Wood.

Military physician Dr. Schlitt in Contalmaison and assistant physician Dockhorn in Mametz Woods have tended to innumerable wounds during days and days of tireless medical work, thus keeping alive many comrades. The work of the orderlies was above and beynd praise. During heavy fire they gave first aid to the wounded, they searched tirelessly for the wounded and carried them back through horrendous fire; there as no sleep; no rest for them. Despite hunger, thirst and fatigue they continued their difficult task.[4]

At dawn, Lieutenant Colonel Harvey, commanding 10 S.W.B., organised a new attack on the Hammerhead from both flanks. Patrols during the night had located the communication trench from Flatiron Copse and a strong picquet was put in to cut the Germans off from further reinforcement. By 05.30 hrs the attack had succeeded, and 24 prisoners were taken.[5]

At about the same time, Brigadier General Horatio Evans of 115 Brigade took over the command of all troops in the Wood, as he had been ordered to do by the G.O.C.[6] He set up his command post on the crossing of the first lateral ride and the central ride and went forward to see the situation. This was something of a surprise. The Operation Order had clearly been written under the impression that the entire Wood was held by 113 and 114 Brigades, but on investigation Evans found that the forward units had, as we have seen, been forced back from their initial lodgement 50 yards short of the northern edge, to about 300 yards at the closest point in the centre astride the ride. It was immediately obvious that his first task was to defend the gains made against the possibility of a strong German counter-attack.

Two of Evans's units, 17 R.W. Fus and 10 S.W.B., were already in the Wood; his M.G. Company and Trench Mortar Battery were in the western end of Caterpillar Copse. He therefore had only two uncommitted battalions available and there was no divisional reserve. These battalions were 11 S.W.B. and 16 Welsh. These he ordered to come forward, leaving two companies of 11 S.W.B. in reserve.[7] As they did so, Evans began the task of straightening and strengthening the defensive line. The battalions of 113 and 114 Brigades were scattered, short of officers and men, disorganised and very tired. 13 and 14 Welsh, in particular, had been in action for 24 hours and they were withdrawn from the Wood to rest.

Once Evans had reinstated some kind of cohesion, the line was occupied by 16 Welsh from Point O along the railway line northwards for about 500 yards. From there, 17 R.W. Fus held the centre of the Wood, inclusive of the central ride. To their right, 11 S.W.B. held the section of the Wood as far as Point V, with 10 S.W.B. to their right across the northern part of the Hammerhead. There were still gaps, however, and accordingly Evans brought forward 16 R.W. Fus, which had had time to rest, to hold the railway line on the extreme left, between Points O and K.[8] The engineers were also put to work constructing strong-points.[9]

During this reorganisation, Lieutenant Colonel J.R. Gaussen recalled that he went forward with Evans and a party of 11 men. They mistook their path and reached the northern edge of the Wood but were not fired on. A little later they were talking in whispers when British artillery opened fire on the northern edge. A shrapnel round burst overhead, killing eight of the men, and wounding Charles Veal, the Brigade Major in the leg.[10] He was evacuated, and as the Staff Captain had also already been wounded the day before, Evans – who had also been wounded in the arm and in the head – sent for Llewelyn Wyn Griffith, attached as a staff learner, to come forward and act as Brigade Major and Staff Captain:

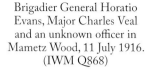

Brigadier General Horatio Evans, Major Charles Veal and an unknown officer in Mametz Wood, 11 July 1916. (IWM Q868)

The enemy was shelling the approach from the South with some determination, but I was fortunate enough to escape injury and to pass on to an ordeal ever greater. Men of my old battalion were lying dead on the ground in great profusion. They wore a yellow badge on their sleeves, and without this distinguishing mark, it would have been impossible to recognize the remains of many of them. I felt that I had run away.

　… it was known that the undergrowth in it was so dense that it was all but impossible to move through it. Through the middle of the Wood a narrow ride ran to a communication trench leading to the German main Second Line of defence in front of Bazentin [i.e. Middle Alley], a strong trench system permitting of a quick reinforcement of the garrison of the Wood. With equal facility, the Wood could be evacuated by the enemy and shelled, as it was not part of the trench system.

　My first acquaintance with the stubborn nature of the undergrowth came when I attempted to leave the main ride to escape a heavy shelling. I could not push a way through it, and I had to return to the ride. Years of neglect had turned the Wood into a formidable barrier, a mile deep. Heavy shelling of the Southern end had beaten down some of the young growth, but it had also thrown trees and large branches into a barricade. Equipment, ammunition, rolls of barbed wire, tins of food, gas-helmets and rifles were lying about everywhere. There were more corpses than men, but there were worse sights than corpses. Limbs and mutilated trunks, here and there a detached head, forming splashes of red against the green leaves, and… one tree held in its branches a leg, with its torn flesh hanging down over a spray of leaf.

Each bursting shell reverberated in a roll of thunder echoing through the Wood, and the acid fumes lingered between the trees... After passing through that charnel house at the southern end, with its sickly air of corruption, the smell of fresh earth and of crushed bark grew into complete domination, as clean to the senses as the other was foul. So tenacious in these matters is memory that I can never encounter the smell of cut green timber without resurrecting the vision of the tree that flaunted a human limb ...

I reached a cross-ride in the Wood where four lanes broadened into a confused patch of destruction. Fallen trees, shell holes, a hurriedly dug trench beginning and ending in an uncertain manner, abandoned rifles, broken branches with their sagging leaves, an unopened box of ammunition, sandbags half-filled with bombs, a derelict machine-gun propping up the head of an immobile figure in uniform, with a belt of ammunition drooping from the breech into a pile of red-stained earth... three men digging a trench, thigh-deep in the red soil, digging their own graves, as it chanced, for a bursting shell turned their shelter into a tomb; two signallers crouched in a large shell hole, waiting for a summons to move ...[11]

Here at the cross-rides, Wyn Griffith found Evans, his arm in a sling, having been also hit by shrapnel. Gaussen also reported that Evans was weak from loss of blood due to his head wound.[12] Evans briefed him on the dispositions and explained that he had also ordered a series of patrols to establish the strength and dispositions of the Germans in the Wood. At 11.00 hrs, a message came in from the G.O.C. six miles away to the rear, saying that the German trenches in front of Bazentin were being shelled and that 'it was quite impossible that he had any strong force in Mametz Wood'.[13] As usual, those far from the point of contact felt sure they knew much more than those on the spot. Watts considered that a determined attack by a small force was all that was needed, and he therefore instructed Evans to occupy the northern and western edges of the Wood 'at the earliest moment.' While Evans was digesting this piece of clairvoyance, Lieutenant Colonel Edward Gossett of the Fourth Army staff arrived and also gave Evans an order to secure the whole Wood:

The Brigadier listened to him with the patience of an older man coldly assessing the enthusiasm of youth. When the Staff Officer had finished, the General spoke.

"I've just had orders from the Division to attack and clear the rest of the Wood, and to do it at once. The defence is incomplete, the units are disorganized, and I did not propose to attack until we were in a better position. My patrols report that the Northern edge is strongly held. I haven't a fresh battalion, and no one can say what is the strength of any unit."

"What do you propose to do?" asked the Staff Officer. "My intention is to take the remainder of the Wood by surprise, with the bayonet if possible; no artillery bombardment to tell him that we are coming. I want a bombardment of the main German second line when we have taken our objective, to break up any counter-attack. Do you know anything about the artillery programme?" "No, I do not. Are you in communication with the Division or with any of the artillery groups?"

"No, except by runner, and that takes a long time. I'm issuing orders to the battalions to get ready to advance quietly at three o'clock, and I'm sending a copy of the order to the Division; if you are going back will you get in touch with them as soon as possible and tell them that I don't want a barrage?"[14]

Gossett then left, and Evans issued orders to the three battalions in the centre to prepare for an attack in three columns at 15.00 hrs. 16 Welsh was to move up the railway line; 17 R.W. Fus up the central ride; and 10 S.W.B. along the eastern fringe of the Wood. Patrols had found that the Wood was only thinly held in front of 11 S.W.B., but that the other two battalions could expect heavy resistance, with several German machine-guns positioned near the centre of the northern fringe of the Wod.

The Germans were in fact in position in hastily-dug scrapes, inside the northern edge of the Wood. This line was held by 5, 6, 7 and 8 Companies, II./184 I.R., supported by No 1 Company 28 Pioneer Battalion; and on the extreme eastern side by 9 and 10 Companies, III./16 Bavarians.[15] The extreme north-easterly corner was still held by 12 Company, III./16 Bavarians. There was also still what remained of the Fusilier Battalion, 9th Grenadiers, on the western edge with some companies of II./ and III./*Lehr*;[16] they did receive around 100 recruits as reinforcements during the night, via the *Shrapnelmulde* route, which was just as well, as their losses had been heavy: one officer killed and two taken prisoner; 82 N.C.Os and men killed, 61 wounded and 254 prisoners or missing. 183 I.R. had been moved back to the second line around Pozières having lost nearly 1,000 officers and men. 122 I.R. was also now in the second line between Pozières and Bazentin le Petit with machine-gun positions forward along the northern edge of Mametz Wood. It too had lost heavily: 13 officers and 217 men on 9 July; 17 officers and 964 men on 10 July – more than a third of its strength in two days, therefore.[17] Also south of Bazentin le Petit Wood were the remainder of the 9th Grenadiers, I./Lehr, and part of I./16th Bavarians.[18]

One personal account details the effect of British fire at this time:

> Battalion Commander Hauptmann von Schauroth [of the *Lehr* Regiment] suffered a shrapnel injury above his left eye. He stumbled against a trench wall. His eye swelled up in no time. A messenger from the battalion headquarters stepped forward, dressed his fore-head and eye, calmly and carefully as there was no enemy around. When the Commander said: 'Stop dressing my wound now, go back to the others or you might fall into the enemy's hands', he said calmly as if it goes without saying: 'If the Commander has to die here, so can I!'[19]

General von Stein, the corps commander, was still determined to hold what he still had of the Wood in order to protect the second line. What remained of I./*Lehr* – 1 and 3 Companies – and No 8 Company of 77 R.I.R. under *Leutnant* Mayer-Ullmann and *Feldwebel* Scheuning, which had been attached to the Guards Fusiliers[20] were ordered to push patrols into the Wood, link up with the remaining German units, discover where the British were, and send back as much information as possible. The 77th was further ordered to clear the area of British troops – a forlorn hope as this would have required a force of at least one German brigade.[21] Contact was made with the in-place units, but with difficulty because of the dense undergrowth, the trees brought down by shrapnel and by the continued harassing fire of the artillery. It was not possible properly to establish the British dispositions, much less expel them, but the Germans estimated, correctly, that the British were 200–300 metres from the northern edge of the Wood.

At noon, 14 R.W. Fus was ordered back into the Wood and took up a position on the first objective where they waited for orders to move up and support 11 S.W.B. Captain Glynn Jones, however, became badly disorientated and the battalion was fired on from the left. Jones decided

Modern photograph of the central ride in Mametz Wood, taken from the probable German line inside the northern edge of the Wood. (A.M. Goulden)

A German communication trench leading to a position in a wooded area, similar to Middle Alley trench from the II *Stellung* to the northern edge of Mametz Wood. (James Payne collections)

Modern photograph of the line of Middle Alley trench. (A.M. Goulden)

Modern photograph of the German Second Line, running this side of the wood, from the northern edge of Mametz Wood and looking up the disused railway line. (A.M. Goulden)

to dig in where he was. This was around 50 yards from the edge of the Wood, according to the War Diary; but which edge is not clear. Later, some men from 13 R.W. Fus under their acting C.O., Captain Hardwick, arrived, but no real contact was made with 11 S.W.B[22]

At 14.45 hrs, Evans's preparations were severely disrupted by a heavy barrage from the British artillery on the northern margins of the Wood; he immediately ordered all units to suspend their assaults and wait for the fire to lift. The divisional headquarters certainly knew that Evans's attack was planned

Mametz Wood, by Henry Handley-Read. (National Museums and Galleries Wales)

as the War Diary records that: 'at 12.50 pm orders were issued by the G.O.C. 115 Brigade for an attack at 3.00 pm'.[23] All the telephone lines were cut so three runners were sent by Taylor, the Brigade Signals Officer, on Wyn Griffith's instructions, by different routes to get the fire lifted.[24] Unbeknown to Wyn Griffith, one of these was his younger brother, Watcyn. Watcyn delivered his message but on the way back was hit and killed instantly by a shell – his body was never found. Wyn Griffith heard of this soon after and recorded his feelings of rage and guilt:

> So, I had sent him to his death, bearing a message from my own hand, in an endeavour to save other men's brothers; three thoughts that followed one another in unending sequence, a wheel revolving within my brain, expanding until it touched the boundaries of knowing and feeling. They did not gain in truth from repetition, nor did they reach the understanding. The swirl of mist refused to move.[25]

At 15.30 hrs, well after the time set by Evans for his surprise attack, the fire *did* lift – but not because any message had got through. Rather it was because this was in accordance with the orders issued to the 7th Division's artillery by Watts, orders that he had not though fit to communicate to Evans. The War Diaries are quite clear on this: 'G Staff order bombardment 2.45–3 p.m. on north edge of wood and 150 yards back. 21st Divn. Artillery will bombard west of Railway, Pearl Wood and Alley. 80th, 35th and 122nd [Artillery] Brigades will bombard northern edge of wood, Flatiron and Sabot Copses. All will lift at 3 p.m. on the German second Line.'[26] The Official History adds that broken telephone lines caused the 30 minutes of delay; 115 Infantry Brigade War Diary adds that: 'At 3.30 p.m. the British artillery ceased firing on the northern edge of the wood.'[27] Lieutenant Colonel F.W. Smith, Commanding 16 Welsh, thought that the mistake had occurred because of the injuries to Evans and Veal,[28] However this seems highly unlikely as the message not to fire a bombardment was taken by Gossett to higher headquarters.

This fire caused heavy casualties among the Welsh battalions even though the range was extreme for the 18-pdrs. However, as soon as the barrage lifted, the battalions assaulted in accordance with their orders. A Company 11 S.W.B. reached the north-west corner by about 17.40 hrs against stiff resistance and heavy machine-gun fire, capturing several prisoners who said that they were nearly starving, as the British artillery fire had stopped all supplies getting through.[29] B Company was slower but also reached the northern edge and extended its frontage to within 75 yards of the central ride, although Middle Alley was still held by German machine-gunners.[30] Gaussen, the Commanding Officer, reported that because of uncut undergrowth and fallen trees, the going was desperately hard and as he had detached to companies to the Hammerhead, he had only two companies avaiable.[31]

17 R.W. Fus and 16 Welsh met even heavier enemy fire and were pushed back to their start lines; 16 Welsh in particular suffered badly from a German flame-thrower, or *flammenwerfer*,[32] probably from No. 3 Guards *Flammenwerfer* Company. Two companies of 10 S.W.B. were brought up and amalgamated into what remained of 11 S.W.B.; and two companies of 16 Welsh were also called forward to support 17 R.W. Fus. Captain Job also brought up guns from 115 M.G. Company and captured some German soldiers. The battalions were told to attack once more – only to be thrown back again, as the German official history records:

> At 7 p.m. [on 11 July], III./Lehr-Infanterie-Regiment which was positioned at the east side of the woods was attacked by 11 South Wales Borderers (115 Brigade). They penetrated a part of 9. Company's position. Their insignificant success, however, was paid for with severe losses.[33]

Evans realised at this point that 11 S.W.B. was out on a limb and in danger of being cut off; he gave Gaussen discretion to pull back if necessary – which Gaussen did. By 21.20 hrs, all these

A German *Flammenwerfer* in action. (http://roadstothegreatwar-ww1.blogspot.co.uk/2013/07/the-german-experience-at-battle-of-somme.html)

battalions were back on their original start lines.[34] 14 R.W. Fus managed at last to contact Evans, who ordered them to remain where they were, on the first objective.

On the far left, 16 R.W. Fus, supported by 10 and 15 Welsh, managed to reach the western edge of the Wood; one platoon bombed its way northwards to come level with the battalions in the centre and briefly reached the north-western corner. At 23.00 hrs, however, heavy fire from 5.9 and 8-inch guns pushed these units back east of the railway line. This artillery fire, along with mortar, rifle and machine-gun fire from 8./II./77 R.I.R. and II./184 I.R., kept up all night, causing many more casualties.[35] What the exhausted Welshmen did not know, however, was that this fire was masking the German withdrawal from the Wood. It was now clear to Von Stein that another heavy British attack the next day would succeed and so at dark, all the remaining German companies pulled back, leaving only a few patrols inside the Wood.[36] *Unteroffizier* Gottfried Kreibohm of 10 Company, III./*Lehr*, recalled the day thus:

> At 4 a.m., I left with three men and took up residence in the field of craters between the company's forward trench and Mametz Wood. We immediately set to work deepening our holes, digging for two hours. Around 8 o'clock the English began to systematically strafe the company sector with heavy-calibre shells. Geysers of earth a 100 feet high shot up from the ground. With my field glasses I could see past Mametz Wood all the way to the village of Mametz. The entire area was swarming with activity…
>
> Thus we waited in our holes for 10 hours – the most fearful 10 hours I ever experienced in my life … around 8.30 pm Tommy's shelling lessened [N.B., this was probably German fire rather than British]. I decided it was useless to stay, so with a shout to my men we ran

German artillery concealed in a wood. (James Payne collections)

as fast as we could towards the rear… There was no-one about. We moved further, eventually reaching a dugout that was blown in by a direct hit. Dead, mangled bodies were strewn and piled everywhere.[37]

The 38th Division was also to be pulled back. Before dawn on 12 July, the four battalions in 62 Infantry Brigade, 21st Division, moved up to relieve the exhausted Welshmen. This had been planned the previous morning by agreement between Watts and Horne at about 08.00 hrs:

> The situation in Mametz Wood was being investigated with a view to clearing it up and establishing a line on the northern edge of the wood. General Watts was of the opinion that if the 38th Division was not in a condition to do so, he had better put one of the battalions of the 7th Division in to do the job. Corps Commander concurred but impressed on General Watts the desirability of not using the battalion of the 7th Division if it were possible to avoid doing so. Corps Commander would direct GOC 21st Division to arrange with General Watts for the relief of the 38th Division in Mametz Wood at the earliest possible moment.[38]

Orders were therefore issued for those battalions of the 38th Division outside the Wood to begin marching that afternoon to billets in the Ribemont – Treux area, about nine miles (13.5 kilometres) away, as shown in the Appendix to this chapter. Those units still in the Wood were to hold until relieved and then march the three miles (4.5 kilometres) to the Citadel, where they would bivouac and then move on to their billeting areas.[39] Llewelyn Wyn Griffith recalled that:

> I have a clear memory of walking up the ride towards the battalions, of tripping over a branch, and of a flash of anger because I hurt my shoulder when I fell. The General went forward to one battalion to make sure that the line was securely held to cover the relief, and I went to another battalion on the same errand. The night seemed to pass in a black film, broken only by the flashes of bursting shells. I am told that I found the battalion…
>
> English voices came out of the dark, enquiring for another battalion of our brigade; more men stumbled by in search of the posts they were to relieve. Our time was drawing to an end.[40]

The first elements of the 21st Division to come forward were *Lewis* gun teams of 12 Royal Northumberland Fusiliers (12 N.F.), who were to make contact with 115 Brigade; they were followed by 7 Green Howards which was to relieve 10 S.W.B. in the Hammerhead. The remaining troops in the relieving force came from 13 N.F., 1 Lincoln, 8 East Yorks and 10 Green Howards, making up 62 Infantry Brigade. They had begun to move at 19.15 hrs on 11 July, but the Lincolns did not reach the Wood, through heavy German shelling, until 03.00 hrs.

Captain John Glynn Jones of 14 R.W. Fus recalled this time:

> About midnight a message was passed that I was wanted on the left. Proceeding there, I found an officer of the Warwicks [sic], who stated that he had come to relieve us. Words cannot express the meaning of that word "relief" as it applied to us at that moment. To a war chronicler it cannot mean more than a trifling operation, but its effect in our case was that after handing over our little line to the new-comers, we were making our way back down

the main ride at a pace that I would never have dreamed us capable of. I remember very little about that long journey back, except that as a parting gift we had a direct hit on our tail, which killed a number of men as we were nearing Mametz village. But I well remember my Quartermaster-Sergeant meeting me somewhere with the words "Thank God you're all right, sir", having a Dixie of hot soup, and falling off into a deep sleep.[41]

Trench digging.

It was not until 06.30 hrs on 12 July that 16 Welsh, the last unit to be relieved, finally left the Wood and 115 Brigade began its march. There was therefore no time for making a stop in bivouacs:

> It was eight o'clock when we reached the old German dug-out and drank a cup of tea. As we were finishing, a Staff Officer from the Division arrived to tell us that we were to get ready to move at short notice. Protest was useless; the battalions must be clear of the bivou-acking ground by five o'clock the next morning, and we must march a distance of 14 miles to another sector of the front.
>
> The day passed in getting ready for the march, and in trying to write a letter to my father and mother to tell them what had happened. When at last I succeeded, I felt in some queer way that an episode was ended, that all feeling had been crushed out of existence within me. Night came, but I could not sleep. At two in the morning we set out to join the battalions, and as dawn was breaking over Bazentin, I turned towards the green shape of Mametz Wood and shuddered in a farewell to one, and to many. I had not even buried him, nor was his grave ever found.[42]

It was left to the 21st Division to complete the final clearance of Mametz Wood, however the German patrols offered no resistance and 62 Brigade found that their job had already been done. Around the northern edge of the Wood, at about noon, they began to find hundreds of dead Germans and 13 heavy guns which had been abandoned, in addition to those already taken by the 38th Division.[43] At dawn on 13 July the Germans launched a heavy counter-attack on 13 N.F., which was beaten back, although the Northumberlands lost 43 men killed and 227 wounded in the five days that they held the Wood.

The 38th Division meanwhile marched away, to take no further part in the Somme campaign:

> The battalions of the brigade were marching in column of fours along the road, and from a little distance it was clear that there was a lack of spine in the column. No ring of feet, no swing of shoulder, no sway of company; slack knees and frequent hitching of packs, a doddering rise and fall of heads, and much leaning forward. Fatigue and exhaustion in a body of men attain an intensity greater than the simple sum of all the individual burdens

of its members warrant. This loss of quality in a unit marching away from the Somme battlefield was made more evident by the rising memory of the sturdy column that swung its way down the hedge-bound lanes in the early mornings of the end of June, a bare fortnight past, singing and laughing in the happiness of relief from the fetters of the trenches in Flanders. To-day the silence was unbroken, save by the shuffling of feet and the clanking of equipment …

… A walk along the column brought a new aspect of our condition into view. A captain was leading a battalion, subalterns and company sergeant-majors were marching at the heads of companies, corporals in front of platoons. Men were marching abreast who had never before stood together in the same file. There are no gaps in a battalion on the march, though many have fallen, but the closing-up that follows losses tells its own tale. The faces of many silent and hard-eyed men showed that they were but half-aware of their new neighbours, newcomers who jostled the ghosts of old companions, usurpers who were themselves struggling against the same griefs and longings, marching forward with minds that looked backwards into time and space… The four battalions marching up from the Somme made a column but little longer than the span of one battalion on the way down: we had left behind us nearly two thousand men of our brigade. The measure of our condition was the measure of the price paid for Mametz Wood; the largest of the woods in the Somme battlefield had reduced a strong division to a shadow. In the capture of this obstacle to our advancing line we had discharged our immediate task, only to be ourselves flung aside as of little worth.[44]

Appendix

38th (Welsh) Division Billeting Areas Following Relief[45]

H.Q. 38th (Welsh) Division	Couin Château
H.Q. 113 (North Wales) Infantry Brigade	Authie
13 R.W. Fus (1st North Wales Pals)	Authie
14 R.W. Fus	St Leger
15 R.W. Fus (1st London Welsh)	Authie
16 R.W. Fus	St Leger
113 M.G. Coy	Authie
113 T.M. Bty	Authie
H.Q. 114 Infantry Brigade	Couin
10 Welsh (1st Rhondda)	Couin
13 Welsh (2nd Rhondda)	Couin
14 (Swansea) Welsh	Couin
15 (Carmarthenshire) Welsh	Couin
114 M.G. Coy	Couin
114 T.M. Bty	Couin

H.Q. 115 Infantry Brigade	Courcelles
10 S.W.B. (1st Gwent)	Courcelles
11 S.W.B. (2nd Gwent)	Left Section (Sub)
16 Welsh (Cardiff City)	Right Section (Sub)
17 Welsh (2nd North Wales)	Coigneux (Divisional Reserve)
115 M.G. Coy	Right Section
115 T.M. Bty	Right Section
19 Welsh (Glamorgan Pioneers)	Thièvres
C.R.A. and Divisional Artillery (119, 120, 121 and 122 Brigades R.F.A.; No 5 M.G. Company, X/38, Y/38 and Z/38 Heavy T.M. Batteries	Remained under command 21st Infantry Division at Mametz
C.R.E.	Couin Château
123 Field Coy R.E.	Rossignol Farm
124 Field Coy R.E.	J.17 Central [N.B., not identified]
151 Field Coy R.E.	Courcelles au Bois (with two sections at Colincamps)
A.D.M.S.	Couin Château
77 Sanitary Section	Couin
129 Field Ambulance R.A.M.C.	Couin
130 (St John's) Field Ambulance R.A.M.C.	Thièvres
131 Field Ambulance R.A.M.C.	Authie
A.D.V.S.	Couin
49 Mobile Veterinary Section	Famechon
H.Q. Divisional Train and S.S.O.	Famechon
330 Company A.S.C.	K.3.d.3.8. (62.d) [N.B., not identified]
331 Company A.S.C.	Famechon
332 Company A.S.C.	Famechon
333 Company A.S.C.	Couin
Supply Column	Freschevillers
Bomb Store	J.17.b. central [N.B., not identified]
Railhead	Belle Eglise
Refilling Points	Road North of Famechon near village

Notes

1   France <www.timeanddate.com> (Accessed 9 May 2018).
2   Interview with Lieutenant W.R.M. Gwynne in *Cambria Daily Leader*, 10 August 1916; see also the account by John Collins of 16 Welsh in Hicks, p. 266.
3   Emlyn Davies, p. 34.
4   Holge Ritter, *Geschichte des Schleswig-Holsteinschen Infanterie-Regiment Nr. 163*, p. 145.
5   T.N.A. WO 95/95/2562/1, 10 S.W.B War Diary.
6   T.N.A. WO 95/2560, Annex IX to 115 Infantry Brigade Operation Order 10 July 1916.
7   T.N.A. WO 95/2560, 115 Brigade War Diary.
8   T.N.A. WO 95/2560, 115 Infantry Brigade War Diary, 11 July 1916.
9   Interview with Lieutenant W.R.M. Gwynne in *Cambria Daily Leader*, 10 August 1916.
10   T.N.A. CAB 45/189, letter from Brigadier J.R. Gaussen.
11   Wyn Griffith, pp. 109–110.
12   T.N.A. CAB 45/189, letter from Brigadier J.R. Gaussen.
13   T.N.A. WO 95/2560115 Infantry Brigade War Diary, 11 July 1916.
14   Wyn Griffith, p. 113.
15   Georg Soldan, p. 34; Brennslecht, p. 190.
16   J. von Hansch & F. Weidling, p. 311.
17   Mügge, *Das Württembergische Reserve-Infanterie-Regiment Nr. 122*, p. 31.
18   Neumann, p. 280; Brennslecht, p. 190.
19   Muhlmann und Mohs, p. 299.
20   Schulenburg-Wolfsburg, p. 135; Alfred Wohlenburg, *Des Res. Inf. Regt. Nr. 77 im Weltkriege 1914–18* (Hildesheim, 1931), p. 185.
21   Muhlmann und Mohs, p. 293.
22   T.N.A. WO 95/2555/2, 14 R.W. Fus War Diary.
23   T.N.A. WO 95/2539, 38th (Welsh) Division War Diary.
24   Wyn Griffith, pp. 112–113.
25   Wyn Griffith, pp. 114–115.
26   T.N.A. WO 95/1639, 7th Division Artillery War Diary and WO 95/1643, 35 Brigade R.F.A. War Diary for 11 July 1916.
27   T.N.A. WO 95/2560, 115 Infantry Brigade War Diary.
28   T.N.A. CAB 45/191, letter from Smith.
29   T.N.A. CAB 45/189, letter from Brigadier J.R. Gaussen.
30   T.N.A. CAB 45/189.
31   T.N.A. CAB 45/189.
32   T.N.A. CAB 45/189.
33   *Somme-Nord*, p. 216.
34   T.N.A. WO 95/2560, 115 Infantry Brigade War Diary.
35   T.N.A. WO 95/2560, 115 Infantry Brigade War Diary.
36   Muhlmann und Mohs, p. 300.
37   Muhlmann und Mohs, pp. 280–282.
38   T.N.A. WO 95/921, XV Corps War Diary, July 1916, Appendix 63/7.
39   T.N.A. WO 95/2539, 38th (Welsh) Division War Dairy, July 1916, Appendix XII.
40   Wyn Griffith, p. 116.
41   Dudley Ward, pp. 211–212.
42   Wyn Griffith, p. 118.
43   Edmonds, Vol II (1916), p. 54.
44   Wyn Griffith, p. 124.
45   T.N.A. WO 95/2539, 38th (Welsh) Division War Dairy, July 1916.

12

'A Dulac picture of some goblin forest': Subsequent Operations Around Mametz Wood

---

As the 38th Division marched away, Rawlinson at Fourth Army Headquarters, who had decided to press on with the attack on Bazentin Ridge as soon as Mametz Wood was penetrated on 10 July, fixed on the 13th for this assault – subsequently postponed for 24 hours by Haig. It was a risky decision. On the 12th, the British artillery began a bombardment of the German positions using one gun for every six yards of front, compared with 20 yards on 1 July, firing some 370,000 shells over two days.[1] After dark on 13 July, the 7th and 21st Divisions moved forward to their start lines and at 03.25 hrs on the 14th, the leading brigades attacked, entering the German lines in the wake of the barrage.

The Germans had been working feverishly to improve their second line and construct a switch position behind it in order to contain the British advance, for a new British attack was daily expected. They had also taken steps to simplify the command structure at corps level and reinforce the Second Army with formations from the Third, Fourth, Sixth and Seventh Armies. The Corps became a *Gruppe*, or Groups, deployed as shown in the Appendix to this chapter.

These changes had been under way since 5 July, and their aim was to provide a stable platform for command and control, especially the provision of intelligence and artillery support, while divisions and regiments were posted around as necessary to contain the British offensive. The down-side of this was that divisions and regiments were shifted rapidly, had little time to establish any sort of relationship with their higher headquarters or flanking formations, and were committed piecemeal – in effect, the same bad practice as was current in the British Army at corps level. Nor did von Falkenhayn support the situation, which was of his making and what he had intended, by shifting heavy guns or aircraft from Verdun to the Somme even when operations on the Meuse were scaled back.[2] The German effort was thus not concentrated in accordance with normal doctrinal practice; moreover the quality of the units – *Landwehr*, recruits and Reserve Infantry Regiments – was not of the same quality as the Prussian Guards, and as a result, the British were able gradually to gain the ground needed to assault the second line.

At the time of the new British assault, the second line north of Mametz Wood and eastwards to Longueval was held, from west to east, by I.R. 183 of 183rd Division; II./77 R.I.R. less No 8 Company from the 3rd Infantry Division; I./184 I.R. from the 183rd Infantry Division and III./165 I.R. from 7th Infantry Division north-west of Bazentin le Petit Wood; next, elements of the 9th Grenadiers, I./ and II./ *Lehr* from the 3rd Guards Division; II./184 I.R. and No 8 Company of II./77 R.I.R.; III./*Lehr;* 91 R.I.R. from the 2nd Guards Reserve Division,

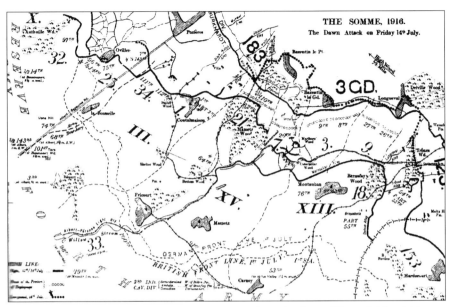

The British and German positions prior to the assault on the Second Line. (Miles, *Military Operations France and Belgium 1916*, Vol. II)

reinforced by what remained of III./16 Bavarians in Bazentin le Petit Wood; part of III./190 I.R. of the 220th Infantry Division and a Recruits Company of the Guards Fusilier Regiment, 3rd Guards Division, in Bazentin le Grand Wood;[3] and finally what remained of I./ and II./16th Bavarians between Bazentin le Grand village and Longueval, with I./190 I.R, behind and in support of the Bavarians.[4] As Jack Sheldon puts it:

> Can there ever have been a greater mixing of units and formations at a critical part of a battle-field? How 6 Guards Infantry Brigade and Generalmajor Rauchenberger,[*] commanding 20 Bavarian Infantry Brigade, who were charged with responsibility for this sector, were expected to exercise effective command over this assortment is anybody's guess.[5]

An additional 14 battalions were also ordered up to the Bazentin ridge to dig and occupy a new switch position. These were also drawn from a variety of divisions, including the newly-arrived 185th Division; 99 R.I.R and 180 R.I.R, the latter with No 3 Company of the Guards Fusiliers, from the 26th Württemberg Reserve Division; and what remained of the 9th Grenadier Regiment of the 3rd Guards Division, as well as some companies of 55th *Landwehr* Regiment. Sixty-five guns and howitzers were also brought forward. This was at first sight a sizeable rein-forcement; however, most of these units were tired and depleted, having been involved in heavy fighting for the past two weeks. The men were also short of ammunition, rations and water, as an account by *Leutnant* W. Steuerwald, a company commander in I./91 R.I.R. made clear after being moved from the Gommecourt area to Bazentin Ridge:

---

*   Otto Rauchenberger, from 1917 Ritter von Rauchenberger (1864–1942)

During the morning of 13th July, the artillery fire eased slightly. Hauptmann von Rauchhaupt ordered that part of the 1st Company under Reserve Leutnant Kaufmann, which was still on the northern edge of Bazentin Wood, was to move forward to the position, to extend the line of 4th Company and to attempt to link up the sector of Major von Kriegsheim (3rd Battalion Lehr Infantry Regiment). The move succeeded. Manning our front line now were the 1st, 4th and 2nd Companies … Artillery fire came down heavily around 11.00 am … Hour by hour the casualty list grew. How would we fare in the event of an attack, which seemed to be ever more likely? It would be extremely difficult to move forward the Reserve Company or other support through the artillery fire. The same applied to trench stores and ammunition. Our men had been rationed for three days, but the shortage of water was already making itself felt … There was a dressing station for the wounded, but this had almost been wrecked by several direct hits … counter battery fire had almost completely accounted for our artillery … The situation was further worsened by the fact that Kreigsheim's men were relieved by two companies of recruits … 1st Company had 45 to 50 men left and 4th Company reported around one 100, some of whom were from 2nd Company. 2nd Company had 60 and 3rd Company 120 men. The company commanders all felt that a further attack on Mametz Wood had absolutely no prospect of success, but they hoped to hold their positions if they had time to work on them.[6]

In the British 7th Division, now once again under the command of Major General Watts and on the right of the Corps, was 1 R.W. Fus. The battalion had been ordered, with the rest of the division, to assault Bazentin Ridge in order to secure the village and the two woods beyond Mametz. The assault was to be delivered when it would be just light enough to distinguish friend from foe, 'preceded by a very effective artillery barrage, swept over the enemy's first trenches and on to the defences beyond.'[7] 20 Brigade was to lead the attack, with 22 Brigade ready to move through and capture Bazentin le Petit village. The diary of the Commanding Officer, Lieutenant Colonel Clifton Stockwell, recorded that on 14 July:

A German panoramic sketch of the view along the Second Line from Longueval towards Bazentin le Grand. (16th Bavarian Regimental History)

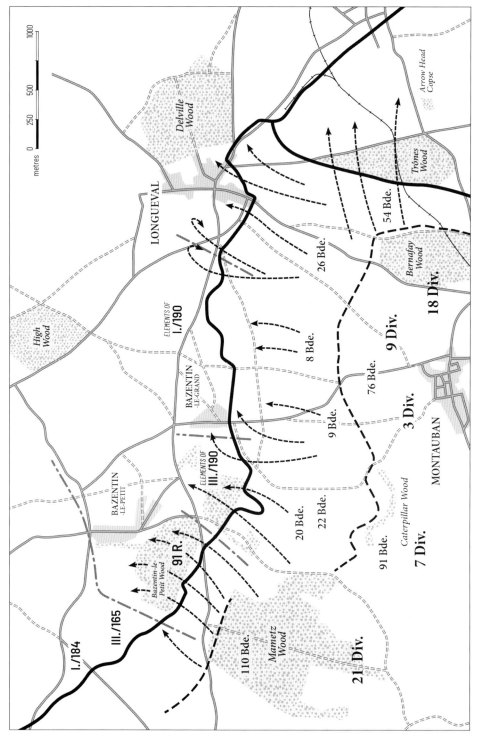

Map 12.i The Assault on Bazentin Ridge.

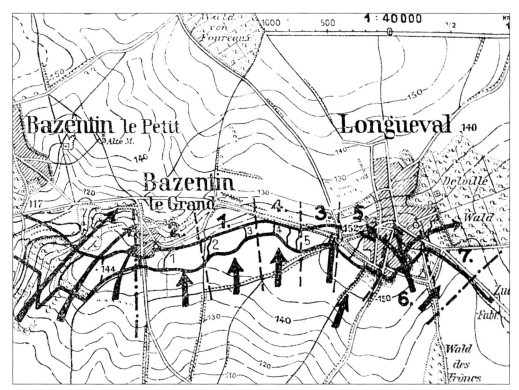

A German sketch of the British attack on the Second Line. (16th Bavarian Regimental History)

We moved off from the Citadel to White Trench. The 20th Brigade are [*sic*] assaulting trenches in front of Bazentin le Petit Wood. The Warwicks and Royal Irish are to go through and consolidate the village as far north as the Cemetery; we are in support … We had some difficulty getting into White Trench as the intense bombardment was on, and we had to dodge the guns.[8]

20 Brigade entered the German second line without difficulty, probably because the position here was held only by the recruit company of the Guards. The account by *Leutnant* Steuerwald tells more:

Fire increased to extreme intensity and involved all calibres. It was dreadful. 8th Company Reserve Infantry Regiment 77 was reduced to its commander (Reserve Leutnant Denicke) and his runner. Our artillery … could not even seriously counter the forward move of British troops …The position was occupied.[9]

22 Brigade was consequently ordered forward, the two leading battalions securing their objectives by 08.15 hrs.[10] During this move, the Regimental Command Post of the 16th Bavarians in Bazentin le Grand was captured. The commander, *Oberstleutnant* Bedall, and all his staff, were taken prisoner and sent to Britain. Bedall's diary was translated in XV Corps War Diary and

A German air photograph centred on Bazentin le Grand. (16th Bavarian Regimental History)

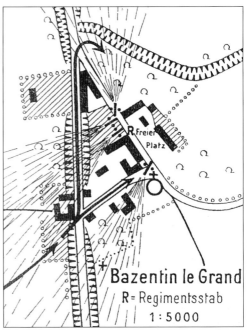

Bazentin le Grand village, depicting location of the captured 16th Bavarians' Regimental Headquarters. (16th Bavarian Regimental History)

has been cited at various times in this account. Bedall also wrote an account of the battle during his captivity, which was committed to memory by the Regimental Surgeon, *Stabsarzt* Dr Eber, who was released and repatriated in October 1916. Eber wrote the account down as soon as he reached the neutral Netherlands:

> At 5.00 am [14 July] I could observe from my command post the adjoining sector beyond my right flank (west). This had been manned by 3rd Battalion Lehr Infantry Regiment, but it had suffered enormous casualties during the night 13/14 July and had been relieved that same night by a company of the [Guards Fusiliers] Recruit Company. I saw men pulling back into the wood [N.B. possibly High Wood?]. As a result, a wide gap through which the British advanced opened up between Bazentin le Grand and Bazentin le Petit. The British were approaching the village of Bazentin le Grand in dense masses at about 5.30 am At once I ordered the machine guns held back in the village to move into fire positions and engage the lines of British soldiers … Once most of the machine gun crews had been killed or wounded and the weapons rendered unusable, the British got into the village.[11]

Stockwell meanwhile pushed 1 R.W. Fus forward one company at a time across the valley in front of Mametz Wood, into positions inside the Hammerhead where there were no trenches but plenty of shell holes. At about 11.00 hrs, the battalion was ordered to follow a cavalry brigade [of the 2nd Indian Cavalry Division] forward, and to take and hold High Wood; however the situation of the rest of the brigade was not comfortable as the Germans were shelling the line heavily, and at 11.30 hrs a strong counter-attack was made by 280 men of the Guards Fusiliers under Hauptmann von Tschirnhaus; but German casualties became so bad and British artillery fire so heavy, that the attack was broken off. At the end of the battle only one *Feldwebel* and 33 of von Tschirnhaus's men had survived; he himself was killed in the assault.[12]

At 12.30 hrs, 2 Gordon Highlanders were ordered to clear the position in Bazentin le Petit Wood, while 1 R.W. Fus cleared the Cemetery and a windmill about 300 yards north of Bazentin le Grand Wood and the same distance east of Bazentin le Petit Wood. Stockwell subsequently observed:

> It took some time to get the battalion out of the wood, what with shells, other units, and pioneers at work, and other battalions advancing. Rallied the battalion on the road to put them in the right direction; while doing so Reeves[*] and I were knocked flying by a big shell which landed about 20 feet from us – one man killed and five wounded alongside me. Pushed the battalion up the hill, under a pretty hot high-explosive and shrapnel fire … Sent patrols out and ordered A and B Companies to attack and hold the line Cemetery to Windmill; B and D in support.[13]

The two assault companies attacked out of a German trench called Circus which ran through Bazentin le Petit Wood and across the open ground to Bazentin le Petit Wood. A Company on the left had a hard fight with Germans in the Cemetery, men of the I./190 I.R., but drove them out. Second Lieutenant James Dadd, the brother of Edmund Dadd, of A Company reported that the counter-attack by the Guard-Fusiliers had forced 2 R. Irish back from the high ground but it had been re-occupied, that contact had been established with the R. Irish at the cemetery and that four machine-guns from 22 Brigade M.G. Company were in position to cover the area. B Company reached the Windmill without opposition and as they reorganised, more Germans were seen advancing, presumably under the impression that they still held the area; these may have been the men of the Guards Fusiliers Recruit Company who had retreated earlier. Fire was brought down on them, and they bolted back towards High Wood. The line was then consolidated using a sunken road – a *Lewis* gun was mounted on top of the Windmill. C Company had also reached its objective. The line occupied gave visibility forward to a slight ridge and denied the Germans the ability to see forward to Mametz Wood. Battalion Headquarters were set up in a shell-hole on the hilltop close to the eastern side of Bazentin le Petit Wood.[14]

The battalion had lost two officers killed – Second Lieutenant Godffrey Morgan and Lieutenant R.H.B. (Richard) Baynes;[†] and four officers wounded – Captain Edward Greaves, Captain Geoffrey Compton-Smith,[‡] Lieutenant Cyril Smith and Second Lieutenant Sebastian

---

[*]   Captain Brian Reeves MC, the Adjutant.
[†]   Some sources call him H.B. Haynes, although there was no officer of that name in the R.W. Fus. Baynes was a native of New South Wales and is commemorated on the Thiepval Memorial.
[‡]   G.L. Compton-Smith DSO (1889–1921) had been commissioned into the Green Howards but transferred into the R.W. Fus in 1915. He was captured off-duty by the I.R.A. in 1921 while working in intelligence and subsequently murdered. He is buried at Fort Carlisle in Ireland, but his cigarette case remains in the Officers' Mess of 1 R.W. Fus.

Brunicardi – 50 men killed and wounded. By the end of the operation, this figure had risen to 14 men killed, 15 wounded and 15 missing.

The attack had taken a heavy toll on the Germans. By the end of the battle, the 16th Bavarians had been reduced by casualties to one officer and 147 in the 1st Battalion; six officers and 365 men in the 2nd Battalion; no officers and 111 men in the 3rd Battalion; and no officers and 21 men in the three machine-gun companies, plus one officer 47 men in the two *M.G. Scharffshutzen-Truppen*.[15] The Headquarters staff and signallers had all been killed or captured. This was a total loss of 82 officers and 2,548 men out of strength of 91 officers and 3,472 men on 1 July and represented a loss rate of 78 percent. *Oberstleutnant* Kumme, the commander of the *Lehr* Regiment, was also captured and I./91 I.R., Steuerwald's battalion, was destroyed: three of the company commanders and six other officers were killed; only two returned unwounded. Six officers were captured and in addition to the dead and wounded, 200 men were also taken prisoner.[16]

There were no trenches between the line now held by the British 7th Division and the German Switch position 1,000 yards to the north, but 1 R.W. Fus was under artillery fire all afternoon. Here they remained throughout 15 July, providing some fire support to the attack on High Wood from the *Lewis* gun on the Windmill. On the 16th, Stockwell was told to hand over to the 1st Highland Light Infantry and withdraw back to Mametz Wood:

> Did so – a rotten place, already full of troops and batteries in position. Got the men to dig in … Saw Duggan of the Irish – he full of thanks. Said our coming up so quick saved him. I was rather lucky to strike off the exact line to hold – done off the map – as it turned out most important, checked all counter-attacks from High Wood, allowed the assault to be launched, and enabled me to deal with the enfilading machine-gun fire from the Windmill.[17]

While 1 R.W. Fus had been in action, 2 R.W. Fus had been moving up with the rest of the 33rd Division, reaching Buire on 12 July from where the Commanding Officer, Lieutenant Colonel 'Tibs' Crawshay* – formerly Brigade Major 114 Brigade – and his company commanders had ridden forward to reconnoitre Mametz. On the 14th, the battalion moved up to a bivouac close to Fricourt where they were observed by a German balloon, shelled, and forced to withdraw behind a reverse slope. On the 15th, the battalion moved off at 04.00 hrs in a thick mist. At noon a halt was ordered, the mist cleared and the battalion found itself in front of Mametz Wood, among the wreckage of battle, a number of large forward ammunition dumps, and the dead of the 38th Division: 'The bodies of several friends were recognised and buried.'[18]

Here, in Mametz Wood, the two Regular battalions of the Royal Welsh Fusiliers had one of their rare meetings. 2 R.W. Fus, in the 33rd Division, had not been engaged in the early days of the Somme battle but had nevertheless been actively engaged in combat operations. On 22 June the battalion had been in the line in the area of Givenchy where it was surprised at 02.30 hrs by the explosion of the huge German mine, their largest in the war to date, which created

---

* Codrington Howard Rees ('Tibs') Crawshay DSO (1882–1937) was commissioned in 1901 and served in South Africa. He commanded 2 R.W. Fus from June 1916 to January 1917 when he was severely wounded at Cléry. He was placed on retired pay but commanded 4 R.W.F from 1921 to 1924. He was greatly liked and respected, Frank Richards thought him the best C.O. he knew.

the celebrated Red Dragon crater. The sector was held by the German Infanterie-Regiment Nr. 134 (10th Royal Saxon), part of 89 Infanterie-Brigade in the 40th Division of XIX (2nd Royal Saxon) Corps. Only determined counter-action by the Royal Welch stopped the Germans from penetrating a large section of the line.[19] The severity of the fighting can be guessed from the casualties – three officers and 49 men killed, and as many more wounded – and the awards following the action, which included a DSO, two MCs, three DCMs and eight MMs.[20] 'Tibs' Crawshay, the Commanding Officer, was set on revenge for this attack and decided on a counter-raid, and it was decided to use gas to achieve surprise. The Gas Officer of the 33rd Division was Lieutenant Christopher Jones, who had originally served with the 16th R.W. Fus but then transferred to the Royal Engineers. Jones had reservations:

> I said that the little scientific common sense I had got from reading Science at Cambridge made me say the plan was impracticable. Even if the new cylinders of chlorine were got … our troops would have to wear masks and the Germans were better equipped than we were to work in masks … but that if I might suggest it, we might stink up a smoke cloud with enough chlorine to panic the Germans while our men, with training, could be going over the top unmasked … In a few days the staff told me to get on with preparations…[21]

The raid was duly mounted by A Company under Captain J.V. (John) Higginson and D Company under Captain Percival ('Peter') Moody. As well as the smoke and gas – which was not mentioned in the war diary – a heavy bombardment by trench mortars, artillery and rifle grenades preceded the raid, 'with an expenditure of 10,000 rounds in ½ an hour.' Another 5,000 rifle grenades were also fired.[22] It was intended that the two companies should get into the German trenches and stay there for two hours, wrecking the mining system, dugouts, trench mortars and communications. The raid was a complete success, with 39 live prisoners taken along with four dead, 14 more identity disks brought in and 'many others known to have been killed and wounded.' A machine gun, a trench mortar and a quantity of other weapons, equipment and documents were also brought back. The raid was not, however, without cost: Second Lieutenant R.A.R. Hollingberry and 10 men were killed, one man was missing, and Lieutenant H.M. Smith and 47 men were wounded.[23] More men were wounded by heavy German retaliatory fire over the following day. The missing man was Corporal Roberts of A Company: the Germans called across No Man's Land the next day to say they had captured him.

Haig, Haking and Herman Landon, G.O.C 33rd Division, all sent fulsome messages of congratulation and the Brigade Commander remarked that the arrangements could not have been bettered. However, when Jones returned to the Divisional Headquarters the following morning, he met with a cold reception from the staff, because gas had been used *offensively* rather than *defensively* without the approval of Army Headquarters![24]

Siegfried Sassoon recorded that: 'The Second Battalion are bivouacked 300 yards away by the Bécordel Road. I had a long talk with Robert Graves, whimsical and queer and human as ever. We sat in the darkness with guns booming along the valleys, and dim stars of camp-fires burning all around in the dark countryside.'[25] Robert Graves recorded seeing the carnage inside Mametz Wood in a passage already quoted in Chapter 10. He also noted that the Germans shelled the Wood around this time with gas shells,[26] as did Frank Richards.[27]

Richards, who was a signaller with 2 R.W. Fus, wrote that German artillery fire was both heavy and accurate at this time; one of his companions remarked that 'If the Jerry gunners were only 50 yards away they couldn't drop their shells more accurately ...'[28] It turned out that a German officer had volunteered to remain concealed in a dugout with a telephone line connecting him to the German guns, which Richards and his companions uncovered a few days later when digging. From his hiding place he had directed the fire of German batteries for days, with the precision noted by Richards. The officer was discovered, shot and wounded by two soldiers of the Middlesex Regiment, then taken prisoner and handed over to 101 Brigade R.F.A.[29]

Robert Graves recorded that around this time he picked up a souvenir, a piece of carved chalk, dropped by a dead German from an artillery ammunition limber.[30] This piece of chalk is now held by the Royal Welch Fusiliers' Regimental Museum. A few days later, on 20 July, Graves was hit by a shell and badly wounded in the left thigh, right shoulder and the chest. He was taken back into Mametz Wood and placed in a German dugout where he lay unconscious for 24 hours. Crawshay was told that Graves was certain to die and so sent a telegram and a letter of condolence to Graves's mother. Nevertheless, on 21 July, Graves was found to be alive, put in an ambulance and taken to the dressing station at Heilly.[31] He eventually recovered and continued to serve in the Regiment until 1919.

Others in Mametz Wood at this time testified to the grim reminders of the struggle. Captain D.V. Kelly of 6 Leicesters,[*] serving in the 21st Division, wrote that on 13 July:

> The wood was everywhere smashed by shell-fire and littered with dead – A German sniper hung over a branch horribly resembling a scarecrow; but half the trees had had their branches shot away, leaving fantastic jagged stumps like a Dulac picture of some goblin forest... Along the west edge ran a trench,[†] from the side of which in places protruded the arms and legs of carelessly buried men, and as our men moved up that night to attack dozens of them shook hands with these ghastly relics. All the old "rides" through the wood were blocked by fallen trees and great shell-holes, and all over hung the overwhelming smell of corpses, turned up earth and lachrymatory gas.[32]

A similar account by Lieutenant Francis St H. Evans of 9 Welsh,[‡] which was serving in the 19th Division rather than the 38th (Welsh), told a similar story on 23 July 1916:

> This spot was lately made famous for all time when it was captured by the Welsh division ... we may claim a share as here we are, holding on and in close support ready to move up ... In this one-time pleasant wood now largely splintered to fragments with whole trunks fallen at all angles and the ground cratered out of semblance we dig for dear life.[33]

Elsewhere, the men of the 3rd and 9th Divisions were not so lucky in the attack on Bazentin Ridge. The 3rd Division included 10 R.W. Fus, a Welsh Army unit not included in the 38th Division. Here, they met unbroken barbed wire, but made progress. 9 R.W. Fus, 5 S.W.B. and

---

*   Later Sir David Kelly KCMG MC (1881–1959), British Ambassador to Moscow.
†   Wood trench.
‡   Commissioned 29 October 1914, *Supplement to the London Gazette*, 13 November 1914, p. 11291.

German dead interred in temporary burials. (James Payne collections)

9 Welsh were also close by in the 19th Division. Llewelyn Wyn Griffith recalled an encounter with Taylor, 115 Brigade Signals Officer, probably shortly before Taylor was wounded. Taylor told him that he had met a Chaplain, referred to as 'Evans' (Wyn Griffith changed many of the names in *Up to Mametz*). Evans had been walking the battlefield for days, trying to find his son, who had been reported killed. Wyn Griffith knew the boy. Taylor did not speak much Welsh and felt this keenly: 'You could not', he said, 'talk English to a man who had lost his son.' Evans never did find the boy or his grave. The Padre was later identified by Mrs Patricia Evans as the Reverend Peter Jones Roberts, a Welsh Methodist minister from Barmouth who had joined up as a chaplain aged 51, beyond the usual age limits. He had four sons, all of whom were commissioned into the R.W. Fusiliers. The second son was captured in late 1916; the third badly wounded in 1918. The youngest got into the war in 1918 and survived. The boy whom Roberts was looking for was his eldest, Glyn, who had been commissioned in 1915 and was serving with the 9th Battalion; he had been killed on 3 July and Roberts had spent a week searching for him.

2nd Lieutenant Glyn Roberts. (RWF Mus)

Although there was fierce fighting in Trônes Wood and Longueval, the opposition soon crumbled and by nightfall the British were established close to the German Switch Line. That night the Germans reinforced this line and, in accordance with their usual doctrine and practice, counter-attacked next morning, recapturing High Wood. From this point on, the fighting in the south of the British sector of the Somme, which had shown the greatest promise of success, degenerated into the same sort of attritional bloodbath as elsewhere.

Haig's despatch in December 1916 at the close of the Somme battles summed up the seemingly unending struggle of those involved in a few short, bland and impersonal paragraphs:

> An attack on Contalmaison and Mametz Wood was undertaken on the 7th July, and after three days' obstinate fighting, in the course of which the enemy delivered several powerful counter-attacks, the village and the whole of the wood, except its northern border, were finally secured … our troops had [also] succeeded at the second attempt in establishing themselves on the 8th July in the southern end of Trones Wood … In the course of this struggle portions of the wood changed hands several times; but we were left, eventually, on 13th July, in possession of the southern part of it. Meanwhile Mametz Wood had been entirely cleared of the enemy, and with Trones Wood practically in our possession we were in a position to undertake an assault on the enemy's second system of defences. Arrangements were accordingly made for an attack to be delivered at daybreak on the morning of the 14th July against a front extending from Longueval to Bazentin le Petit Wood, both inclusive… The preliminary bombardment opened on the 11th July. The opportunities offered by the ground for enfilading the enemy's lines were fully utilised and did much to ensure the success of our attack.[34]

A contemporary view from Bazentin le Petit Wood looking north-east towards 1 R.W. Fus' position.

Modern photograph taken from the Windmill towards Bazentin le Petit Cemetery – the line held by 1 R.W. Fus. (A.M. Goulden)

Modern photograph taken from 1 R.W. Fus' position towards the direction of the attack by the Guards Fusiliers. (A.M. Goulden)

Modern photograph of Bazentin le Petit Cemetery. (A.M. Goulden)

Appendix

```
( Sixth Army
(_____ x x x x _____
( Second Army
( Gruppe von Stein (XIV Reserve Corps)
(     3rd Guards Div
(     183rd R.D.
(     26th I.D.
(     28th R.D.
(     52nd I.D.
(_____ X X X _____
( Gruppe von Arnim (IV Corps)
(     7th I.D.
(     8th I.D.
(_____ X X X _____
( Gruppe Gossler (VI Reserve Corps)
(     11th R.D.
(     12th R.D.
(     12th I.D.
(_____ X X X _____
( Gruppe von Quast (IX Corps)
(     121st R.D.
(     22nd R.D.
(     Div von Frentz
(     11th I.D.
(     44th R.D.
(_____ X X X _____
( Gruppe von Pannewitz (XVII Corps)
(     35th I.D.
(     36th I.D.
(     Guard Gruppe
(       1st Guards Div
(       2nd Guards Div
(       15th Landwehr Div
(_____ River Somme _____
```

Note
(Denotes direction of frontline

Notes

1   T.N.A. WO 95/431, Fourth Army War Papers (G.S.), File A, Operation Orders 1–31 July 1916.
2   General der Infanterie z.V. Fritz von Loßberg, *Meine Tätigkeit im Weltkriege* 1914–1918 (Berlin, 1939), pp. 222–223.
3   Schulenburg-Wolfsburg, p. 140.
4   Sheldon, p. 81; Neumann, p. 283; Brennslecht, p. 191; Wohlenburg, p. 190.
5   Sheldon, p. 81.
6   Leutnant des Reserve A.D. Adolf Kümmel, *Res.-Inf-Regt. Nr 91 im Weltkriege 1914–1918* (Oldenburg, 1926), pp. 216–217.
7   Stockwell's Diary for 14 July.
8   Stockwell's Diary for 14 July.
9   Kümmel, p. 217.
10 Dudley Ward, p. 217.
11 Kriegsarchiv Munich, 16. Inf. Regt. (WK) 3, *Bericht über den Gefechtstag Bayr. 16.Inf.R. am 14.7.1916*, account of Oberstleutnant Bedall as transcribed by Dr Eber on 22 November 1916. See also Brennslecht, p. 192.
12 Schulenburg-Wolfsburg, pp. 140–141.
13 Stockwell's Diary for 14 July.
14 Dudley Ward, p. 219.
15 Brennslecht, p. 194.
16 Kümmel, p. 217.
17 Stockwell's Diary for 16 July.
18 Dudley Ward, p. 214.
19 The explosion is described in the accounts of Captain H.M. Blair, Captain p. Moody and others in *Regimental Records of the Royal Welch Fusiliers*, Vol. III, pp. 167–170.
20 T.N.A. WO 95/2423, 2 R.W. Fus War Diary 4 July 1916.
21 Account by Captain C. Jones in RWF Mus/Archives.
22 T.N.A. WO 95/2423, 2 R.W. Fus War Diary 5 July 1916; *Regimental Records*, Volume III, p. 175.
23 T.N.A. WO 95/2423, 2 R.W. Fus War Diary 6 July 1916. See also the account *in Regimental Records*, Vol. III, p. 174–175.
24 Account by Captain C. Jones in RWF Mus/Archives.
25 Sassoon *Diaries 1915–1918*, p. 93.
26 Graves, p. 254.
27 Richards, p. 130.
28 Richards, p. 131.
29 Renshaw, p. 129.
30 Graves, p. 258.
31 Graves, pp. 261–264 ; Sassoon *Diaries 1915–1918*, p. 98. The telegram and letter of condolence, along with a second letter to Graves expressing pleasure at learning he was alive, are in the RWF archive collections.
32 D.V. Kelly, *39 Months* (London, 1930), pp. 28–29.
33 Frank Delamain (ed.), *Going Across: Extracts from the war letters and diaries of Lt. St. H. Evans* (Newport, no date given), p. 46.
34 Haig's Second Despatch is in the *London Gazette*, 29 December 1916.

13

Aftermath: 'The price paid for Mametz Wood'

There was, both in the immediate aftermath of the capture of Mametz Wood and in subsequent accounts after the war, adverse criticism of the performance of the 38th (Welsh) Division. This has been both well documented and refuted in the past by Colin Hughes and Michael Renshaw and also more recently by Jonathan Hicks and Chris Williams. It is not therefore intended wholly to repeat their important work, either in terms of redeeming the reputation of the 38th Division or of capturing so much personal experience, but to summarize the arguments and add the perspective of a former division and corps commander. I also aim to prove their contention concerning the undeserved slights on the Welsh division's reputation by employing accurate casualty figures for both sides to demonstrate the ferocity of the fighting, the stubbornness of the defence and determination of the attack.

Adverse criticism began as early as 1919, when Lieutenant Colonel J.H. (John) Boraston co-wrote, with G.A.B. (George) Dewar, *Sir Douglas Haig's Command.* This work is in two volumes and is now largely forgotten. It was however written directly after the events of the war, using the first-hand knowledge of those involved at all levels and published in 1922. This was at a time when Haig's star was shining very brightly and the adverse criticisms of him in the late 1920s and 1930s had not surfaced; nor the more bitter accounts of veterans appeared, such as those of Siegfried Sassoon and Edmund Blunden on the British side, and Erich-Maria Remarque in Germany. The book is extravagantly pro-Haig, dismissive of Lloyd George and damns the French and Americans with faint praise. In it, Boraston castigated 38th Division for its supposed failure to secure Mametz Wood before 14 July and pinned the blame for the failure to make more progress on Bazentin Ridge on this 'delay':

> The days lost here were of the greatest value to the enemy. They gave him the opportunity he needed to restore order among his defeated battalions, to bring up fresh troops and to reorganise his defences. Though he could not prevent us from carrying his second line system in our next assault, he was enabled so to strengthen his last remaining defences on the crest and reverse slopes of the ridge beyond that our advance was held up there when within measurable distance of effecting an actual breakthrough.
>
> There is little risk of exaggerating the effect of three day' delay at this stage of the battle, when every hour was of importance… trench systems, switch lines, strong points, and belts of wire were multiplied across the whole space from High Wood to Bapaume. That was a part of the price paid for the check at Mametz Wood.[1]

This is a serious charge, as Colin Hughes has noted.[2] However the facts do not stand up to the charge. Boraston speaks of a delay of three days – from 7 to 10 July – rather than the five days that it actually took to capture the Wood. But what of the period of *six days* before 7 July, when according to him, every hour was of importance? Mametz Wood was not part of the objective on 1 July and in the days following it was the possession of Contalmaison, not Mametz Wood, that occupied British commanders' attention – even though it was, wrote Launcelot Kiggell, 'of such importance to secure possession of Mametz Wood that it must be captured and held.'[3] The 38th Division had no part in the failed assaults on Contalmaison. If Mametz Wood was of such importance, why was it not the objective of a set-piece attack immediately after the capture of Mametz Village and Fricourt? Major G.P.L. (Geoffrey) Drake-Brockman, a Regular officer, was one of the staff officers of the 7th Division who moved with Watts after 7 July to the 38th Division. He had served in the infantry with the Border Regiment and won a Military Cross in 1915.[4] Drake-Brockman was on the staff of the 7th Division on 3 July, and wrote that there had been a feeling within the headquarters and among the troops that:

> A great opportunity was being let slip on the evening of 1 July… the enemy's resistance had been well broken on the front of the 30th, 13th and 7th Divisions. Certain localities outside the final objective could have been captured with very small loss, which subsequently were very costly to take.
>
> The most notable of these were Mametz Wood and Caterpillar Wood. To my certain knowledge there were hardly any of the enemy in the former at this time: our infantry in Bunny Alley and White Trench were very keen to push on, but right up to the time of the division relief on 6 July no concerted forward move on Corps front was permitted, other than by patrols …
>
> An advance by 17th Division through 7th Division from the south against Mametz Wood could have been undertaken at dawn on 2 July, as the whole front here was stable, and defined, by 6 p.m. on 1 July. Moreover, the capture of Mametz Wood by that division in conjunction with an advance by the [III] Corps on the left, would have facilitated and shortened the operations which were so long drawn out and costly, subsequently undertaken to capture Contalmaison and the area between that village, Mametz Wood itself and Fricourt Farm. Had this been done, German reinforcements could have been prevented from trickling down to this area.[5]

Edmonds' official history says much the same: 'XV Corps headquarters had received many reports to show that on its front the enemy had not yet rallied, and at 3 p.m. [3 July] patrols found that Mametz Wood and Quadrangle Trench were empty.'[6] Edmonds goes on to say that at 17.00 hrs that day, Horne gave permission for the 7th Division to occupy the southern edge of Mametz Wood, Strip trench, Wood trench and Quadrangle trench during darkness. Giving permission is not the same thing as actively directing the vigorous prosecution of the offensive, of seizing and maintaining the initiative, that such moments demand. It was at this point that guides sent to take forward the paltry force of two battalions – 1 R.W. Fus and 2 R. Irish – went astray. Edmonds is somewhat more diplomatic, saying that 'if the XV Corps had encouraged a more vigorous action on the afternoon of the 3rd, a hold on Mametz Wood could have been secured, and Wood Trench and Quadrangle Trench occupied.'[7] This was the crucial delay that was to lead to the loss of so many lives and so much time and the blame lies squarely at the feet of the Corps Commander, Horne. Pilcher, G.O.C. 17th Division, was explicit in this:

> There is no doubt in my mind that on the front of XV Corps the battle was terribly misman-aged, and I consider that of the 4,000 casualties incurred by the 17th Division only 1,500 were what one may call unavoidable, and that the remaining 2,500 were the direct result of orders issued by the corps which were in defiance of common sense and every rule of tactics.[8]

Peter Hart has also written of the 'collective failure of generalship within the Fourth Army [that] can never be adequately explained or excused', blaming Rawlinson in particular for 'an abrogation of clear responsibility to personally oversee [*sic*] the performance of command tasks.'[9]

Even after this piece of dereliction of duty, three days could have been saved if the attack on Bazentin Ridge had been launched on 11 July when all but the very northernmost edge of Mametz Wood, close to the German second line, had been captured. The Germans were at this point moving troops from the second line at Bazentin le Petit to defend the Wood and they would have been badly caught out by an assault. Instead, Haig pondered, and the artillery was not used to destroy the German wire in front of the second line, something which was not properly completed on 13th, never mind the 11th.[10]

Between the two set-piece attacks on 1 and 14 July, operations were fragmented and unco-ordinated, using small numbers of troops, with minor matters being directed from remote headquarters and too little discretion given to those who would have to execute the task. This made success impossible especially on 7 July. XV Corps dictated methods of attack that were unsuited to the terrain and the enemy, resulting in troops assaulting over ground that allowed the German artillery and machine-guns to wreak havoc. It made no effort properly to co-ordi-nate the assaults by the 17th and 38th Divisions in time or space. It issued orders that had no chance of reaching those who had to carry them out in a timely manner. No wonder the staff officers of the Great War came in for so much hatred from the men in the line: '… a bloody nuisance, inefficient where it isn't actually crooked' as John Masters reported the common view; or more specifically: 'The function of the staff is so to foul up operations, by giving contradictory orders and misreading their maps, that wars will be prolonged to a point where every staff officer has become a general.'[11]

On the other hand, many staff officers were inexperienced and they, like their commanders, were engaged in a struggle beyond anything which the British Army had ever known, wrestling with a scale of resources and problems greater than anything that could have been imagined only two years before. They were also working under pressure of time themselves and, because of the system of rotation of divisions, no Corps ever had a permanent order of battle; there was thus no chance for corps and divisional commanders and their staffs to establish proper working relationships and mutual trust. David Kelly said that:

> Our professional officers, with certain defects and virtues… were inferior to none, but they were totally inadequate, both in numbers and staff experience for the work of handling millions of men. Why should one expect a man who had never commanded more than a battalion to make no mistakes in charge of a division or a corps?[12]

What gave the Germans time to 'restore order among his defeated battalions, to bring up fresh troops and to reorganise his defences', as Boraston puts it, was in fact the failure by the corps level of command in particular, but also the army level, to fight their formations *as* formations, and not as collections of pieces. There was, at these levels, a woeful want of command, of control and of co-ordination; no sense of urgency, nor determination, nor initiative. Nor was there any sense of continuity or forward planning – how the achievement of one objective on one part of the front would set up operations on another.

Headquarters XV Corps seems to have been far more ready to interfere with, and proscribe, the work of its divisions, than to command, control and co-ordinate their actions – possibly because Horne did not trust either Philipps or Pilcher. Pilcher himself, who was like Philipps removed from command, disputed the orders he had been given and did his best to mitigate the casualties which he knew would follow: 'It is very easy', he wrote, 'to sit a few miles in the rear, and get credit for allowing men to be killed in an undertaking foredoomed to failure …'[13] XV Corps Headquarters also failed repeatedly to allow sufficient time for the passage of orders and made no allowance for any breakdown in communications or for the operation of Murphy's Law – that anything that can go wrong, will go wrong.

Brigade commanders, who might have been able directly to influence the situation, seem to have been instructed from the divisional or even corps level to remain in their command posts on the end of the telephone line, rather than to move with the troops on the ground. This often led to one of the Commanding Officers being given de facto command of the brigade in combat – and most of the Commanding Officers had no experience of commanding anything in combat, let alone a brigade.

Bearing all this in mind, to place the blame for the later delay on the main assault on Bazentin Ridge on a single division, one of 24 engaged in operations on the Somme front,[14] and which did not become engaged until after the key time period had already past, is little short of ludicrous.

Another view is given by Drake-Brockman. In 1930 he recalled his view of the fighting men of the 38th Division as 'really good material', but he was appalled by the lack of command by Philipps prior to his removal:

> The 38th Division suffered from having a number of senior officers who owed their appointments to their political positions or to being friends of Mr Lloyd George… *Major General Philipps* was appointed to the command of the division in early 1915 … promoted over the heads of many more senior and meritorious officers. As a divisional commander it is hardly surprising that he was ignorant, lacked experience and failed to inspire confidence… It is not therefore to be wondered at that an influential political atmosphere permeated the whole division and was in some cases the cause of considerable friction. Brigadiers found it difficult to get rid of officers who were useless, since… they were often the constituents or political supporters of the divisional commander, who held a high opinion of their capabilities.[15]

Drake-Brockman thought it was fortunate that the G.S.O. I of the division, Lieutenant Colonel ap Rhys Pryce, was very capable. He 'in reality commanded the division himself.' He thought also that some of the Commanding Officers, especially those seconded from the Indian Army, were 'excellent'. But with Philipps in command, Drake-Brockman thought it hardly surprising that the 38th Division 'did not distinguish itself in its first engagement, though later in the war, under different commanders, it did extremely well.' Drake-Brockman was highly critical of Philipps for committing only a single brigade on 7 July and sending troops into the attack piecemeal, and for making it known that attacks should not be pressed too hard if stopped by machine-gun fire, but rather that battalions were to retire to their start lines and await further artillery preparation:

> By the time, therefore, that General Watts took over command of the division on 9 July, it is not to be wondered at that the infantry were considerably discouraged and exhausted after three days' fighting of this nature.[16]

Drake-Brockman commented on the political influences in the 38th Division, saying that Lloyd George's pulling of strings on behalf of certain individuals was:

> … almost a record instance for political interference and dishonesty with the fighting portion of the army in France. Particularly is it an illustration of the disadvantages under which the 38th Division functioned, which in no small measure accounts for the very poor performance put up by it during the period under review.[17]

Drake-Brockman went on to comment on the effect of delaying an assault on Mametz Wood until 7 July, and of the single-brigade attack that day:

> … these half-hearted attacks encouraged the enemy considerably so that instead of evacuating Mametz Wood as he appears to have intended, he kept reinforcing his troops in the wood. This, coupled with the thick and impenetrable nature of the wood rendered the final attack a very much more formidable affair than it would have been three days earlier – in fact Mametz Wood on 10 July was a really tough proposition and the division deserves credit for what it did do after being "messed about" for three days.[18]
>
> Consequent to the elimination of this political atmosphere under the leadership of Major General Blackader the division did extremely well during the rest of the war. I served with the 38th Division for 10 months, but for the whole of this period the stigma of Mametz Wood stuck to the Division and it was common talk in the British Expeditionary Force that 38th Division had "bolted" and the fact remains that 38th Division was never employed again on the Somme.[19]

It is clear, in spite of Drake-Brockman's emphasis on Philipps's inability and the political aspects of command in the 38th Division, that its headquarters was very heavily directed from Corps and it may therefore be going too far to place all the blame for piecemeal attacks on Philipps; it was after all Horne who had directed the attack from two opposing directions on 7 July, from positions over a mile apart. That said, Philipps had certainly failed to organise supporting fire even though 113 Brigade's task, as ordered by Horne, was to be ready to enter the wood via the southern strip.

Despite all the evidence to the contrary, there was a widely-held view for some months that the Welsh Division had run from the enemy. Drake-Brockman had spoken of 'stigma' and the idea that the troops had 'bolted'. Lieutenant Colonel Hugh Lloyd Williams of 9 R.W. Fus had called the battle 'a disaster';[20] J.C. Dunn remarked that the Welsh division had been 'mishandled';[21] and Sassoon used terms like 'massacre and confusion', 'pandemonium' and 'a disastrous muddle',[22] even though none of them had been anywhere near the scene of the action. This was certainly a view held in the 7th Division, perhaps because it was to Major General Watts that Price-Davies had submitted his report and Watts had then returned to the 7th Division. The chief author of this view may well therefore be Price-Davies: the man whom Llewelyn Wyn Griffith described as 'the second most stupid soldier I met … too dull to be frightened …' and 'a daily plague to his brigade.'[23] This view may well be the explanation for the fact that the honours and awards given to the 38th Division for the period of the battle were few and included no Commanding Officers, brigade commanders or senior staff. The senior Regimental officers had done their duty towards their subordinates by putting in recommendations, that much is clear; but it is also clear that neither Watts nor Horne had exerted themselves on behalf of the more senior officers, in spite of the severity of the casualties among them.

That this view was a wrong view can be seen from the large amount of evidence that records the grim nature of the fighting in the Wood and the determination of the Welsh to carry out their task, rather than bolting. As Colin Hughes and Michael Renshaw say, the battle: 'set the standard for this type of combat that was never surpassed on the Somme battlefields.'[24] Mametz was the biggest wood on the Somme and the most easily dominated by the defence, because of the proximity of the second line on the high ground behind it. Bernafay, Bazentin le Grand and Bazentin le Petit were smaller, well forward of the second line and fell easily; but Trônes Wood, which was situated in a similar position to Mametz, was not taken until the main assault on Bazentin ridge on 14 July.[25] Delville Wood, similarly, was not captured until 27 August.[26] High Wood did not fall until 15 September when tanks were used. The capture of Mametz Wood in a mere five days was therefore a significant achievement. The early adverse criticism soon faded in the light of the serious difficulties encountere subsequently.

The casualty figures on both sides, both German and British, bear out the ferocity of the fighting at close quarters. The fighting strength of the 38th Division on 7 July was around 15,500 if the Pioneers, Engineers, machine gun companies and trench mortar batteries are added to the infantry battalions; losses were 4,040, or 26 percent of the fighting strength. The detailed figures are contained in Appendix I to this chapter and include all units of the

Modern photograph showing the enduring effects of British artillery fire, shell-holes and unexploded ordnance inside Mametz Wood. (A.M. Goulden)

division, not just the infantry brigades; they thus differ from other published accounts. There are also differences between sources, and when this has occurred, I have used the latest dated figure in order to take account of those who died of their wounds or were missing but turned up. These figures are therefore slightly higher than those cited by Jonathan Hicks from Marden's *History of the Welch Regiment*. These are comparable with the losses of the 17th Division, against whom no adverse criticism was directed: 91 officers and 1,634 men killed or missing, 106 officers and 2,940 men wounded: a total of 4,771.[27]

German losses inflicted by 38th Division and supporting artillery have not been properly codified. This is, however, possible if German sources are examined. First, there is the matter of prisoners taken. One German source already cited said that more than 400 prisoners were lost to the British. This is an over-estimation as the figures for prisoners taken by the British were recorded in the 38th Division's A.A. & Q.M.G. War Diary,[28] as shown in Appendix III to this chapter: a figure of 348. The figure of 'more than 400' therefore includes men missing and assumed to have been captured.

Many other, mostly British, accounts speak of very large numbers of dead Germans throughout the Wood and especially at the northern edges. Although they give no figures, it is clear that these were on the same scale as the British losses and many were caused by artillery fire.[29] Other German accounts previously cited speak of men being buried alive in collapsed dugouts and shelters.[30] The account by *Oberstleutnant* Bedall, the Commander of the 16th Bavarian Regiment, claimed that the II./*Lehr*, II./184 and the Pioneers in the Wood on 10 July had been reduced to a total of 140 men. This claim can be supported by the figures cited in Chapter 10 which give the losses of II./*Lehr* as one officer and 82 men killed; two officers captured; 61 men wounded; and 254 men missing or taken prisoner: a total of 400. III./*Lehr* recorded losing three officers and 78 men on 8 and 9 July with 'many wounded or buried alive'. The Regimental History of the Lehr gives the full breakdown, which is provided in Appendix II of this chapter. The Regiment lost more than two-thirds of its fighting strength and had to be temporarily re-formed into two small battalions of three weak companies each.[31]

The 16th Bavarian Regiment incurred serious losses, to the extent that the Regiment had subsequently to be completely re-formed. The Regiment's strength on 1 July 1916 was 91 officers and 3,572 men. By the end of the battle, this had been reduced to eight officers and 711 men, a loss of 83 officers and 2,548 men killed, wounded, missing and prisoner, or 78 percent of its strength.[32]

Other detailed figures are contained in the various German regimental histories held by the Imperial War Museum, the British Library and archives in Germany. In the 3rd Guards Division, the 9th Grenadiers entered the battle with a strength of 65 officers and 2,767 men in the headquarters staff, the three battalions and the M.G. companies; on 14 July they reported their strength as 35 officers and 1,115 men, a loss rate of 54 percent among the officers and 40 percent among the men.[33] The Guards Fusiliers, who were close by at Ovillers and supplied some companies to support the fighting in and around the Wood, recorded casualties over the period of three officers and 215 men killed, 14 officers and 776 men wounded, three officers and 206 men missing.[34]

In other divisions, the History of 122 I.R. gives their losses as 40 officers and 1,675 men between 7 and 10 July in the infantry battalions, the M.G. and Trench Mortar Companies.[35] 163 R.I.R. recorded seven officers and 137 men killed, 33 officers and 728 men wounded and 88 men missing from a start state of 65 officers and 2,957 men: a total of 993 lost, or 32 percent[36]

One source gives losses of 1,000 officers and men from 183 I.R., although the Regimental History of the 183rd gives the parade state of the Regiment on 12 July as 56 officers and 1,857 men of whom 1,577 were fit for duty, and 184 horses, a loss of 49 officers and 1,883 men from its strength at the start of the battle, of 105 officers and 3,434 men.[37] 184 I.R. lost 33 officers and 1,566 men, at least 40 percent of its strength.[38]

The established strength of a German infantry battalion at this time was 25 officers and 1,050 N.C.O.s and men, a total of 1,075; with the headquarters staff and the two M.G. companies, each with six guns, five officers and 45 men, an unreinforced Regiment totalled 83 officers and 3,440 men. I have already assumed when calculating the force ratios that German battalions in the Wood were on average at about 80 percent of full strength before the main action began, which would reduce their effective strength to around 850. In Appendix II, I have provided full casualty figures for all German units in and around Mametz Wood, for completeness. To make a comparison, however, then as well as modifying the total figures by assuming a reduced strength at the start of the battle, one must also subtract the total of prisoners to avoid double counting. One must also deduct a percentage, as noted in the Appendix, from those Regiments which were only partly engaged around the Wood. These were chiefly the Guards Fusiliers, the 9th Grenadiers, and 184 I.R.

This methodology produces a German casualty figure in and around Mametz Wood of 8,900 killed, wounded, missing and prisoners. If the 15 German battalions engaged were at a reduced fighting strength of around 13,000, then losses of 8,900 are 68 percent. If the M.G companies, T.M. companies and pioneers are included, then the percentage drops to around 60 percent. This is more than twice the loss rate of the 38th (Welsh) Division and at least equal to the total combined losses of the 17th and 38th Divisions. If this figure seems excessive to readers then I would ask them to consider that the German Military Cemetery in Fricourt, albeit admittedly containing casualties from other years of the war, holds more than 17,000 dead in individual and mass graves.

Various bodies of evidence suggest that when casualties reach around 25 percent, units rapidly decline in their effectiveness. This figure seems not to have varied greatly over the last 200 years,[39] and is a compound of the inability to execute tasks with smaller numbers, fatigue and the moral effect of seeing comrades killed and wounded. It is interesting that 38th (Welsh) Division was at this figure when it was relieved; the Germans were in many cases well above it and therefore deserve considerable respect for having kept up the fight. Possibly the isolation of sub-units in the confines of the Wood made soldiers less aware of the losses being suffered. One must also acknowledge that the quality of the mainly-professional soldiers of the *Lehr* Regiment, the Guards Fusiliers and the 9th Grenadiers was high, as has already been described. The 16th Bavarians and the 122nd Württembergers were also well trained and professionally led. The training, equipment and motivation of such units meant that they would stand longer than most. The achievement of the amateurs of the 38th Division is therefore all the more marked.

The battle of the Somme continued until it was formally closed down by Haig on 18 November 1916. By that time, most authorities agree that the British had lost close to 420,000 men killed, wounded, missing and captured, and the French 204,000. The fighting had cost the Germans nearly half a million men, on top of the 340,000 they had lost at Verdun, making a total of 840,000.[40] The Somme was indeed, as one German writer put it: 'the muddy grave of the German Field Army.'[41] This is not the place to describe in detail the effects of the Battle

Fricourt German cemetery. (A.M. Goulden)

of the Somme on Germany and the German Army, simply because the battle continued long after the end of the Welsh Division's involvement and in any case, other authors have done this already.[42] What is clear however is that casualties on the scale of those I have postulated at Mametz contributed to the overall consequence that Hans von Hentig described. Its effect was felt not just on the quantity of men available, but also on the quality of the Army. Crown Prince Rupprecht summed this up, saying that: 'What still remained of the old first-class, peacetime-trained, German infantry had been expended on the battlefield.'[43] As a contemporary source observed:

> Soldiers returning from leave rejoined their troops on a daily basis in order to protect their threatened fatherland together with their comrades. Maybe they would die within minutes of returning to the front. Maybe they went missing and nobody knew where they were. If they were still alive after a few days, they considered it a gift from heaven which no-one expected anymore.[44]

As has already been pointed out, the class of new recruits liable for call-up to the German Army in 1918 had to be brought forward to late 1916, a measure of just how deeply the corrosive effects of the fighting of this year had penetrated the quantity and quality of the German Army. From as early as August 1916, in spite of shifting 42 divisions from the eastern and south-eastern fronts to the west, the Germans realized that victory on land, at least in the short term, was not possible in the west. They turned to an operational and strategic defensive here with the construction of the *Hindenburgstellung* and the introduction of unlimited submarine warfare

– with the miscalculations that followed.[45] This was not at all what von Falkenhayn had had in mind at Christmas 1915 and it led directly to his dismissal and replacement by the Hindenburg-Ludendorff partnership.

Just as the Germans were forced to compromise on their pre-war standards by calling up new classes two years ahead of their time, so too Douglas Haig had been obliged by circumstances to compromise: he had committed Kitchener's – and Lloyd George's – Army to battle before it was properly ready to take the field, but in strategic terms, as we have seen, he had no choice if the French Army was not to be destroyed in detail at Verdun and the wartime coalition thus undone. In this context, then, although the clearance and capture of Mametz Wood was not a tidy affair and was certainly not well managed at battalion, brigade or divisional level – with a few notable exceptions such as Marden's command of 114 Brigade on 10 July – it remains the case that an imperfectly trained, poorly prepared and indifferently led New Army division, with limited experience, committed to battle a year before it had been intended to undertake anything so complex, had pushed back some of the best units in the German Army – the 9th Grenadiers, the Guards Fusiliers, the *Lehr* Regiment and the 16th Bavarians – more than one mile (1,600 metres). It was, therefore, an achievement as great as any in the Battle of the Smme.

Mametz Wood Memorial in 1987. (*The Western Mail*)

Battle centenary, 7 July 2016.

As Chris Williams has pointed out, the battle has an iconic cultural position in Welsh history and folklore, standing as an example of the Welsh experience of the whole war.[46] It was, as Llewelyn Wyn Griffith recalled, a 'high point of the war, where for me and so many other Welshmen the tragedy reached its culmination.'[47] It has been commemorated in literature by David Jones, Llewelyn Wyn Griffith, Robert Graves and Owen Sheers, among others; in art by another Christopher Williams; in music by the Welsh National Opera. In 1986 a memorial was unveiled at the Wood and it was here in July 2016 that the centenary celebrations, led by Carwyn Jones, First Minister of Wales, took place. The battle stands, as Chris Williams correctly states, as Wales's first day of the Somme: 'For an audience whose grasp of the First World War remains profoundly influenced by the tropes of "Lions led by Donkeys", *Oh! What a Lovely War* and *Blackadder Goes Forth*, it fits neatly as an example of the courage of ordinary soldiers, the stupidity of generals, and the futility of the war as a whole.'[48] If the brave soldiers are all, however wrongly, identified as Welsh and the stupid Generals as English, then the centenary has failed to dispel another inaccurate myth of the war.

Years later, Siegfried Sassoon chose the conditions in and around Mametz Wood to sum up the experience of this war in his evocative poem *Aftermath*:

> *Do you remember the dark months you held the sector at Mametz –*
> *The nights you watched and wired and dug and piled sandbags on parapets?*
> *Do you remember the rats; and the stench*
> *Of corpses rotting in front of the front-line trench…*
> *Do you remember the stretcher-cases lurching back*
> *With dying eyes and lolling heads – those ashen-grey*
> *Masks of the lads who once were keen and kind and gay?*[49]

Lloyd George, the father and founder of the Welsh Army, addressed the symbolic place of Mametz Wood in Welsh consciousness as early as 21 August 1916 when addressing drafts for the 38th Division at Kinmel Park Camp, and the last word should belong to him:

I know the dangers you have to face. You will face them like men. The men belonging to the division you have the honour to belong to are a credit to their race. They had a very difficult piece of work to do on the Somme in that great battle. They accomplished much with honour to themselves and to the land to which they belonged. The attack on Mametz Wood was one of the most difficult enterprises which fell to any division. It was left to the Welsh division, and they swept the enemy out of it. From end to end there is not a living German in the wood now. He has been driven far beyond it, and it will be your task to drive him further still and I think in time you will accomplish it.[50]

Appendix I

38th (Welsh) Division Casualties, 7–13 July 1916[51]

Unit	Officers		O.R.s		Missing	Totals
	killed/d.o.w.	Wounded/ sick	killed/d.o.w.	Wounded/ sick		
Divisional Staff	–	1	–	–	–	1
113 Brigade H.Q., 113 T.M. Bty and 113 M.G. Coy	2	1	10	18	10	41
13 R.W. Fus (1st North Wales Pals)	5	5	40	182	12	244
14 R.W. Fus	4	13	53	311	49	430
15 R.W. Fus (1st London Welsh)	1	9	34	185	19	244
16 R.W. Fus	3	5	47	209	63	327
114 Brigade H.Q., 114 T.M. Bty and 114 M.G. Coy	2	3	3	4	4	16
10 Welsh (1st Rhondda)	4	13	38	220	32	307
13 Welsh (2nd Rhondda)	3	9	52	206	73	343
14 Welsh (Swansea)	1	15	36	276	75	403
15 Welsh (Carmarthen)	4	3	42	118	61	228
115 Brigade H.Q., 115 T.M. Bty and 115 M.G. Coy	1	4	5	27	1	38
17 R.W. Fus (2nd North Wales)	6	12	37	217	37	309
10 S.W.B. (1st Gwent)	4	9	28	154	6	201
11 S.W.B. (2nd (Gwent)	4	10	35	143	36	228
16 Welsh (Cardiff City)	4	15	66	199	87	371
Divisional Troops						
19 Welsh (Pioneers)	1	3	14	106	15	139
Divisional Artillery						
119 Brigade	–	3	3	5	–	11
120 Brigade	–	–	–	24	–	24
121 Brigade	–	1	5	10	–	16
122 Brigade	–	5	–	–	–	5
38 Trench Mortar Battery	–	–	1	1	5	7
Divisional Engineers						
38th Signal Company	–	1	2	3	1	7
123 Field Company	–	1	4	21	–	26
124 Field Company	–	4	4	25	5	38
151 Field Company	–	1	2	24	–	27
R.A.M.C.						
129 Field Ambulance	1	–	–	–	–	1
130 Field Ambulance (St John's)	–	2	4	2	–	8
131 Field Ambulance	1	–	1	8	–	9
Unit R.M.O.s	1	2	–	–	–	3
Total	**53**	**132**	**566**	**2,698**	**591**	**4,040**

Appendix II

German Casualties

An analysis of figures provided in the Regimental Histories of the Regiments involved, held in the British Library, Imperial War Museum, and archives in Germany as listed in the Bibliography.

Regiment/Battalion	Officers	N.C.O.s and men	Total	Remarks
Guards Fusilier Regiment				
I./, II./ and III./ and M.G. coys – *Regimental total*	20	1,197	1,217	Regimental History p 141
9th Grenadier Regiment				
R.H.Q.	2	–	2	
I./	10	391	401	
II./	10	522	532	
Fusiliers	11	444	455	
M.G. coys	1	21	22	
Regimental total	33	1,378	1,411	Regimental History, p 311
***Lehr* Regiment**				Regimental History p 290
I. /and 2 M.G. Coy	16	896	912	
II./	12	743	755	'Reduced to 140 officers and men with the pioneers and II./184' Regimental History p 290
III./ and 1 M.G. Coy	14	796	810	Regimental History p 301–304
Regimental total	42	2,435	2,477	
16th Bavarian Infantry Regiment		3	3	According to Bedall, the Regimental Commander Regimental History, p 194
Regimental staff	24	778	802	
I./	31	878	901	
II./	19	560	579	According to Bedall
	18	727	745	Regimental History, p 194
III./	25	814	839	According to Bedall
	26	940	966	Regimental History, p 194
1, 2 and 3 Bavarian M.G. Companies	6	100	106	According to Bedall Regimental History p 194
44 M.G. SS Tp	0	44	44	Regimental History p 194
77 M.G. SS Tp	1	63	64	
Regimental total	74	2,252	2,326	According to Bedall
No 1 Coy 28 Pioneer Bn	82	2,548	2,630	Regimental History, p 194
			Around 65?	'Reduced to 140 officers and men with II./Lehr and II./184'
122 I.R.				
I./	10	536	546	Regimental History, p 31
II./	10	472	482	
III./.	13	575	585	
1 and 2 M.G. Coys	6	45	51	
122 T.M. Coy	–	45	45	

Regiment/Battalion	Officers	N.C.O.s and men	Total	Remarks
Regimental total	*49*	*1,673*	*1,722*	
163 I.R.				Regimental History p 146
Regimental total	*40*	*953*	*993*	
183 I.R.				Regimental History, p 91
Regimental total	*49*		*1,883*	
17th Royal Saxon I.R. No 184				Regimental History, p 288.
Regimental total	*33*	*1,566*	*1,599*	
No 8 Coy 77 R.I.R.	*0*	*13*	*13*	Regimental History lists only those
TOTAL			13,224	killed, no wounded or missing
Subtract PoWs			−348	
Subtract 20 percent			−1,500	No unit was up to full strength at the start of the battle
Subtract 2/3 of 9th Grenadiers			−920	
Subtract 2/3 of Guard Fusiliers			−934	
Subtract 2/3 of I.R. 184			−1,060	
Projected Final Total			**8,900**	

Appendix III

Germans Captured

Taken by (unit/formation)	Officers	N.C.O.s and men
113 Infantry Brigade (unit not known)	–	41
13 R.W. Fus	–	99
14 R.W. Fus	–	2
15 R.W. Fus	–	3
114 Infantry Brigade (unit not known)	2	139
10 Welsh	–	21
15 Welsh	–	7
115 Infantry Brigade		
17 R.W. Fus	2	28
10 S.W.B.	–	4
151 Field Company R.E.	–	2
TOTAL	**4**	**348**

In addition, one 77 mm gun, three 15 cm guns, one large calibre howitzer and 12 machine-guns were taken as well as 13 other guns found abandoned in the Wood by the 21st Division after 12 July.

Notes

1   George A.B. Dewar and Lieutenant Colonel J.H. Boraston, *Sir Douglas Haig's Command*, Vol. 1 (London, 1922), pp. 113–116.
2   Hughes, p. 130.
3   Rawlinson MS, Item 87d, 8 July 1916.
4   *Supplement to the London Gazette*, 5 February 1915, p. 1546.
5   T.N.A. CAB 45/189, letter from Drake-Brockman.
6   Edmonds, Vol. II (1916), p. 16.
7   Edmonds, Vol. II (1916), p. 17.
8   T.N.A. WO 45/190, Letter from Pilcher.
9   Chris Williams, 'A Question of Legitimate Pride', p. 735; Peter Hart, *The Somme* (London, 2008), p. 262.
10   Edmonds, Vol. II (1916), p. 65.
11   John Masters, *The Road Past Mandalay*, (London, 1961), p. 83.
12   Kelly, p. 159.
13   T.N.A. CAB 45/190, letter from Major General Pilcher, 1930.
14   Hughes, p. 134.
15   T.N.A. CAB 45/189, letter from Major G.P.L. Drake-Brockman dated 7 February 1930 with attachments.
16   T.N.A. CAB 45/189, letter from Drake-Brockman.
17   T.N.A. CAB 45/189, letter from Drake-Brockman.
18   T.N.A. CAB 45/189, letter from Drake-Brockman.
19   T.N.A. CAB 45/189, letter from Drake-Brockman.
20   Chris Williams, 'A Question of Legitimate Pride', p. 733, citing Williams's personal papers in the IWM.
21   Dunn, p. 226.
22   Sassoon, *Memoirs of an Infantry Officer*, pp. 61–63.
23   Wyn Griffith, pp. 132, 133.
24   Renshaw, pp. 14, 134; Hughes, p. 134; Chris Williams, 'A Question of Legitimate Pride', p. 736.
25   Christopher Duffy, *Through German Eyes: The British and the Somme 1916* (London, 2007), p. 179.
26   Edmonds, Vol II (1916), p. 204.
27   Renshaw, p. 116.
28   T.N.A. WO 95/??? NOTE: Leave note for author to provide remainder of source nomenclature. Michael
29   Graves, pp. 252–253; Emlyn Davies, pp. 31–32; Frank Richards, 130; numerous citations in Jonathan Hicks, Chapter 9.
30   *Leutnant* Köstlin, *Grefrieter* Kreibohm and others.
31   Mühlmann und Möhs, pp. 303–304.
32   Brennslecht, pp. 194, 483.
33   J. von Hansch & F. Weidling, pp. 288, 289, 311.
34   Schulenburg-Wolfsburg, p. 141.
35   'The Other Side of the Hill' No. 2, p. 247; Ernst Mugge, *Das Württembergische Reserve-Inf.-Regiment, Nr. 122 im Weltkrieg 1914–1918* (Stuttgart, 1922), p. 31.
36   Ritter, p. 146.
37   'The Other Side of the Hill', No. 2, pp. 258–259; Armin Hase, *Das 17 Königleichten Sachsen Infanterie Regiment Nr 183* (Dresden, 1922), pp. 24, 28.
38   Georg Soldan, p. 91.
39   See, for example, Matthew Bradley, et al, 'Combat casualty care and lessons learned in the last 100 years', in *Current Problems in Surgery*, Vol 54, No. 6, June 2017, pp. 315–351.
40   See especially, for the German figures, Holger Herwig, 'War in the West, 1914–1916' in John Horne (ed.), *A Companion to World War One* (Cambridge, 2010), pp. 62–63.
41   Hans von Hentig, *Psychologische Strategie des großen krieges* (Heidelberg, 1927).
42   See, for example, John Terraine, *The Western Front* (Hertford, 1997); Jack Sheldon, Anthony Farrar-Hockley, and other writers cited previously and in the bibliography. See also most recently 'A Turning

Point in Military Methods and Mentality: Germany and the Significance of the Battle of the Somme'
<www.undergraduatelibrary.org/48.pdf> (Accessed 11 May 2018).

43 Rupprecht of Bavaria, cited in John Terraine, p. 122.
44 Muhlmann und Mohs, p. 305.
45 Roger Chickering, *Imperial Germany and the Great War 1914–1918* (Cambridge, 2004), p. 88.
46 Chris Williams, 'A Question of Legitimate Pride', p. 738.
47 Wyn Griffith, 'The Pattern of One Man's Remembering', p. 289.
48 Chris Williams, 'A Question of Legitimate Pride', p. 738.
49 'Aftermath' in Siegfried Sassoon, *Collected Poems*, p. 118
50 *The Times*, 21 August 1916.
51 Compiled from War Dairies; brigade returns; summaries in WO 95/2541/1, H.Q. 38th Division AA & QMG returns; Part II Orders; and accounts in T.N.A. CAB 45/189.

Annex A

Honours and Awards, December 1915–July 1916[1]

Name	Unit	Date of Award
Distinguished Service Order (DSO)		
Captain G.R. Owen	15 R.W. Fus	19 May 1916
Captain R.J.A. Roberts	10 Welsh	19 May 1916
Lieutenant J. Edwardes	13 Welsh	August 1916
Military Cross (MC)		
2nd Lieutenant A.D.C. Clarke	122 Bde R.F.A.	March 1916
Lieutenant J.F. Venmore	14 R.W. Fus	23 March 1916
Lieutenant E. Gill	10 S.W.B.	23 March 1916
Captain J.G. Jones	14 R.W. Fus	June 1916
Major P. Hammond DSO	No 5 M.M.G. Coy	June 1916
Lieutenant J. F. Bligh	119 Bde R.F.A.	June 1916
Lieutenant J.S. Strange	14 Welsh	June 1916
Lieutenant A.L. Jones	14 R.W. Fus	June 1916
Lieutenant W.J. Peters	Y 38 T.M. Bty	June 1916
2nd Lieutenant J.A. Wilson	14 Welsh	June 1916
RSM J. Rees Jones	15 R.W. Fus	July 1916
2nd Lieutenant J.C. Griffiths	119 Bde R.F.A.	August 1916
2nd Lieutenant J.P. Connor	119 Bde R.F.A.	August 1916
2nd Lieutenant P. McDonough	19 Welsh	August 1916
2nd Lieutenant C.H. Stork	14 R.W. Fus	August 1916
CSM F. Thompson	14 R.W. Fus	August 1916
Lieutenant J. Evans	15 Welsh	August 1916
Lieutenant J. Edwardes	13 Welsh	August 1916
Lieutenant D. Yorke	14 Welsh	August 1916
Lieutenant L.W. Fox	X 38 T.M. Bty	August 1916
Major A.P. Bowen *Shrops L.I.*	B.M. 114 Inf Bde	August 1916
2nd Lieutenant A. Green	10 Welsh	August 1916
Lieutenant J. McMurtrie *R.E.*	151 Fd Coy R.E.	August 1916

Name	Unit	Date of Award
Captain E. Evans *R.A.M.C.*	Att. 11 S.W.B.	August 1916
Captain D.C. Stephenson	121 Bde R.F.A.	September 1916
2nd Lieutenant H.L.O. Gill	13 R.W. Fus	October 1916
2nd Lieutenant T.T. Taylor	10 S.W.B.	October 1916
2nd Lieutenant G.R. Paton	13R.W. Fus	October 1916
2nd Lieutenant W.M. Morgan	15 R.W. Fus	October 1916
2nd Lieutenant T.R. Wilson-Jones	15 R.W. Fus	October 1916
2nd Lieutenant R. Bowes	15 R.W. Fus	October 1916
Captain G.H. Lees	13 R.W. Fus	October 1916

Bar to the Military Cross

2nd Lieutenant A.D.C. Clarke	122 Bde R.F.A.	September 1916

Distinguished Conduct Medal (DCM)

Corporal L.C. Gardner	38 T.M. Bty	April 1916
Corporal W. Williams	14 R.W. Fus	23 March 1916
Sergeant F. Owen	151 Fd Coy R.E.	6 April 1916
Corporal D.W. Bloor	15 R.W. Fus	19 May 1916
Private J. Heeson	15 R.W. Fus	19 May 1916
Private P.F. Witten	15 R.W. Fus	19 May 1916
Sergeant H. McHals	14 R.W. Fus	June 1916
Private J. Hughes	16 R.W. Fus	June 1916
Private A.R, Hole	16 R.W. Fus	June 1916
Corporal C. Lewis	38 T.M. Bty	August 1916
Sergeant J.H. Williams*	10 S.W.B.	August 1916
CSM F. Thompson	14 R.W. Fus	August 1916
CSM J. Jones	14 Welsh	August 1916

Military Medal (MM)

Private H.S. Ellison	15 R.W. Fus	15 April 1916
Private A.E. Constant	10 Welsh	20 April 1916
Private A. Coles	16 Welsh	20 April 1916
Private G.A. Thomas	10 S.W.B.	27 April 1916
Private H.E. Evans	10 S.W.B.	27 April 1916
Private G.H. Beech	10 S.W.B.	27 April 1916
Private H. Benjamin	13 Welsh	3 May 1916
Sergeant G.P. Jones	15 R.W. Fus	19 May 1916
Corporal F.T. Rosser	15 R.W. Fus	19 May 1916
Private F. Langdon	15 R.W. Fus	19 May 1916
Private I. Downs	15 R.W. Fus	19 May 1916
Lance-Corporal Ll. Jones	10 Welsh	19 May 1916
Corporal G.H. Rees	13 R.W. Fus	June 1916

Name	Unit	Date of Award
Lance-Corporal T.H. Davies	13 R.W. Fus	June 1916
Lance-Corporal N. James	13 R.W. Fus	June 1916
Private C. Edwards	13 R.W. Fus	June 1916
Private J. Soar	13 R.W. Fus	June 1916
Sergeant F. Gardner	14 R.W. Fus	June 1916
Corporal O.H. Hughes	14 R.W. Fus	June 1916
Lance-Corporal S. Soar	14 R.W. Fus	June 1916
Private H.R. Noble	14 R.W. Fus	June 1916
Private W. Hall	14 R.W. Fus	June 1916
Private T.C. Jones	14 R.W. Fus	June 1916
Sergeant R. Kendall	10 Welsh	June 1916
Private E. Griffith	10 Welsh	June 1916
Corporal P. O Brien	14 Welsh	June 1916
Bombardier E. Harling	119 Bde R.F.A.	June 1916
Bombardier G, Sparkes	122 Bde R.F.A.	June 1916
Lance-Corporal P.D. Rogers	151 Fd Coy R.E.	June 1916
Sapper R. Millington	151 Fd Coy R.E.	June 1916
Bombardier J. Nelson	Y 38 T.M. Bty	June 1916
Gunner D. Noland	Y 38 T.M. Bty	June 1916
Gunner J. Pearson	Y 38 T.M. Bty	June 1916
Sergeant F. Appleyard	X 38 T.M. Bty	July 1916
Corporal L. Culver	Y 38 T.M. Bty	July 1916
Bombardier W.B. Williams	Z 38 T.M. Bty	July 1916
Gunner S. Bushell	X 38 T.M. Bty	July 1916
Gunner A. Berry	X 38 T.M. Bty	July 1916
Gunner W. Holt	X 38 T.M. Bty	July 1916
Gunner T. Corcoran	Z 38 T.M. Bty	July 1916
Sergeant A. Green	Y 38 T.M. Bty	July 1916
Corporal E.J. Smart	Z 38 T.M. Bty	July 1916
Gunner J. Walmsley	Y 38 T.M. Bty	July 1916
Driver E. Descer	119 Bde R.F.A.	July 1916
Gunner W. Morgan	119 Bde R.F.A.	July 1916
Sapper J. Barnet	123 Fd Coy R.E.	July 1916
Corporal A.J. Williams	13 R.W. Fus	July 1916
Lance-Corporal J.R. Roberts	14 R.W. Fus	July 1916
Corporal T. Pudner	14 R.W. Fus	July 1916
Private H. Jones	14 R.W. Fus	July 1916
Private W. Lowe	14 R.W. Fus	July 1916
Lance-Corporal F. Bird	17 R.W. Fus	July 1916
Private W. Hughs	13 R.W. Fus	July 1916
Lance-Corporal J.T. Davies	15 R.W. Fus	July 1916

Name	Unit	Date of Award
Private J. Schofield	15 R.W. Fus	July 1916
Private O. Foster	10 Welsh	August 1916
Sergeant G. Buse	14 Welsh	August 1916
Private G. Hale	14 Welsh	August 1916
Sergeant J. Higgson	16 R.W. Fus	August 1916
Sergeant W. Howe	10 Welsh	August 1916
Sergeant W.J. Beavan	10 Welsh	August 1916
Private R.W. Jones	10 S.W.B.	August 1916
Private D. Thomas	129 F.A. R.A.M.C.	August 1916
Gunner B. Parr	122 Bde R.F.A.	September 1916
Corporal E.T. Morgan	122 Bde R.F.A.	September 1916
Bombardier L.P. Evans	122 Bde R.F.A.	September 1916
Gunner W.G. Waters	122 Bde R.F.A.	September 1916
Sergeant R.A. Culverwell	123 Fd Coy R.E.	September 1916
Sergeant A.M. Darrock	123 Fd Coy R.E.	September 1916
Corporal W.P. Langman	123 Fd Coy R.E.	September 1916
Corporal T.H. Rogers	123 Fd Coy R.E.	September 1916
Corporal W.H. Gale	124 Fd Coy R.E.	September 1916
Sapper W.T. Jones	124 Fd Coy R.E.	September 1916
Sapper P.D. Davey	124 Fd Coy R.E.	September 1916
Corporal T.C. Walker	119 Bde R.F.A.	September 1916
Driver F. Ball	120 Bde R.F.A.	September 1916
Bombardier L.C. Morris	120 Bde R.F.A.	September 1916
Bombardier G.V. Hall	121 Bde R.F.A.	September 1916
Sergeant R. Williams	121 Bde R.F.A.	September 1916
Bombardier M. Weston	121 Bde R.F.A.	September 1916
Gunner A.E. Hartley	122 Bde R.F.A.	September 1916
Driver W.J. Howells	122 Bde R.F.A.	September 1916
Driver J. Halstead	122 Bde R.F.A.	September 1916
Private R. Harding	13 R.W. Fus	September 1916
Private H.J. Dye	13 R.W. Fus	September 1916
Private R.E. Jones	14 R.W. Fus	September 1916
Private Ll. S. Rogers	15 R.W. Fus	September 1916
Private R.J. Shoulder	113 M.G. Coy	September 1916
Private W. James	10 Welsh	September 1916
Private J.M. Thomas	10 Welsh	September 1916
Private G.H. Stokes	10 Welsh	September 1916
Lance-Corporal H. Davies	10 Welsh	September 1916
Corporal J. Jones	14 Welsh	September 1916
Private T.J. Dyer	14 Welsh	September 1916
CQMS H.V. Burnhill	15 Welsh	September 1916

Name	Unit	Date of Award
Private J.J. Davies	15 Welsh	September 1916
Corporal D.A. Evans	114 T.M. Bty	September 1916
Private T.T. Oliver	17 R.W. Fus	September 1916
Private A. Hewer	19 Welsh	September 1916
Lance-Corporal E. Elias	19 Welsh	September 1916
Private D. Thomas	129 F.A. R.A.M.C.	September 1916
Sergeant T.G. Hopkins	130 F.A. R.A.M.C.	September 1916
Private W.H. Jones	130 F.A. R.A.M.C.	September 1916
Private W.J. Ridgeway	130 F.A. R.A.M.C.	September 1916
Lance-Corporal T.J. Nicholls	130 F.A. R.A.M.C.	September 1916
Private E.B. Thomas	131 F.A. R.A.M.C.	September 1916
Private T. Allen	130 F.A. R.A.M.C.	September 1916
Sergeant W.T. Jones	13 R.W. Fus	October 1916
Sergeant T.G. Pickering	13 R.W. Fus	October 1916
Private W.T. Griffiths	14 R.W. Fus	October 1916
Private R. Johnson	16 R.W. Fus	October 1916
Lance-Sergeant P.F. Evans	10 S.W.B.	October 1916
Sergeant E.J. Hughes	13 R.W. Fus	October 1916
Lance-Corporal E. Westwood	13 R.W. Fus	October 1916
Private S. Frost	13 R.W. Fus	October 1916
Private G.A. Briggs	15 R.W. Fus	October 1916
Private A.H.E. Ford	15 R.W. Fus	October 1916
Private A.E. Lewis	15 R.W. Fus	Ctober 1916

Albert Medal (AM)

2nd Lieutenant N.M. Morgan (2nd Class)	15 R.W. Fus	21 May 1916
Lance-Corporal G. Broadbent (1st Class)	11 S.W.B.	July 1916

Mentioned in Despatches (MiD)

Colonel E.H. de V. Atkinson CIE	C.R.E. 38 Div	15 June 1916
Captain H.R. Bently *Cheshire*	B.M. 113 Inf Bde	15 June 1916
Brigadier General T.O. Marden *Welsh*	Comd 114 Inf Bde	15 June 1916
Major H.H. Pryce-Jones *Coldm Gds*	D.A.A. & Q.M.G. 38 Div	15 June 1916
Brigadier General W.A.M. Thompson CB *R.F.A.*	C.R.A. 38 Div	15 June 1916
Lieutenant Colonel R.J.W. Carden *17L*	C.O. 16 R.W. Fus	15 June 1916
Lieutenant Colonel J.H. Hayes *Shrops Yeo*	C.O. 14 Welsh	15 June 1916
Lieutenant Colonel P.J. Paterson DSO *R.F.A.*	C.O. 119 Bde R.F.A.	15 June 1916
Lieutenant Colonel H.G. Pringle *R.F.A.*	C.O. 121 Bde R.F.A.	15 June 1916
Lieutenant Colonel W.C.E. Rudkin DSO *R.F.A.*	C.O. 122 Bde R.F.A.	15 June 1916
Captain D.C. Stevenson *R.F.A.*	121 Bde R.F.A.	15 June 1916
Captain H.P. Jesson *R.E.*	O.C. 38 Div Sig Coy	15 June 1916
Lieutenant J.G. Jones *R.W. Fus*	14 R.W. Fus	15 June 1916

Name	Unit	Date of Award
Lieutenant Colonel R. Gaussen	C.O. 11 S.W.B.	15 June 1916
Lieutenant D. Yorke *Welsh*	14 Welsh	15 June 1916
Sergeant T. Rattle	13 Welsh	15 June 1916
Captain H.M. Hoare *A.S.C.*	H.Q. 38 Div	15 June 1916
Colonel F.J. Morgan *R.A.M.C.*	A.D.M.S. 38 Div	15 June 1916
Sergeant J.H. Williams	10 S.W.B.	August 1916

Notes

* Later VC, MM and bar, also M.i.D.; commissioned into 3 R.W. Fus in 1918.
Compiled from the 38th Division A.A. & Q.M.G. War Diary, T.N.A. WO 95/2541.

Annex B

Welsh Army Corps Outside 38th Welsh Division

Although the idea of a Welsh Army Corps was abandoned, as described in Chapter 2, enough infantry units were actually formed to field a complete corps. Some of these were assigned to other brigades and divisions; some were garrison battalions formed for static duties throughout the Empire; and others were holding and training units whose role was to supply replacements for casualties in the service battalions overseas. There were no equivalent units in the Royal Artillery, Royal Engineers, Army Service Corps or Royal Army Medical Corps.

The sections below describe these units and what happened to them during the course of the War. At the end of this annex is a section describing the formation of the Training Reserve.

Royal Welsh Fusiliers

8th (Service) Battalion
Formed at Wrexham in August 1914 as part of K1 and came under the command of 40 Infantry Brigade, 13th (Western) Division. The brigade moved to Salisbury Plain but by February 1915 was at Blackdown in Hampshire. It moved to Mudros in July 1915 and subsequently served in Gallipoli, Egypt and Mesopotamia.[1]

9th (Service) Battalion
Formed at Wrexham on 9 September 1914 as part of K2 and came under the command of 58 Infantry Brigade, 19th (Western) Division. It then moved to Tidworth but by December 1914 was in Basingstoke. It returned to Tidworth in March 1915 and embarked for France, landing at Boulogne on 19 July 1915. It remained with the 19th Division for the rest of the war.[2]

10th (Service) Battalion
Formed at Wrexham on 16 October 1914 as part of K3 and came under the command of 76 Infantry Brigade, 25th Division. It moved to Codford St Mary in Wiltshire but by November 1914 was in Bournemouth. It moved to Romsey on 29 April 1915 and to Aldershot on 3 June 1915. It then embarked for France and landed at Boulogne on 27 September 1915. On 15 October 1915 it transferred with the rest of the brigade to the 3rd Division. On 8 February 1918 it was disbanded in France, having been one of those units selected for reduction because of manpower shortages; the men were transferred to the 8th Entrenching Battalion.[3]

11th (Service) Battalion

Formed at Wrexham on 18 October 1914 as part of K3 and came under the command of 67 Infantry Brigade, 22nd Division. The brigade then moved to Seaford and by December 1914 the battalion was in billets in St Leonards. It returned to Seaford April 1915 but moved on to Aldershot in June 1915. The brigade landed in France early September 1915 but by 5 November 1915 it was in Salonika where it remained throughout the war.[4]

12th (Reserve) Battalion

Formed in Wrexham in October 1914 as a Service Battalion of K4 and came under the command of 104 Infantry Brigade, originally in the 35th Division. It moved to Tenby in February 1915. On 10 April 1915 it became a Reserve Battalion and moved to Kinmel Park, Rhyl, where it remained until on 1 September 1916 it was converted into 62nd Training Reserve Battalion of 14 Reserve Brigade. [5]

18th (Reserve) Battalion (2nd London Welsh)

Formed at Gray's Inn in London in February 1915 as a Service battalion. Moved to Bangor in June 1915 and until August 1915 it was part of the 38th (Welsh) Division. It was then converted into a Reserve Battalion. On 1 September 1916, with the 20 R.W. Fus, it became the 63rd Training Reserve Battalion in 14 Reserve Brigade.[6]

19th (Service) Battalion

Formed March 1915 by the Welsh National Executive Committee as a Bantam Battalion. It served with the 38th (Welsh) Division at Deganwy until August 1915. In September 1915 it was transferred to 119 Brigade, 40th Division at Aldershot. The battalion landed in France in early June 1916. On 6 February 1918 it was one of the battalions selected for disbandment in France because of manpower shortages; the men were transferred to the 8th Entrenching Battalion.

20th, 21st and 22nd (Reserve) Battalions

Formed in North Wales as Reserve battalions for the 38th (Welsh) Division. The battalions moved to Kinmel Park (Rhyl) in May 1915 and on 1 September 1916 the 20th Battalion, with 18 R.W. Fus, became the 63rd Training Reserve Battalion; and 21st and 22nd formed the 64th Training Reserve Battalion. Both units were assigned to 14 Reserve Brigade. [7]

26th (Service) Battalion

Formed from the 4th Garrison Battalion (see below) on 16 July 1918. Was at the time under the command of 176 Infantry Brigade, 59th (2nd North Midland) Division.

1st Garrison Battalion

Formed at Wrexham in July 1915, then to Gibraltar where it remained throughout the war.[8]

2nd Garrison Battalion

Formed at Garswood Park, Wigan, on 21 October 1915. In March 1916 it moved to Egypt where it remained throughout the war. After going first to Zagazig, in August 1917 the battalion moved to Sollum, via Alexandria. It then remained Sollum until after the Armistice, when elements returned to Cairo to relieve the 6th Garrison Battalion which was about to go to Salonika. [9]

3rd (Reserve) Garrison Battalion
Formed at Wrexham in February 1916. It moved to Abergele in November 1916 and from thence to Rhyl and Gobowen. It moved again to Oswestry in June 1917 and to Ireland in November 1917, when it went to Cork. It moved on to Crosshaven in March 1918 before being disbanded.[10]

4th Garrison Battalion
Formed at Bebington on 15 April 1916. It embarked for France and landed at Le Havre on 7 June 1916, where it was attached to the Army Troops of the Third Army. It was renamed 4th Garrison Guard Battalion in 1918. On 16 May 1918 it came under the command of 176 Infantry Brigade, 59th (2nd North Midland) Division and was converted to the infantry role. On 16 July 1918 it was renamed 26th (Service) Battalion.[11]

5th (Home Service) Garrison Battalion
Formed at Wrexham in August 1916 but moved immediately to Barrow-in-Furness. It became the 12th Battalion, the Royal Defence Corps in August 1917.[12]

6th Garrison Battalion
Formed at Aintree on 18 September 1916 and moved to Egypt in January 1917, and was based at the Citadel, Cairo. The battalion moved to Salonika on 1 November 1918. After a brief stay embarked for Bulgaria, landing at Dede-Agach on 10 November, where it was employed in guarding the Salonika-Constantinople railway until its disbandment.[13]

7th Garrison Battalion
Formed in January 1917 but disbanded the following month.[14]

South Wales Borderers

4th (Service) Battalion
Formed at Brecon in late August 1914 as part of K1 and came under the command of 40 Infantry Brigade, 13th (Western) Division. It moved to Park House Camp at Tidworth and in October 1914 went on to Chiseldon. It was in Cirencester by December 1914. It moved to Woking in March 1915 and embarked at Avonmouth on 29 June 1915 for Gallipoli via Mudros, landing on 15 July 1915. It returned to Mudros in January 1916 and subsequently served in Egypt and Mesopotamia until disbanded.

5th (Service) Battalion (Pioneers)
Formed at Brecon in September 1914 as part of K2 and came under the command of 58 Infantry Brigade in the 19th (Western) Division. It moved to Park House Camp at Tidworth. It was at Basingstoke by December 1914. On 10 January 1915 it was converted into a pioneer battalion. It moved to Burnham in January 1915 and to Bulford in March 1915. It moved again in April 1915 to Perham Down. It landed at Le Havre on 16 July 1915 and served in France until its disbandment at the end of the war.

6th (Service) Battalion (Pioneers)

Formed at Brecon on 12 September 1914 as part of K3 and came under the command of 76 Infantry Brigade, 25th Division. It moved to Codford on Salisbury Plain but was in Bournemouth by November 1914. In February 1915 it was converted into a pioneer battalion. It moved to Hursley Park in April 1915 but went on to Aldershot soon after. It embarked for France and landed at Le Havre on 25 September 1915. On 2 July 1918 it transferred to the 30th Division and remained in France until the end of the war.

7th (Service) Battalion

Formed at Brecon on 14 September 1914 as part of K3 and came under the command of 67 Infantry Brigade, 22nd Division. It moved to Seaford but by December 1914 was in St Leonards. It returned to Seaford in April 1915 and moved to Aldershot by the end of May. It embarked for France and landed at Boulogne on 6 September 1915 but sailed at Marseilles on 10 October for service in Salonika, where it remained until the end of the war.

8th (Service) Battalion

Formed at Brecon on 19 September 1914 as part of K3 and came under the command of 67 Infantry Brigade, 22nd Division. Its subsequent service was the same as that of the 7th Battalion but it sailed from Marseilles 30 October 1915.

9th (Reserve) Battalion

Formed at Pembroke Dock on 31 October 1914 as a Service Battalion of K4 and came under the command of 104 Infantry Brigade, in the original 35th Division. On 10 April 1915 it became a Reserve Battalion and moved to Kinmel Park, Rhyl. On 1 September 1916 it was converted into the 57th Training Reserve Battalion of 13 Reserve Brigade. Later, it became the 52nd (Graduated) Battalion (see below).

12th (Service) Battalion (3rd Gwent)

Formed at Newport in March 1915 by the Welsh National Executive Committee as a Bantam Battalion. In March 1915 it came under the command of the Welsh Bantam Brigade. It moved in July 1915 to Prees Heath. In September 1915 it moved to Aldershot, where the formation was renamed as 119 Bantam Brigade, 40th Division. It embarked for France and landed at Le Havre on 2 June 1916. On 10 February 1918 it was disbanded in France as one of those battalions selected for reduction because of manpower shortages.

13th (Reserve) Battalion

Formed at St Asaph in July 1915 as a Reserve Battalion. It moved in September to Kinmel Park, near Rhyl. On 1 September 1916 it was converted into the 59th Training Reserve Battalion of 13 Reserve Brigade.

14th (Reserve) Battalion

Formed at Prees Heath in September 1915 as a Reserve Battalion. It moved to Conway in October 1915 but moved on to Kinmel Park near Rhyl in January 1916. On 1 September 1916 it was converted into the 65th Training Reserve Battalion of 14 Reserve Brigade.

15th (Service) Battalion

Formed at North Walsham in June 1918 and next month absorbed the cadre of the 10th Cheshires. It moved to Aldershot around September 1918 and appears to have been disbanded by November 1918.

51st (Graduated) Battalion

Up to 27 October 1917, this was known as the 230th Graduated Battalion and had no regimental affiliation. Before that it had been the 58th Battalion of the Training Reserve and up to September 1916 had been the 12th (Reserve) Battalion of the Welsh Regiment. A training unit based at Aldeburgh, it was part of 204 Infantry Brigade of the 68th (2nd Welsh) Division. By April 1918 it had moved to Stowlangtoft in Suffolk and was disbanded at the end of the war.

52nd (Graduated) Battalion

Up to 27 October 1917, this was known as the 282nd Graduated Battalion and had no regimental affiliation. Before that it had been the 57th Battalion of the Training Reserve and until September 1916 had been the 9th (Reserve) Battalion of the South Wales Borderers. A training unit based at Patrickbourne near Canterbury, it was part of 201 Infantry Brigade in the 67th Division. By January 1918 it had moved to Broadstairs and in April went to Foxhall Heath, near Ipswich. It was disbanded at the end of the war.

53rd (Young Soldiers) Battalion

Until 27 October 1917, this was known as 59th Young Soldiers Battalion and had no regimental affiliation. A basic recruit training unit based at Kinmel Park, it was part of 14 Reserve Brigade.

Welsh Regiment

8th (Service) Battalion (Pioneers)

Formed at Cardiff in August 1914 as part of K1 and came under the command of 40 Infantry Brigade in the 13th (Western) Division. The battalion moved to Salisbury Plain and was at Chisledon in October 1914. It then went to Bournemouth in December. In January 1915 it was converted into a pioneer battalion, remaining in the 13th Division. It moved to Aldershot in February 1915. On 15 June 1915 the battalion embarked at Avonmouth and landed at ANZAC cove, Gallipoli, on 5 August 1915. In
December 1915 it was evacuated and went to Egypt via Mudros. In February 1916 it moved to Mesopotamia for the rest of the war and was disbanded there.

9th (Service) Battalion

Formed at Cardiff on 9 September 1914 as part of K2 and moved to Salisbury Plain, where it came under the command of 58 Brigade in the 19th (Western) Division. It was at Basingstoke in November 1914. It moved to Weston-Super-Mare in January 1915 and then to Perham Down in May 1915. It embarked for France and landed at Boulogne mid July 1915. It remained in France for the rest of the war.

11th (Service) Battalion

Formed at Cardiff in September 1914 as part of K3. It moved to the South Downs and came under the command of 67 Infantry Brigade in the 22nd Division. It moved to Hastings in December 1914 and on to Seaford in April 1915. It went to Aldershot in May. The battalion embarked for France and landed at Boulogne on 6 September 1915. It sailed from Marseilles on 30 October 1915, eventually to Salonika, where it remained for the rest of the war until disbanded.

12th (Reserve) Battalion

Formed in Cardiff on 23 October 1914 as a Service battalion, part of K4 and came under the command of 104 Infantry Brigade in the original 35th Division. On 10 April 1915 it became a Reserve Battalion at Kinmel Park. On 1 September 1916 it was converted into the 58th Training Reserve Battalion of 13 Reserve Brigade and lost its connection to the regiment.

17th (Service) Battalion (1st Glamorgan)

Formed at Cardiff in December 1914 as a Bantam Battalion. In December 1914 the battalion moved to Rhyl and was attached to the 43rd (Wessex) Division. It moved to Rhos in February 1915 and in July went on to Prees Heath. In July 1915 it was transferred to 119 Brigade in the 40th Division. It moved to Aldershot in September. From there it embarked for France and landed in June 1916. It was disbanded on 9 February 1918.

18th (Service) Battalion (2nd Glamorgan)

Formed at Cardiff in January 1915 as a Bantam Battalion. It moved to Porthcawl and attached was to the 43rd Division. In July it went on to Prees Heath. In July 1915 it was transferred to 119 Infantry Brigade, 40th Division. It moved to Aldershot in September. from there it embarked for France and landed in June 1916. On 5 May 1918 it was reduced to cadre strength after suffering heavy casualties. After re-formation, on 18 June 1918 it was transferred to 47 Infantry Brigade in the 16th (Irish) Division in England. It then went to North Walsham. On 20 June 1918 it was fully reconstituted by absorbing the 25th Battalion and moved to Aldershot. It returned to France again on 29 July 1918 and remained there until disbanded.

20th (3rd Rhondda) (Reserve), 21st (Reserve) and 22nd (Reserve) Battalions

Formed in Wales in July and September 1915 as Reserve battalions. Moved to Kinmel Park and on 1 September 1916, the 20th Battalion became the 60th Training Reserve Battalion and the 21st became the 61st Training Reserve Battalion, both in 13 Reserve Brigade. The 22nd formed the 66th Training Reserve Battalion in 14 Reserve Brigade. All three battalions lost their connection to the regiment at this time.

23rd (Service) Battalion (Welsh Pioneers)

Formed at Porthcawl in September 1915 and moved to Aldershot in March 1916. Between May and June 1916, it was attached to the 69th Division at Thetford. It embarked at Devonport on 13 July 1916 for Salonika. On 24 August 1916 it was attached as a pioneer battalion to the 28th Division and remained there until it was disbanded.

25th Battalion

Formed at North Walsham on 1 June 1918 but absorbed by the 18th Battalion on 20 June 1918.

51st (Graduated) Battalion

Until 27 October 1917, this unit was known as the 226th Graduated Battalion and had no regimental affiliation. Before that it had been 63rd Battalion of the Training Reserve and up to September 1916 had been the 18th and 20th (Reserve) Battalions of the Royal Welsh Fusiliers. A training unit based at Halesworth, it was part of 203 Infantry Brigade in the 68th Division. It moved to Yarmouth in the winter of 1917–18 and by May 1918 was at Herringfleet until its disbandment.

52nd (Graduated) Battalion

Up to 27 October 1917, this was known as the 234th Graduated Battalion and had no regimental affiliation. Before that it had been the 65th Battalion of the Training Reserve and until September 1916 had been the 14th (Reserve) Battalion of the South Wales Borderers. As a training unit based at Herringfleet, it was part of 205 Infantry Brigade in the 68th (2nd Welsh) Division. It moved to Lowestoft in the winter of 1917–18 and by May 1918 was at Saxmundham where it remained until its disbandment.

53rd (Young Soldiers) Battalion

Until 27 October 1917, this was known as the 64th Young Soldiers Battalion and had no regimental affiliation. Before that it had been 21st (Reserve) Battalion of the Royal Welsh Fusiliers. A basic recruit training unit based at Kinmel Park, it was part of 14 Reserve Brigade.

Formation of the Training Reserve

A considerable reorganisation of the reserve infantry battalions took place on 1 September 1916. Before this date, most infantry regiments contained one or more reserve battalions of the Regular and New Armies. Recruits would be posted to these battalions for basic training, before they were sent on to an active service unit. With the introduction of conscription, the Regimental system simply could not cope with numbers. A new structure was put into place: The Training Reserve. The local nature of recruitment for infantry regiments was abandoned and the entire system centralised.

After 1 September 1916, Regimental distinctions disappeared, and the reserve units of Regiments were instead re-designated as battalions of the Training Reserve and were organised into new brigades. No Guards, Irish or Territorial battalions converted to the T.R. The reorganisation did not affect the Special Reserve or Extra Reserve battalions of the Regular Army

The official complement of the Training Reserve was a around 208,500 soldiers. Men posted to T.R. battalions were not allocated to any particular Regiment and from this time on it is not safe to assume that a recruit would serve with his local regiment. Later, from May 1917, this arrangement was again altered when the units of the T.R. became Graduated and Young Soldiers Battalions and were once again aligned with specific regiments.

T.R. units dropped the cap badges and shoulder titles of their former Regiments and instead wore a large General Service button on a red disc on the cap and the letters 'TR' as a shoulder title. All N.C.O.s and men wore the number of their T.R. Brigade on their sleeve in the form of a cloth patch. The most senior battalion wore its number in white, the others in red, yellow, green, brown and blue in descending order. The T.R. shoulder titles were discontinued from June 1917 and the sleeve number in December of that year. The cap button was also dropped and a red number of the T.R. battalion replaced it. Officers of the T.R. continued to wear their Regimental uniform and badges.

Notes

1   T.N.A. WO 95/5162, 8 R.W.F. War Diary.
2   T.N.A. WO 95/2092, 9 R.W.F. War Diary.
3   Lt. Col. F.N. Burton (ed.) *The War Diary of 10th (Service) Battalion Royal Welch Fusiliers* (Plymouth, 1926).
4   T.N.A. WO 95/4858, 11 R.W.F. War Diary.
5   Brig. Gen. E.A. James, *British Regiments 1914–1918*, p. 67.
6   T.N.A. WO 380/17.
7   Welsh Army Corps, 1914–19. Report of the Executive Committee (Cardiff, 1921).
8   T.N.A. WO 380/17.
9   T.N.A. WO 380/17 and James, *British Regiments 1914–1918* (Uckfield, 2009), p. 68.
10   Army Council Instruction No 1528 of 1916 and *British Regiments 1914–1918*, p. 68.
11   T.N.A. WO 95/409.
12   Army Council Instruction No. 2364 of 1916, T.N.A. WO 380/17, and *British Regiments 1914–1918*, p. 68.
13   T.N.A. WO 380/17 and *British Regiments 1914–1918*, p. 68.
14   James, *British Regiments 1914–1918*, p. 68.

Annex C

Welsh Regular, Special Reserve and Territorial Force Units

Wales's contribution to the Army during the Great War also included its Regular, Special Reserve and Territorial Force (TF) units. This annex provides a summary of units and parent formations.

1. Regular Army and Special Reserve Regiments and Battalions

Regiment/Battalion	Brigade	Division
3rd (Prince of Wales's) Dragoon Guards	6 Cavalry	3rd Cavalry
9th Royal Lancers	5 Cavalry	2nd Cavalry
1 Welsh Guards	3 Guards	Guards
1 R.W.Fus (23rd Foot)	22	7th
2 R.W. Fus (23rd Foot)	19	33rd
3 (S.R.) R.W. Fus (23rd Foot)		Western Command
1 S.W.B. (24th Foot)	3	1
2 S.W.B. (24th Foot)	87	29th
3 (S.R.) S.W.B. (24th Foot)		Home
1 Welsh (41st Foot)	84	28th
2 Welsh (69th Invalids)	3	1
3 (S.R.) Welsh (41st/69th Foot)		Western Command

2. Yeomanry Cavalry (Territorial Force)[*]

Regiment	Brigade	Division
Denbighshire Hussars	Welsh Border Mounted	74th Yeomanry
Welsh Horse	South Wales Mounted	74th Yeomanry
Montgomeryshire	South Wales Mounted	74th Yeomanry
Glamorgan	South Wales Mounted	74th Yeomanry
Pembrokeshire	South Wales Mounted	74th Yeomanry

---

[*] Later formed into infantry battalions of the R.W. Fus and Welsh Regiment in 231 Brigade, 74th (Yeomanry) Division.

3. 53rd (Welsh) Division (Territorial Force)

Headquarters 53rd (Welsh) Division

Divisional Troops

Artillery	Engineers	Medical Services
265 (I Welsh) Brigade R.F.A.	436 (1 Welsh) Field Company R.E.	1st Welsh Field Ambulance R.A.M.C.
266 (II Welsh) Brigade R.F.A.	437 (2/1 Welsh) Field Company R.E.	2nd Welsh Field Ambulance R.A.M.C.
268 (III Welsh) Brigade R.F.A.	53rd Division Signal Company R.E.	3rd Welsh Field Ambulance R.A.M.C.
Welsh (Caernarvonshire) Heavy Brigade R.G.A.	**Other Divisional Troops**	53rd Division Mobile Veterinary Section
53 M.G.C.	53rd Division Cyclist Company	53rd Sanitary Section
53rd Division Ammunition Column	53rd Divisional Supply Train A.S.C.	

158 (Royal Welsh) Infantry Brigade	**160 (South Wales) Infantry Brigade**	
1/5 (Flint) R.W. Fus	1/4 Welsh	
1/6 (Caerns & Anglesey) R.W. Fus	1/5 Welsh	
1/7 (Montgomery & Merioneth) R.W. Fus	1/1 Brecknock (S.W.B.)	Later 5th (Mhow) Division, India
158 Light Trench Mortar Battery	160 Light Trench Mortar Battery	
158 M.G. Company	160 M.G. Company	

4. 68th (2nd Welsh) Division (Territorial Force)

Headquarters 68th (2nd Welsh) Division

203 (Royal Welsh) Brigade	204 (Welsh Border) Brigade	205 (South Wales) Brigade
2/4 (Denbigh) R.W. Fus	2/1 Brecknock (S.W.B.)	2/1 Monmouths
2/5 (Flint) R.W. Fus		2/2 Monmouths
2/6 (Caerns & Anglesey) R.W. Fus		2/3 Monmouths
2/7 (Montgomery & Merioneth) R.W. Fus		

5. Other General Service Territorial Force Units

Unit	Brigade	Division
1/4 (Denbigh) R.W. Fus	3 Infantry	1st
1/1 Monmouths	84 Infantry	28th, later 46th
1/2 Monmouths	12 Infantry	4th, later 29th
1/3 Monmouths	83 Infantry	28th, later 46th
1/6 (Glamorgan) Welsh	84 Infantry	28th, later 1st

6. Other Home Service Territorial Force Units

Western Command

3/4 R.W. Fus

3/5 R.W. Fus

3/6 R.W. Fus

3/7 R.W. Fus

3/1 S.W.B.

3/1 Monmouths

3/2 Monmouths

3/3 Monmouths

2/4 Welsh

3/4 Welsh

3/5 Welsh

3/6 Welsh

2/5 Welsh

1/7 (Cyclists) Welsh

3/7 (Cyclist) Welsh

Eastern Command

23 R.W. Fus

4 Monmouths

2/6 (Glamorgan) Welsh

2/7 (Cyclist) Welsh

Annex D

British and Imperial Divisions World-Wide Deployment 1916

B.E.F. Western Front
See Chapter 2 Appendix for the list of British and Imperial Divisions: Total 62⅓

42 corps and army artillery brigades (of regimental size) – 3⅔ divisions
5 Army tank Brigades – 1⅔ divisions
Engineer Special (gas) Brigade – ⅓ division
10 Royal Flying Corps/Brigades – 3⅓ divisions
5 Labour Corps groups, each of divisional size – 5 divisions
Western Front total: 76⅓

Middle East
XX Corps
74th Yeomanry T.F.
10th (Irish)
53rd (Welsh) T.F.
60th (2nd London) T.F.

XXI Corps
52nd (Lowland) T.F.
54th (East Anglian)
75th (Territorial and Indian)

Desert Mounted Corps
ANZAC Mounted Division
Australian Mounted Division
Yeomanry Mounted Division
Imperial Camel Brigade
Light armoured brigade
Middle East total: 11⅓

Mesopotamia and Persia
III Indian Corps

13th (Western)
3rd (Lahore) Indian
6th (Poona) Indian
7th (Meerut) Indian
12th Indian
14th Indian
15th Indian
16th Indian
17th Indian
18th Indian
7 (Meerut) Indian Cavalry Brigade
11 Indian Cavalry Brigade
South Persia (Indian) Brigade
Mesopotamia total: 11

Salonika
XII Corps
22nd
26th
7 Mounted Brigade
8 Mounted Brigade
16th Wing R.F.C.
Salonika total: 3

India
1st (Peshawar) Indian
2nd (Rawalpindi) Indian
4th (Quetta) Indian
5th (Mhow) Indian
8th (Lucknow) Indian
9th (Secunderabad) Indian
11th Indian
16th Indian
1st Indian Cavalry
Burma Division
Aden Brigade
Bannu Brigade
Derajat Brigade
Kohat Brigade
India total: 11⅓

Egypt
IX Corps
11th (Northern) Division
42nd (East Lancashire)

20 Indian Brigade
29 Indian Brigade
Imperial Cavalry Brigade
Western Frontier Force (Egypt) – 1 brigade
Cyprus Garrison
Alexandria and Suez Canal Garrison
Middle East Brigade R.F.C.
Egypt total: 5

Africa
Somaliland Camel Corps – 2 battalions
West African Frontier Force – 1 division
King's African Rifles (East Africa) – 3 divisions
South African Division
Rhodesian Regiment
Africa total: 5⅓ divisions

Home Service and Training
63rd (2nd Northumbrian)
64th (2nd Highland)
65th (2nd Lowland)
67th (2nd Home Counties)
68th (2nd Welsh)
69th (2nd East Anglian)
71st
72nd
73rd
2/2nd Mounted
3rd Mounted
4th Mounted (2nd Cyclist)
Total at home: 12

Final total: 135⅓

Annex E

Mametz Wood Writers, Poets and Artists

Bernard Adams

John Bernard Pye Adams (1890–1917) was born in Beckenham and educated at Malvern College and St. John's College, Cambridge. He was awarded a prize for one of his odes written in Latin and gained a First Class Honours Degree. In 1914, he volunteered for service in the Army and was commissioned into the Royal Welch Fusiliers, being posted to the 1st Battalion, with whom he served in front of Mametz before the Mametz Wood fighting of July 1916. He was one of the first writers to publish his memoirs of service. This was written whilst convalescing from a wound sustained in June 1916. *Nothing of Importance: A Record of 18 Months at the Front with a Welsh Battalion, October 1915–June 1916* was published in 1918. Adams returned to active service on the Western Front on 31 January 1917. He was gravely wounded whilst leading his men in an attack near Serre on 26 February 1917. He died of wounds the following day.

James Dunn

James Churchill Dunn DCM (1871–1955) is best known for his memoir *The War the Infantry Knew*, first published in 1938. It was originally published anonymously, in a private limited edition, and was described by *The London Review of Books* as 'a magnificent tour de force, the length of three ordinary books. Dunn had previously served with the Imperial Yeomanry in South Africa where he had been awarded the DCM. He qualified as a doctor and served as Regimental Medical Officer in The Royal Welch Fusiliers during the Great War and is mentioned in the memoirs of both Graves and Sassoon. Dunn famously wrote of his official role that: 'The first duty of a battalion medical officer in War is to discourage the evasion of duty… not seldom against one's better feelings, sometimes to the temporary hurt of the individual, but justice to all other men as well as discipline demands it.'

Robert Graves

Robert von Ranke Graves (1895–1985) was a poet, historical novelist, critic, and classicist. Graves produced more than 140 works. His poems, many volumes of which record his military service, together with his translations and interpretations of the Greek myths; his memoir of his early life, including his role in the Great War, *Good-Bye to All That*; his historical dramas *I Claudius* and *Claudius the* God; and his study of poetic inspiration, *The White Goddess*, remain widely read. He enlisted and was commissioned into the 3rd (Special Reserve) Battalion of The Royal Welsh Fusiliers and served with the 1st and 2nd Battalions on the Western Front. He was badly wounded in the leg, arm and chest and never fully recovered. *Good-Bye to all That* contains a record of his impressions of Mametz Wood. His son David was killed serving with the 1st Royal Welch Fusiliers in Burma in 1943 having been recommended for a Victoria Cross.

Llewelyn Wyn Griffith

Llewelyn Wyn Griffith CBE *CdeG* (1890–1977) was a Welsh-speaking poet and writer, who was commissioned into the 15th Battalion, Royal Welsh Fusiliers (1st London Welsh) in 1915. He served throughout the war, from mid-1916 on wards chiefly as a staff officer at brigade, division and corps level. He received the MBE, the French Croix de Guerre and was twice mentioned in despatches. He is best known for his memoir, *Up to Mametz* which he wrote in the early 1920s, although the work was not published until 1931. His other works include *Beyond Mametz* and *The Pattern of One Man's Remembering*. In these he left a vivid account of the Battle of Mametz Wood.

David Jones

Walter David Jones CH CBE (1895–1974) was a painter, engraver, calligrapher and one of the first British modernist poets. As a painter he worked chiefly in watercolour, painting portraits and animals, landscapes, legendary and religious subjects. T.S. Eliot considered him a writer of major importance, and Jones's work *The Anathemata* was thought by W.H. Auden to be the best English long poem of the 20th century. His lengthy dramatic poem *In Parenthesis* chronicles his military experiences, especially those in Mametz Wood. Inspiration for his work originated with the author's Catholic faith and Welsh heritage. In 1914 Jones joined the 15th Battalion Royal Welsh Fusiliers (1st London Welsh) and served on the Western Front from 1915 to 1918. He was wounded in Mametz Wood but recovered and rejoined the battalion. He served longer at the front than any other British war writer. The consequences of this long period in the trenches on Jones's health were serious in the long term.

Harold Gladstone Lewis

Harold Lewis served as a Lieutenant and Captain in 15 R.W. Fus. He emigrated to Australia in 1910, returning to Britain to serve in the war but returning to Australia in later years. He wrote two autobiographical books, *Crow on a Barbed Wire Fence* and *Bluey*. His account of Mametz Wood is short and inexact.

Thomas Marden

Major General Sir Thomas Owen Marden KBE CB CMG (1866–1951) susequently commanded 6th Division. After the war, he commanded the British occupying force in Turkey during the Chanak Crisis in the early 1920s. He was Colonel of the Welch Regiment in the 1950s. He wrote the Regiment's official history covering the war years.

Frank Richards

Francis Philip Woodruff DCM MM (1883–1961) was born in Monmouthshire, orphaned at the age of nine, and was then brought up by his aunt and uncle in the Blaina area of the South Wales Valleys. The uncle, his mother's twin brother, and surnamed Richards, adopted Frank who then changed his surname. Richards enlisted into The Royal Welch Fusiliers in 1901, serving in India and Burma from 1902–1909, when he transferred to the reserves. He was recalled to the Colours in 1914 and served throughout the Great War in 2 R.W. Fus. He is best known his two volumes of memoirs, *Old Soldier Sahib*, about his service in India; and *Old Soldiers Never Die* in which he describes his service on the Western Front, including at Mametz.

Siegfried Sassoon

Siegfried Loraine Sassoon CBE MC (1886–1967) was a poet, and prose writer. He was decorated for bravery on the Western Front in 1916 and became one of the leading poets of the Great War. His poetry both described the horrors of the trenches, and satirised the false patriotism of those who, in his view, were responsible for continuing the war unnecessarily. Sassoon made a lone protest against the continuation of the war in his 'Soldier's Declaration' of 1917, and as a result was admitted to the military psychiatric hospital at Craiglockart. Here he formed a close friendship with Wilfred Owen, who was greatly influenced by him. Sassoon later won acclaim for three-volume fictionalised autobiography of the Great War, *memoirs of a Fox-Hunting Man, Memoirs of an Infantry Officer* and *Sherston's Progress.* He took part in the initial attack on Mametz from 1–3 July. Like his close friend Robert Graves, he enlisted and was commissioned into the 3rd (Special Reserve) Battalion of The Royal Welsh  Fusiliers and served with the 1st and 2nd Battalions on the Western Front. He also served in Egypt with the 24th Battalion, where he formed a friendship with the poet Vivian de Sola Pinto (1895–1969).

W.A. (Bill) Tucker

Bill Tucker attempted to join the Army under age twice and succeeded at the third attempt. He served in 15 R.W. Fus and the Divisional Cyclist Company. He served at Mametz but oddly his account of the war, *The Lousier War*, makes no mention of the battle. He was captured in early 1918 and spent the rest of the war in German prison camps. His book is one of the few accounts of life as a P.O.W. during the Great War. He later worked on *The Times* and was instrumental in launching *The Times Atlas of the World.*

Wynn Wheldon

Sir Wynn Powell Wheldon KBE DSO (1879–1961) was a left-leaning academic, educator, broadcaster, administrator, lawyer and writer who served in 14th Battalion Royal Welsh Fusiliers, commanding the battalion in 1917 in the Ypres Salient. He was mentioned in despatches and awarded the DSO for bravery and distinguished conduct. His letters and dairies, and a collection of short stories, record his service with the 14th Battalion in Mametz Wood. His son Sir Huw Powell Wheldon also served with The Royal Welch Fusiliers in the Second World War and was awarded the MC. Wheldon later became B.B.C. Controller.

Bibliography

British

Primary Sources

The National Archives (Kew)
German Foreign Ministry Paper GFM 34/215, *Der Weltkrieg (geheim) Bd. 2.*
CAB /18/24
CAB 45/189, 190, 191, letters and correspondence from veterans to the author of the British
    Official History (Fourth Army)
PRO 30/57/53
WO 20/Gen. No. 3449 (A.G.1)
WO 95/224, 38 Heavy Battery R.G.A. War Diary
WO 95/431, Headquarters Fourth Army War Diary
WO 95/547/2, 215 Fortress Company R.E. War Diary
WO 95/881, XI Corps War Diary
WO 95/921, XV Corps War Diary
WO 95/1365, 2 R.W. Fus War Diary
WO 95/1631, 7th Division War Dairy
WO 95/1639, 7th Division Artillery War Diary
WO 95/1643, 35 Brigade R.F.A War Diary
WO 95/1660/1, 1 R.W. Fus War Dairy
WO 95/1660/5, 22 Infantry Brigade War Diary
WO 95/1981, 17th (Northern) Division War Diary
WO 95/2539/4, 38th Division War Diary (G.S.)
WO 95/2541, 38th Division War Diary (A.A. & Q.M.G.)
WO 95/2542, 38th Division War Diary (Artillery)
WO 95/2545/3, 122 (Howitzer) Field Battery R.F.A. War Diary
WO 95/2546, 38th Division Ammunition Column War Diary
WO 95/2546/1, 119 Field Battery R.F.A. War Diary
WO 95/2546/2, 120 Field Battery R.F.A. War Diary
WO 95/2546/3, 121 Field Battery R.F.A. War Diary
WO 95/2547/1, 123 Field Coy R.E. War Diary
WO 95/2547/2, 124 Field Coy R.E. War Diary
WO 95/2547/3, 151 Field Coy R.E. War Diary
WO 95/2548, 38th Division Signal Company War Diary

WO 95/2548/2, 19 Welsh (Pioneers) War Diary
WO 95/2549/1, 129 Field Ambulance War Diary
WO 95/2549/2, 130 Field Ambulance War Diary
WO 95/2549/3, 131 Field Ambulance War Diary
WO 95/2550, 38th Division Supply Train War Diary
WO 95/2550/2, 38th Division Field Ambulance Workshop War Diary
WO 95/2551/1, 113 Brigade War Dairy
WO 95/2555/2, 13 R.W. Fus War Diary
WO 95/2555/3, 14 R.W. Fus War Diary
WO 95/2555/4 and 2556, 15 R.W. Fus. War Diary
WO 95/2555/5, 16 R.W. Fus War Diary
WO 95/2557, 114 Brgade War Diary
WO 95/2559/1, 10 Welsh War Diary
WO 2559/2, 13 Welsh War Diary
WO 95/2559/3, 14 Welsh War Diary
WO 2559/4, 15 Welsh War Diary
WO 95/2560, 115 Brigade War Diary
WO 95/2561/3, 16 Welsh War Diary
WO 95/2562/1, 17 R.W. Fus War Diary
WO 106/46/E2.10
WO 256/10
Welsh Office and Wales Office Records, 1890–1914

National Library of Wales, Aberystwyth
MS 3556E, Welsh Army Corps Draft Report, prepared for The Executive Committee.
GB 0210 LL WGRIF G3/10 Llewelyn Wyn Griffith papers, National Library of Wales (Army Book 136 – notebook containing a partial diary and draft poems, 1916–1917); P1/2 (letters 1914–1974); P2/2 letters to his wife 1915–1953); P3/1 (diaries 1915–1932); P4/1 (officer's record).

Churchill College Cambridge
RWLN, Lord Rawlinson of Trent (Rawlinson MS), Vol I.

Royal Welch Fusiliers Archives, Wrexham
3684, Personal notes on the operations about Mametz Wood, as far as the 115th Brigade was concerned, by Brigadier H.J. Evans
Concise History of the 15th RWF (1st London Welsh) 1914–1924 (compiled and published by the Committee of the 15th RWF Association).
David Jones Papers
Diary of Sergeant John Bradshaw for 1915 (Permission of Mr John Griffiths)
Diary of Robert Keating, RWF Mus 9203
Harold Diffey letters, RWF Mus 7133
E.L. Kirby, *Officers of The Royal Welch Fusiliers 1689–1914* (privately published, 1997)
Diary of Brigadier General Clifton Inglis Stockwell (Permission of the Stockwell family)

'Notes on the 1914–18 War by Regimental Signaller W.R. Thomas Reg. No. 20214 on active service with the 14th and 1st Bns. The Royal Welch Fusiliers (38th & 7th Divisions)'

War Diary (1914–1918) of 10th (Service) Battalion Royal Welch Fusiliers (edited by Lt-Col F.N. Burton and Lt A.P. Comyns MC, Plymouth, 1926)

War Diary of the 14th (Service) Battalion Royal Welch Fusiliers 1914–1919 (Gale & Polden, Aldershot)

Museum of the Royal Welsh (Brecon)
The Monmouthshire Regiment TF World War I. Fact Sheet: 7-B07-11.
'Story of the Attack on Mametz-Wood, July 1916' by J.H. Hughes, 11 S.W.B. 2014 252.1–3
Dairy of Lieutenant Colonel C.D. Harvey DSO, C.O. 10 S.W.B., 1.88 Box 17

Parliamentary Papers and Documents
An Act to make provision with respect to Military Service in connexion with the present War. 5 & 6 Geo. 5 c. 104
Hansard's *Parliamentary Debates,* as listed in reference notes
Report of the War Office (Reconstitution) Committee, 1904 (Esher Report) (Parliament Command Paper 1932)
Memorandum by the Secretary of State for War on Army Reorganisations, 30 July 1906 (Haldane Report) (Parliament Command Paper 2993)

Archaeological Reports
Richard Osgood MLitt AIfA FSA FSA (Scot) for *Bearhug Television*, 'A Certain Cure for Lost of Blood. Archaeological Excavation Report Mametz Wood', 2015.

Military Manuals and Publications
Army List (H.M.S.O., London, August 1914 to September 1919)
Army Orders (H.M.S.O., London, 1915)
Field Service Regulations, Vol. I (Organisation and Administration) 1908. WO 26/Regs/1849.
Field Service Pocket Book 1926. WO 26/863
General Routine Orders Issued to the British Army in the Field by Field-Marshal Sir Douglas Haig, K.T., G.C.B., G.C.V.O., K.C.I.E. (H.M.S.O., London, 1916–1918)
C.H. Dudley Ward, *Regimental Records of the Royal Welch Fusiliers, Vol. III, 1914–1918* (London, 1928)
Brig. Gen. Sir J.E. Edmonds, *History of the Great War based on Official Documents, by direction of the Historical Section of the Committee of Imperial Defence. Military Operations France and Belgium 1916,* Vol. I (London, 1932)
H.A. Jones, *The War in the Air, Being the Story of the Part Played in the Great War by the Royal Air Force,* Vol. II (Oxford, 1928)
H.A. Jones, *The War in the Air, being the part played by the Royal Air Force in the Great War 1914–1918,* Vol. III (Oxford, 1931)
Timothy J. Lupfer, *The Dynamics of Doctrine: The Changes in German Tactical Doctrine During the First World War* (Leavenworth papers No. 4, U.S. Command and General Staff College, July 1981).

Capt. Wilfred Miles, *History of the Great War based on Official Documents, by direction of the Historical Section of the Committee of Imperial Defence. Military Operations France and Belgium 1916*, Vol. II (London, 1938)

Lt.-Col. J.E. Munby CMD DSO (ed.), *A History of the 38th (Welsh) Division* (London, 1920)

Secondary Sources

Anon., *The Times History of the War* (London: 1914–1919)

Bernard Adams, *Nothing of Importance: A Record of Eight Months at the Front with a Welsh Battalion, October 1915 to June 1916* (London, 1917)

Sidney Allinson, *The Bantams: The Untold Story of World War One* (Barnsley, 2009)

Major General W.H. Anderson CB, *An Outline of the Development of the British Army up to the Commencement of the Great War 1914. Notes on four lectures delivered at the Staff College, Camberley* (London, 1920)

C.T. Atkinson, *History of the South Wales Borderers* (London, 1931)

Ian Beckett and John Gooch (ed.) Politicians and Defence: Studies in the Formulation of British Defence Policy (Manchester, 1981)

John Blacker (ed.), *Have You Forgotten Yet? The First World War Memoirs of C. P. Blacker* (Barnsley, 2000)

Robert Blake (ed.) *The Private Papers of Douglas Haig 1914–1919* (London, 1952) Victor Bonham-Carter, *Soldier True: The Life and Times of Field Marshal Sir William Robertson* (London, 1963)

Gerald Brennan, *A Life of One's Own* (London, 1962)

M.V. Brett (ed.) *Journals and Letters of Reginald Viscount Esher,* Vol. II (London, 1934)

Malcolm Brown and Shirley Seaton, *Christmas Truce* (London, 1994)

Henry Cadogan, *The Road to Armageddon* (Wrexham, 2009)

Roger Chickering, *Imperial Germany and the Great War 1914–1918* (Cambridge, 2004).

Winston Churchill, *The World Crisis 1911–1918* (London, 1931)

Tim Coates, *Patsy: The Story of Mary Cornwallis-West* (London, 2003)

Arthur Conan Doyle, *The British Campaign in France and Flanders 1916* (London, 1918)

Rose E.B. Coombs, *Before Endeavours Fade: A Guide to the Battlefields of the First World War* (London, 1983)

Martin Van Creveld, *Command in War* (Springfield, Massachusetts,1985)

Emlyn Davies, *Taffy Went to War* (Knutsford, 1976)

Frank Delamain (ed.), *Going Across: Extracts from the war letters and diaries of Lt. St. H. Evans* (Newport, n.d.)

George A.B. Dewar and Lieutenant Colonel J.H. Boraston, *Sir Douglas Haig's Command*, Vol. I (London, 1922)

Thomas Dilworth, *David Jones in the Great War* (London, 2012)

Timothy C. Dowling, *The Brusilov Offensive* (Bloomington, Indiana, 2008)

Dudley Ward, C.H. *Regimental Records of The Royal Welch Fusiliers, Vol. III 1914–1918, France and Flanders* (Wrexham, 1991)

Christopher Duffy, *Through German Eyes: The British and the Somme 1916* (London, 2007)

Col. John R. Dunlop *The Development of the British Army 1899–1914* (London, 1938)

Captain J. C. Dunn, *The War the Infantry Knew 1914–1919* (London, 1994)

A.H. Farrar-Hockley, *The Somme* (London, 1966)

David French and Brian Holden Reid (ed.), *The British General Staff: Reform and Innovation 1890–1939* (London, 2002)

Robert T. Foley, *German Strategy and the Path to Verdun: Erich von Falkenhayn and the Development of Attrition* (Cambridge, 2005)

Martin Gilbert, *The First World War* (London, 1994)

Gerald Gliddon, *The Battle of the Somme: A Topographical History* (Stroud, 1996).

Robert Graves, *Goodbye to All That* (London, 1929)

Llewelyn Wyn Griffith (Jonathon Riley ed.), *Up to Mametz … And Beyond* (Barnsley, 2010)

Llewelyn Wyn Griffith, *Hiraeth* (Privately Printed, 1929)

Llewelyn Wyn Griffith, *Spring of Youth* (London, 1935)

Paul Guinn, *British Strategy and Politics 1914 to 1918* (Oxford, 1965)

B.H. Liddell Hart, *History of the First World War* (London, 1970)

Edward Hancock, B*azentin Ridge* (Barnsley, 2001)

Peter Hart, *The Somme* (London, 2008)

Jonathan Hicks, *The Welsh at Mametz Wood: The Somme 1916* (Talybont, 2016)

Michael Howard *The Continental Commitment: The dilemma of British defence policy in the era of the two world wars* (London, 1989)

Colin Hughes, *Mametz: Lloyd George's Welsh Army at the Battle of the Somme* (London, 1982)

Alistair Horne, *The Price of Glory, Verdun 1916* (London, 1962)

Anthony Hyne, *David Jones, A Fusilier at the Front* (Bridgend, 1995)

David Jones, *In Parenthesis* (London, 1937)

David Jones, *The Anathemata* (London, 1951)

D.V. Kelly, *39 Months with the Tigers, 1915–1918* (London, 1930)

T.O. Marden, *History of the Welch Regiment, 1914–1918* (Cardiff, 1932)

John Masters, *The Road Past Mandalay*, (London, 1961)

Kenneth O. Morgan (ed.), *Lloyd George; Family Letters 1885–1936* (Cardiff and London, 1973)

David A. Pretty, *Farmer, Soldier and Politician: The Life of Brigadier-General Sir Owen Thomas, MP Father of the 'Welsh Army Corps'* (Wrexham, 2011)

Frank Richards, *Old Soldiers Never Die*, Annotated by H. J. Krijnen and D. E. Langley (Peterborough, 2004)

Peter Robinson, *The Letters of Major General Price-Davies VC CB CMG DSO* (London, 2013)

D. Rogers (ed.), *Landrecies to Cambrai: Case Studies of German Offensive and Defensive Operations on the Western Front 1914–17* (Solihull, 2010)

Michael Renshaw, *Mametz Wood* (Barnsley, 1999)

Michael Renshaw, *The Welsh on the Somme* (London, 2015)

Peter Rowland, *Lloyd George* (London, 1975)

Siegfried Sassoon, *Memoirs of an Infantry Officer* (London, 1930)

Siegfried Sassoon (Rupert Hart-Davis ed.), *Diaries 1915–1918* (London, 1983)

Hugh Sebag-Montefiore, *Somme: Into the Breach* (London, 2016)

Gary Sheffield, *Forgotten Victory: The First World War – Myths and Realities* (London, 2001)

Gary Sheffield and John Bourne (eds.), *Douglas Haig: War Diaries and Letters 1914–1918* (London, 2005)

Peter Simkins *Kitchener's Armies: The Raising of the New Armies, 1914–16* (Manchester, 1988)

E.M. Spiers, *Haldane: An Army Reformed* (Edinburgh, 1980)

A. J. P. Taylor, *Illustrated History of the First World War* (London, 1974)

A.J.P. Taylor (ed.), *Lloyd George: A Diary by Frances Stevenson* (London, 1971)

W.A. Tucker, *The Lousier War* (London, 1974)

E.S. Turner, *Gallant Gentlemen. A History of the British Officer, 1600–1956* (London, 1956)

S.R. Williamson *The Politics of Grand Strategy. British and French Preparations for War, 1904–1914* (Oxford, 1969)

Jean Moorcroft Wilson, *Siegfried Sassoon. The Making of a War Poet. A Biography 1886–1918* (London, 1998)

Journals and Anthologies

'The German Defence during the Battle of the Somme: Mametz Wood and Contalmaison, 9th–10th of July 1916', 'The Other Side of the Hill' series, Army *Quarterly*, Vol. 9, No. 2 (January 1925)

Ian Beckett, 'Henry Rawlinson' in Ian Beckett and Steven Corvi (eds.), *Haig's Generals* (London, 2006)

Matthew Bradley et al, 'Combat casualty care and lessons learned in the last 100 years' in *Current Problems in Surgery*, Vol. 54, No. 6, June 2017

P.A. Crocker, 'Some Thoughts on The Royal Welch Fusiliers in the Great War' in *Y Ddraig Goch – Journal of The Royal Welch Fusiliers*, September 2002

Llewelyn Wyn Griffith, 'The Pattern of One Man's Remembering' in *Promise of Greatness* (George A. Panichas ed.) (London, 1968)

Holger Herwig, 'War in the West, 1914–1916' in John Horne (ed.), *A Companion to World War One* (Cambridge, 2010)

T.M. Holmes, 'Absolute Numbers: The Schlieffen Plan as a Critique of German Strategy in 1914'. *War in History,* No. 21 (April 2014)

John Hussey, 'Portrait of a Commander-in-Chief', in Brian Bond and Nigel Cave (eds.) *Haig: A Reappraisal 80 Years On* (London, 1998)

Siegfried Sassoon, 'Fight to a Finish', *Cambridge Magazine,* 27 October 1917

Chris Williams, 'A Question of "Legitimate Pride"? The 38th (Welsh) Division at the Battle of Mametz Wood, July 1916' in *Welsh History Review*, No. 28/4 (2017)

Chris Williams, 'Taffs in the Trenches: Welsh national identity and military service, 1914–1918' in Matthew Cragoe and Chris Williams (eds.), *Wales and War: Society, Politics and Religion in the Nineteenth and Twentieth Centuries* (Cardiff, 2007)

Newspapers

Caernarvon and Denbigh Herald
Cambria Daily Leader
Daily Mail
Daily Mirror
Daily News

Daily Post and Mercury (Liverpool)
Daily Telegraph
Economist
Llandudno Advertiser,
London Gazette
Manchester Guardian
The Spectator
The Times
Sunday Telegraph
Welsh Outlook
Western Mail
Wrexham Advertiser
Y Dinesydd Cymreig

German

Primary Sources

***Reichsarchiv Militär-Verlag,* Berlin**
S. 71 (1927) *Geschichte de Lehr-Infanterie-Regiment und seiner Stammformationen.*

***Militärarchiv, Deutsche Bundesarchiv,* Dresden**
N44/2 Wild Nachlass
PH3/607 *Nachrichtenabteilung West*, Report dated 14 November 1915
W10/51523; W10/51318

***Bayerisches Hauptstaatsarchiv – Kriegsarchiv,* Munich**
Die Bayern im Grossen Kriege 1914–1918 (Bayerischer Kriegsarchiv, Munich, 1923)
PH3 Catalogue Band 5, 16th Bavarian Infantry Regiment: 555 AOK 2, January–July 1916
HS 2106, *Tagebuchaufzeichnungen von Dr. H. Gareis s. Z. Vizefeldwebel in 1/16 Infanterie-Regiment.*
Generalstab 18, 14. Abteilung, 'Denkschrift über die Festung Verdun,' 1910
3rd Battalion 16th Bavarian Infantry Regiment, *Garde-Infanterie-Division I.*
16. Inf. Regt. (WK) 3, *Bericht über den Gefechtstag Bayr. 16.Inf.R. am 14.7.1916*, account of
   Oberstleutnant Bedall as transcribed by Dr Eber on 22 November 1916.

Landesarchiv Baden-Württemberg, Hauptstaatsarchiv Stuttgart
M411 band 2594, Reserve-Infanterie-Regiment Nr. 122 Kreigtagebuch 11. April-31 Juli 1916
M1/11 Bü 127, Reserve-Infanterie-Regiment Nr. 122 Mai 1915–Oktober 1916 [official account
   of actions]
M1/11 Bü 462, Reserve-Infanterie-Regiment Nr. 122 an der Westfront 1915–1917
M110, Bü 127, Reserve-Infanterie-Regiment Nr. 122 various papers

Printed Contemporary Sources

The Assault. War Experiences of a front-line Officer (Hauptmann v. Brandis of 24 Infantry Regiment)
Published by the Chief of the General Staff of the Field Army, 15 September 1917

Published Sources

Major Eduard Bachelin, *Das Reserve-Infanterie-Regiment Nr. 111 in Weltkrieg 1914 bis 1918* (Karlsruhe, n.d.)

Hermann Cron, *Imperial German Army 1914–18: Organisation, Structure, Orders-of-Battle* (Solihull, 2006)

Hermann Cron et al, *Die 26 Reserve Division 1914–1918* (Stuttgart, 1920)

Erich von Falkenhayn, *General Headquarters, 1914–1916 and its Critical Decisions* (London, 2009)

Fritz Fischer, *Germany's Aims in the First World War* (English translation of *Griff nach der Weltmacht*, Düsseldorf, 1967)

Matteus Gerster, *Das Württembergische Res. Inf. Regt. Nr 119 im Weltkrieg 1914–1918* (Stuttgart, 1920)

J. von Hansch & F. Weidling, *Das Colbergsche Grenadier-Regiment Graf Gneisenau (2. Pommersches) Nr. 9 im Weltkriege 1914–1918* (Berlin, 1929)

Dr Armin Hase, *Das 17 Königleichten Sachsen Infanterie Regiment Nr 183* (Dresden, 1922)

Georg von Holtz, Das *Württembergische Res. Inf. Regt. Nr 121 im Weltkrieg 1914–1918* (Stuttgart, 1920)

Leutnant des Reserve A.D. dolf Kümmel, *Res.-Inf-Regt. Nr 91 im Weltkriege 1914–1918* (Berlin, 1926)

General der Infanterie z.V. Fritz von Loßberg, *Meine Tätigkeit im Weltkriege 1914–1918* (Berlin, 1939).

Hauptmann Ernst Freiherr von Lutz, *Das Königlich. bayerische 16. Infanterie-Regiment Großherzog Ferdinand von Toscana in Kriege 1914–1918* (Passau, 1920)

Paul Mühlmann und Wilhelm Möhs, *Geschichte de Lehr-Infanterie-Regiment und seiner Stammformationen* (Stuttgart, 1931)

Ernst Mügge, *Das Württembergische Reserve-Infanterie-Regiment im Nr.122 im Weltkrieg 1914–1918* (Belserche Derlagsbuchhandlung, Stuttgart, 1922)

Ernst Neumann, *Vierzig Monate Westfront : Geschichte des Infanterie-Regiments 184, Teil 1: 1915–1916* (Berlin, 1934)

G. Pfeffer, *Geschichte des Infanterie-Regiments 186* (Berlin, 1926).

Major Karl Roth, *Das K.B. Reserve-Infanterie-Regiment N.23* (München, 1927)

H. Ritter, *Geschichte des Schleswig-Holsteinschen Infanterie-Regiment Nr. 163* (Hamburg, n.d.)

Crown Prince Rupprecht of Bavaria, *In Treue Fest: Mein Kriegstagebuch, Vols. I and II* (Munich, 1929)

Generalmajor a.D. Carl Graf von der Schulenburg-Wolfsburg, *Geschichte des Garde-Fusilier-Regiments*, Preuß. Anteil, Band 157 (Berlin, 1926)

Franz *Freiherr* von Soden, *Die 26. (Württembergische) Reserve-Division im Weltkrieg 1914–1918, I. Teil* (Stuttgart, 1939)

George Soldan, *Das Infanterie-Regiment Nr. 184* (Berlin, 1920)

Gerhardt Stalling, *Deutsche Reichsarchiv, Schlaten des Weltkrieges* (Berlin, 1930), '*Anlage zu Band 20, Pt I, Somme-Nord*'

A. Stosch, *Somme Nord, Die Brennpunkte der Schlacht im Juli 1916, Druck und Verlag von Berhard Stalling*, (Berlin, 1927)

Herbert Sulzbach (tr Richard Thonger), *Zwei lebender Mauern* English edition, (London, 1931)

Hermann Wendt, *Verdun 1916* (Berlin, 1931)

Oberstleutnant d.R.a.D. Rektor Alfred Wohlenburg, *Das Reserve-Infanterie-Regiment Nr. 77 im Weltkriege 1914–1918* (Hildesheim, 1931)

Electronic Sources

Sir Iain Colquhoun's Diary <www.valeofleven.org.uk>

Robert T. Foley, 'A New Form of Warfare? Erich von Falkenhayn's Plan for Victory in 1916' <https://kclpure.kcl.ac.uk/portal/files/10060338/Foley_1916_New_Warfare.pdf>

Graham Watson, *1914 Indian Army Order of Battle* <http://www.orbat.info>

1914–1918 Online <http://www.1914-1918-online.net/>

Measuring Worth <www.measuringworth.com>

Roads to the Great War: The German Experience at the Battle of the Somme <http://roadsto-thegreatwar-ww1.blogspot.co.uk/2013/07/the-german-experience-at-battle-of-somme.html>

Soldiers Died in the Great War <www.forces-war-records.co.uk>

CEF Study Group – Orders and Medals Society of America <https//http://ww1weatherreports.wikifoundry.com/page/Somme>

Index

People

Adams, Bernard 116, 147, 160, 324
Albrecht, *Hauptmann* 255
Allenby, Sir Edmund 92
Angus, James 194
Anthony, P. 57, 243
ap Rhys Pryce, H.E. 55, 58, 187, 189, 191, 207, 291
Asquith, Herbert 22, 27, 32, 125
Atkinson, E.H. de V. 55, 308

Ballard, J.A. 58, 110, 243, 244
Barne, Miles 125
Bell, R.C. 57, 110, 236, 238, 251
Bedall, *Oberstleutnant* A. 227, 253, 256, 277, 278, 294, 300
Behr, *Leutnant* 253, 254
Below, Fritz von 76, 78, 80-81, 82, 165, 166
Bennett, T.E. 56
Benson, H.W. 57
Bently, H.R. 56, 308
Bethmann-Hollweg, Theobald von 63
Blackader, C.G. 55, 212-213, 292
Blacker, Carlos 118, 122
Bloor, D.W. 137
Bond, C. 57, 238, 240
Bonham-Carter, A.L.B. 218
Boraston, J.H. 288-289, 291
Borchers, *Leutnant* 254
Boss, *Leutnant* 201
Boston, Lord 39
Bowen, A.P. 57, 304
Bowen, I. 57
Bowintel, P. 255
Bowyer, S. 55
Brace, William 33
Bradshaw, John 41-42, 114, 120
Brennan, G. 235
Brusilov, Aleksei 69, 82, 95
Brynmor-Jones, David 33
Burrell, R.E. 55

Carden, R.J. 57, 211, 231, 232, 233, 240, 308
Clarke, Lieutenant 244, 304, 305
Colquhoun, Sir Iain 123-125
Compton-Smith, G. 279
Cory, F.H. 56
Cowie, H. 234
Cracroft, R.B. 244
Crawshay, C.H.R. ('Tibs') 57, 280, 281, 282
Cundall, H.J. 57, 205

Dadd, Edmund 155, 160
Dadd, James 279
Dagge, Captain 232
Darhroeben, von Humboldt 253
Davies, David, Lord Davies 10, 57, 141-142
Davies, Emlyn 42, 45, 110, 111, 112, 113, 136, 187, 193, 236, 247, 249, 259
Davies, H. 307
Davies, J.E. 42
Davies, J.E.H. 56
Davies, J.J. 308
Davies, J.T. 306
Davies, Reginald 194
Davies, T.H. 306
Denicke, *Leutnant* 77
Derby, Lord (Edward Stanley) 34, 52, 92
Dewar, G. 288
Dietz, *Oberstleutnant* 254
Diffey, Harold 124
Downes, I. 137
Drake-Brockman, G.P.L. 48, 141, 142, 218, 289, 291, 292
Dreyer, *Oberleutnant* 254
Dunn, J.C. 292, 324
Dunn, R.H.W. 45, 56, 57, 110

Eber, Dr 278
Edwards, C. 306
Edwards, D.A. 57
Edwards, J.E. 57

Edwards, G. d'A. 57, 232
Edwards, W.G. 56
Eid, *Hauptmann* 254
Esebeck, Major *Freiherr* von 254
Evans, D.A. 308
Evans, E. 305
Evans, Ellis Humphrey (Hedd Wyn) 111-112
Evans, F. St H. 282
Evans, F.W. 58
Evans, H.E. 305
Evans, Horatio 47, 58, 189-193, 196-197,
    198-200, 202, 203, 204, 259-263, 265, 267
Evans, J. 304
Evans, L.P. 307
Evans, Noel 40
Evans, P. 57
Evans, P.F. 308
Evans, Sir Vincent 35
Evers, *Leutnant* 254

Falkenhayn, Erich von 63-68, 69-70, 78. 80-82,
    105, 106, 107, 165, 273, 279
Felstead, Bertie 120, 122
Fincht, *Leutnant* 254
Fisher, H.F.T. 56
Flower, C.S. 46, 56, 57, 241, 242, 248
Fox-Pitt, William 35, 45, 57, 111
Frankenberg-Lütwitz, *Hauptmann* von 253
Franz, *Hauptmann* von 253
French, Sir John 25, 91, 101, 111
Fuchs, Arnold 153

Gaja, Major von 255
Gardner, F. 306
Gardner, J. 55
Gardner, L.C. 305
Gaskell, Frank 37, 58, 138
Gaussen, J.R. 58, 260, 262, 266, 309, 181, 247
Gauter, Karl 255
Gibson, Lance-Corporal (a.k.a. Kendle) 161
Gifford, W. 57
Girndt, Ernst 153
Godfrey, L.G. 253
Gossett, E. 241, 262, 263, 265
Grant-Dalton, D. 55
Graves, Robert 17, 36, 44, 111, 118, 125, 136,
    151, 161, 228, 236, 281, 282, 298, 325
Greaves, Edward 160, 279
Greenwood, Hamar, Lord Greenwood 40, 58, 189
Greiner, *Leutnant* 255
Griffith, E. 306
Griffith, Ellis 39
Griffiths, J.C. 304
Griffiths, W.C. 308

Grünert, Paul 165
Gwyther, G.H. 57, 142, 210, 212, 233, 234, 238
Gwynne, W.P. 56, 271

Haig, Sir Douglas 91, 92, 93, 95-100, 104, 106,
    118, 125, 158, 166, 169, 209, 212, 213, 238,
    250-251, 290, 295, 297
Haking, Sir Richard 48, 126, 281
Hamer, Thomas Pryce 196
Hampe, *Oberleutnant* 255
Hardwick, H.W. 57, 248, 265
Harris, Charles 194
Harris, Henry 192
Hase, *Hauptmann* von 255
Hauscheld, Robert 158
Hayes, J.H. 57, 234, 238, 243, 308
Hayes-Sheen, T. 56
Hawkins, F.J. 232
Hayward, G.W. 55
Head, C.O. 55, 224
Heathcock, T. 244
Heeson, J. 137, 305
Herbert, Ivor, Lord Treowen 33
Hetschold, *Gefreiter* 240
Hindenburg, Paul von 64, 65, 66
Hinton, Harold 58, 198
Hohenborn, Adolph Wild von 67
Holloway, E.L. 57
Holmes, William 151
Horne, Sir Henry 48, 98, 141, 172, 190, 202, 204,
    209, 211, 212, 213, 217, 251, 268, 289, 290,
    291, 292, 293
Hosang, *Leutnant* von 254

Jachman, Major 253, 254
Jacob, Sir Claude 141
Job, E.D. 58, 189, 197, 266
Joffre, Joseph 69, 81, 90, 92, 93, 95, 96, 106, 161
Jones, A.L. 304
Jones, C. 281
Jones, David 35, 43, 49, 111, 113, 115, 122, 136,
    140, 236, 238, 241, 242, 250, 298, 326
Jones, G.P. 137, 305
Jones, H. 306
Jones, J. 305, 307
Jones, J. Brynmor 33
Jones, J.G. 304
Jones, J. Glynn 219, 233, 234, 236, 238, 240, 263,
    268, 308
Jones, J.R. 304
Jones, Llewellyn 305
Jones, R.E.
Jones, R.T. 33, 192
Jones, R.W. 307

Jones, T.C. 306
Jones, Thomas 39
Jones, W.H. 308
Jones, W.T. 307, 308
Josesofski, *Unteroffizier* 301
Joshua, William 194, 197

Kaufmann, *Leutnant* 275
Keating, Robert 122-124
Kelly, D.V. 282, 290
Kendle, see Gibson
Kenyon, Lord 33
Kessler, O. 256
Kiggell, Sir Launcelot 105, 169, 204, 209, 289
Killermann, O. 256
King, G.C. 244
King, L.R. 57
Kirkwood, J.R.N. 56
Kitchener, Lord 26-28, 34, 36, 37, 38, 39, 52, 91, 95, 105, 142, 297
Kirchner, Felix 153
Koch, *Leutnant* 229, 244
Köhler, *Hauptmann* 255
Köstlin, *Leutnant* 214, 229, 231, 243, 244, 250
Kleist, Major von 253
Kreibohm, *Unteroffizier* G. 231
Kreigsheim, Major von 242, 248, 254, 275
Kriger, *Leutnant* von 253
Kumme, *Oberstleutnant* 254, 280
Kummetz, *Leutnant* 242, 247, 248

Lakemaker, Oswald 153
Lamonby, I.W. 56
Langdon, F. 137, 305
Leffe, *Leutnant* 254
Lenser, *Leutnant* 254
Lettow-Vorbecht, Major von 254
Leyshon, Ernest 194
Lloyd, Sir Francis 33
Lloyd George, David 32, 35, 36, 39, 40, 42, 47, 48, 49, 53, 111, 113, 142, 213, 288, 291, 292, 298
Lloyd George, Gwilym 41, 42, 48, 213
Lloyd George, Richard 41, 42, 48
Lossberg (Loßberg), Fritz von 81, 165, 166
Ludendorff, Erich 64, 65, 297
Ludwig, *Hauptmann* 201, 214, 240, 254
Lutz, *Hauptmann* Ernst *Freiherr* von 256
Lyons, R. 234

Macdonald, Captain 237
McKenna, Reginald 33
Mackinnon, Sir Henry 34, 49, 51
McLellan, J.R.H. 232

Marburg, *Unteroffizier* 201
Marden, T.O. 57, 110, 194, 217, 219, 238, 243, 247, 251, 252, 297, 308, 327
Marschall, F. 256
Marsh, Edward 161
Mills-Roberts, R.H. 56
Minshull Ford, J. 149, 155
Moltke, Helmut von, the Younger 61
Montgomery, Sir Archibald 106, 212, 213
Morgan, Charles 196
Morgan, E.T. 307
Morgan, F.T. 55, 309
Morgan, G. 279
Morgan, John 153, 155, 156
Morgan, N.M. 308
Morgan, W. 306
Morgan, W.M. 305
Mostyn, Llewelyn, Lord 33
Mostyn, H.R.H. Lloyd 58, 110, 189
Müller, H. 255
Mühlman, Major von 253, 254

Neville, R. 189
Niehoff, *Leutnant* 254
Niemeyer, *Hauptmann* 255
Nivelle, Robert 69
Noel, K.E. 58

Oliver, Albert 196
Oliver, Ernest 196
Oliver, T.T. 308
Osbourne-Jones, Noel 41, 137
Ostermener, *Leutnant* 254
Otto, Major 255
Owen, F. 305
Owen, Goronwy 136, 137, 304
Owen, O.W. 33, 55

Packe, F.E. 57
Paget, V. 40
Pannewitz, Günther von 86, 165, 286
Parkinson, T.W. 57
Parvus, Alexander 69
Paterson, P.J. 55, 308
Pearson, C.A. 38, 55
Pearson, J. 305
Perriman, Sergeant 204
Pétain, Philippe 69, 81, 95
Pfeiffer, *Leutnant* 240, 254
Philipps, Sir Ivor 45, 47, 48, 49, 55, 58, 142, 190, 200, 202, 209, 211, 212, 213, 217, 218-219, 291, 292
Pilcher, Thomas 188, 202, 212, 213, 290, 291
Plessen, Hans von 65

Plumer, Sir Herbert 92
Porter, H.E. 58, 189
Posse, R. 201
Price, T.J. 197
Price-Davies, Ll. A.E. 56, 110, 111, 125, 133,
    137, 141, 189, 210, 211, 212, 217, 219, 224, 240,
    241, 243, 247, 249, 251, 252, 257, 293
Pringle, H.G. 55, 308
Pryce, H.E. ap Rhys 55, 187, 191, 218, 247, 291
Pryce-Jones, H.M. 55, 308
Psister, A. 256
Pudner, T. 236, 306

Rauchenberger, *Ritter* Otto von 274
Rauchhaupt, *Hauptmann* von 275
Rahman, Major 214, 255
Ratzmer, *Oberleutnant* von 253, 254
Rawlinson, Sir Henry 93, 96, 97, 98, 100,
    106-107, 109, 173, 205, 209, 212, 250, 273, 290
Rede, *Leutnant* 354
Rees, G.H. 305
Rees, R.G. 242
Rees-Jones, J. 237, 304
Reeves, Brian 156, 279
Reiche, *Hauptmann* von 254
Reinhard, *Hauptmann* 254
Reiss, Major von 255
Reithe, *Hauptmann* 253
Reitz, F. von 256
Ricketts, P.E. 57, 234, 240
Roberts, E.E. 36
Roberts, Glyn 283
Roberts, J.R. 306
Roberts, Rev P.J. 283
Roberts, R.J.A. 304
Roberts, W. 57
Robertson, Sir William 91, 95
Rohbeiter, *Leutnant* von 254
Rosenegt, Ridisch von 253
Rosser, A. 249
Rosser, F.T. 137, 305
Rudkin, W.C.E. 55, 308
Rupprecht, Crown Prince of Bavaria 76, 78, 80,
    81, 82, 165, 296

St David's, Lord 48
Sassoon, Siegfried 111, 117-118, 136, 151, 153,
    156, 158, 160, 161-162, 173, 175, 281, 288,
    293, 298, 328
Schauroth, *Hauptmann* von 254, 263
Scherer, T. 182, 256
Schluga, August 66-67
Schmeling, *Unteroffizier* von 201
Schwarz, Richard 155

Scobie, M.J.G. 57
Sebersen, *Hauptmann* von 254
Seelhorst, Major von 254
Seidel, *Oberleutnant* 244
Seitz, M. 256
Seymour, Lord Henry 124
Sicht, *Obetsleutnant* 255
Simons, R.J. 46, 56
Smith, C. 279
Smith, F.W. 58, 138, 189, 297, 265
Smith, H.M. 281
Soden, Fritz von 85, 166
Soder, E. 256
Soldan, G. 255
Stadebacher, Rudolf 204
Stein, Hermann von 78, 82, 85, 249, 263, 267,
    286
Steinau-Steinrud, W. Von 255
Stevens, Robert 155, 156, 160
Stevenson, Frances
Strange, J.S. 243, 304
Stroh, H. 182, 256
Stockwell, C.I. 116, 151, 153, 155, 156, 158, 159,
    160, 161, 162, 275, 278, 279, 280
Stork, C.H. 236, 304
Sykes, H.E. 56

Taggart, Herbert 137
Taylor, A. 58, 190, 191, 197, 265, 283
Thomas, D. 307, 308
Thomas, E.B. 308
Thomas, G.A. 305
Thomas, J.M. 307
Taylor, T.T. 305
Thomas, Sir Owen 38-39, 42, 45, 48-49, 56,
    110-111
Thomas, Richard 194, 196
Thomas, W.R. 141, 183, 210, 227, 228, 234
Thompson, F. 236, 304, 305
Thompson, W.A.M. 55, 197, 308
Thynne, U.O. 55
Tighe, F.A. 55
Tregaskis, Arthur 194, 196
Tregaskis, Leonard 194, 196
Tschirhaus, *Hauptmann* von 253, 297
Tucker, W.A. 35, 42, 50, 111, 136, 138, 328

Umann, Major von 253, 254
Umpfreville, Major 46, 57

Veal, Charles 46, 58, 190, 196, 197, 260, 261,
    265
Venables, A.V. 233
Voight, *Oberstleutnant* 254

Wahlen, *Unteroffizier* 231
Wald, A. 255
Walter, *Grenadier* 158
Watts, Herbert 55, 150, 151, 213, 218, 224, 243, 251, 262, 268, 275, 289, 292-293
Watts, Sir W. 57
Weede, *Hauptmann* 255
Weisse, *Hauptmann* 255
Weiterer, *Leutnant* 254
Wellhausen, *Leutnant* 254
Werner, *Leutnant* 255
Westbrooke, G.C. 233
Wilhelm II, Kaiser 61, 64, 65, 66, 79, 80, 184
Willes, C.E. 55, 57
Williams, A.J. 306
Williams, D. Llewellyn 56
Williams, Harry 251
Williams, Howard 153, 155, 160
Williams, H. Lloyd 292
Williams, H.P. 138
Williams, J.H. 305, 309
Williams, John 194
Williams, M. 56
Williams, Milbourne 232

Willimas, O.M. 136
Williams, R. 307
Williams, W. 305
Williams, W.B. 306
Wilson, J.A. 232, 304
Wilson-Jones, T.R., 305
Windsor-Clive, Robert, Earl of Plymouth 33
Witten, P.F. 137, 305
Wittig, *Leutnant* von 254
Wölsl, J. 256
Wyn Griffith, Llewelyn 21, 41, 44, 47, 58, 99, 110, 111, 113, 114, 118, 120-121, 122, 124, 126, 129, 133, 136, 137, 140, 190, 192, 193, 199, 100, 259, 260, 262, 265, 268, 283, 293, 298, 325
Wyn Griffith, Watcyn 45, 265
Wynne-Edwards, T.A. 57

Yorke, D. 249, 304, 309

Zeppelin, Major Herman von 231, 244, 245, 246, 255
Zippelskichen, *Oberst* von 254
Zschwimmer, *Leutnant* 255
Zukow, Alfred von 255

Places

Abergavenny 46, 50
Acheux 141
Aire 113
Arras 81, 93, 97
Auchy 136

Bapaume 97, 141, 183, 226, 288
Bazentin cemetery 284, 285
Bazentin Ridge 169, 173, 174, 273, 274, 275, 280, 288, 290, 291, 293
Bazentin village 70, 83, 144, 180, 261, 262, 269, 274, 275, 277, 278
Beaumont Hamel 74, 85, 98, 153
Béthune 138
Blaenau Ffestiniog 39
Brecon 33, 312, 313

Caernarvon 36, 41
Cambrai 97, 185
Cardiff 33, 34, 37-38, 39, 42, 138, 196, 314, 315
Carnoy 156, 189, 192
Chantilly 90, 91, 92
Colwyn Bay 42, 45
Contalmaison 70, 85, 144, 148, 153, 169, 172, 174, 175, 183, 185, 188, 191, 205, 209, 214, 218, 224, 229-230, 249, 250, 260, 284, 289

Douai 97

Festubert 129, 133
Flers 97, 185
Frelinghien 116
Fricourt village 80, 82, 85, 98, 144, 147, 153, 155, 156, 158, 162, 165, 166, 169, 185, 280, 289, 295, 296
Fromelles 126, 138

Givenchy 113, 129, 135, 136, 280
Gommecourt 78, 80, 81, 84, 98, 100, 274
Grandcourt 100
Grove Town, Grovetown – see Meaulte

Happy Valley 172, 233
Hébuterne 92, 95
Heilly 162, 251, 282

Kinmel Park 51, 52, 298, 311, 313, 314, 315, 316

Lassigny 92
Laventie 118, 119, 120, 125, 136
Leipzig Redoubt 98
Llandudno 39, 42, 45, 48, 49

Longueval 144, 169, 174, 180, 273, 274, 275, 283, 284

Mametz village 82, 85, 98, 141, 142, 143, 144-149
Maricourt 95, 97
Meaulte (Grove Town) 219
Minden Post 198
Miraumont 97
Monchy le Preux 97
Morlancourt 198
Montauban 98, 100, 144, 158, 174, 175, 189, 192, 215, 244

Neuve Chapelle 129, 131, 138, 140
Noyon 78

Ovillers 74, 80, 98, 166, 175, 185, 294

Péronne 93
Picantin 113, 129
Pommiers Redoubt 190, 192, 199
Portmadoc 50
Pozières 70, 74, 85, 97, 98, 180, 185, 214, 263
Prestatyn 50
Pwllheli 50

Queen's Nullah 175, 179, 189, 211, 219, 224, 226, 249

Rancourt 97
Richebourg l'Avoué 130, 132
Richebourg St Vaast 129
Rubempre 141
Rivers
    Ancre 78, 147
    Scharpe 93
    Scheldt 93
    Somme 70, 78, 80, 81, 82, 86, 92, 93, 147, 165, 286
Rhondda Valley 35, 39
Rhyl 35, 39, 42, 45, 311, 312, 315

St Pol 141
St Venant 114
Salisbury Plain 50-51, 310, 313, 314
Schwaben Redoubt 98, 153
Serre 74, 78, 97, 98, 100, 200, 324
Shrapnelmulde 174, 229, 263
Shrewsbury 33, 46
Stuff Redoubt 98

Theipval 85, 97, 98, 147, 166
Trenches
    Apple Alley 144, 155

Bois Français 144, 147, 149, 155, 162
Bottom Alley 158, 160
Caterpillar 189, 198
Circus 279
Danzig Alley 155, 187, 189, 211
Fritz 187, 189
Kaisergraben 175, 229
Loop 189, 190
Middle Alley 201, 224, 242, 243, 248, 261, 264, 266
Montauban Alley 189, 190, 191
Orchard Alley 144, 155
Quadrangle 158, 159, 160, 161, 166, 183, 187, 289
Quadrangle Alley 160, 187, 188, 233, 244
Quadrangle Support 188, 192, 201, 213, 214, 218, 219, 229, 244, 250
Rectangle, The 155, 156
Rectangle Support 155
Strip 158, 175, 188, 205, 210, 211, 212, 217, 222, 224, 234, 241, 242, 289
Sunken Road   124, 125, 155, 156
White 187, 189, 190, 211, 217, 219, 222, 224, 232, 277, 289
Willow Avenue 144
Wing Corner 156
Wood 158, 159, 160, 161, 166, 175, 182, 188, 205, 210, 229, 233, 236, 238, 282, 289
Zinc 155
Triangle Post 189, 198, 199
Treux 141, 268

Verdun 67-70, 78, 80, 82, 93, 95-96, 165, 273, 295, 297

Winchester 50, 113
Woods
    Acid Drop Copse 169, 172, 174, 175, 187-188, 244
    Bailliff 173
    Bazentin le Grand 169, 174, 274, 293
    Bazentin le Petit 169, 174, 263, 273, 274, 275, 277, 279, 284, 290, 293
    Bernafray 158
    Bottom 144, 159, 172, 174, 187
    Caftet 189
    Caterpillar Copse 158, 172, 174, 175, 176, 177, 178, 187, 189, 190, 191, 192, 193, 196, 197, 198, 199, 205, 218, 219, 224, 260
    Delville 144, 293
    Flatiron Copse 174, 175, 178, 182, 185, 187, 191, 194, 196, 197, 201, 202, 205, 222, 229, 240, 242, 260, 265
    Fricourt 144, 147

Hammerhead (part of Mametz) 174, 178, 179, 183, 188, 190, 196, 202, 222, 223, 224, 231, 232, 239, 240, 242, 247, 248, 249, 260, 266, 268, 278

Hidden 144

Mametz 102, 143, 158-161, 166, 169-273, 288-298

Mansell Copse 155

Marlborough 172, 174, 176, 178, 187, 189, 205, 224

Railway Copse 144, 187

Sabot Copse 174, 175, 178, 182, 185, 187, 191, 194, 196, 197, 201, 202, 205, 222, 229, 240, 242, 260, 265

Trônes 169, 172, 209, 252, 283, 284, 293

Wrexham 33, 310, 311, 312

Ypres 25, 45, 61, 63, 65, 78, 93, 106, 329

Military Formations and Units

British

Armies
First 138
Second 133
Third 100, 141, 312
Fourth 93, 97-98, 102, 104, 105, 169, 172, 213, 241, 250, 273, 290

Corps
II 100, 141
III 98, 144, 172, 205, 250, 289
VII 100, 104
VIII 98, 99
X 98, 99, 130
XI 91, 113, 126, 129, 133
XIII 98, 99, 144, 172, 187
XV 48, 98, 141, 151, 166, 172, 187, 189, 192, 193, 199, 202, 205, 209, 251, 277, 289, 290, 291

Divisions
1st Cavalry 100
2nd Cavalry 100
3rd Cavalry 100
2nd Indian Cavalry 100
3rd Infantry 282, 310
7th Infantry 25, 142-143, 149, 150, 165, 203, 213, 218, 222, 251, 265, 268, 275, 280, 289, 293
8th Infantry 30
9th (Scottish) 282
12th (New Army) 100
17th (Northern) 159, 175, 187, 192, 193, 197, 202, 205, 210, 212, 213, 218, 219, 224
18th (Eastern) 187
19th (Western) 98, 113, 114, 125, 126, 129, 133, 252, 282, 283, 310
21st (New Army) 98, 144, 153, 187, 218, 265, 268, 269, 273, 282, 301
23rd (New Army) 218, 250, 187

25th (New Army) 100
26th Infantry 87
28th Infantry 87
29th Infantry 91
31st (New Army) 98, 107, 108
33rd (New Army) 136, 280, 281
34th (New Army) 98, 107
35th (New Army) 107, 108, 133
36th (Ulster) 98
37th (New Army) 30, 100, 107
40th (New Army) 30, 52, 107, 108
43rd (Welsh) 30, 47
46th (North Midland) 30, 108
48th Infantry 100
49th (West Riding) 98
56th (London) 100, 107, 108
68th (2nd Welsh) 33, 34, 53, 319, 323

Brigades
South Wales Mounted 34, 318
Welsh Border Mounted 34, 318
20 Infantry 144, 151, 153, 155, 156, 275, 277
22 Infantry 144, 151, 155, 156, 275, 277, 279
50 Infantry 155
52 Infantry 201
62 Infantry 269
91 Infantry 144, 155, 158
113 (North Wales) 49, 110, 114, 125, 126, 187, 189, 190, 202, 205, 210-213, 217-219, 224, 231, 233, 236, 241, 243-244, 248, 251, 292, 299, 301
114 Infantry 49, 57, 110, 114, 125, 187, 190, 201, 217-219, 224, 231-232, 242-243, 251-252, 260, 270, 297, 299, 301
115 Infantry 47, 50, 58, 125-126, 187, 189-192, 195, 199-202, 205, 218-219, 243, 260, 265-266, 268, 270, 299, 301
119 Bantam 52

Regiments
3rd Dragoon Guards 33, 318

12th Lancers 33, 318
Monmouthshires 33
Welsh Guards 33, 318
Wiltshire Yeomanry 47, 55

Artillery Brigades and Batteries
35 Brigade 159, 265
101 Brigade 252
119 Brigade 55, 271, 299, 304
120 Brigade 55, 224, 271, 299
121 Brigade 50, 224, 271, 299
122 Brigade 55, 265, 271, 299
38th Heavy Battery 55, 265, 271, 299

Engineer companies
123 Field 56, 218, 229, 271
124 Field 46, 56, 190, 210, 271, 299
151 Field 46, 48, 56, 189, 224, 271, 299, 301
215 Fortress 50, 56
38th Divisional Signal Company 46, 48, 55, 57, 191, 197, 226, 247, 265, 299, 319

Battalions
7 Northumberland Fusiliers 159, 160
12 Northumberland Fusiliers 268
13 Northumberland Fusiliers 268-269
2 R. Warwicks 149
1 Lincoln 268
9 Devons 155
7 E. Yorks 244
7 Yorks (Green Howards) 268
10 Yorks (Green Howards) 268
6 Leicesters 282

1 R.W. Fus 25, 29, 149-150, 153, 156, 158-160, 162-164, 275, 278-280, 284, 289, 318
2 R.W. Fus 280, 282, 318
9 R.W. Fus 282, 292
10 R.W. Fus 282
13 R.W. Fus (1st North Wales Pals) 56, 187, 189, 211, 236, 241, 247-248, 265, 270, 299, 301
14 R.W. Fus 40, 57, 129, 133, 138, 141, 162, 187, 189, 210-212, 231, 233-234, 236,236, 238, 240, 242, 247-248, 265, 270, 299, 301
15 R.W. Fus (1st London Welsh) 35-36, 110, 111, 114, 118, 120-124, 136, 187, 189, 190, 192, 205, 210, 236, 241, 249, 270, 299, 301
16 R.W. Fus 57, 113-114, 142, 187, 189, 190, 189, 193, 199, 205, 243-244, 247-248, 260, 263,266, 299, 301
17 R.W. Fus (2nd North Wales Pals) 45, 58, 110, 114, 187, 189, 190, 193, 199, 205, 243-244, 247-248, 260, 263, 266, 299, 301
18 R.W. Fus (2nd London Welsh) 48, 52

19 R.W. Fus (Bantam) 48
20 R.W. Fus 51
21 R.W. Fus 51
22 R.W. Fus 51

1 S.W.B. 33, 318
2 S.W.B. 33, 318
5 S.W.B. 282
10 S.W.B. (1st Gwent) 40, 42, 58, 114, 190, 197, 198-199, 203, 224, 243, 247-249, 260, 263, 266, 268, 270, 299, 301
11 S.W.B. (2nd Gwent) 58, 114, 189-191, 194, 196-197, 203-204, 247, 260, 263, 266, 270, 299
12 S.W.B. 48
13 S.W.B. 52
17 S.W.B. 51

6 Dorsets 244, 247

1 Welsh 25, 142, 318
2 Welsh 25, 318
9 Welsh 282-283
10 Welsh (Rhondda) 57, 138, 190, 234, 236, 240, 243, 248, 251, 270, 299, 301
13 Welsh (Cardiff City) 37, 42
14 Welsh (Swansea) 35, 238, 252
15 Welsh (Carmarthenshire) 42, 44, 190, 242-243, 247, 267, 299, 301, 314
16 Welsh 46, 58, 136, 138, 189-191, 194, 196-199, 201, 203, 260, 263, 265-266, 269, 270, 299
19 Welsh (Pioneers) 47, 114, 189-190, 203, 210, 224, 247, 271, 299
21 Welsh 51
22 Welsh 52

20 Manchesters 149, 155
22 Manchesters 155
1 South Staffords 155
2 R. Irish 158 – 160, 175, 279, 289
2 Border 151
2 Gordon Highlanders 279

M.G. Companies
5 Motorised 57, 224, 304
113 57, 248, 270, 299
114 57, 270, 299
115 58, 266, 270, 299

Trench Mortar Batteries
113 57, 270, 299
114 57, 270, 299
115 58, 270, 299

Air Units (R.F.C.)
  9th (H.Q.) Wing 102
  Brigades
    IV 102
    VIII 104
  Squadrons
    1 (Kite Balloon) 102
    3 102, 103
    4 102, 103
    5 (Kite Balloon) 102
    8 104
    9 103
    15 102, 103
    21 102
    27 102
    60 102
    70 102

R.A.M.C. and Veterinary units
  129 Field Ambulance 46, 56, 271, 299
  130 (St John's) Field Ambulance 42, 45, 53, 56,
    198, 271, 299
  131 Field Ambulance 56, 271, 299
  No 5 Bacteriological Section 56
  49th Mobile Veterinary Section 56

Army Service Corps Companies
  330 Company 56, 271
  331 Company 56, 271
  332 Company 56, 271
  333 Company 56, 271

Cyclist Companies
  38th Division 50, 55, 187, 319

Transport Companies
  38th Divisional Company 56

German

Armies
  Second 76, 78, 80-82, 83-87, 102, 165, 166,
    273, 286
  Sixth 66, 76, 78, 80-82, 286

Corps
  Guards 78, 80
  IV 286
  VI Reserve 286
  IX 286
  X 98, 130
  XIV Reserve 78, 81, 82, 85, 144, 166, 249,
    286
  XVII 78, 80, 82, 141, 165, 166, 286

Gruppe
  von Arnim 286
  Gossler 286
  von Pannewitz 286
  von Quast 286
  von Stein 286

Divisions
  2nd Guards 81, 83, 130, 253, 273, 286
  3rd Guards 83, 166, 183, 185, 187, 253,
    273-274, 286, 294
  2nd Guards Reserve 81, 84, 130, 253, 273
  3rd Infantry 254, 273
  7th Infantry 273
  10th Bavarian 82, 84, 166, 181, 256
  11th Reserve Infantry 144
  12th Infantry 86
  12th Reserve Infantry 86
  15th *Landwehr* 86
  26th (Westphalian) Reserve Infantry 74, 82,
    85, 162, 166, 274, 286
  28th (Baden) Reserve Infantry 70, 82, 85,
    144, 152, 162, 165-166, 182, 183, 238, 249,
    286
  35th Infantry 86, 286
  36th Infantry 87, 286
  52nd Reserve Infantry 85, 286
  111th Infantry 84, 144, 183, 255
  183rd Reserve 85, 185, 226, 229, 253, 255, 273,
    286
  185th Infantry 274
  220th Infantry 274

Brigades
  6 Guards 83, 274
  20 Bavarian Infantry 87, 274

Battalions/Regiments
  I./ Guards Fusiliers 185, 229, 253, 263, 274,
    300
  II./ Guards Fusiliers 185, 253, 263, 266, 300
  III./ Guards Fusiliers 185, 253, 263, 300
  Recruit Company G.F.R. 274
  I./ 9 Grenadiers 185, 254, 263, 274, 300
  II./ 9 Grenadiers 185, 254, 263, 274, 300
  Fusilier/ 9 Grenadiers 185, 214, 229, 254, 273,
    300
  I./ *Lehr* 229, 263, 259, 263, 273, 300
  II./ *Lehr* 185, 226, 229, 240, 253, 254, 263,
    273, 273, 294, 300
  III. / *Lehr* 185, 214, 216, 231, 240, 254, 263,
    267, 273, 294, 300
  I/16th Bavarian 185, 226, 254, 274, 300
  II/16th Bavarian 185, 274, 300

III/16th Bavarian 166, 185, 226, 254, 263, 274, 279, 280, 274, 300
I./ 77th 254, 273, 300
II./ 77th 249, 253, 254, 263, 267, 273, 300
III./ 77th 249, 254, 300
I./ 91st 273, 254, 279, 280
I./ 110th 153, 165
II./ 110th 153, 162, 165
I./ 111th 162, 165
I./ 122nd 214, 229, 254, 229, 300
II./ 122nd 185, 214, 229, 229, 300
III./ 122nd 185, 214, 229, 300
I./ 163rd 301
II./ 163rd 183, 185, 254, 301
III./ 163rd 254, 301
I./ 165th 273
III./ 165th 254, 273
I./ 180th 274
I./ 183rd 185, 254, 301
II./ 183rd 185, 214, 254, 301
III./ 183rd 185, 214, 254, 301

I./ 184th 229, 254, 273, 301
II./ 184th 185, 226, 242, 247, 249, 253, 254, 263, 267, 273, 294, 301
III./ 184th 254, 301
III./ 186th 158, 165
I./ 190th 274
III./ 190th 190, 274

28th Pioneer Regiment 249, 253, 254, 263, 279

Military organisation (British):
    Battalion and below 40
    Brigade 45-46
    Division 47, 50, 55-58, 127
    Corps and Army 97, 102
Military organisation (German):
    Battalion and below 295
    Regiment 83-87, 254-256
    Brigade 83-87
    Division 83-87, 105, 254
    Corps and Army 85-87, 112, 286

General

Air power, Allied 104, 185, 215
Air power, German 69, 76
Allied situation and plans in 1915/1916 90-109, 144-146, 169-172
Artillery and mortars
    role and use of 45, 50, 70, 72, 74, 96, 98, 100, 101, 102-103, 106, 125-126, 141, 180, 187-189, 191, 197, 210, 222, 224, 231, 238, 240, 243, 247, 249, 262, 265, 281-282, 290, 292, 293-294
    types and calibres of 40, 45, 47, 50, 55, 199, 265, 271, 319, 321
    effectiveness of 67, 69, 101, 105, 106, 123, 133, 137, 153, 155, 159, 165, 192, 193-194, 197, 199, 210, 202, 204-205, 209, 214, 232-233, 234, 241-242, 252, 260, 266, 267, 273, 275
Artists and writers 111, 324-329
Attrition 67-69, 106, 107, 284

British Army strength and deployment in 1916 90-92, 107-108, 321-323
British Army manpower 21-22, 90-92

Casualties at Mametz
    British 133, 142, 145, 156, 160, 190, 196, 197, 198-199, 203, 204, 212, 230, 234, 238, 247, 266, 267, 281, 290, 299
    German 102, 212, 216, 230, 234, 278, 279, 280, 294, 295, 300-301

Casualty rates 52, 66, 90, 95, 295-296
Christmas Truces 1914, 1915 116-125
Communication
    Telephones 72, 81, 102, 105, 106, 137, 159, 165, 192, 193, 199, 200, 202, 226, 240, 243, 247, 265, 285, 291
    Wireless 81, 102, 159, 197, 199
    semaphore 226
    runner 40, 192, 193, 202, 211, 226, 238, 240, 265
Conditions of service
Conscription 21, 27, 63, 112, 316

Derby Scheme 34, 52, 92

Expeditionary Force (British) 21-30

Flame-throwers, *flammenwerfer* 69, 189, 266

German situation and plans in 1915/1916 61-89

Haldane Reforms 22

Intelligencence 48, 66, 67, 80, 82, 105, 180, 219, 226, 273

Lice and other pests 138
Logistics and supply
    British 47-48, 153, 214, 241
    German 101-102, 153, 214, 241

Machine guns
    allocation to units 70, 82, 101, 105, 140, 141
    effects of 67, 106, 204
    employment of in Mametz Wood
    German 155, 150, 161, 180, 182, 191, 192,
        193, 194, 199, 200, 201, 204, 205, 209, 214,
        232-233, 234, 242, 243, 244, 247, 248, 250,
        251, 253, 263, 266, 267
    British 187-188, 189, 197, 224, 229, 231
Mametz Wood
    descriptions of 169-171, 173-182, 234-235,
        260-261
    significance of169, 172, 180, 267, 268,
        289-293
    German defences in and around 175-186, 201,
        226-229, 232, 234, 264
Manpower bill for the war effort in Wales 34-35
Medical treatment in battle 42, 45, 104, 105, 149,
    155, 199, 260
Mines and mining 136, 152, 153, 280

Poets, poetry, poems of the battle of Mametz
    111-112, 122, 136, 156, 236, 242, 250, 298,
    324-329
Prisoners 25, 26, 35fn 61, 66, 76, 78, 80, 142, 152,
    153, 156, 2019, 212, 214, 217, 219, 234, 238,
    247, 252, 253, 260, 263, 266, 277, 280, 281,
    294-295, 301

Raids, raiding 76, 94, 116, 126, 136-138,
    210-212, 214, 281
Railways, railway lines 67, 80, 102, 104, 105, 144,
    158, 160, 172, 177, 188, 210, 220, 222, 241,
    248, 260, 263, 264, 267
Rations 104, 115, 117, 200, 219, 259fn, 274,
    275

Recruiting and Training organisation (British) 22,
    24, 25, 27, 34, 35-36, 37, 38, 51-52
Somme
    Assault on Mametz Wood, 7 July 169-207
    Assault on 8-9 July 209-215
    Assaults on 10, 11, 12 July 217-257, 259-270
    battlefield description 92-93, 94, 96, 97, 99
    Evaluation of the attacks on Mametz Wood
        212, 238, 250, 281, 284, 288-297
    First assault on Fricourt and Mametz, 3 – 5
        July 144-167
    German intelligence on 66, 76, 78, 80-81
    German reactions to the attacks 165-166, 167,
        249, 263
    Haig and the High Command's views on 158,
        169, 209, 212, 238, 281
    plans for the battle 92-97
    views of various commanders 99-100, 105-106

Tactics and innovation for trench warfare
    149-150, 155
Training, for British units and formations 42, 44,
    45, 50-51, 112, 113, 114, 125, 140, 141, 150
Training, for German units and formations
    112-113, 183-185, 295
Trench construction 47, 70, 72, 74, 76, 101, 104,
    115, 117
Trench routine and conditions 115-116, 129, 133,
    138, 140

Welsh Army Corps
    formation of 32-52
    Executive Committee for 34-36, 42, 46, 48-49,
        52
Welsh language and culture 43, 52-53, 111-113